THE LANGUAGE OF VISUAL ART

THE LANGUAGE OF VISUAL ART

Perception as a basis for design

Jack Fredrick Myers

Formerly
Associate Professor of Art
University of Dayton
and the Cooper School of Art

Harcourt Brace Jovanovich College Publishers

Fort Worth   Philadelphia   San Diego
New York   Orlando   Austin   San Antonio
Toronto   Montreal   London   Sydney   Tokyo

Acquisitions Editor: Karen Dubno
Production Manager: Spectrum Publisher Services, Inc., Evelyn Tucker
Designer: Connie Szcwciuk
Art Layout: Fred Pusterla
Cover Design: Gloria Gentile
Photo Editor: Elsa Peterson

Library of Congress Cataloging-in-Publication Data
Myers, Jack Fredrick.
  The language of visual art.

  Bibliography: p.
  Includes index.
  1. Visual perception.   2. Composition (Art)
3. Communication in art.   I. Title
N7430.5.M9 1989   701'.8   89-1848
ISBN 0-03-012604-5

Printed in the United States of America

1 2 3 4 5 6 7 8 9 0   061   9 8 7 6 5 4 3 2 1

ISBN 0-03-012604-5

Harcourt Brace Jovanovich, Inc.
The Dryden Press
Saunders College Publishing

The Language of Visual Art is intended to serve as the two-dimensional design component in a one-year foundation, or core, program in visual art. Its broad base is a deliberate attempt to establish adequate grounding in design appropriate to whatever area of the visual arts students' individual interests may lead them—fine art, applied art (in all its forms such as graphic design, advertising art, and textile design), photography (both still and motion picture), animation, and computer graphics. By providing technical, physical, and psychological data about visual perception, this text offers a cross-fertilization of concepts, methods, and understandings that will enhance alternative creative possibilities available to all artists whatever their field.

Although the topics presented in this text are intended to cover two or three terms (a school year), including one term that would focus principally on color, they can be adapted to cover a single term. Some information included in this book will prove of importance to working professionals.

The text aims to provide theoretical support for any appropriate series of project topics but does not propose any set routine. It is not a workbook. Student projects, for example, are included primarily to illustrate the topic under discussion, not necessarily to mandate particular class assignments. In spite of this, there is an abundance of specific "how to" information provided to help make various principles more understandable.

A wide variety of possible projects, assignments, and demonstrations to accompany this text will be found in the *Instructor's Manual,* which is available from the publisher.

On the basis of more than 30 years of evaluating student work produced at many institutions, two major deficiencies observed in young artists' work are repetitiousness of idea and an inability to formulate good compositions consistently, that is, to organize patterns well. It appears that a major part of the problem may be the emphasis placed on so-called design elements or components (line, form, color). This fractionalizes, rather than focuses, attention on pattern-making, in which such elements function as mere tools. Current approaches leave novice artists on their own and shift the burden of learning to the individual and to that individual's resources. No other discipline leaves its advocates so poorly prepared, technically, for their profession.

Traditional approaches to design are rooted in an intuitive understanding of visual perception learned primarily through a process of trial and error. Little attention has been given to recent research findings in visual perception and their application to teaching design. This is limiting in two ways: (1) artists and students can explore only a limited number of problems, thereby increasing the time needed to gain an understanding of the interrelationships of meaning, image, and perception; and (2) lacking a sense of the bigger picture of relationships, they are also restricted to using the solutions they have previously seen or have accidentally uncovered. No one would think of asking a computer programmer, a physicist, or a physician to rediscover all his or her profession's technology before entering the field. Design students are asked to learn design by a hunt-and-pick approach.

Studies suggest that a substantial number of instructors assume that a student will pick up technical background not covered in a basic design course in due time either through experience or through instruction given in other art courses. That assumption is simply not true for the vast majority of students.

The fact is that many points covered in this text have never become functional alternatives even at the professional level. Though this text may appear more rigorous than many basic design texts, perhaps it is because most make so few demands of design students. Even so, a course based on this text can cover only a small part of the materials essential for a graduate to function effectively in highly competitive fields.

Patternmaking is the substance of all the arts. Music is patterned sound: dance is patterned movement; spoken language is patterned speech and written language is patterned graphic form.

Patternmaking in the visual arts and the patternmaking of our perceptual processes coincide. Understanding how perceptual mechanisms work can help an artist understand how all elemental visual components like line, shape, color, space, and texture fit together. All those components commonly found in other basic design texts are included here but in a contextual framework. *The Language of Visual Art* places emphasis on the associative qualities inherent in these visual fragments, not on the components themselves. It is not the fact that *lines* are used in a work that matters, but how lines are organized to express the emotional and conceptual objectives set by the artist. The professional artist is not primarily concerned with visual components—line, shape, color—but with how such design fragments fit together to make patterns. Rather than with visual components, the professional is concerned with *qualities* like concept, aesthetics, coherence, expression, harmony, and so on, which are fundamental to communication.

Communication is an essential ingredient of the arts. Few texts suggest how visual fragments might well be used to enhance communication. Yet each one possesses inherently a wealth of attributes, *cues,* that stimulate emotional and intellectual responses through which a viewer may deduce meaning.

Patternmaking and meaning are the fundamental components of perception. Their characteristics form the basis for *visual literacy.* Once understood, they provide artists with as many innumerable options in managing images as any literate person has in managing words. Artists are image managers.

This book is about *visual literacy* and *image management.*

It is focused on concepts and understanding; on the what, how, when, where, and why; on defining advantages and disadvantages of particular choices in a wealth of choices. It provides a basis for understanding how to warp two-dimensional space, how to stimulate a sense of balance and movement, how to emphasize or to subordinate any graphic elements whatever the goal or purpose, and how to expand knowledge and to energize thinking. The goal is to stimulate, in a geometric progression, the numbers of alternative possibilities. Exploring alternatives is the essence of creativity.

The focus is not on graphic accomplishment, but on knowledge. Design is conceptual, not media specific.

The Language of Visual Art is divided into four sections. Section 1, *Awareness,* develops an understanding of organizational principles (patternmaking) in terms of our perceptual mechanisms, including concepts such as those proposed by Gestalt psychologists. This section emphasizes patternmaking at the rudimentary level perceptually as well as according to traditional practices of artists. In essence, the brain is not only the subject of this section, but is the subject of the entire book. How we process and respond to visual data depends on both our physiological and psychological mechanisms.

Section 2 deals with the all-but-ignored subject of *visual weight.* It enlarges upon concepts presented in Section 1 with detailed specifics that establish bases for all visual patternmaking. Chapters concerning the topics of *space* and *change* deal in some depth with these two most significant components of visual perception. The degree of emphasis on visual weight is unique to this text, yet it is one of the most necessary, basic, and universal qualities of visual organization. The same is true of *leveling and sharpening* (the application of the *concept of contrast*) though I am aware of only one other basic design text that even mentions the subject by that term. *Stereotyping* is not discussed in any similar text although it appears with unflagging regularity in virtually every aspect of student work. Stereotyping is not only a component of simplification, but a characteristic of the manner in which our perceptual mechanisms operate. It is a conceptual element to avoid or to utilize as circumstances dictate in any form of visual communication as well as a social phenomenon with which we have to deal on a more or less regular basis. As such, stereotyping exhibits strong emotional constituents both positive and negative.

Section 3 deals with *The Anatomy of Meaning,* a subject that addresses the inherent symbolism contained in the visual expressions of the elemental components of design and concerns creativity as stimulated by a recognition of the similarity of dissimilars (cross-modalities). Everything is interwoven—interconnected. Deducing *meaning* from sensory data about our environment is a *perceptual imperative* with which our subconscious brain is forever preoccupied. Do visual components of design mesh with known characteristics of our perceptual mechanisms? Is there a correlation between artists' methods, theories, and aesthetic concepts and our brains' visual processing mechanisms? Recent scientific studies suggest that the answer to these questions is "Yes." That information is *useful* to us. It is knowledge that vastly extends creative alternatives. It enriches the storehouse of tools available for *thinking* as well as for doing. An understanding of perceptual mechanisms can multiply an artist's options many times.

Color is a complex and difficult-to-manage component of design. For this reason, it has its own section, *The Anatomy of Color,* yet a perceptive reader will find continual references to color throughout the text, not just in Section 4. Color cannot be separated from design any more than it can be separated from vision. Color, like perception in general, is compromised by *perceptual constancies,* by "set" concepts determined not by reason, but by fashion, tradition, style, and —most often—arbitrary preference and personal idiosyncrasies. It is the most telling, the most expressive, and the most *psychologically emotional.* Although color is as diverse as artists are individual, guidelines exist for both physical and psychological applications of color to works of art. This book acquaints artists with many of these.

The color section supplies scientific facts about light, vision, and pigment we need to know in order to use them more productively, both in the art itself and in the process of making art. It includes information about fundamental color-mixing systems and how they apply to creative art forms. It includes a technique that allows a relatively limited number of pigments to produce a full spectral range of hues at close to maximum purity; it includes a never-fail method to create color "harmony;" and it also includes information that helps an artist produce an illusion of light emanating from the canvas whether endeavoring to simulate the naturalistic qualities of illumination or employing *abstract light cues* for conceptual purposes. Concluding with Chapter 18, we return to the perceptual characteristic of *meaning* as specifically related to color and color psychology. Also, we look briefly at the influence of color as a psychological determinant and at the uses of color in society, in language, and in art forms.

To assist readers, a "summary" follows each chapter.

Because this text relates the science of perception to art and design, there are a number of terms from psychology, physics, and biology not common to all basic design texts. In addition, there is an attempt to use some art terms more precisely to clarify meaning. Unfamiliar terms are fully explained in the body of the text as well as in a list of key terms following each chapter and the full glossary. Those likely to present the most difficulty for persons with previous knowledge of art are *luminance, purity,* and *hue circle.* Let us take a moment to look at the reasons for their use.

Luminance is the dimension of color more often called "value," a term whose popularity is attributed to Albert H. Munsell. Luminance is the relative energy level (intensity) of light reflected from a surface, that is, the relative light energy that strikes the retina of the eye. It is a "subtractive" measure. Luminance pertains to the lightness or darkness of a hue but *not* to its vividness or grayness.

In the Munsell system, white is rated 10.0, the presence of all light; and black 0.0, the absence of all light. These are "additive" measures pertaining to the mixing of light sources. Yet, in character, most two-dimensional design and painting are *subtractive,* a term that pertains to light (or color) reflected from the surface of pigments. Some respected color authorities like Joseph Albers have refused to use the term *value* because they reasoned that careless use of the term and false examples in books destroyed it as a means of measure. The author agrees with that, as well as with all the other objections Albers raised to the term *value* in his book, *The Interaction of Color.* Albers proposed *luminant level,* however, this text prefers the single root word *luminance* as a less ambiguous and more precise and workable alternative to *value.* In addition, the term *luminance* is able to accommodate a gray scale based on density, a subtractive measure, which is of more practical benefit to students of design. Density is discussed in Chapter 16 as well as in the glossary.

Instead of the term *intensity,* or *saturation,* this text uses *purity* to describe the dimension of color that establishes a scale ranging from the most vivid hue physically possible to neutral gray. It *does not* involve the lightness/darkness of a color. There is no universally accepted descriptive term for this dimension. Although some persons use *purity* as we will be doing, other persons prefer *intensity,* and still others prefer *saturation.* Some say intensity and saturation mean different things, and both terms are required. Some persons prefer the term *brightness,* but that is a term most frequently used to describe a combination of dimensions rather than a single one. In the Munsell system, this dimension of color is called by yet another term, *chroma*. Although intensity is probably used by more artists and luminance by more scientists and technicians, no single term is accepted by a clear majority of any group. The term *purity* can be defined in its most vivid expression as monochromatic light of a single wavelength, giving it a precise meaning. For that reason, it is preferred in this text. Then purity, for example, is a measure of how close a color reflected from a surface comes to the light of a single wavelength.

The term *hue circle* is preferred to *color wheel* simply because color wheels usually deal only with *hue*. Artists should learn to use a specific term when only one dimension of color is meant, reserving the term *color* for use when referring to two or more dimensions combined. All terms just mentioned, as well as some other common synonymous terms, are cross-referenced in the glossary.

Throughout the text, many theories are mentioned, and many facts presented. A reader should clearly distinguish between what is a fact and what is a theory. Terms such as *suggest, infer,* and *indicate* should provide cues to the reader that concepts, ideas, or theories are being discussed. A theory is one explanation or answer as to why a certain event or phenomenon takes place. A fact is a proved theory. A theory becomes a fact if a universally acceptable test can be devised that everyone agrees will prove the theory and if that test can be replicated (repeated exactly) by independent researchers time after time with identical results.

For example, *additive color mixing* is a physical characteristic of light. Colors of the rainbow as dispersed by a prism can be reassembled into white light using another prism. In the presence of one 100-watt light bulb, if we turn on another 100-watt bulb, we will have *added* to the light in the room (doubled it in this example). Even if these bulbs were colored or of a different wattage, the same basic effect would occur. Anyone can try these tests and will come up with the same results every time. The red, yellow, and blue hue circle (or color wheel) artists commonly use represents a theory, not a fact. As proposed by Louis Prang in 1876,[1] there are no artists' pigments available that meet theoretical primary hue requirements. This means that a full range of pure (vivid) colors *cannot* be mixed from just these three. Nor are permanent, monochromatic pigments available for a more scientific *subtractive mixing system*, which offers magenta, yellow, and cyan as primaries. Even in its best-expressed forms, color slide film and the color printing in this book, the subtractive system also remains essentially theoretical because, in application, a combination of the three primary hues cannot produce absolute blacks (the absence of all visible light) as the theory says that it should. When we mix red, yellow, and blue dyes, inks, or paints together, we do not get "black."

There is no reason, however, why a theory, proved or not, cannot be put to worthwhile use if it can be demonstrated that *it works* as the subtractive system does with printing and film. For more than a hundred years before Prang, artists were doing just that with concepts that formed the basis for the red-yellow-blue (RYB) theory—they made the hue circle work.

The same thing can be done with new understandings about the way in which the body's sensory mechanisms work, perception, even though not all the data are in. After all, we do not have to be automotive engineers in order to drive a car from here to there. We can act on the preponderance of the evidence. Artists have been doing some of these things intuitively for over 25,000 years.

Contents

Section four.   The anatomy of color

References are to figure numbers unless indicated plates.

PHOTOGRAPHIC CREDITS

The author and publishers wish to thank the custodians of the works of art for supplying photographs and granting permission to use them. Photographs have been obtained from sources listed in the captions, unless listed below.

A/AR: Alinari/Art Resource, New York
AR: Art Resource, New York
B/AR: Bridgeman/Art Resource, New York
BPK: Bildarchiv/Preussischer Kulturbesitz, West Berlin
G/AR: Giraudon/Art Resource, New York
HB: Hedrich-Blessing, Chicago
JFM: Jack Fredrick Myers
JS: Joseph Szaszfai, Branford, Conn.
M/AR: Marburg/Art Resource, New York
MOMA/FSA: Museum of Modern Art, New York/Film Stills Archive
N/AR: Nimatallah/Art Resource, New York
NASA: National Aeronautic and Space Administration
PR: Photo Researchers, New York
RMN: Service de Documentation Photographique de la Reunion des Musees Nationaux, Paris
S/AR: Scala/Art Resource, New York

Color Plates 1, 3, 5: JFM. 6: Clive Corless. 7: JFM. 8: From THE AMERICAN WILDERNESS: The Grand Canyon. Photographs by Harald Sund. © 1972 Time-Life Books, Inc. © 1988 Harald Sund. All Rights Reserved. 9, 11–16: JFM. 17, 18: Paul Brierley. 19: Evelyn Hofer, New York. 20, 21, 23, 24: JFM. 25: Fred English Photographs, Inc. 26–29: JFM. 30: Zindman/Fremont. 31: JFM. 34: © 1988 Kenneth Snelson.

Chapter One 1.2: Sylvia Plachy/Archive Pictures. 1.5: Lockheed Electronics Company. 1.6: Bettmann Archive. 1.7: From PERCEPTION by Irvin Rock. Copyright © Scientific American Books, Inc. Reprinted with permission. 1.9: J.C. Lozouet/The Image Bank. 1.10: © J. Alex Langley/Click/Chicago.

Chapter Two 2.1: Bayerisches Staatsgemaldesammlungen, Munich. 2.5: JFM. 2.7: Stan Wayman/LIFE Magazine © 1965 Time, Inc. 2.10: © 1988 M.C. Escher Heirs/Cordon Art, Baarn, Holland. 2.11: Courtesy Lanny Sommese Design. 2.21: Copyright 1982 Lonni Sue Johnson.

Chapter Three 3.1: © Lee Lockwood/Black Star. 3.2: NASA. 3.4: JFM. 3.8: Charles Campbell/Taurus Photos. 3.11: © Verlag C.J. Bucher GMBH, Munich. 3.13: © Gerald Fisher, University of New Castle Upon Tyne. 3.15b, c: Adapted from "A Special Type of Visual Illusion," L.S. Penrose and R. Penrose. *British Journal of Psychology* (1958) 49, 31–33, figures. By permission of the British Psychological Society. 3.16: © 1988 M.C. Escher Heirs/Cordon Art, Baarn, Holland. 3.18: © 1984 Victor Moscoso. 3.20: Alison Frantz, Princeton, N.J. 3.23: RMN. 3.24: Mark Kaufman, LIFE Magazine, © Time, Inc. 3.25: JFM. 3.26: Richard Hartt, LIFE Magazine © Time, Inc. 3.28: DDB Needham WorldWide. 3.30: G/AR.

Chapter Four 4.1: Siggraph Conference Office. 4.7: JFM. 4.8: Teri Leigh Stratford/PR. 4.11: RMN. 4.16: A.C. Cooper, Ltd., London. 4.17: © 1972 Wucius Wong. 4.19: From PATTERN DESIGN, Lewis F. Day (New York: Taplinger, 1979). Used by permission. 4.20: Vignelli Designs, New York. 4.22: Reproduced from *Environment and Planning B: Planning and Design,* Vol. 13, 1986, page 171, by permission of Pion Ltd., London. 4.23: By permission of McGraw-Hill Book Company. 4.31: John Webb FRPS. 4.32: JFM. 4.33: Courtesy Charles Swedlund. 4.34: Phototeque. 4.38: © 1980 John Martin. Originally painted for the May 1980 issue of *The Financial Post Magazine,* Toronto. 4.41: All Rights Reserved. The Metropolitan Museum of Art. 4.42: Courtesy C. Michael Dudash.

Chapter Five 5.3: © 1967 Tomi Ungerer.

Chapter Six 6.5: © Frank Frazetta. 6.8, 6.9, 6.10: © 1972 Wucius Wong. 6.11: JS. 6.12: S/AR. 6.20: Geoffrey Clements/Staten Island, New York. 6.21: HB. 6.25: NASA. 6.27: AR. 6.28, 6.29, 6.30: RMN.

Chapter Seven 7.2: Jacqueline Duvoisin/Sports Illustrated © Time, Inc. 7.3: © 1982 Baron Wolman/Woodfin Camp and Associates. 7.6: JFM. 7.8: Carmelo Guadagno.

Chapter Eight 8.6: Courtesy Igarashi Studio, Tokyo. 8.7: From *Pictorial Perception and Culture* by Jan B. Deregowski. Copyright © 1972 by Scientific American, Inc. All Rights Reserved. 8.9: Road Atlas © 1981 by Rand McNally & Co. 8.11: Photo courtesy F. Fox, Chester, England. 8.12: Reproduced by permission of Mitchell Beazley London Ltd. 8.15: © Pat O'Hara. 8.17: Walter Wick. 8.23: From *The Processor of Vision* by Ulric Neisser. © 1968 by Scientific American, Inc. All Rights Reserved. 8.24: © Alexander Lowry/PR. 8.25: JFM. 8.26: JS. 8.27: M/AR. 8.30: All Rights Reserved, The Metropolitan Museum of Art. 8.37: Joseph S. Dydek. 8.38: © 1985 The National Geographic Society. 8.41: © 1981 by EARTHings Corp.

Chapter Nine 9.1: S/AR. 9.5: From E.J. Marey, *Movement,* 1895/New York Public Library, Astor, Lenox and Tilden Foundations. 9.7: © Harold Edgerton. Courtesy Palm Press. 9.16: A/AR. 9.17: D. James Dee, New York. 9.18: JFM. 9.26: © 1988 Hans Namuth. 9.31: All Rights Reserved. The Metropolitan Museum of Art.

Chapter Ten 10.1: Magnum Photos, Inc. 10.2: Michael Evans/Sygma. 10.3: JFM. 10.6, 10.7: JFM. 10.8: All Rights Reserved. The Metropolitan Museum of Art.

Chapter Eleven 11.1: BPK. 11.5: N/AR. 11.7: Pelka/Noble. 11.10: © Arnold Newman. 11.13: Image by Andrew de Lory. 11.15: B/AR. 11.17: Copyright 1941, renewed © 1969 by The Viking Press, Inc. All Rights Reserved. Reprinted by permission of Viking Penguin, Inc. 11.19: From Roy Paul Nelson, *The Design of Advertising,* 5th edition. © 1985 Wm. C. Brown Publishers, Dubuque, Iowa. All Rights Reserved. Reprinted by permission.

Introduction

The science of perception

The science of perception is relatively new. Its progress has been impeded by its interdisciplinary nature. That is, it requires extensive knowledge in more than one field, for example, psychology, physiology (biology), and physics. In recent years, scientists have made astonishing discoveries about how we see (how our eyes receive and transmit visual data to the brain) and how our brain processes, interprets, and stores this information.

Much is still to be learned.

What is significant is how much of this material correlates with the intuitive feelings of outstanding visual artists over the centuries. Individual artists have clearly employed their own perceptions, though imperfectly understood, as a basis for their works. These approaches were expanded and preserved to form the basis for the artistic tradition we find in societies of differing times and in differing parts of the world. The arts have always used perceptual characteristics to convey ideas and information — to communicate. They have used a visual language.

That vision, the primary perceptual tool in human beings, constitutes a form of language should not be surprising. Visual symbols, pictures, were the first language.

In the attempts by researchers to understand perception, a major stumbling block was the inability to see the forest for the trees. The visual field is with us every waking and, often, dreaming moment. It is, in many ways, so diverse, personal, and individual that it seems to possess no structure, no perceived units of organization.

Studies in perception are now beginning to reveal some of that basic structure. It may be decades or centuries before we fully understand how it all works. The brain's intricate mechanisms do not easily yield to analysis. Today's techniques are rudimentary, yet the evidence is already overwhelming. Our brain appears to have specific operational modes that control the manner in which all of us, artists as well as everyone else, analyze visual fields. These modes are innate characteristics derived from natural selection — our survival characteristics. At a primitive level, they govern just about everything we understand about our real world.

Perception, as a science, deals with the body's biological and mental mechanisms applicable to our entire species. It concerns how we acquire information and knowledge about our world through the action and interaction of our sensory organs and our brain. Place this in opposition to the "perception" of the individual, a discernment or understanding of a particular subject, object, or event. Science looks for *likenesses* among human beings. Individual perception emphasizes *differences* between them. It is only through the science of perception that someday we may understand something about individual perceptions.

When the terms *real* or *natural world* are used in this book, we will be talking about *veridical reality*, which is a reality that we can measure. It is the reality of the scientist who deals with physical elements and the way in which we negotiate our world whatever we think or make of it. This is to contrast veridical reality with metaphysical philosophy, which contends that it may never be possible to know what true reality is. The term *veridical* applies to things we consider objectively without reference to viewing conditions. For example, diameters that pass through the center of a circle and end at its circumference can be measured with a ruler to show that they are all equal. Yet the projection of a circle on the retina of the eye or on the film in a camera is usually an ellipse. The diameters of an ellipse are not equal in any direction. In this instance, there is a conflict between sensory data (an ellipse focused in the eye) and knowledge. Our brain tells us that what we are actually looking at is a circle in perspective (with equal diameters). We call this faculty *perceptual constancy*. It shows how knowledge is frequently used to alter perceptions.

The grammar of a language

Before we proceed further, it may be worthwhile to examine the characteristics of the "grammar" of a language, any language, as the term is generally understood.

Language is a form of communication. Its symbols, the letters of an alphabet, must be organized in a manner in which we can comprehend them. If letters are not coherent, that is, do not have an orderly and logical arrangement of parts, then no communication can take place. Let us look at some examples.

The quick brown fox jumps over the lazy dog.

This sentence is a common one for testing typewriters and other composing machines because it includes all letters of the alphabet. The sentence has

both meaning (message) and structure. Though it does not say anything very important, it is nevertheless easily understandable, clear, and concise. Compare it to the following:

Abc defgh ijklm nop qrstu vwx yz.

Though we may recognize this as the alphabet, we do not accept it as a sentence. The letters, simply divided into wholly arbitrary groups, have been given a kind of structure that in no way contributes to understanding. In other words, even though the individual letters (language symbols) can be recognized, there is no "message" because the sentence does not have *semantics*; that is, the words do not *mean* anything to us. Examine the following:

Dow agllps cf inor bhju qy erkm tiyxzm.

This is pure gibberish. Yet this sentence also contains all the letters of the alphabet and seems to have a kind of structure. That structure makes no contribution to understanding, no sense at all. Like the former sentence, the words have no basis in any language. Why? Because they are purely an arbitrary arrangement of letters, the result of mere random selection, pure chance. This sentence does not have any semantics either. As a communication, it is worse than the previous sentence. At least that one consisted of letters in alphabetical order.

Fda mgey xnkst bxt fgilo kran fda hwvu zkc.

This sentence looks like the one above it, like gibberish. Within it, however, is one cue that suggests that it may be something more. It contains a repetition of the same three letters in the same sequence. Actually this sentence is the same as the very first one,

I.I In the circle, **a**, every diameter is the same length. In the ellipse, **b**, diameters vary in length.

a

b

I.2 Dik Browne. *Hi and Lois.* This cartoon illustrates a failure in communication due to differences in the perceptions of words (slang phrases) between the younger boy and his older brother. They are not speaking the same language. Reprinted with special permission of King Features Syndicate, Inc.

I.3 Jim Benton. *Mrs. Hubbins.* Ink and watercolor, 18 × 24" (45.7 × 61 cm) © Jim Benton 1985 for *The Artist's Magazine.* An example of what psychologists call *cognitive dissonance.* It is brought about by a conflict between what we believe and what we do—our behavior. Sometimes we cannot accept objective reality even when it is obvious for everyone else to see. Often we alter it to fit our perceptions as the artist in the cartoon has done (although it is usually a mental rather than a physical adjustment).

transposed, or encoded, in a simple cypher. Each letter of the alphabet has been moved forward five places: *a* is *e*, *b* is *f*, *c* is *g*, and so on. We could analyze it and ultimately decode its message. On the surface, however, it appears to be a totally different language, one that we do not understand. In fact, it is precisely like a foreign language that we have never learned. The sentence has both meaning (message) and structure, but it is not comprehensible to us. This sentence has no *pragmatics*; that is, the words have no associational meaning for us. *There is no shared knowledge.* If no words used in a communication have ever been seen before, they can never have been "learned" and, therefore, never assimilated into our memory.

If we cannot figure out such a puzzle quickly, we usually become frustrated and give up, concluding that it probably is not worth the effort anyhow. This kind

of reaction to a circumstance is what psychologists call *cognitive dissonance.* See Figure I.3. When a belief and a behavior are in conflict, either the belief or the behavior must change to conform. Such a conflict, or dissonance, cannot be tolerated by anyone for very long. The ceaseless duel between thinking and behavior allows the brain continually to test and reassess beliefs.

Next consider the following:

Jumps lazy the over brown quick dog fox the.

This sentence contains meaning, but poor structure. The structure of grammar—the way in which words are strung together, their associative quality—is the *syntax* of a sentence. It is syntax that makes communications clear, understandable, concise, and effective. The sentence permits several equally valid

The science of perception   **3**

interpretations. We are able to deduce a sort of "general message" in short order. But because the sequence of the words is jumbled, we do not know, nor can we ever know, who jumps over whom and who is brown, who is quick, or who is lazy. Therefore, the sentence is *ambiguous,* neither clear nor effective as communication.

The ordinary and principal function of language is direct communication: making others understand, do, or feel something we want them to. Whenever we talk about language, it is important to remember that it is a means to an end. Language is a conveyer of ideas (messages), a kind of vehicle.

As we have seen, for a clear communication in any language, written, spoken, or visual, the rules of grammar require that at least three conditions must be present: (1) *semantics,* that is, the recognition of the meaning of a word or image; (2) *syntax,* or structure, the way that the words, phrases, sentences, or images are put together — their relative agreement and position; and, (3) *pragmatics,* the interconnection, or inter-relationship with the reader, listener, or viewer — *the existence of shared knowledge.* When any one of these is missing, or unclear, meaning is likely to be impaired, distorted, or, simply, nonexistent.

The same thing is true for the visual language.

Meaning: A requisite of visual fields

Perceptually, all visual fields must have meaning for human beings. Whatever we see, our brain interprets, desperately seeking recognizable forms, objects, or evidences of humanity. The process is autonomic (subconscious) and uncontrollable, one that goes on all the time in spite of anything we may try to do to stop it. It is a survival characteristic that we could call the *perceptual imperative.* When our brain is unable to decipher meaning from the visual field, we turn off, tune out, ignore, or disregard it because we cannot deal with such a situation emotionally. Studies in sensory deprivation suggest that the failure to observe and define meaning in our environment may lead to mental disorientation and, ultimately, to mental illness. We must make sense out of nonsense. If it cannot be done logically, we may invent a meaning!

Visual literacy

The term *literacy* implies an ability to decode messages in a written language: an understanding of word meanings, associations, and grammar. When the term *visual* is added to it, the implication is that *visual literacy* is an ability to decode visual messages. Visual literacy is heavily dependent on *semiotics,* that is, the study of "signs" and their perceptual significance to human communication. Interpreting a visual language requires a recognition and experiencing of the interacting relationships of diverse visual sensory data. This involves *syntactics,* which pertain to the interpretation and significance of abstract signs and their relationships or expressions — in short, the way in which words (or images) are put together to form "phrases" or "sentences." Because the elemental components of visual processing are abstract (dot, line, color, texture, dimension, movement, and so on), they have perceptual significance in the way in which they are observed to form figures in any visual field. This gives them recognition and meaning like words (semantics). As with words, their orderly association with one another, their syntax, forms visual "strings," that is, visual phrases or sentences. Ultimately, the whole relates to our previous experience and understanding. Visual literacy, then, depends on our ability to retrieve sensory data from any visual field and decode its "message." The wonderful advantage of the visual language is that its spontaneous evidence lends immediacy to communication.

In studies of basic design, the emphasis is usually placed individually on the abstract elemental visual components such as line, form, and color. They have no meaning in the accepted sense of the term, even to aspiring artists, until one learns how to employ them to create a work of "visual art." Like the letters in the alphabet, the significance of these elemental visual components lies in how they are used, their pattern or structure.

Structure has limitless forms, as one might glimpse, for example, in the infinite variety of structures that nature devises. Structure is the single most significant element in any entity, including works of art. Without structure, the whole falls apart, no matter how attractive the individual parts may be. Perception and structure are intricately intertwined.

To function confidently the aspiring artist needs to acquire an understanding of how perceptual mechanisms work. Ultimately, such understanding should become very deep and intuitive. The quality that has distinguished those artists throughout history who somehow have divined how visual communication takes place, and who spoke with clarity and insight, we call "genius."

The historic problem with the study of basic design is that it is often viewed as having no overall discernible grammar like written language. Studies of visual perception suggest that this assumption is not correct.

Realistic images ("representational" figure-objects portrayed in natural settings) have always had meaning for everyone. That is because these images are familiar. They evoke familiar—shared—memories.

Elemental visual components like line, shape, color, space, and motion are like the alphabetical letters in this sentence; they are symbols, abstract visual components, which depend on recognition (semantics), association (syntax), and shared understanding or knowledge (pragmatics) to produce a visual communication.

The signs and symbols of mathematics are abstract. The physicist's formulas, which describe the fundamental way in which physical forces act in our universe, are abstract patterns that, like mathematics, must be learned through academic study. The geneticist must learn in infinite detail the patterns that make up the human physiology. The note patterns and symbols that a composer uses to create music, patterned sound, are likewise abstract. Dance is patterned movement. Language is patterned thought.

The elemental components of visual composition are also abstract. The organizational mechanisms of perception which govern our response to such patterns demand specialized study just as an engineer must learn and understand aerodynamics in order to design an automobile or an airplane that can travel safely at high speeds.

The *product* of none of these disciplines, or "arts," is abstract. Abstract symbols, concepts, theories, and methodology are a means to an end. That end is tangible: a satellite to beam images around the world instantly, ultimately a cure for AIDS or the common cold, safer travel on the nation's highways, a book, a screenplay, a dance, a musical score, a painting or design. "Appreciation" of arts forms can be construed as possessing utility. It is believed that Homo sapiens would not have invented "art" if there were not some deep-rooted emotional compulsion to fulfill. Psychologist Morse Peckham insists that artistic behavior is not a pretty ornament to life but a terrible necessity that keeps human beings vital and enables them to innovate. Of all the burdens we bear, art is one of the most unendurable and yet one of the most necessary.

Deprived of art, humans could not continue to be human.[2]

Art is largely a matter of feeling. Every visual field, *all visual art,* leads to a fundamentally emotional experience. The viewer is the other half of any art experience or engagement. The extremes of positions on this subject are taken by some fine artists who disregard the public altogether as insignificant or view them as a sort of by-product, necessary but subordinate to their own process of artistic expression. At the opposite end of the scale are many clients of applied artists who take the position that the viewer's participation is the only one that counts and that the artist is only a tool—a means to an end.

Realistically, every practitioner of art must develop and maintain an intense sensitivity to the emotional character of works and the interchange of feelings with the viewer, without whom there would be little need for art. However, no artist is a tool; otherwise the creation of art could be left to computers. It would be a dull art. Human beings are important because they can make *inferences;* that is, people can join dissimilar things in their minds to create new concepts. No computer yet created can do that.

The principles of visual perception provide artists with an analytical basis for the evaluation of visual art to place beside our subjective considerations. Unless we recognize that there is a problem, we cannot possibly solve that problem—we cannot grow or change. Problem recognition is fundamental to any successful person—the computer programmer, the corporation president, the economist, or the artist whatever the field (design, illustration, painting, sculpture, photography, acting, writing, or composing).

Understanding perception allows visual artists to express themselves in language that is clear, precise, and effective. Whatever mode of expression visual artists choose, from photographic realism to totally abstract, nonobjective works, understanding how perceptual processes work expands their capability to express their intentions more precisely—to clarify or, if they choose, to obscure meaning.

Understanding perception expands our visual vocabulary in direct proportion to the degree of that understanding. Knowledge provides artists with tools to exert a greater influence over a viewer's emotional response to their work and over the precision with which visual communication takes place. That is how visual literacy works.

Review of key terms

abstract, abstraction Theoretical rather than applied or practical; something considered apart from physical existence. *In art:* a type of work that uses representational shapes or forms as a point of departure but freely adapts or subjugates these to the aesthetic purposes of the artist.

ambiguity Doubt or uncertainty in meaning. *Ambiguous:* capable of being understood in two or more possible senses; equivocal.

cognitive dissonance An internal conflict between one's beliefs and one's knowledge or behavior, for example, the opposition to the killing of animals and the eating of meat. It is a theory articulated by Leon Festinger, which states that when belief and behavior are in conflict, either one or the other must change.

inference The act or process of drawing a conclusion from evidence or premises. Inferences are not necessarily the result of step-by-step logic but are often a consequence of deduction and supposition (a kind of sixth sense) that sees similarities in dissimilar things, activities, or mechanisms.

perception An awareness of everything around us obtained through our sensual organs: sight, hearing, smell, touch, and taste.

perceptual imperative An autonomic psychophysical drive to find meaning in every visual field or, more broadly, to derive meaning from all sensory data.

pragmatics That part of language that depends on social or cultural interrelationships — the existence of shared knowledge.

semantics In the grammar of any language, a recognition, tagging, or naming of a word or "figure" — its fundamental meaning.

syntax Language structure, that is, the way in which words, sentences, or images are put together to form phrases or sentences — visual "strings" — in relative agreement and position sequentially.

veridical Pertaining to properties of things considered objectively that can be determined by measurement and without dependence on viewing conditions. Veridical reality is the reality of the scientist.

visual literacy Comparable to literacy in language, it is the ability to understand and to use effectively all characteristics of the visual language.

Awareness

"True, you're a butterfly now, but you still think like a caterpillar."

CHAPTER ONE

The nature of perception

Understanding perceptual processes

Perception is awareness of the world around us derived from data supplied by all sensory organs, of which vision is foremost, accounting for about two-thirds of everything we know. We are dominated by visual concepts.

Our perceptions are derived from (1) biological structure, (2) experience, and (3) knowledge. Each of us has an array of sensory equipment: eyes, ears, nose, skin, and tongue. Every waking moment our brain is inundated with bits of sensory data that are continually compared with *paradigms* (definitive models) derived from past experience. How one interprets this information (the stimuli) depends partly on one's physical state. Sickness affects perception, for instance, as do exhaustion, happiness, and depression.

Our brain not only codifies and stores experiences, but it also allows us to control and to synthesize (create and recreate) experiences in our minds.

How knowledge affects perception

How many readers believe that the earth is flat? Today, how many believe that the earth is the center of the universe and that the sun, stars, and other planets all revolve around the earth? For thousands of years even educated people believed these things to be true. No wonder; they all seemed perfectly logical. When standing on the earth, we cannot "see" it as a globe or "see" the earth as traveling around the sun. It was knowledge that changed people's minds. We know that the moon is not glowing yellow but that its light is coming from the sun, reflected from a cold surface.

Knowledge provides us with the information needed to change our perceptions. If we depended on our senses alone, the earth would still be flat, and the Greek god Apollo might still be dragging a fireball across the dome of the sky in his chariot. Perhaps we never would have developed the science of astronautics and never ventured into space.

Our perceptions are largely based on elements of which we are hardly aware and are influenced by previous experience and preconceived notions of every kind. It should be clear by now that the world that we see, hear, taste, smell, and feel is not directly related in any simple way to the world of the scientist. The brain interprets everything we see. Two people act differently for the same reasons or will act the same for different reasons.

Attaching a meaning to sensory awareness is perception.

The perceptual processes

Our perceptual processes are not objective reproducers of reality like a camera or a tape recorder. They are subjective (interpretive) processes more comparable to computer processing (as long as we do not push the comparison too far). The brain takes bits of sensory data, sorts, allocates, and restructures them. The analysis of sensory data "bits" is affected by age, culture, environment, education (knowledge), and intelligence—it is a kind of "programming." Computers are only as accurate and effective as the quality of their programs and the accuracy of input data allow. Human programming is incredibly random, sheer happenstance (whatever personal experiences occur throughout a lifetime, in whatever order, and in

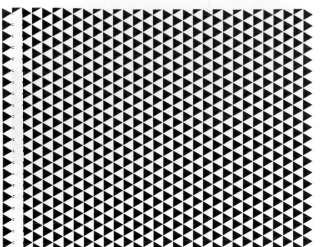

1.1 Concentrate on this pattern of triangles. Within moments they begin to group and regroup in differing formations as the brain frantically searches for meaning. Some seem to be lighter—some darker—than others. After awhile one begins to feel nervous and disturbed because the pattern cannot be resolved into a meaningful figure.

1.2 Rubik's Cube. Only a few years ago, it was driving everyone a little crazy—except for those with methodical minds who were able to master the complex, repetitive moves required to solve the puzzle and to do it in a few minutes.

whatever context). Perception is not a constant but an accumulative and evolving entity. Although once a percept is "set," it may take a considerable effort to change it, if it can be changed at all.

We have the notion that our senses provide us with an accurate picture of the world around us. Nothing could be further from the truth.

The perceptual imperative

One of the foremost properties of perception is the brain's insistence on creating "meaningful patterns." (See Fig. 1.1.) Our brain disregards virtually everything that does not hold immediate meaning for us. This relentless drive of our brain goes on all of the time without any conscious effort on our part. It is fundamental to survival in a hostile environment, to natural selection (the survival of the fittest), and such characteristics have been honed to a fine edge over millions of years.

Our drive toward meaning is inextricably tied to emotions that arise within us uncontrollably. Meaning may be derived from sensory (visual) experiences that exist only in our minds. This may occur whether we want it to or not and in spite of any effort we make to the contrary because the perceptual imperative is linked to the strongest biological drive we possess—the instinct for self-preservation.

Many of us have agonized over the solution to Rubik's Cube (Fig. 1.2), become frustrated when we were unable to find missing pieces to a jigsaw puzzle, or are angered when a storyteller withholds the answer to a riddle. The problem is a failure to find the meaningful pattern in the puzzle, like our reaction to the arrangement of triangles in Figure 1.1. Once a problem is solved, a certain smugness and good feeling always come over us. Our brain psychologically rewards us for this kind of achievement.

Although our perceptions are generally subjective, individual and peculiar to each person, the biological and mental processes by which they are formed are the same for all normal human beings. All persons share some understanding and respond similarly to some things. The narrower a group's interests, the greater the number of shared experiences.

Communication begins with shared experiences.

Illusion versus reality

Much of what we think we understand is illusion. For all of us, it is this illusion that is reality. The physical and the perceptual worlds are both different. Yet both are real.

Understanding the nature of this paradox and how to use this knowledge provide the key to more effective visual images in all the visual arts: in adver-

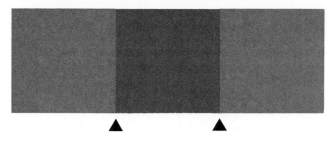

1.3 If the edges between the darker gray tone in the center and the lighter tone on each side appear fluted as if they raised up forming a crease in the paper, it is because of perceptual *irradiation*.

1.4 The small gray spots that are seen at the intersections of the white bars in this field of black squares are strong evidence of the process of *irradiation*. The brain is actually *forcing the edge*. Where the white paper is next to black, the paper is seen to be "whiter" than when next to itself (the white bar). The gray spots are entirely illusionary and disappear whenever we try to look at them.

tising, graphics, industry, theater, photography, film—in all that is commonly called fine art.

The business of the artist is creating illusions.

Studies in fundamental design must enlarge vision because seeing is a prerequisite to the formation of new or fresh ideas, and it is ideas that are the basic commodity in the visual arts, not "art" (a craft of the hands).

Most persons have not the slightest understanding of what happens when they look at something, that is, an understanding of the mechanisms of viewer response to any visual field. Our primary and secondary educational systems provide little basis for such a conception.

How visual perception works

Perception is a patternmaking process. It involves only two primary, or basic, functions. These are **(1)** organization (pattern structure) and **(2)** meaning (recognition).

Organization has to do with separating *figure* from *ground*. A "figure" is what we look at; everything else is "ground." Ground is neutral; figure is not. Figures separate themselves from ground (background) and become the focus of our attention. They are separated from each other by *edge*.

One way in which we locate, or identify, an edge

involves a psychological organizational principle called *irradiation* (Fig. 1.3). In this process, the eye moves back and forth across any detectable separation between light and dark areas in our field of vision. In order to clarify such a separation or edge, the brain perceptually accentuates the observed difference by making the lighter edge lighter and the darker edge darker as can be observed in Figure 1.4. This accentuation of light-dark differences, the contrast, is entirely illusionary. Once an edge is detected, the brain seeks to follow it until it encloses an entire shape. Edges extend into a contour; the contour encloses and defines a shape or mass creating a "figure." Even if there are breaks in the contour, the brain will fill in, *close*, missing parts. These processes are autonomic and subconscious, and they occur every waking moment.

Recent studies suggest that an area of unified lightness-darkness, color, or texture (that is, a mass) in motion establishes, or helps to establish, the edges or contours of a shape or form. Thus our brain appears to possess differing processing modes for figures that remain still and for those that are moving.

We are primarily aware of "change." *Change* is any perceived difference or alteration to a visual field.

As long as we understand that in many fundamental ways the brain is very unlike any computer, there is an interesting correlation between the manner in which we recognize (identify) figures through perceptual brain activity and the combination of the video camera, digital data processing, and computer modeling. This may have come about because human beings must devise the machines to do these things. Perceptual processes are very different from the objective recording mechanisms of a conventional camera or tape recorder. Perhaps a look at the methodology researchers have invented to teach a computer to identify an object visually, to "see," will help us to understand how we must process similar visual data. The technique is shown in Figure 1.5.

Our brain begins the process by comparing the figure detected — the visually perceived pattern — with stereotypical patterns stored in the memory (paradigms). For example, these may be compared at all points where the direction of the line changes until a match occurs, that is, until the figure is "recognized." To confirm the original match (a hypothesis), a series of additional tests are made by comparing additional paradigms (model patterns) that, like subcategories, provide finer and finer degrees of discrimination. These might include spatial position (which helps to determine size), texture, color, and so on, which are appropriate to the original hypothesis.

1.5 **a** An easy job for humans, the computer's goal is to find the tank in this aerial photograph of scrubby desert.
b First, it identifies areas that are neither very light nor very dark, that is, masses with relatively equal luminances.
c Next the computer looks for objects whose surfaces are comparatively smooth.
d Combining decisions on luminance and smoothness, it then focuses on an area that possesses both qualities (center).
e The computer isolates the edges of this shape, which is compared to patterns (model shapes) stored in its memory.
f The computer's program then develops a hypothesis. "Guessing" that the object is a tank, it may go back to the original picture, **a**, to look for other identifying features.

Paradigms of space and size, texture, line, color, and the like, are often cited as the "elemental visual components of design." Therefore, the so-called elements of design are not artistic devices invented by a person or abstracted concepts created by artists or aesthetics, but fundamental mechanisms of visual perception, biologically significant to our existence.

In every visual field we seek evidence of life—in particular, human life. Life at the primitive level is a battleground: prey or predator, friend or foe. To help us evaluate visual fields, to detect living things, we developed paradigms of movement, of spatial position, and of symmetry.

Of these, movement (a "change") may be the most important to survival because all movements are potentially threatening. The type of movement enables us to determine whether a figure is a living creature or an inanimate object, whether it is prey or predator. Depth perception may be next in importance because it enables us to determine the size of a figure and its location in space, an absolute necessity if we are to obtain food or avoid disaster.

In our original visual field, if we have detected a figure whose contour (shape) fits our paradigm of "dog," but whose size is "elephant," then something is obviously wrong. There is an ambiguity in the perceptual visual field that is unacceptable; either that, or we are observing an elephant-sized dog, an equally unacceptable idea.

In simple terms: Perception involves comparisons between a series of model shapes or forms developed from our storehouse of experience that first helps us to recognize the similarity of a figure (a match) and then, subsequently, seeks to clarify or refine the initial identification by applying more and more paradigms to test and confirm the first. It is a process of discrimination: a recognition of the novel or unique qualities of any figure. This is the reason why qualities of difference always attract our attention.

If our dog figure is "blue," then something is wrong again; our color models for dog do not include blue simply because we are not familiar with any blue dogs. If we can determine that the "blue" is simply a covering, we may get around the problem. If the dog, hair or skin, is simply bright blue, it does not conform to any of our original models (previous knowledge). Such a situation is confusing, irritating, and frustrating until, somehow, that ambiguity is resolved. It may be resolved (1) by completely rejecting what we see as false and irrational (cognitive dissonance) or (2) by incorporating the color blue into our paradigms of colors acceptable for dogs.

Our disbelief—(1) above—could be refocused to include "artificial" or "surrogate" dogs, such as a painting, a statue, a poster, or special effects photography as in a science-fiction movie. In fact, all performance arts (theater, television, motion pictures) require us to *suspend our disbelief* if we are to derive any pleasure from them at all. We would probably find that our elephant-size dog belongs to one of their pictorial fields.

We have paradigms for texture. These are perceptions of what are acceptable characteristics of hair (texture) varying from short to long that are appropriate to dogs. If each succeeding paradigm continues to fit with our initial model, we may not only have concluded that the figure is a dog, but through increasing degrees of discrimination, we will have also determined which breed of dog.

So far there is one critical element missing: dogs are alive. Paradigms that detect the quality of life are movement and symmetry.

The paradigms of movement

The criteria for determining if a perceived figure is alive or is inanimate (not alive) involve (1) how it moves against the ground (its environment) and (2) whether it possesses component parts that move independently of the body mass and the environment. Most objects have the potential for movement. Objects that are not alive, however, must be moved by an outside force—wind, water, any force applied to the object, including gravity or the action of a living creature. If the figure appears to move of its own volition, that is, moves by itself and independent of the environment, that is one of the paradigms for a living creature. If a figure moves against the wind, for instance, then such a figure must possess a force equal or superior to the force of the wind. In our brain, only a living creature is capable of such an action contrary to nature.

The paradigm of symmetry

All living creatures appear to have symmetrical characteristics. This impression is so strong that we find it difficult to "see" differences that exist between the right and left halves of any living creature, especially other human beings. We may be startled when such a perception is overridden. We can hardly take our eyes off a scar or an exposed birthmark because these destroy a person's symmetry. For another example, see Figure 1.6, which shows two right halves and

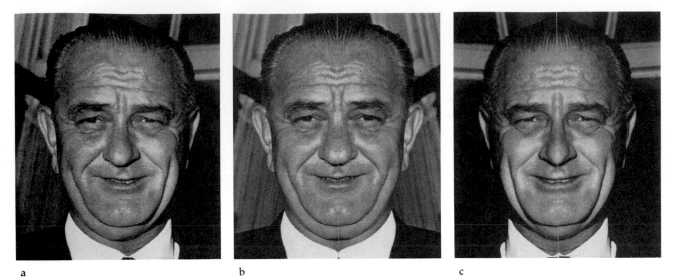

a   b   c

1.6   From a single photograph of one person, **a**, two prints were made, one a mirror image of the other (a flopped image). These prints were split down the center and reassembled placing the left hand of one print next to the right hand of the other, and vice versa. Part **b** combines two left halves; and **c**, two right halves of the person's face. The result is a startling transformation — almost the creation of two different persons from one. On comparative examination, then, body symmetry is also an illusion. The person in the photo is President Lyndon Baines Johnson.

1.7   One tends spontaneously to perceive symmetrical patterns as *figures*. In the patterns of **a**, it is the black shapes that stand out, in **b**, the white shapes. Symmetry possesses a heavy visual weight because we see it as a characteristic of living creatures — particularly human beings.

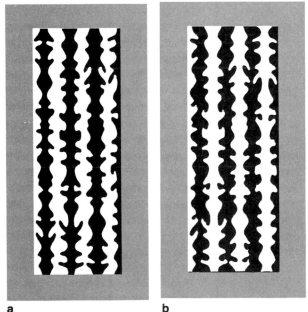

a   b

two left halves of one person's face as well as a normal photograph. We perceive a character change: the altered photographs look like the person, but also they do not. It is fascinating, yet, at the same time, uncomfortable.

All this brain activity, the many comparisons to paradigms — the tests applied to recognized figures — take place in fractions of a second, like the fastest computer.

Unlike any computer, our brain has developed short cuts, the mechanisms of which are not very well understood. This ability to make *inferences* permits human beings to reach conclusions that are not an obviously logical consequence of a series of orderly steps.

Elements in our environment that are seen to be symmetrical stand out as having the potential to be living creatures. Ten thousand years ago, when we were hunter-gatherers and had not yet built towns and developed agriculture, a form mostly hidden in the tall grass or partly obscured by bushes and trees could be a lion (predator) or a deer (prey — food). The figure could be a friend or an enemy lying in wait for us. Our survival depended on quick and accurate recognition. We "understand" that the right and the left sides of a central axis drawn through living creatures are mirror images of one another. This understanding is so strong that symmetry is a viable means of figure recognition (Fig. 1.7). In any visual field, symmetrical

1.8 Edward Weston. *Rocks and Pebbles, Point Lobos.* 1948. © 1981 Arizona Board of Regents, Center for Creative Photography. The random, asymetrical qualities of nature have been captured by Weston in one example of its infinite variety.

1.9 Chateau of Villandry. Early 17th century, France. This formal European garden is typical of the symmetrical arrangement of many Western gardens although few are built on such a scale.

figures will always stand out; that is, they possess a comparatively greater "visual weight."

Visual weight is the degree to which any figure in the visual field commands our attention and sustains our interest. Casual observation is a light weight; extreme emotional involvement—fear, anger, love, hate—is a heavy weight.

Because perceived symmetry is seen as a characteristic of the human species, it may well account for the fact that we perceive symmetrical things to be beautiful. That symmetry is the most beautiful aesthetic state was a fundamental tenet of the Renaissance. The idea probably came from the Greeks originally and became one of the foundations of Western cultural tradition.

The natural landscape (inanimate figures or objects) is seldom, if ever, symmetrical to the casual observer. Fields, mountains, lakes, streams—the entire panorama of geology spread before us—displays little evidence of symmetry. Intermediary figures, like plants, display asymmetrical characteristics in their location and overall form, and their movements are perceived to be subject to natural elements. Any symmetry they possess is detectable only on close examination. Thus, on purely visual data alone, persons (living creatures) are symmetrical; nature is asymmetrical.

It is our knowledge that tells us that all matter and the universal forces that apply to them (energy) are symmetrical and balanced, not our senses.

The Orient and asymmetry

Why Oriental cultures found beauty in asymmetry would be pure conjecture. Their focus seemed to be on nature, and their art may have intentionally reflected nature's forms rather than those of living creatures.

To Western eyes, trees that are symmetrical seem to be beautiful and carry a heavier visual weight simply because they are not commonly seen in that form. In formal gardens, trees are cut, bent, and shaped to conform to symmetrical concepts. All forms of symmetry attract our attention and approval. Western artists have learned to appreciate asymmetrical organization just as Oriental artists have come to appreciate symmetrical forms.

Twentieth-century Western art is based on a virtual denial of Renaissance traditions which grew out of the concept of symmetry. It incorporates a new and unfamiliar language consisting of abstractions of nature rather than its representation; of asymmetrical balance; and of subjects like color, line, and shape rather than images of persons or objects. It is a language that the general public has not learned—and does not understand.

Our ordinary life experiences do not prepare us to decode many of the visual messages written in such a language. Understanding is possible only if we learn a language's coding system—its grammar (the seman-

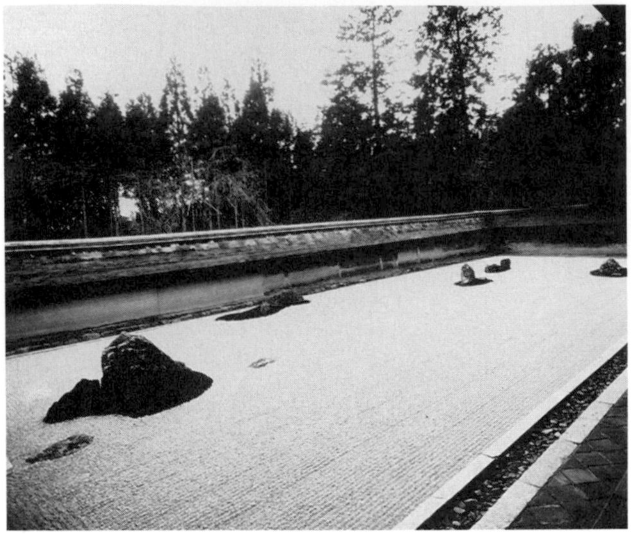

1.10 Ryoan-ji Temple, Kyoto. A formal Oriental garden of raked sand and rocks in an asymmetrical design. The Japanese construct these abstract dry landscapes to encourage quiet contemplation rather than typical garden activities.

tics, syntax, and pragmatics)—and if we do not draw impenetrable boundaries around our expectations.

How we derive understanding from sensory data

Any organism is more than the sum of its parts. Without any preconceived notion or picture of the whole mechanism and the way that it functions (a concept or a hypothesis), how can we possibly understand how the parts fit together? Would not an arbitrary arrangement be reasonable and functional? Even though the science of perception did not come along until three hundred years later, the 20th-century mathematician Christian Huygens observed that a person who has worked out a hypothesis that leads to a consequence is deceived easily and believes in the reality of what he or she hopes to see. Though not impossible, it is certainly very difficult to study parts of an entity and draw conclusions about that entity that are accurate.

Consider the problem of an interlocking jigsaw puzzle. If we do not have the picture, an idea of what the final result will look like (the concept or hypothesis), we have utterly no idea where to begin to solve the puzzle. Our only option is to look for edges of distinctly separated masses of light, dark, color, or texture. Suppose these do not exist. All conceivable configurations (that is, pure chance) are possible bases for organization.

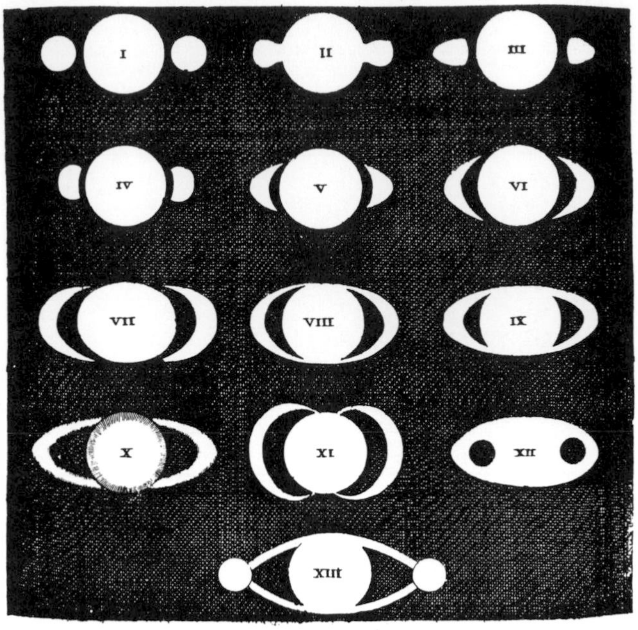

1.11 Drawings of the planet Saturn made by astronomers before Huygens. **I** illustrates Galileo's observations made in 1610. He visualized Saturn as a triple object, one large circle with two smaller ones on each side. Huygens also saw similar images when using a small, relatively primitive telescope. Some observations are thus accounted for by defects in the telescopes and by the fact that bright objects of any shape appear round when they are seen indistinctly. Other drawings are based on observations and theories proposed by a number of scientist-astronomers. For example, Riccioli thought the two "handles" of the planet were unequal in size—and consistently drew them that way (**III**, **VIII**, and **IX**). In a flash of insight, Huygens wrote, "[*W*]*hen someone has worked out a hypothesis which leads to a consequence, he easily deceives himself and believes in the reality of what he hopes to see*" (from Huygens, 1659, *Systema Saturnium*).

Perhaps a more concrete example is to be found in early scientific concepts about the nature of the rings of Saturn (Fig. 1.11). As there was no accepted theory or hypothesis (paradigm) that explained the odd shapes seen through the telescopes of the early 17th century, competitive theories evolved. The idea of rings, as such, was not even considered until 1659, when Christian Huygens, whose brother had built an improved telescope, was able to explain the phases of Saturn on the basis of a ring theory. Once a hypothesis has been accepted by independently applied tests that can be repeated exactly, it becomes a new paradigm, a "fact," by which all associated data are measured or compared, as it was in the case of Huygens' theory.

1.12 Close to one-third of gray matter in the brain is used to process visual information. In this cutaway view of the cerebral cortex, area **V1** appears to sketch the outlines of a scene, analyzing details of depth, color, motion, and orientation. Of six layers in **V1**, the fourth receives the sensory data sent along the optic nerve to the brain. Areas **V2, V3,** and **V3a** deal with analysis of edges, orientations, and depth. Cells in areas **V2** and **V1** respond to color, but only when it is defined by shape. The superior sulcus (STS) is predominantly concerned with motion. Sixty percent of the cells in area **V4,** discovered by neurophysiologist Semir Zeki in 1977, are coded specifically for color, with no regard for the shapes of the objects perceived. Compared with the eye's photoreceptor "rod" cells, which respond primarily to lightness and darkness, cells in **V4** respond only to precise red, green, and blue hues (narrow wavelengths of visible light). The retina's highly sensitive fovea with its concentration of "cone" cells (those that respond to red, green, and blue light) is given an overriding status in the visual cortex. *Areas in* **V1** *that respond to data from the fovea are 10,000 times the size of the fovea* and many times larger than those that respond to peripheral vision. Only the foveal areas of **V1** send impulses to the color area **V4.** The *fovea* is a small spot on the retina of the eye that resolves fine detail and provides our color vision.

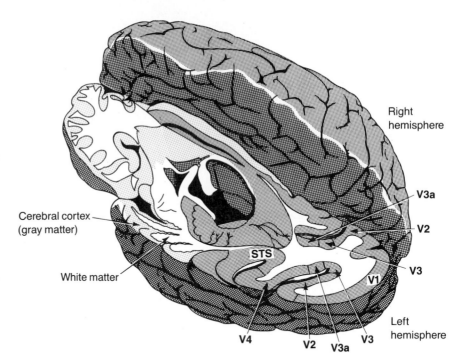

Examples like this show clearly how sensory data may lead us astray and point out that we must be wary of drawing conclusions from incomplete data or data that are *delimited* (surrounded by arbitrary boundaries). Yet this is the manner in which all perception operates. We do not normally apply the criteria of measurement to determine the accuracy of sensory data: what we see, feel, taste, smell, or touch. We regard our world as we perceive it. We use sensory data primarily as a means of getting around.

We pay attention to only a small part of all the sensual stimuli that surround us. The amount of sensory messages bombarding our brain at any given moment is so overwhelming that if we were not able to tune most of it out, we would cease to function.

This ability to give attention to some things while filtering out all others is called *perceptual selectivity*. The problem is that because we are selective in what we pay attention to, we often see only what we expect to see. An aspect of perceptual selectivity is a tendency not only to see what we expect to see but also to remain unaware of those things we do not expect. Psychologists call this *perceptual set*. Unfortunately, this latter characteristic often governs the way that we react to everything around us. We do not want our stable environment or any preconceived notion to be disturbed by the unexpected, so we simply ignore everything that fails to conform or view such things as irrelevant.

Some perceptual psychologists now believe that a good deal of what we currently call knowledge may be nothing more than perceptual accommodations to the negotiation of our environment.[3]

How the brain attaches meaning to visual figures

After separating figure from ground, the next activity of the brain is to attach a meaning to the figure, that is, to satisfy the perceptual imperative. To accomplish this task, the brain searches in its stored memory for a model or paradigm. Once a match occurs, the figure is "recognized" or given a name.

This procedure goes on millions of times every waking day. We are normally completely unaware of this process, yet it is basic to all activities in which we engage and is responsible for our ability to function in the physical world.

In this text, the term *meaning* is used in its most generic sense: to refer to perceptual *recognition*, the naming or identification of any figure-object. The term does not necessarily imply *message*, which is a correlation of meanings in a specific context for the purpose of communication — transmitting a purposeful thought, concept, or idea.

For the process of recognition and meaning to work efficiently, new patterns or paradigms must be constantly added to our memories and retained there for future comparison. This brain function is called *assimilation*. It appears that patternmaking is a learning process that begins even before birth, with outside sounds (mother's voice, for instance) penetrating into the womb. Some psychologists are now considering the possibility that conditions in the womb may determine, for an entire lifetime, both the attainable intellectual level and the learning capabilities of the child. There is little disagreement that experiences in the early months of life exert significant impact on these aspects. Like heart or lung processes, perceptual activity of the brain is an inseparable part of our physiology.

Almost one-third of the cerebral gray matter is involved in processing visual information. Much of the sensory data appear to be stored in discrete parallel processing areas that Michael S. Gazzaniga calls "modules."[4] Research by the neurophysiologist S. Zeki in Great Britain and C.R. Michael and P. Gouras in the United States, among others, has revealed a wealth of new information about the visual cortex. Some results of their studies may be seen in Figure 1.12. This information provides insights into the way that the brain processes and stores data related to edges, orientation, spatial depth, and color.

Realism and nonobjective abstraction: Two sides of the same coin

A large part of an artist's initial study is learning "how to see." We spend a lifetime using our vision incidentally in order to carry out some larger activity. We do not really look at the switch we use to turn off a light, nor do we examine the texture and construction of a baseball we catch. We are only vaguely aware of the character of almost everything until we have to draw it.

Completely objective re-creation of surface characterisics of anything may well be impossible. Much

of what constitutes any surface is invisible to the naked eye. A magnifying glass or a microscope is required, for example. Even the color that we attribute to surfaces is not a characteristic of the surface at all, but a phenomenon of light partly absorbed, partly reflected or transmitted, by the molecular structure of that surface.

No one perceives a painting as a window even though it may recall sensory data from the natural environment in its images. A painting is always a painting no matter how realistic we declare it to be. We know it can never duplicate actual reality; at best it merely imitates the image projected upon the retinas of our eyes.

In *Optics, Painting, and Photography,* Maurice Pirenne, lecturer in Physiology at Cambridge University, appraises similar ideas:

> . . . representation evidently is not, in itself, the aim of representational art. It is only one of the artist's means of expression . . . the belief has become widespread that an exact, complete and objective representation of the visible world could be made by an artist, but that this "mere imitation" would not be Art. Furthermore, it is believed that such a representation can be obtained "scientifically" by the use of photography . . .

> But, in fact, such a perfect, objective, representation can be obtained neither in painting nor photography. So, the striving of an artist after the (unattainable) ideal of "copying nature" does not necessarily entail any loss of originality.[5]

In this text we will use the term *representation* to indicate any subject that is pictured in a recognizable form. If it is very accurately portrayed, we may call it "realistic" or "naturalistic." An *abstraction* is a type of painting that clearly departs from the natural appearance of things, but the images may be still very recognizable. Degrees of abstraction vary from fairly realistic (just simplified shapes) to works called "nonobjective" or "pure" abstraction which make no reference at all to nature. If we mean to identify a composition that consists of lines, shapes, and colors that do not describe anything but themselves, the term *nonobjective,* by itself or together with the term *abstraction,* is preferred as it is more specific.

A *nonobjective abstraction* is the other side of the coin from realism. It is a composition laid bare, deprived of all nonessentials and reduced to pure structure composed of components of visual processing like line, shape, and color. All works of visual art are made up of these bits or fragments of visual data as our bodies are made up of cells, tissues, and bones.

A nonobjective abstract design (pure patternmaking) not only may be an end in itself but also serves as the underlying skeletal structure for any artwork in any form or in any style, including the most naturalistic realism. It always has.

Based on abstract visual components, works possess the elegant pattern of a mathematical formula or a manuscript for a symphony. Thus, inherent in basic abstract organization may be the very character (an unfamiliar language) that may cause a layperson to reject it. At the same time, no representational or naturalistic work possesses much aesthetical worth without excellence in its underlying nonobjective (skeletal) organization.

Patternmaking (perceptual organization), as a process, is purely abstract both in concept and realization. It is the syntax of the visual language, telling us how elemental visual components fit together.

Conclusion

Simply put, perception is a process of forming patterns from bits of data received by our senses, a biological function. The perceived patterns are compared and tested against paradigms (models) acquired through experience and knowledge, a mental function.

When we make distinctions between paradigms, our perceptual processes look for and evaluate the same visual components that artists have, for thousands of years, designated as elemental to visual fields.

Our perceptions govern everything that we do — whether we pay attention to something or not, what meaning we deduce from an experience, and commonly what action (response) we take in any given situation.

Perception operates, in its most rudimentary form, at the survival level. Our senses deliver raw data to the brain, which the brain, in turn, utilizes in ways to protect us from harm, to obtain nourishment (food and drink), and to reproduce. As such, it is likely that some perceptual responses are significantly influenced by genetic memory. Our perceptual responses have been created by natural selection (biological adaptations over thousands on thousands of years) and possess inherent emotional characteristics like fright, pain, anger, and love.

Just a few years ago, the majority of scientists believed that environmental influences (nurturing) overwhelmingly determined individual behavior. Recent exhaustive studies of twins separated at birth and reared apart show that genes play a far greater role in behavior than was once thought. Textbooks will have to be rewritten.

Visual language has grammar. It is based on perceptual processes, and its organizational structure is keyed to stimulating viewer responses. That is, visual language is rooted in the way that we see, integrate, and respond to visual sensory data.

Random notes on a musical instrument produce noise. Random letters or words produce gibberish — literary noise. Lacking any cohesive structure, random visual elements produce visual noise.

In any situation where there is no coherency between the sensory data and our experience or knowledge, meaning is diffused or nonexistent. It is just "noise." Visual elements, like notes in music or words in a sentence, are associative in application. It is in this context that the basic principles of perception (organization and meaning) become operational.

Review of key terms

assimilation A process by which a meaningful percept (a figure or impression) obtained by one or more of the senses is compared to the vast body of past personal knowledge and experience; placing things physically or psychologically in a familiar context.

asymmetry The principle of the seesaw transposed into pictorial form. Parts of a composition, unequal in area (size), are balanced in visual weight in either side of an imaginary fulcrum. The fulcrum is the center of visual balance, not the center of the picture.

autonomic Spontaneous or involuntary.

behavioral conditioning A term that encompasses anything learned by experience and practice: observation, imitation, formal education, and any behavior modification due to reward and punishment. This concept is often generalized as "nurture" as opposed to "nature," which consists of innate or genetic characteristics.

change A transition from one state to another, altered state; a movement from one place to another place; a passage from one moment in time to another; any sort of slow transformation, such as metamorphosis, growth, decay, and erosion.

contour The outline of a figure-object or mass. Commonly refers to the shape of a three-dimensional body as represented on a two-dimensional surface.

contrast Opposing qualities of things when compared or set side by side; or the accentuation or sharpening of such differences.

delimit To establish limits or boundaries.

figure In this text, the term describes any shape or form enclosed by a boundary or contour line, which is seen as separate from the ground or background. Ground is neutral; figure is not. The term, as used in science, psychology, and in this text, does not necessarily imply a person as in the common expression *figure drawing*.

genetic, genetic memory Pertaining to the biology of heredity. Physiological body processes or characteristics, mental or physical predispositions, or actions due to the genetic makeup of an organism. These are often called *innate*. Genetic memory in humans is generally allied to what we call "instinct" in lower animals and is often generalized as "nature" versus "nurture." *See* **behavioral conditioning.** *In this text, every reference is to the genetic characteristics all human beings share, NOT to individual or family traits.*

ground The background against which figures are perceived. Grounds are fluctuating entities depending on whatever in the visual field is the focus of our attention. *Note:* The term is also commonly applied to any of several materials, like gesso, applied to a support in preparation for painting or drawing. Do not confuse the two meanings.

irradiation A perceptual illusion in which our brain makes a dark edge darker and a light edge lighter in order to clarify and strengthen the formation of the edge. Some psychologists call this "contrast"; this text prefers the term *irradiation* to avoid confusions with the broader meanings of the word *contrast*.

mass Any body of matter perceived to be unified but without regard to specific shape; any cohesive group of objects so perceived.

nonobjective "Pure" abstraction, that is, figure-objects that make no reference or bear no resemblance to the forms of nature or the natural world or to man-made objects or structures; nonrepresentational.

paradigm A model or a blueprint, especially one perceived to be definitive.

perceptual selectivity and set A process allied with assimilation. Everyone of us sees what we look for, that is, *what we expect to see,* while remaining unaware of things we do not expect to see. This process may become fixed and prevent acceptance or recognition of new knowledge even when it is explicitly clear. Where any strongly held belief is challenged, contrary knowledge may so destabilize an individual's personal world that he or she chooses denial as a means of escape. This condition is referred to as *perceptual set.*

recognition A simple act of identification that gives a name to a familiar figure-object—the most fundamental level of deriving *meaning* from sensory data.

Renaissance A period of revived intellectual and artistic enthusiasm from roughly the 14th century to the 16th century; also pertaining to the styles, characteristics, and attitudes of that period.

stereotype A vastly oversimplified model, concept, opinion, or belief in which things typify or conform in an unvarying manner and without individuality.

symmetry or symmetrical balance Exact repetition or correspondence of shapes on opposite sides of an axis or a point. When correspondence is not exact, but still similar, it is called "approximate" symmetry.

visual weight The degree of attention, or sustained interest, which any single figure-object (or mass) commands related to all other elements in any visual field.

CHAPTER TWO

Coherence: Visual structure and unity

The dominance principle

Human beings are psychologically disturbed and often deeply upset by imbalance, disorder, chaos, tension, and conflict. Our lives are filled with struggles against such elements which we try to resolve—which we are driven to resolve. Life is characterized by decisions, decisions, decisions. We are comfortable only when we feel in *equilibrium*, that is, balanced and in control not only of the world immediately surrounding us but also of our own person, mentally and physically.

We attempt to maintain our equilibrium in several ways. One way is by escaping whatever upsets us. This is the most common solution to any circumstance that appears insoluble. We can observe the escape motive in lower animals whose first reaction to danger (a predator) is to run. An animal fights only when it is trapped or must protect its defenseless young. Human beings are likely to react to a life-threatening situation in a similar manner, a fact easy to understand. Not so easy to understand is the mental escape, which is a means of avoiding less obvious, less immediate, or often less terminally threatening problems. It is a far more common reaction, a feeling that if we just ignore a problem or turn our backs on it, it will go away.

Another way to maintain equilibrium is to achieve

dominance. A conflict is resolved by exercising our ability to control, absolutely if possible, all those things over which we can exert or impose influence. We use our physical power, mental power, or combine these to reshape or to redirect an event. Achieving dominance is a natural survival characteristic. Samuel Johnson observed that no two men can be together a half hour before one will acquire an evident superiority over the other.

If we cannot escape or dominate, the problem may produce a festering mental wound that never heals, with consequential mental instability.

Life: A never-ending series of decisions

It is important to realize that every function we perform requires hundreds, perhaps thousands, of decisions. For example, each of us needs to decide when to eat the next meal, where it will be eaten, and what it will consist of. There is the matter of getting from here to there, what sort of transportation might be needed, or what route to take, how soon it is nec-

2.1 Walter Crane. *The Horses of Neptune.* 1892. Oil on canvas, 33⅞ × 84⅝" (86 × 215 cm). Neue Pinakothek, Munich. Observe the lines of movement and rhythmic repetition of line and shape—the arcs. Horse shapes and the curves of waves are motifs interwoven into the composition. Note arcs (compressed, expanded, and anamorphically distorted) are repeated everywhere, including in the horses' manes.

essary to leave the place where we are in order to arrive where we want to be at a predetermined time, and so on. True, many decisions are small, and we make them without conscious awareness, but they are all elements in the continual stream of decision making.

Life consists of unending conflicts that no one can escape. In virtually every situation, incompatible responses compete for our attention all at once. If we are mentally healthy, such conflicts are resolved by dominance, and equilibrium is temporarily restored. Alternately, one response is permitted to dominate, then another, creating an cyclic pattern of behavior. Dominance restores equilibrium, which initiates another cycle. This is a normal behavioral pattern that continues throughout our lives.

Artistic conflicts are also resolved by dominance.

Ways to achieve dominance in a pictorial field

The focal point of a work of art is the most dominant feature in a hierarchy of primary and secondary figures or masses. The term *hierarchy* means to arrange things in a graded series with each level subordinate to the one above. (See Fig. 2.2.) Establishing the *visual hierarchy* provides a logical sequence of images through which a statement or message can be understood. The dominance principle is the major instrument of coherency in the visual language. It is also a major contributor to its syntax.

The hierarchy of dominant and subdominant figures not only provides viewers with something to look at first, second, third, and so on, but also sets up all of the basic patterns of movement throughout the work that lead the eye from one point to another. Parts of the work are observed in the sequence desired by the artist rather than at the pleasure of the viewer. If the viewer's eyes are permitted to wander at will through a work, then the artist has lost control or has deliberately relinquished control for a defined purpose. Losing control should never occur accidentally.

Equilibrium is maintained in a pictorial field by establishing a sequence of dominant and subordinate elements.

There are two primary means of establishing dominance: coherence and visual weight. *Coherence* results from the understanding and management of visual qualities like proximity, similarity, continuity, and closure. These qualities help to produce consonance (rhythm and harmony), which unifies works of art. They are part of a collection of techniques we call "connections of the narrow kind." A stronger force for managing dominances is *visual weight*. Six factors give artists their primary ability to manage dominances in a work of art. These are balance, orientation, attraction, space, change, and psychological force. We may emphasize or de-emphasize any part of a work at will; push or pull (warp) a two-dimensional surface to create any sort of spatial effect; imply actual movement or stimulate movement in visual terms. Visual weight may be balanced in much the same way as we would balance a physical scale like a seesaw.

The rest of this chapter will deal with the characteristics of coherence that Gestalt psychologists first identified as the primary ways in which visual fields are organized. In later chapters, we will examine visual weight in considerable detail.

Gestalt psychology

The beginning of Gestalt psychology is generally attributed to a paper published in 1912 by Max Werthheimer. The German word *Gestalt* is not easily translated into English. It unites the concept of "wholeness" with ideas of form, shape, and pattern. Gestalt psychology emphasizes the fact that behavior and experience must be studied as organized wholes and cannot be understood by analyzing parts. One must have a concept of how the whole functions in order to determine what relationship one part has to another and to the whole. Responses are not seen as a sum of independent sensations or other elementary processes but are dependent on and serve the requirements of the whole mechanism.

The Gestalt psychologists developed the theory that patterns or groupings are the primary elements of perception. Werthheimer proposed certain principles that explained how the brain organizes parts of visual fields into "figures" and "grounds."

These concepts have provided a reliable psychological basis for spatial organization and graphic communication.

The principles of Gestalt

The original Gestalt psychologists formulated a number of "laws" or principles related to the organization of visual fields. We will be concerned only with those that follow. These have been modified to reflect contemporary thinking and terminology. It is important to keep in mind that each principle does not operate independently but always works in concert with every one of the others.

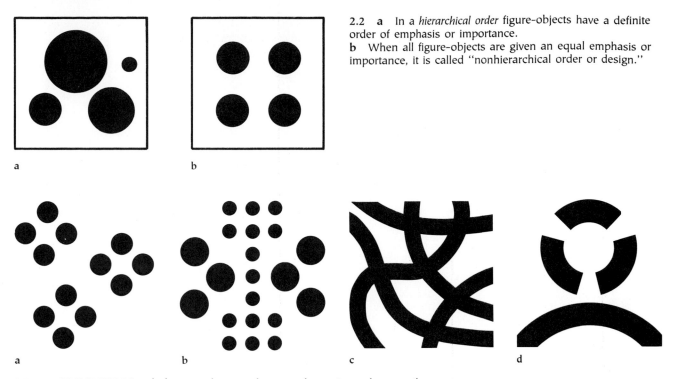

2.2 **a** In a *hierarchical order* figure-objects have a definite order of emphasis or importance.
b When all figure-objects are given an equal emphasis or importance, it is called "nonhierarchical order or design."

a   b

a   b   c   d

2.3 **a** PROXIMITY. Visual elements that are close together unite and are easily seen as a figure.
b SIMILARITY. Visual elements that resemble one another, whether in size, shape, or color, unite and are seen as a figure.
c CONTINUITY. Organization tends to flow in one direction. We have no difficulty following any single line or contour through a maze of lines.
d CLOSURE. Visual elements in close proximity that suggest contours of a form, though incomplete or separated by gaps, will visually join to become a closed form.

All principles of Gestalt psychology deal with coherent factors, that is, grouping—the joining together and orderly (or logical) relationship of parts, which lead to recognition and comprehension.

1. *Proximity.* What is closest together unites. Elements that are near to one another join together to form patterns or "groupings," figures against the ground (Fig. 2.3 **a**).

2. *Similarity.* Visual elements that resemble one another in some way (form or shape, size, color, direction) unite to form a homogeneous group *figure* (Fig. 2.3 **b**). Modern psychologists believe that the orientation—or slope—of lines is the major factor in similarity grouping.

3. *Continuity.* Perceptual organization tends to move in one direction; thus we can follow the path of a single line (or contour) even in a maze of many overlapping lines (Fig. 2.3 **c**).

4. *Closure.* We possess an innate tendency to perceive multiple elements as a group or totality, to close gaps and to make wholes. The result is more visually stable. When we can achieve this, we are both physically and psychologically rewarded. We feel good. If edges, contours, or masses are not joined, our brain may connect them together if it can find evidence of continuation. The fewer the interruptions or discontinuities, the more likely closure will occur. Such "closed" areas are readily seen as a figure (Fig. 2.3 **d**). Closure is a confirmation by the brain of a *preexisting idea*; it is not a verification of knowledge.

5. *Equilibrium (balance and orientation).* Every visual field tends toward excellence or precision—completeness—just as all physical activity is directed toward attaining physical balance or achieving equity in opposing forces. The idea is reflected in the ancient Chinese concept of the yin and the yang.

Coherence: Visual structure and unity   **23**

2.4 The Gestalt principle of *similarity* compares likenesses of things. It combines with *equilibrium,* a principle that states that figure-objects tend to assume their most regular form, so that the brain "expects" that when visible parts of half-covered figure-objects are alike, the whole is also alike. Therefore, when we observe figures that are overlapping like those seen in **a** and **e**, we expect the partly hidden form to be a duplicate of the one in front of it, such as two pennants **b** or two rectangles **f**, because these are the *simplest or most regular explanation*. We do not expect to see shapes like **c** and **d** or **g** and **h** although they are equally reasonable.

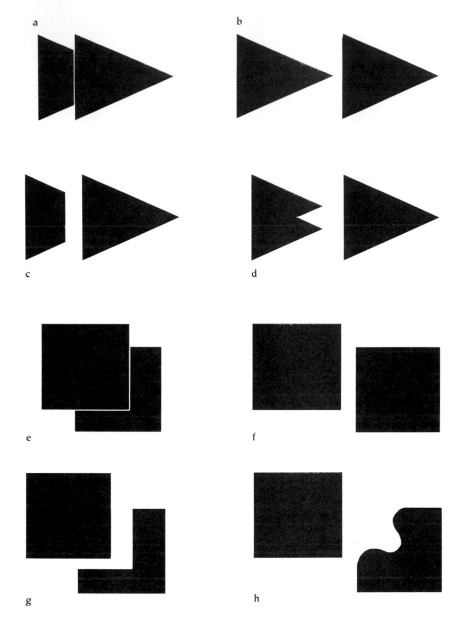

Psychologically, we are very uncomfortable — sometimes frightened — by anything perceived to be out of balance whether or not it is something we are experiencing physically or perceiving visually. It is a condition that we will not tolerate for very long.

Nature strives for the most regular organization possible. Evidence of this may be observed in a water droplet; stretched out as it starts, it gradually changes to a spherical form as it falls. Consider minerals whose crystalline structure is the most regular (simple) organization of their molecules.

Our visual perception conforms to this concept. We prefer or are attracted to, figures that exhibit the fewest alternative modes of organization. The brain tends to see the stimulus as more correct than it really is by mentally altering the configuration of any figure-object or thought perceived to fit the simplest interpretation. It is a process of stereotyping or model making.

We assume that objects viewed have a regular organization. When we see matching parts of over-lapped figures, as seen in Figure 2.4 **a** and **e**, we expect them to appear like **b** or **f** when viewed separately. We assume that the image is a consequence of the overlapping to two figures of exactly the same shape (the simplest interpretation). Yet all the other

2.5 *Isomorphic correspondence* is a relationship between the visual appearance of a figure-object and a comparable response in human behavior. What kind of a reaction do these rose thorns produce?

configurations shown are equally as reasonable.

Modern psychologists now believe that two other organizing principles play primary roles in perception: assimilation and irradiation.

6. *Assimilation.* This is a process by which a percept (a meaningful impression) obtained by any one or more of the senses is related to the vast storehouse of past experience and knowledge.

Assimilation is responsible for a characteristic that psychologists call "isomorphic correspondence." This is the relationship between the appearance of a visual form and a comparable response in human behavior. We know the glowing red coils on an electric stove will burn us; we will recoil and shout at a small child about to touch them. We can *feel* the hurt. Seeing an image of broken glass or of sharp thorns may cause most viewers to shiver (see Fig. 2.5). We are reminded of a previous uncomfortable experience with these and respond emotionally to the visual image. The image — sometimes the mere thought — of a gun or a knife disturbs some persons because the function of guns and knives is well understood. In the arts, isomorphic correspondence is an especially valuable concept. When the correct groundwork is laid, the emotional response may be very strong.

During the climactic moments of the film *The Empire Strikes Back*, many in the audience actually feel the horror and pain when Darth Vader cuts off Luke Skywalker's hand with his light saber. In this instance, empathy plays a role. *Empathy* is a strong identification with another person's feelings, situation, and motives. The entire acting profession depends on arousing such emotional responses from an audience.

7. *Irradiation.* This is a perceptual mechanism that locates edges by comparing areas of lightness and darkness (contrast), a subject we discussed in the last chapter.

Everything we understand is subjective

Absolutely everything that we learn is subjective. No true objectivity probably exists. We can attempt to be objective only when the desire is very strong and highly motivated; even then it may be impossible to overcome deep-seated (rooted-in) prejudices—habits of thinking and behavior developed over a lifetime.

Although individually we may draw widely divergent conclusions from identical sensory data, the manner in which the brain receives and processes this information appears to be the same for all normal individuals. Perceptual mechanisms are a function of biology.

Separating figure from ground

Before we can "see" anything, we must separate it from ground, its background or field. Whatever we look at automatically becomes "figure" and is always seen against a "ground." Figure and ground may reverse or flip-flop, but we can see only one figure at a time. Our perception that a field may be filled with figures is a product of the brain's reconstruction and stabilization of the visual field, not of visual processes themselves. Some figure-ground relationships may be observed in Figure 2.6.

In order to survive, our species had to learn to search for meaningful shapes in the environment, for example, a lion or a tiger half-hidden in tall grass waiting to pounce on us (Fig. 2.7). We had to distinguish the animal's shape mostly blocked by tall blades

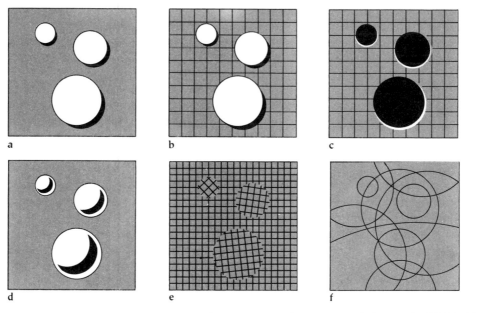

RELATIONSHIPS BETWEEN FIGURES AND GROUNDS
2.6 **a** Figures usually sit on top of, or appear in front of, a simple (plain) ground. The ground is seen as a surface.
b On complex ground, a figure may stand out sharply or merge with the ground, depending on how the artist handles the distribution of visual weight.
c Figures seen as a holes in the ground rather than as objects in front of it.
d Ground seen as space—figures float in it.
e Figure and ground merge (meld).
f An ambiguous visual field. We cannot determine what is figure and what is ground.

of grasses of the same color as its hide, its *camouflage*. If an early human was unable to see a concealed predatory animal, that person's genetic structure was not passed on to the next generation because he or she became the animal's dinner. It is characteristic of our eye-brain processes to seek out and separate such shapes (camouflaged figures) from the general or common texture and color.

Ambiguous figures

Determining what is figure and what is ground is not always easy. All visual fields exhibit potential ambiguities. Supplementary data obtained by our other senses is often inadequate to resolve such problems. From the moment of our birth, we begin to acquire a set of *cues*, a kind of bag of tricks. They work so well for us in our day-to-day activities that we normally are unaware of their existence. A few diagrams will show that these cues (coded visual data) do not work in all instances, and they also provide us with an opportunity to see and understand how cues work.

In Figure 2.8 **a**, which cross is the figure? What is seen first? As a rule, the smaller elements are seen as figure, but wider segments may be seen as figure, simply by willing to do so or by blackening them as in Figure 2.8 **b**. The principles of contrast and of similarity are at work here. When the shading is eliminated and the segments of the 12-sided figure separated only by lines (Fig. 2.8 **c**), the result is more ambiguous. Yet it is still possible to view either one set or the other set of segments as figure, whichever one we focus attention on. It is impossible to see both as figure simultaneously.

Seeing: Not the goal of vision

In her *Lectures on Visual Psychology*, Anna Berliner writes, "Seeing depends not only upon the environment, but also the state of the person . . . activities planned or completed, change the look of things. . . . In daily life seeing is generally not the goal, but it serves some activity in which it is imbedded."[6]

If seeing is not the goal, what is the goal? Our goal is to get around, that is, to negotiate our world.

We do not usually look at steps in order to use them; a quick glance tells us all we need to know. We have gone up and down steps thousands of times

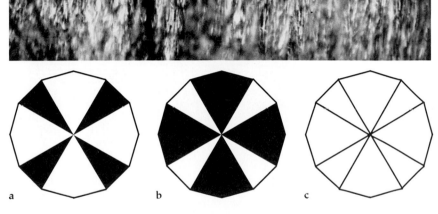

2.7 A majority of living creatures have acquired the ability to conceal themselves from another's eyes. Protective camouflage enhances concealment when stalking prey, thus improving chances of capturing food; or, conversely, it reduces chances of being caught by a predator and eaten.

a   b   c

2.8 Smaller units are usually seen as figure. In these examples, however, what appears to be figure can be changed simply by willing to do so. Like other equivocal (fluctuating) figures, we cannot see both the small and the large wedges as figures at the same time.

before, and they usually conform to a certain range of height versus depth. If they were not similar, they would not be functional. Unless steps exhibit unusual characteristics, we will ascend or descend them without even looking at our feet.

How many tines does a common dinner fork have? How many buttons are there on a touch phone or holes on a dial phone? When asked to draw a phone from memory, most persons leave off something, usually the cord that connects the phone to the phone line. This is because that cord is not normally used when making a call.

Artists must learn to see—to observe objects and conditions in ways contrary to the manner in which we normally use our sight.

Seeing artistically is something that does not happen automatically. Our powers of observation must be cultivated.

When figure and ground coincide

In some abstract works there may be no clearly defined figure and ground any more than there is in Figure 2.8. Ambiguity is part of the design concept in Figure 2.9, a work by Victor Vasarely, which is the same right side up as upside down. One way, the black figure becomes dominant because it is more easily identifiable as a person in that position; turned around, the white figure dominates for the same reason. Numerous works of M. C. Escher, like Figure 2.10, explore the figure-ground relationships. Simply by focusing our attention on one area versus another, we see different figures, always present, but which cannot be seen simultaneously. In some works these metamorphose into other figures. All two-dimensional space is included; figure and ground are at once, one and the same!

2.9 Victor Vasarely. *Catch.* 1945. Gouache, 17¾″ × 13″ (45 × 33 cm). Vasarely Center, New York. Turn this painting upside down. Ground has become figure; figure has become ground.

far right: **2.10** M. C. Escher. *Symmetry Drawing C.* M. C. Escher Foundation. Haags Gemeentemuseum, The Hague. Note how figure becomes ground and vice versa. Perhaps it seems like just a fascinating trick. Yet, Escher's work points up an important compositional truth: *grounds are EQUALLY as important as figures.*

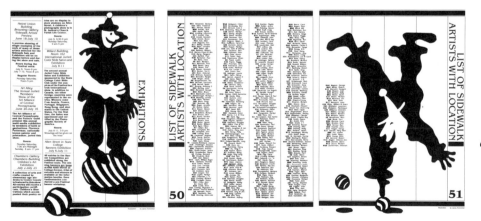

2.11 Lanny Sommese (Art Director, Artist, Designer), Andrea Hemmann and Carla Frank (Designers). Program for Central Pennsylvania Festival of the Arts. 1982. Cut paper; each page 11 × 7¾″ (28 × 19.7 cm). This work shows how the figure-ground concept may be used to create visually challenging illustrations.

2.12 Michael Vanderbyl. Symbol proposed but not adopted for the California Conservation Corps. 1976. One figure surrounds a space (ground) that becomes another figure in this logotype.

Figure-ground reversals are effective ideas for painting, illustration, and design. In this announcement for a sidewalk art exhibition, Figure 2.11, the arm and hand of the clown, left, is carved out of negative space. When we look at it, the arm becomes positive, that is, a figure, and the black body becomes ground. At right, a similar technique produces the clown's head. In a logotype for the California Conservation Corps, Michael Vanderbyl creates mother bear and cub using the same black configuration (Fig. 2.12).

Sometimes the position from which we view a figure transforms it. Figure 2.13 comes from a book whose illustrations are created to depict one scene rightside-up and a completely different scene later in the story when turned upside down. The illustration changes by virtue of its "orientation," as a scene, for example, featuring a giant bird becomes an island with an attacking fish. *Orientation* refers to the alignment (or position) of a thing with respect to a specific direction, reference system, or axis. Gravity is the most predominate reference system. Orientation is discussed in Chapter 6.

Closure: Complete figures from incomplete data

The principle of closure enables us to join elements together to form a meaningful figure. Question: How far can the elements of a figure be dispersed and still join together? How little of the object can be visible in order for assimilation and identification to occur? The "word" in Figure 2.14 is shown progressively dismembered. At each stage, recognition becomes more difficult. Cover all the stages except the last. Is it possible to make it out now?

Chunks of the line drawing, Figure 2.15, are added progressively. At which stage does it become

2.13 Gustave Verbeek. From *The Incredible Upside-Downs of Gustave Verbeek*. 1963. Copyright The Rajah Press 1963. The text from this children's book not only begins the story rightside-up and concludes it upside-down, but the illustrations also invert to depict the appropriate action in the story. Turn this one upside down, and take a look.

2.14 Cover all but the lowest image **d** in this figure. Now, can the word be read? Uncover the next **c**. Now is it readable? What about **b**? Conclusion: for recognition and meaning to occur, forms or shapes must conform to expectations within fairly narrow limits.

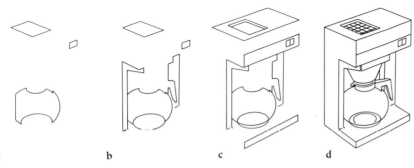

2.15 Cover all but the far left image. Is that enough to identify the object? Uncover the others in sequence. Compare the results with Figure 2.14. Do the shapes of familiar objects have broader recognition factors than the abstract symbols (letterforms) required for the written language?

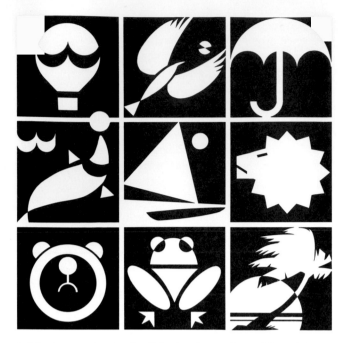

2.16 An exercise in simplification for students. Nine objects are reduced to minimal detail of shape, yet remain easily identifiable. Such simplification is a basis for the creation of trademarks, icons, and other symbols. Is it also an example of stereotyping?

2.17 Ted Trinkhaus (Designer and Art Director) and Sherman Wiseburd (Photographer). *The Miracle Worker,* promotional advertisement for the film. © 1962 Playfilm Productions, Inc. All Rights Reserved. Is the fuzzy image disturbing? Does this contribute to its effectiveness?

possible to identify it? How much can be deleted from an image and still maintain recognition? Find out by tracing objects from photographs in magazines. Trace only outlines, dropping out whole segments. Try them out on friends or associates. Very few are likely to be unidentifiable. How much can be left out, and how much must be retained? How significant is contour to recognition? Are some things more important than others? This is not only an exercise in the principle of closure but also one in simplification. (See Fig. 2.16.) The exercise points out how important visual stereotyping (creating models-paradigms) is to the recognition process.

Conclusion. Even though our perceptual capability to combine and extend visual fragments to form whole figures is quite remarkable, it has definite limitations. In creating works of art, the artist knows what she or he is portraying; a fraction of an object may meet the artist's own personal expectations — expectations that the viewer may not share. Unresolvable elements become an exercise in frustration for everyone. We can look at such a field for a short time and try to figure it out, but then we lose patience, ignore or reject it, and go on to something else.

Emotional correspondences in visual fields

We simply cannot deal with an unresolvable field for very long; it arouses our emotions: unpleasant feelings, instability, nervousness, and ultimately anxiety.

Obviously, this knowledge can be used creatively to stimulate emotions appropriate to solving some kinds of visual problems. The effectiveness of the poster for the film *The Miracle Worker* in Figure 2.17 depends on such ambiguities in the photograph: figures not easily made out and the sense of distortion and movement. The image is disturbing. It is an image that captures the highly charged emotional character of the film, a story of the pivotal point in the life of Helen Keller, blind and deaf from birth, when she first establishes contact with the world outside herself.

If we can somehow obstruct or prevent closure of a split object normally seen as a whole entity, we can create tension at that point in the design or composition. (See Fig. 2.18.) It's a "foot in the door" technique commonly used in films of suspense.

Notice how the eye attempts to define patterns in the field of dots in Figure 2.19 **a** (like Fig. 1.1). If we change the *interval* (spacing between elements) to

2.18 Our urge to close shapes is so strong that when closure appears to be prevented, considerable visual tension occurs at that point. It is a "foot in the door" technique. How could the idea be used in an illustration or a painting?

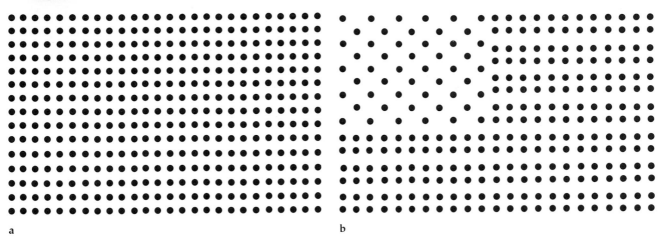

a   b

2.19 Why does the field of dots in **a** appear to form spontaneous patterns as we concentrate on it—rows horizontal, or rows vertical? What is different about the field of dots in **b**? Is an object instantly recognizable? Which Gestalt principles are at work?

assist this process, proximity and closure combine to create a familiar image, Figure 2.19 **b**. Because the dots are all similar, similarity is not a factor, but assimilation is. In this case, the pattern (model-paradigm) recognized suggests the American flag.

Assimilation

Assimilation is a term used to describe the vast storehouse of past experiences stored in our memory that each of us accumulates over a lifetime. It is what enables us to recognize a particular shape or form, the figure, as representative of something. Once a figure recognized, our brain has assigned a fundamental *meaning*. There are three stages of meaning:

   a. *Representation:* simple identification or naming of a figure or object based on stored paradigms (assimilated visual patterns).

   b. *Association:* an understanding of the relationship of one figure-object to another by function— bolt, nut, and washer, for example, or fingers, hand, wrist, arm.

   c. *Symbolism:* an understanding of figure-objects as

signs that stand-in for broad concepts or ideas—a kind of shorthand.

The coherency theory: A correspondence between parts

The coherency theory combines the concept of coherence, which is a logical and orderly arrangement of parts, with consonance, which is agreement or accord between parts (similarity). It is the syntax of the visual grammar. A major component of coherence is the dominance principle. In addition, the Gestalt principles of continuity and equilibrium, which we have already discussed, reinforce dominance and make their own contribution to the orderly sequencing of events within a visual field (a composition or design).

Harmony: Consonance through natural order

Consonance suggests that a composition may be made whole or unified by creating agreement between visual elements throughout a work of art. We can accomplish this by giving such things as line, shape, color, space, and motion qualities that are alike or that are very similar. When people view pictures, it is the

Coherence: Visual structure and unity   31

qualities of consonance that most of them recognize as being harmonious. Colors that are in sequence according to the spectrum (around the hue circle) or comprise a section of the hue circle (analogous colors) are consonant because each successive hue appears to contain a part of both the preceding and following hues. Lines or motions that go in one direction (have one orientation) are consonant, and they remain so even if they change direction *so long as we can observe the change* as it occurs.

What all these things have in agreement is *natural order*. Natural order is a sequence of logical and progressive steps in any event, activity, or procedure. One kind of natural or regular order would be an ordinary numerical sequence, for example: 1, 2, 3, 4, 5, 6, 7, and so on. A range of grays from white to black — or black to white — in even steps is a natural order, like black, middle gray, white, or a sequence of any such gradual change in the shape, volume, interval, or spatial position of any figure. One reason we perceive a rainbow to be beautiful is that it consists of a spectral hue sequence in natural order from purple-blue to green to yellow to red. Natural order may proceed backward as well as forward as long as the correct sequence is maintained. Arranging things alphabetically would be placing them in a natural or customary order, but an order that is a culturally based response.

Natural order produces strong "affective (emotional) influences" on a viewer: familiar, comfortable, easy, fast, correct, right, normal, nonthreatening, harmonious, like nature. Obviously, this places a viewer at ease.

Affective responses are not only emotional constituents of a sequence, like natural order, but also of varieties of line, shape, color, space, and movement, for example. It is the goal of the majority of art forms to touch the viewer, the listener-audience, or the reader *emotionally*. As we proceed through this text, the subject of "affective responses" will grow in importance and significance. In order for references to be easily located later, mark all information such as that in the preceding paragraph with a distinctive color highlighting marker, like orange or pink, different from one, if any, being used to mark general points of interest.

Unnatural order. Unnatural order is any arbitrary sequence not in a regular progression, for example, 7, 1, 5, 9, 2; or black, white, middle gray. Objects in unnatural order do not appear to share common traits with their neighbors. They are not consonant (similar); consequently, unnatural order is more difficult to make work in a composition because other forces must be used to create balance.

Unnatural order carries with it all meanings opposite to natural order: uncomfortable, difficult, slow, incorrect, jarring, chaotic, against nature, insane, threatening, and disturbing. Here a viewer is upset, perhaps agitated; there is definite arousal and excitement, the degree depending on everything in the visual field as related to a contrast range from natural and lifelike (mild interest) to the opposite pole (a highly disturbed state.)

Consonance through agreement in shape

One of the most effective means of creating consonance in a pictorial field is through repetition of a shape in whole or in part throughout a composition, painting, design, layout, or illustration. Repetition creates a quality called *rhythm*. Such a shape becomes a "motif." A *motif* is a pictorial fragment that is repeated throughout a composition or design. Observe how the repetition of arcs (the motif) produces rhythms throughout Walter Crane's *The Horses of Neptune*, Figure 2.1. A single motif can be used to create an entire rhythmic structure, or several motifs may be woven together (interlaced). To be effective, a motif should be simple; remember, it is a fragment on which complexity is built. Complex motifs, therefore, tend to be self-defeating. Motifs yield to all sorts of variations: They can be divided, decomposed, sectioned, intertwined, intersected, and so on.

In any single composition, a motif may appear fragmented (just a portion rather than the entire motif), in differing sizes (large, intermediate, small), in differing colors, in differing luminances (lightness or darkness), in differing orientations (right side up, upside down, sideways), or in altered states such as anamorphosis (that is, in a compressed or expanded form, as well as in its original configuration). Some figures may even be dismembered and reassembled so long as they are perceived to have a family resemblance to the original figure or to have been created from modules of the original figure.

Important: **Where a single motif is clearly and unequivocally stated in the composition, attention is irresistibly drawn to that spot.**

In Figure 2.20 **c**, a pattern of nine figures, the motif is invisible. Each completed shape seen is constructed on a square composed of 16 circles which is the actual motif. As resulting shapes all rely on the same underlying grid configuration (a modular

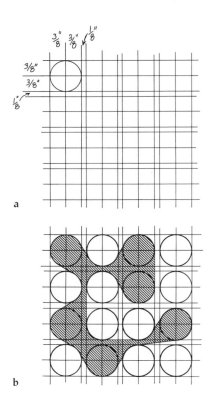

a

b

c

2.20 Using a grid such as that shown in **a**, a field of 16 circles may be constructed. All figures constructed with the 16-circle matrix, like the one shown in **b**, are harmonious because they share a common origin and some common contours. They are also inherently rhythmic. Why? Part **c** is an exercise for students consisting of an arrangement of nine such figures. (After an exercise devised by Armin Hofmann.)

system), their relationship is *symbiotic*; that is, though each one is different, their rhythmic similarities provide a unique family resemblance that makes them work together in harmony.

The pattern network

The overall composition of every work of art is not a single entity, but a combination of a number of individual patterns. The most important of these are the luminance (light-dark) pattern, the linear pattern, and the color pattern. In hierarchical compositions, all these patterns (abstract design structures) include dominance characteristics that overlay one another so that the dominances of all are in the same relative location in the composition.

These basic structural patterns work best when they are relatively simple, balanced (in equilibrium), and suggest wholeness or completeness. As a rule, the pictorial space should be filled (Fig. 2.21). White space is more often seen as mere emptiness (wasted

2.21 Lonni Sue Johnson (Artist) and Tom Laidlaw (Designer). *Untitled (Shipyard)*. 1982. Watercolor and ink, approximately 8½ × 11″ (21.6 × 27.9 cm). Chelsea Industries Annual Report. Open areas suggest emptiness, a void, or, at worst, a failure of the artist to complete the work. Perceptual fields are always perceived to be complete. Therefore, it is important to "fill" pictorial space. Notice how the boat is distorted to conform more closely to the given space. If the boat had been drawn with realistic proportions, what would have happened to the composition?

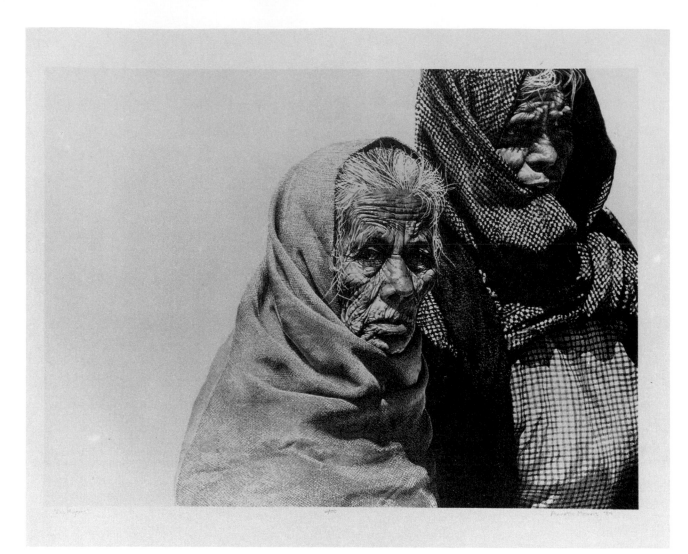

2.22 Annette Morris. *Dos Mujeres.* Stone lithograph, 19″ × 14″ (48.2 × 35.5 cm). The white left side of this lithograph perfectly balances the right. A fulcrum is firmly anchored at the old woman's eyes (just above center), which stare directly out at us. For "empty" space to become functional space, it must be perceived as if it were a figure and balanced as such, a difficult problem for the young artist.

space)—unfinished rather than functional space. In order for white space to work, it must be perceived as a figure, balanced as if it were a figure, and be appropriate to the concept (Fig. 2.22).

The emotional qualities or mood of a work become strongest when all the patterns have affective responses (emotions or "moods") that are either exactly alike or are quite similar.

A critical factor. The *luminance pattern* is especially important when work done originally in color must also be reproduced in black and white. This would

include all work designed for television, for instance. In any sort of realistic or naturalistic work, the luminance pattern generally outweighs all other color considerations. Only in abstraction, color-field, op art, and some graphic design does the color pattern assume the right of dominance. For thumbnail sketches, the *luminance pattern* can often be reduced to three or four tones: black, white, and one or two grays.

Remember, contours are lines. There are bold lines, thin lines, curved lines, straight lines, scratches, wrinkles, furrows, linear objects (string, wire, railroad tracks), paths or routes, margins or gutters. Each of

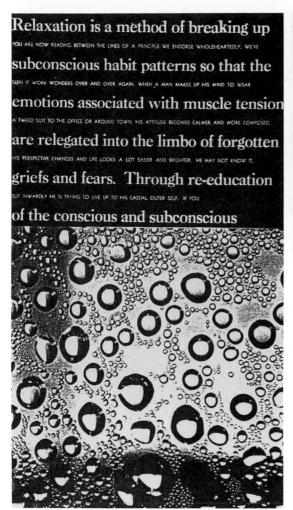

Relaxation is a method of breaking up

YOU ARE NOW READING BETWEEN THE LINES OF A PRINCIPLE WE ENDORSE WHOLEHEARTEDLY. WE'VE

subconscious habit patterns so that the

SEEN IT WORK WONDERS OVER AND OVER AGAIN. WHEN A MAN MAKES UP HIS MIND TO WEAR

emotions associated with muscle tension

A TWEED SUIT TO THE OFFICE OR AROUND TOWN, HIS ATTITUDE BECOMES CALMER AND MORE COMPOSED.

are relegated into the limbo of forgotten

HIS PERSPECTIVE CHANGES AND LIFE LOOKS A LOT EASIER AND BRIGHTER. HE MAY NOT KNOW IT,

griefs and fears. Through re-education

BUT INWARDLY HE IS TRYING TO LIVE UP TO HIS CASUAL OUTER SELF. IF YOU

of the conscious and subconscious

2.24 Bradbury Thompson (Designer) and Somoroff (Photographer). *Westvaco Inspirations 210: Rain, Rain, Rain,* 1958. Reprinted with permission of Westvaco Corporation. Although the type design and photographs in this advertisement pertain to weather prediction, that concept is quickly related to the business climate—a metaphor. Rows of type have become pictorial elements. Portions of the text are almost obliterated by the images. Could that ever be a problem? What about the difficulty of reading type oriented vertically? Note the rhythms created by repetitions of lines and shapes.

2.23 John David, Inc. © 1958. A simple, easily understood example of how more than one pattern can be interlaced (or interwoven) with another, whether image, symbol, literature, or concept.

these may possess differing orientations (position and attitude). There are invisible construction lines, which are connections of the "narrow" kind. There are lines of movement within any flat, two-dimensional work, including the eye movements of a viewer throughout a work as programmed and directed by the artist; and there are lines of direct or simultaneous motion in television, film, and film animation. These are all part of *the linear pattern.*

Consistency is essential between subject matter, the hues selected, the intended visual communication or expression, and the psychological associations appropriate to that overall concept. Color is the most inherently emotional visual component. For a *color*

pattern, artists always keep principles governing effective color schemes in mind, as well as the influence of visual weight. We will discuss all these things as we proceed through the book.

Two examples

The large water drops form one distinct pattern, and the small drops another distinct pattern, both of which are "interlaced" (alternated) in the advertisement in Figure 2.23). This pattern is precisely echoed in the manner in which the text is handled. We have no difficulty reading the large type as a continuous statement, any more than we do the small type. Similarity grouping in this case establishes the overall patterns and sets up *alternating rhythms.* Similarity also is at work in the spread from *Mademoiselle* magazine (Fig. 2.24). Similarity joins figures together, thus unifying the design; repetition sets up interesting rhythms; and variations from one to the other suggest motion —viewing a sequence of events simultaneously.

The two examples from applied art were chosen to illustrate these points because of their straightforward simplicity, obviously a virtue in each case. We ought to be able to recognize exactly the same sort of conceptual thinking and structure in works of fine art. Artists must sensitize themselves to the presence of

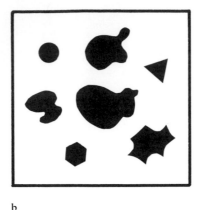

a　　　　　　　　　　　　　　　　b　　　　　　　　　　　　　　　　c

2.25 **a** *Monotonous shapes.* All the shapes, both figures and ground shapes, are very much alike and boring, even though they are relatively well placed in the picture frame. **b** The *polka-dot effect* results when all shapes are neatly centered in all spaces even if the shapes are interesting by themselves. Be wary of our urge to fill centers. **c** The *bull's-eye effect* occurs when everything is clustered in the center of a composition, with very little or no activity that extends to frame edges.

opposite: **2.26** *Form interrelationships:* **a** When two figures are completely *coinciding,* only one may be seen. **b** When one figure is *overlapping* another, it appears to rise above, and be in front of the other. **c** Similar to transparency effects, *penetration* tends to place emphasis on the altered figures (black parts of this diagram) though *intersection* tends to place emphasis on the alteration itself (white part). **d** In a *union* (or meld), figures fuse to become a new shape without any sort of dividing lines. **e** In *subtraction* (or decomposition), objects are sectioned or divided into parts. **f** *Touching* establishes tangents or points of tension. **g** *Detachment* is pulling things apart, creating gaps. **h** *Interlacement* intertwines figures like a basket weave or the way cloth is woven.

such techniques in every form of art and should observe how they often contribute to effectiveness — or how their absence tends to diminish the result.

Three most common coherency problems

Monotonous shapes. Although in certain design work, wallpaper and textiles, for example, repetitive shapes may be a virtue, in most painting, design, and illustration, such monotony is a most undesirable characteristic (Fig. 2.25 **a**). Deliberately vary area (mass), shape (contour), visual weight (attraction), and spacing (interval) so that figures and grounds will be distinctly different and interesting. Assess the quality of negative shapes by outlining them with a black marker on tracing paper and filling them in solid so they may be perceived as figures rather than grounds. Compose with simple, large shapes; these can be broken down into more complex configurations so long as the total integrity of each is not compromised.

The polka-dot effect. The polka-dot effect results from having spaces surrounding figures (above, below, and on each side) that are approximately equal throughout the work (Fig. 2.25 **b**). Before proceeding too far,

always check to see if spacing between figures, *the interval,* is visually different in the same way that the size of the figures and their shapes should differ.

The bull's-eye effect. Figure-objects are centered within the picture frame. Commonly, subordinate figure-objects — or compositional divisions — are centered also. Be sensitive to the fact that odd configurations or divisions of space are more dynamic than even divisions. Be conscious of the urge to fill centers, and avoid it like the plague. (See Fig. 2.25 **c**.)

Interestingly enough, there is also a reverse bull's-eye. This is where everything is arranged around the perimeter of the pictorial field or actually connected to the edges, leaving the center empty. *Good idea:* When attempting to work out a composition, cut basic shapes from sheets of wrapping paper or cheap construction paper. Move them around, overlap them, run some off the edges of the picture frame, and try some larger or smaller. Fool around with the organization until it looks good.

Visual problems are best solved visually.

Four ways to unify a composition

1. *Unit theory.* Figure-objects group or unite to pro-

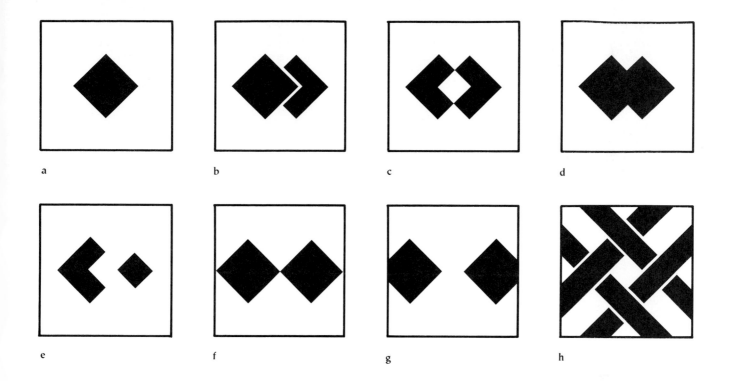

a b c d

e f g h

duce as few separate units as possible—*one unit* if at all possible. The primary techniques are those of the coherency theory and of Gestalt psychology: proximity, similarity, continuity, and closure; but other methods include coinciding, overlapping, penetration, intersection, union, and interlacement. The last six are "form interrelationships." (See Fig. 2.26.) Other *form interrelationships,* as identified by Wucius Wong,[7] are subtraction, touching, and detachment although these do not necessarily contribute to unity.

2. *Color tonality.* There are three alternate possibilities.

   a. A coordinated, rhythmically balanced pattern of hue, luminance, and purity—individually or all together. What this means is that we put a little bit of every color in every part of a work.

   b. A dominant tint technique, or a chromatic light technique. A bit of one hue pervades all other hues in the work.

   c. A monochromatic technique, one color *only* plus black, white, and a variety of grays created from mixtures of black and white or of gray and the single color (chromatic grays).

Though tonality may be more heavily dependent on luminance than any other dimension of color, it is usually regarded as an emotional quality that establishes the general mood through particular choices of hues, luminances, and degrees of purity.

3. *Dominant light pattern.* Shadows and chiaroscuro (shading or modeling) originate from a single light source, such as the sun. The single light is seen to suffuse and stabilize the entire visual field. Multiple light sources tend to flatten a visual field and rob it of its spatial dynamics; this increases ambiguity, is often confusing, and sometimes is very disturbing psychologically.

4. *Interaction of elements.* When figures-objects-elements look or point to one another or to a single point, unity is enhanced. Tension is increased or decreased as objects become closer together or spread apart. Watch out for the following problems. Tension between an internal element and the picture frame leads the eye out of the composition; tension tends to be completely neutralized when objects are centered, which ordinarily compromises all dynamics. (Do you recognize the bull's-eye and its reverse?)

Although not usually considered a visual design component, a single compelling idea may also contribute to unity. All elements will then be chosen that are appropriate to the purpose; that is, they will belong. Nonfunctional, superfluous, or extraneous parts will be excluded as inappropriate. It is knowing what is to be said, then saying it directly, clearly, and economically.

In almost any noisy environment, a spoken word stands out (advances) over extraneous sounds (noise recedes). This is because words have coherency that we immediately recognize and respond to. Their sound possesses a logical order and interrelationship that we recognize as language. This draws our rapt attention (figure) as opposed to the noise (ground), which we ignore as less important. The spoken word will usually override even distinct, directional environmental sounds.

All possible visual elements that we might use in a composition constitute a kind of visual noise. Every artist must continually struggle with these in order to reshape them into a coherent design.

Creating variety

Some persons are comfortable when everything is absolutely the same. They like to have familiar things about them, go to familiar places, eat familiar foods; in short, they like to have their perceived world disturbed as little as possible. Though we all prefer to have a very strong connection with a home ground (familiarity) because it makes us feel safe and secure, at least from time to time, most of us want to go to different places, do different things, try new foods. Variety, the old saying goes, is the spice of life. It is also the spice of visual fields.

To capture and retain a viewer's interest, we need to create variety everywhere. Of course, certain formal symmetrical or conceptual works may require absolute conformity, but, generally, within the framework of coherency, a work should exhibit a great deal of difference. We usually give our attention to the things in our visual field that are different, not to the things that are familiar (the same).

Though it is not as easy as it might appear, we can be sure we have created enough difference between parts of any pictorial field if we would just follow these four simple rules:

Do not give any figures, grounds, or any of their parts (1) the same visual weight, (2) the same shape, or (3) the same area or mass, and do not (4) space them at the same interval (distance apart).

Summary

Pattern selecting and patternmaking are at the heart of all works of art as they are at the heart of perception. Any work of art is generally viewed as more or less successful in accordance with the sense of completeness of wholeness perceived. This sense of unity is the result of the application of coherency to visual elements. Depending on the degree of that achievement, the work will tend to be emotionally satisfying. When we fail to discover a discernible pattern with a relatively easy point of reference, we quickly turn off and tune out.

Perceptual patternmaking, the grouping (or unification) of visual components, is facilitated if components (1) are reasonably distinct from their background (a figure-ground discrimination); (2) are close to one another (proximity); (3) are similar in shape, color, texture, size, and so on, and/or appear to have the same illumination (similarity); (4) have the fewest interruptions in contour, movement, or direction (continuation); and (5) permit formation of a shape identifiable as a figure (closure).

Few works of art consist of one single overall pattern. Each usually is made up of a number of different patterns overlaid on one another. Most commonly, there are a luminance pattern, a linear pattern, and a color pattern. One important point to remember is that the psychological associations (the mood) created for each pattern should all be very much alike, yet the pictorial elements should have variety in order to capture and sustain interest.

In addition, any truly effective composition normally requires a focal point and a coordinated pattern of dominant and subdominant elements, which we achieve by managing visual weight.

Review of key terms

closure Gestalt principle that describes an innate perceptual tendency to perceive multiple objects as a group or totality; to close "gaps" and to make "wholes" out of discontinuous lines, masses, or contours.

coherence A logical or orderly arrangement of parts, particularly one that provides comprehension and recognition.

consonance Agreement, conformity, harmony. *See* **rhythm**.

continuity A Gestalt principle of organization that states that perception tends to move in one direction. Thus, we can easily follow the path of a single line, for example, even in a maze of many overlapping lines. This faculty is part of a survival characteristic required to distinguish contours and thereby separate figure from ground. Also, more broadly, continuity means to carry forward in natural order. In television, film, slide presentations, and storyboards or multipanel art, it is a natural flow of events in *chronological* sequence.

cue A sign or signal that prompts someone to do something. In psychology, it is a perceived signal for action that produces an operant response.

dominance principle A perceptual characteristic that establishes psychophysical equilibrium in human beings. It is a rippling pattern of behavior in which first one thing, then another, is seen to dominate our field of view, mental state, or priority of action, preventing the sheer mass of sensory data from overwhelming us.

equilibrium A Gestalt principle of organization that states that every psychological field tends toward "excellence" or precision, that is, the most regular organization possible. The concept reflects physical activity of natural forces that strive for balance. A water drop changes into a sphere as it falls; water seeks its own level; and so on.

harmony Agreement, or consonance, between forms, shapes, colors, concepts or ideas, and so on. A perceptual characteristic identified by Gestalt psychologists as the principle of similarity.

hierarchy A clearly defined relationship between things that establishes differing levels of dominance, emphasis, or influence, with each level subordinate to the one above. Overall patterns with equally emphasized figures are sometimes called "nonhierarchical designs."

interval The amount of spatial separation between things such as lines, figures, colors, luminances, areas, spaces, times, and so on. Intervals are *regular* when spacing is all the same and *progressive* when the spaces change in natural order whether a simple numerical progression or based on a geometric ratio.

motif A design fragment, reduced to its most simplified form or configuration, that is used as a basic theme in a work of art. The motif may be repeated rhythmically, fractionalized, enlarged, and elaborated on; however, its presence always helps to provide coherency and unity in the work.

natural order In regular or normal order or sequence: hues according to their spectral sequence (red, orange, yellow, green, blue); even steps or gradations of gray from white to black or vice versa; and so on. Such sequences are psychologically comfortable, natural, easy, fast, and so on. *See* **unnatural order.**

orientation To align or position anything with respect to a specific direction, reference system, or axis, especially gravity.

proximity In Gestalt psychology, the principle in which things close together in a visual field join to make a perceptual "whole" or figure.

rhythm Repetition of any visual component—interval, shape, color, or motif (figure)—in a regulated patternmaking process. Shapes or motifs may be repeated in their entirety, fractionalized, compressed, or expanded, throughout a design.

similarity The Gestalt psychology principle that states that like elements, (similar shapes, or sizes, or colors . . .) perceptually join to form "wholes" or figures.

unnatural order Any arbitrary sequence like 7, 1, 5, 9, for example, or orange, blue, and red. Typical affective responses are "unnatural," slow, disturbing, jarring, and chaotic. *See* **natural order.**

visual field Essentially anything we see before us although, in specific instances, a visual field may be conceptually limited by perimeters such as a picture frame. In that case, it may be referred to as a *pictorial field.*

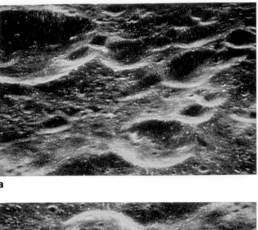

a

b

CHAPTER THREE

Illusion

Pictures have a dual reality

Flatness and three dimensions are perceived simultaneously in the same picture. Human beings examine a photograph or a realistic painting and "assimilate" it, bringing all their past experience with visual fields to bear on the image. The brain automatically decodes cues, both innate and learned, through which interpretations or understandings are obtained. The result is in the mind—a synthetic projection of the image. If a dog sniffs at the same picture, it will identify the picture for what it is, a piece of paper.

In *Perception of Pictures* (Vol. I), Ralph Norman Haber writes:

> . . . perceivers use the same perceptual processes when looking at pictures as when looking at natural scenes. This implies that with normal viewing, pictures, unlike scenes, have a dual reality: They are perceived as flat surfaces because head movements and binocular disparity produce retinal patterns indicative of flatness, and they are perceived as representative of three-dimensional scenes because the momentary pattern to either eye alone

is the same as that reflected from the actual scene represented by the picture.[8]

Visual ambiguity

Virtually every visual field has potential for visual ambiguity. Has anyone ever seen a two-headed camel? Because photographs, like all two-dimensional works, impose limitations on perceptual cues, the brain attempts to interpret pictures in accordance with the cues that do exist.

In our environment, *equilibrium*, that is, the assumption of what is "good" or "simple," generally

above left: **3.1**   Of course, cameras always record images factually and without distortion. That is correct is it not? No one should have a problem, then, with this two-headed camel. *All photographs are ambiguous* just as any two-dimensional field is likely to be. It is often impossible to know where volumes are located and to determine spatial relationships between figure-objects. Photographing a subject from many angles helps to overcome these problems.

above right: **3.2**   In the photo of the moon **a**, the craters are clearly visible. In **b**, they have mysteriously become mounds. Turn **a** upside down to discover where photo **b** came from. The effect witnessed is a phenomenon of light constancy in which all original light sources are perceived to be overhead.

40

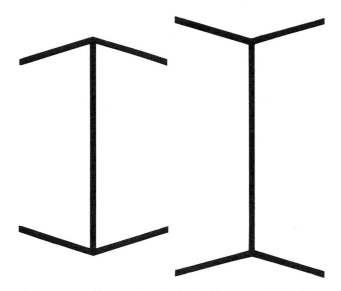

a ▲

above: **3.3** *Müller-Lyer Illusion* devised by Franz Müller-Lyer in 1889. Both vertical lines are exactly the same length even though they do not appear to be.

right: **3.4** One theory proposed to explain the Müller-Lyer illusion is that the brain unconsciously interprets the arrowlike figures as skeletal three-dimensional structures resembling the outside corner **a** or the inside corner **b** of a building. A perceptual mechanism appears to shrink the former and to enlarge the latter.

works in our favor. It enables us to achieve dominance and eliminate problems posed by such ambiguities. For example, we have the perception that light comes from above; therefore, interpretations of convexity or concavity are often dependent on that assumption (Fig. 3.2).

When we view pictures that reduce sensory data by eliminating or simplifying visual information, the remaining cues may cause contradictory responses. Let us take a look at a few such images, which psychologists call visual or perceptual illusions.

Size illusions

One of the best-known illusions is the Müller-Lyer illusion (Fig. 3.3). It may take a ruler to convince ourselves of the fact the lengths of the two vertical lines are exactly the same. This illusion is not fully explained after nearly a century of study. Most scientists believe it results primarily from spatial (depth) cues related to the arrowlike configurations formed by the corners of buildings, homes, and workplaces, as seen in perspective (Fig. 3.4). One reason for this explanation is the fact that Zulus who live in round dwellings do not appear to share the illusion.

b ▼

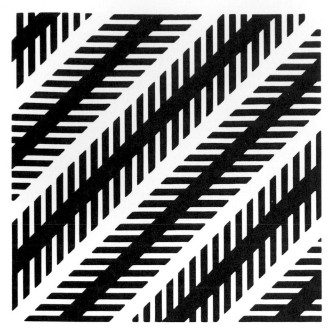

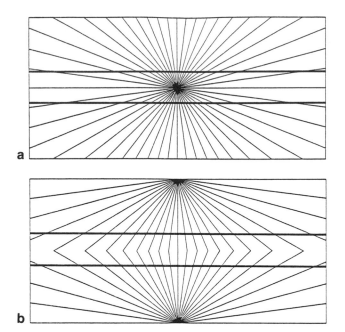

above: **3.5** *Zöllner Illusion,* published in 1860, was one of the first of the distortion illusions. Diagonal white bars and black bars are perfectly parallel. Smaller vertical and horizontal black bars pass straight through vertical bars, even though they appear to be offset. This illusion explains why straight lines sometimes appear crooked in a picture.

above right: **3.6** **a** *Hering Illusion,* first published in 1861, raised a question among physicists and astronomers about the reliability of visual observations. The horizontal bars are perfectly straight and parallel.
b A reverse of the Hering illusion was devised by Wilhelm Wundt in 1896. Both illusions explain why straight lines sometimes appear curved in a picture. How would we go about optically compensating for the effect?

right: **3.7** Devised by British psychologist J. Frazer, the illusion of a spiral is so strong in this figure that most persons find it hard to believe that it is composed of concentric circles even after they trace around each one. When an environment is very strong, it may completely overwhelm (and distort) our perception of any figure.

We tend to perceive acute angles as sharper and obtuse angles as wider than they actually are. The manner in which one line crosses another commonly affects how we view such lines. Parallel lines distort the oblique white and black bars in Zöllner's illusion (Fig. 3.5). Zöllner suggested that diverging lines lead the eye outward and make the space between seem larger than it really is. Further examples, in Figure 3.6 **a** and **b**, distort perfectly straight lines perceptually so that they appear curved. More astonishing is the design created from concentric circles (Fig. 3.7).

Both horizontal bars in Figure 3.8 **a** and **b** are exactly the same size. In Figure 3.8 **a**, the upper bar appears larger than the one below it. Like viewing railroad tracks as they run off to the horizon (Fig. 8 **b**), the converging lines are cues that trigger the illusion because *we know* (1) that figures that are higher in the visual field are further away and (2) that objects identical to one another will appear smaller when further away than when seen close up. Both of these illusions are related to depth cues discussed in Chapter 8.

Apparent size may be altered by association. The center letters *N* in Figure 3.9 **a** and **b** are identical, yet the one looks larger because we make comparisons between the object and its surrounding elements. Figure 3.9 **c** and **d** present another pair of images

3.8 a Both horizontal bars are exactly the same length in the *Ponzo Illusion,* proposed by Mario Ponzo in 1913. The converging lines suggest elements of Renaissance perspective.

b If the rectangles in this photograph were real objects lying between the rails, we would know at once that the more distant one was larger. Such illusions involving perspective are unusually constant for all human observers. Because we know distant railroad tracks are as large as near ones, the size of any object lying between the rails will be evaluated accordingly. This important size/depth cue provides one example of how the brain ignores retinal images to maintain rough size constancy for familiar objects located at differing distances.

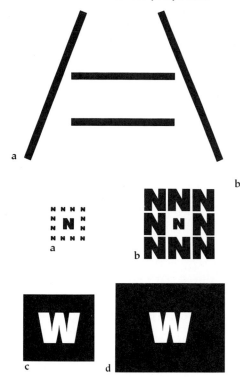

3.9 Our perceptions of an object's size whose dimensions are unknown are always related to what is next to them in their immediate environment. The center squares in both **a** and **b** are exactly the same size although they do not appear to be. The two W's in **c** and **d** are also identical in size.

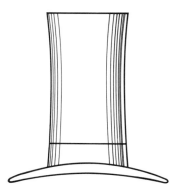

3.10 The illusion, whose horizontal and vertical dimensions are identical, is commonly known as the *Top Hat Illusion.* It shows that a vertical line appears longer than a horizontal line of the same measure.

3.11 Both **a** and **b** are squares identical to **c**; yet **a** looks taller, and **b** appears to be wider. The orientation effects of these stripes provide one way to make something appear to be wider or taller than it really is, a person or an automobile for example.

employing a similar illusion. The letter *W* appears larger in **c** because it fills the box and seems confined. The identical letter seems smaller by comparison when the surrounding space is enlarged and there appears to be ample space for growth or expansion.

The Top Hat illusion (Fig. 3.10) shows us that vertical lines appear taller than horizontal lines of the same measure. About a 15 percent increase in the length of the horizontal is needed to make the lines appear the same. One proposed explanation is that it requires more effort to raise the eyes than to follow horizontal motion. Three squares (Fig. 3.11 **a**, **b**, and **c**) are identical in size, yet **a** appears taller than **c**, and

b appears to be wider. The eye moves more easily along with the light or dark bars rather than across them because colliding with light and dark spots many times produces considerably more sensory data for the brain to process.

It should be obvious that these illusions trigger all sorts of brain activity that clearly distort the truth, truth that we can measure. The most reasonable explanation lies in the manner perceptual processing mechanisms are physically organized.

Equivocal, or alternating, figures

Another common illusion is Schröder's Staircase

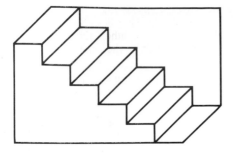

left: **3.12** *Schröder's reversible staircase.* This is a typical *equivocal figure,* that is, one that can be interpreted by the brain in more than one way. The brain alternates between recognition of the staircase as if viewed from the top (a bird's-eye view) and as if viewed from the bottom (a worm's-eye view).

right: **3.13** Is the image a rabbit or a duck? It is not possible to see both simultaneously.

a   b   c

left: **3.14** This young girl/old woman illusion was brought to the attention of psychologists by Edwin G. Boring in 1930. As created by cartoonist W. E. Hill, the young woman's chin is the old woman's nose. Some psychologists say that whichever image we see first is determined by our *mindset*—our current emotional relationship with an old or a young woman.

3.15 A series of "impossible" figures. We cannot accept these as representations of real objects, yet for some of them, it is possible to construct solid objects that will look the same when viewed from one particular direction. However, when viewed from some other direction, the actual objects appear as strange as the drawings.

(Fig. 3.12). Stare at it a moment. The perspective will spontaneously reverse. At one moment it will appear we are looking down on the stairs; in another moment we will be looking up. As the conflict between the two cannot be resolved, the brain gives dominance first to one idea and then the other because they are equally reasonable. Such a figure is often called equivocal.

What image is seen in Figures 3.13 and 3.14? Are there other possibilities? Is the rabbit really a duck (or vice versa)? Is the young girl really an old woman?

Impossible figures

Though the brain alternates between equivocal figures because each possibility is valid, it eventually rejects figures that present totally confusing cues as impossible. Figure 3.15 shows three such figures. M. C. Escher has carried these ideas to an intriguing extreme; an example is shown in Figure 3.16.

Figure-ground illusions

The brain's bag of tricks we call perceptual cues can lead to other forms of illusions. For instance, we can see "figures" where none exist except in our minds. The figures, a triangle and a square, seen in Figure 3.17 **a–b** are implied in each case by the configuration of the other elements. Our brain has manufactured them. When they are perceived, we seem to see a separation, and the figures tend to float somewhat above the ground. Is it possible to organize the spots seen in Figure 3.17 **c,** or are they random designs? Is there anything unusual about the cover design for the May 1974 issue of *Art Direction* magazine (Fig. 3.18)? Was it possible to figure this out before reading the caption?

These are often called figure-ground illusions because the brain oscillates between what portion of the visual field is viewed as figure and what as

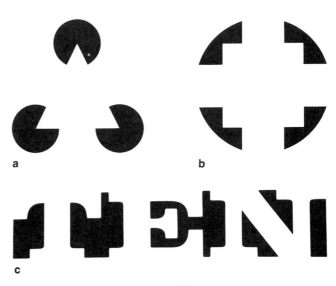

a   b

c

above right: **3.17** **a–b** In these examples, the brain fabricates a triangle and a square out of the grounds. When they are perceived, the brain "closes" the inferred contours, which separate from the ground and advance.

c Are these abstract shapes or a word? We are so perceptually tied to letterforms that we are hardly aware of the shape of the space that surrounds them. Correct spacing of letters in a headline for a poster or an advertisement depends on making the *space between letters about as equal in area as possible.* In any composition, **ground is always as important as figure!**

right: **3.18** Victor Moscoso. Cover illustration, *Art Direction.* May 1974. Is there anything to be seen in the artist's illustration that is not obvious at first glance?

3.19 Kaiser Porcelain Ltd., London. *Royal Silhoutte Vase,* 1977. Another equivocal figure. This vase was created for Queen Elizabeth's Silver Jubilee. Depending on how the visual pattern is organized, one can see either a vase or two profiles.

3.20 *The Parthenon.* 447–432 B.C. Marble. Acropolis, Athens, Greece. Would anyone believe that there are many curved lines everywhere in the architectural plan for this building?

ground. Another example is the picture of a vase (Fig. 3.19), or is it a picture of the profiles of Queen Elizabeth and Prince Philip of Great Britain? Block off the background at the top and bottom with pieces of white paper. Are the silhouettes strengthened?

Why study these illusions?

Recognition of principles involved in perceptual illusions reveals important facts that provide advantages to every artist.

1. They enable us to discover that we have important gaps in our sensory apparatus: We do not see what we think we see. This helps to acquaint us with the manner in which our brain organizes and processes sensory data — perception.

2. This understanding of how visual fields may be interpreted enables the artist to avoid ambiguous events in works of unabashed realism; conversely, they provide experimental bases for an intriguing variety of deliberate ambiguous visual events in other types of works.

3. The knowledge often leads to superior solutions for visual problems of all types, both for the fine artist

and the applied artist — a point that should not be lost on the communication designer. One simply capitalizes on the perceptual cues required to invoke the appropriate illusion (response).

The business of the artist: Creating illusions

Straight beams of wood rendered with prominent cross grain may appear to bend or curve; we may want to compensate for that or, conversely, make straight lines appear more organic and less rigid. Solutions to these opposing visual problems are seen in Figure 3.6.

If we wish to create convincing illusions of three dimensions on a flat surface, we must employ every depth cue possible while carefully sidestepping every single ambiguous possibility seen in the equivocal examples. Conversely, if we wish to celebrate the flatness of the two-dimensional surface, we can deliberately employ such devices to confuse and to confound the viewer's spatial perceptual organizational systems. For experimenters, fascinating results are possible by taking both of these approaches at the same time.

As the illusions show, we can make things seem

larger or smaller than they really are; we can make identical objects look different in size or make differing size objects look similar in size. We can make figures on a canvas, a magazine ad, or a breakfast cereal box look wider or taller than they really are by running design masses, respectively, horizontal or vertical. In other words, we can optically compensate for visual irregularities or, conversely, create them at will, deliberately, for whatever specific reasons we have in mind.

Space can be apparently expanded, made airy and open, by spacing figures at declining intervals, by giving smaller figures open spatial relationships, by using light colors. Space can be contracted, made claustrophobic, by filling it completely, by crowding figures together, by using strong and dark colors.

When it may be necessary to increase the apparent size of a room or hide a disagreeable architectural feature, such knowledge can be applied equally well to interior design or architectural design as it can to two-dimensional works. In the performance arts, these applications can make the set designer equally versatile in creating whatever ambience is required.

Optical compensation is not a new idea

In the arts, "optical compensation" is nothing new. As long ago as the classical age in Greece some artists were aware of deficiencies in certain visual mechanisms (perception). For example, if we look up at a tall rectangular building, the walls appear to converge at the top. This conflicts with perceptual constancy—we know the walls are perpendicular. Photographers can now buy a special PC (perspective correction) lens that will make the walls vertical in a photograph. *Optical compensation* is a broad term that covers a variety of techniques that artists may use to correct what viewers may regard as "distorted images" in works of art or, conversely, to employ deliberate distortions to increase a sense of naturalism.

Nearly two thousand five hundred years ago (around 450 B.C.), the Greeks of Athens built a temple, the Parthenon (Fig. 3.20), dedicated to their patron goddess, Athena. With all its apparent precision of line and symmetry, the Parthenon is considered an architectural masterpiece. The fact is that the architects Ictinus and Callicrates designed the temple with hardly a straight line anywhere. Columns fatten in the center, lean back precariously from the vertical; and the interval between columns is different at the corners than it is in the centers of the sides. At the corners of the building, the columns themselves are thicker overall than those in the center. The pediments and other structural features supported by the colonnade, the platform, and the steps leading up to the temple all bulge up in the center.

Not the result of some natural catastrophe, these things are evidence of *an attempt to deliberately apply optical refinements* designed to make the temple appear perfectly linear and symmetrical to approaching viewers. Even the inscriptions on some Greek temples were optically compensated by making letters on the top row taller in order to make words appear to be the same height as those in the row beneath. Normally the higher the row, the smaller the letters appear.

The differing spacing and thicknesses of columns in the corners were a compensation for the effects of irradiation, where a dark object against a light ground (the sky) appears smaller than a light object against a dark ground (the shadowed walls). With equal spacing, the shadowed spaces in the center would have been seen to be narrower than the sky intervals viewed at the corners, and the corner columns would have appeared to be skinnier than ones in the center.

Of course, the Greeks knew nothing about modern perceptual psychology; they were keen observers who used their intuitive knowledge for calculated effect.

Constancy in an inconstant world

How do we see reality? How is it possible for the same image to produce differing perceptual responses? How do we see figures as separated from ground, that is, as distinct and segregated objects? How is it that this can flip-flop from moment to moment? The images projected on the retinas of our eyes are constantly varying in size and sharpness. Why does this not change our perception of things? How is it possible for a tiny image of a person in the distance to be perceived as the same size as a large image of a person standing close by? How is it possible that this extraordinary size difference on the retinas of our eyes fails to produce a similar perceptual size difference? How is it possible to see a white object in shadow as white, when it may actually be as dark as a black object in sunlight? Furthermore, how is it that this may occur in the same visual field without perceptual conflict? All these things happen to us almost every waking moment of our existence.

Differences in retinal images are resolved by a mechanism of the brain that stabilizes our visual field, a characteristic needed for biological survival. This mechanism is called *perceptual constancy*.

Scientists do not completely understand how and

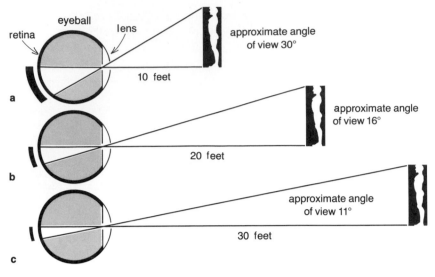

3.21 These diagrams show the variations in the size of the retinal image of a person who is standing at differing distances from us. Note how much of a size discrepancy has occurred between **a** and **c**. Yet we do not perceive that the person has changed size.

3.23 Leonardo da Vinci. *Mona Lisa.* 1503. Oil on canvas, 30″ × 21″ (77 × 53 cm). Louvre, Paris. A small painting with a very large reputation.

3.22 All drawings of the man shown in this illustration are exactly the same shape and size. Why does the one on the right look like a giant and the one on the left look like a midget?

3.24 Michelangelo Buonarroti. *David.* 1501−04. Marble, height 18′ (5.5 m). Accademia, Florence. Although most art books provide dimensions of works, they usually have little impact. Very few books or slides provide visual evidence of *scale,* often an indispensable aspect of both the creation and the viewing of works of art.

48   Awareness

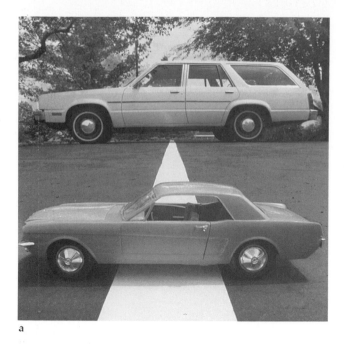

a

b

3.25 **a** Two automobiles the same size? It all depends on the point of view. Photo **b** reveals the actual scale of the objects shown in photo **a**.

why perceptual constancy works, but it appears to be based on desperate necessity. What would it be like if our perception of the world changed every time our retinal image varied? In spite of all ambiguities and continually changing images on the retina, the mind can extract essential data regarding the inherent properties of figures-objects and adjust our perceptions accordingly.

We have constancies related to the intensity of illumination, "brightness" constancy; size constancy; color constancies (for all three dimensions); shape constancy; spatial constancies; worth constancy; etc.

Constancies that affect our understanding of color, of brightness (light), of space, and of movement will be discussed in their appropriate chapters. Here we will deal with constancy as it affects our perception of size, worth, and shape.

Size constancy

Size constancy is a process by which the brain takes into account changing distances and other associative visual cues in order to perceive objects as remaining the same size despite radical changes in the retinal image. Some of these cues appear to be innate; others are learned. Figure 3.21 shows how the retinal image varies for a person standing at differing distances from us. If men are an average of five feet ten inches tall, we always see them that way, whether standing next to us or far off, even though the retinal size of the first may be more than ten times the other.

We know how large an automobile is—or a bicycle.

The brain assumes that functional figure-objects are always of a closely similar size regardless of the size of their retinal image. As a rule, we see these familiar objects in relationship to their environment. The size of objects next to them can be gauged with relative ease no matter what their distance from us. Concepts of size deal with relative magnitude.

Does anyone believe in giants? The figures in 3.22 are all identical in size, yet we are virtually forced to see those at the right as being successively larger than the one at left. *Scale* in works of art is not necessarily consistent with reality or with our mental perceptions of reality. Would most of us be surprised to learn that the *Mona Lisa* is a small painting, about 30 × 21 inches (77 × 53 cm)? Or that Michelangelo's sculpture *David* is as high as a two-story house? In realistic figure paintings, landscapes, or cityscapes, persons, buildings, and animals are seldom pictured in a scale that is true to life. Nor do snapshots of relatives or friends picture them actual size, yet we relate to them easily. This was not always true; primitive societies used to see pictures as a form of magic.

Size constancy can turn the tables on viewers, permitting artists to create worlds of fantasy and imagination. Surprising and compelling images may be based on differences in perceptual scale.

Are there two full-size autos in Figure 3.25 **a**? No, one is a toy; the actual scale is seen in Figure 3.25 **b**.

3.26 A confusion of scale. In this photograph, Californian Ollie Johnson chugs around his backyard on a 16-inch-high working model of a steam locomotive. The point of view (camera angle) and the convincing detail on the model engine, track, and landscape combine to turn Johnson into an alarming godlike being.

above right: **3.27** Merian C. Cooper and Ernest Schoedsack (Producers), David O. Selznick (Executive Producer) and William H. O'Brien (Chief Technician). *King Kong.* © 1933 RKO Pictures, Inc. Ren. 1960 RKO RADIO PICTURES, a division of RKO General, Inc. Courtesy Turner Entertainments. Two-dimensional confusions of scale allow many of the wonderful special effects in the theater and films. They also provide any artist with enormous conceptual possibilities.

right: **3.28** In this advertisement, a large amount of open space helps the designer say "small" visually. © Volkswagen United States Inc. Used by permission.

In the absence of other visual cues, we generally assume that a camera is positioned at our eye level. In another example, this fact distorts our perception of the relative size of a person observed in the same photograph with a steam locomotive (an extremely realistic scale model) because it shifts our understanding of the position of our feet relative to the horizon line—a subject discussed further in Chapter 8. Though a physiological characteristic that enables us to negotiate our world more comfortably, perceptual constancies may produce confusions of scale when point of view or other distal or perspective cues are confusing or contrary to expectations (Fig. 3.26).

Motion pictures have long used miniaturization to stage difficult, costly, or impossible scenes. Figure 3.27 is a frame from the film *King Kong* where the giant ape's head more than fills an entire window. In the original film, most photography was done with articu-

lated models about 20 inches high although some full-scale parts were used for certain scenes. On the stage as well as in films and other commercial photography, *forced perspective* is often used to simulate extraordinary depth in a limited space. This technique involves greatly diminishing the size of background props or scenery in natural order. When a set is viewed from a relatively fixed frontal position, the trick is not revealed.

Scale figures prominently in an advertisement for Volkswagen, (Fig. 3.28), one in a successful advertising campaign that launched sales in the United States. Scale also contributes conceptually and aesthetically to the effectiveness of the composite photograph used for the cover of an annual report (Fig. 3.29).

Size as a scale of relative worth

In the Middle Ages, scale often served a different

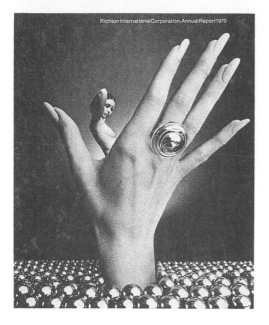

above left: **3.29** Robert Miles Runyon & Associates (Agency), Bill Tobias (Art Director), Bob Pellegrini (Designer), Ryszard Horowitz (Photographer). Annual Report, Richton International Corp., 1970. Black and white photograph. The company specializes in fashion and accessories.

above right: **3.30** Enguerrand Charenton. *The Coronation of the Virgin.* 1454. Musée Hospice, Villeneuve-les-Avignon. Here is another use of scale in art. Contrast in size between persons was used to indicate a difference in relative worth or importance.

left: **3.31** One common stereotypical model for a house.

purpose. It was used as an indicator of status. In this altarpiece painted in 1454 (Fig. 3.30), Jesus and His mother, Mary, are several times larger than the saints, who, in turn, are several times larger than the ordinary people. Religious art of this time commonly depicted persons in a scale related to their importance rather than their physical size. In this way the artist visually communicated how the status of a person differed from that of ordinary people. The same thing was being done by Egyptian artists at least as early as the 15th century B.C.

Although artists deliberately varied scale in deference to exalted persons, everyone tends to see valued persons/objects as closer, larger, more vivid. Psychologists call this characteristic *perceptual accentuation.* In one study, poor children perceived the size of coins as larger than did children from more affluent families.

To most of us, coins appearing in photographs or paintings look too small when made actual size; they appear correct when made about 8 percent (one-twelfth) larger. A circle that contains a number of elements or parts tends to appear smaller than one that contains nothing. Test these premises out with friends or acquaintances.

Shape (or form) constancy

Most persons will respond to constancies rather than to individual differences. When children draw houses from imagination, the house looks like the one in which they grew up, or it looks like the house symbol though few homes really do (Fig. 3.31). Unless modeled on a pet, drawings of dogs from imagination are usually stereotypes rather than individual dogs or breeds.

3.32 a Are these two figures different?
b Are these figures identical, or are they slightly different?
c Recognize this shape? Turn it on its side and see if that helps.

Shape constancy leads us to draw generic (stereotypical) images, not individual images that are far more interesting. There is a strong tendency to make grass green, sky blue, and roses red—a tendency that must be studiously avoided. As we shall learn in chapters on light and color, grass is not green, nor the sky blue, nor even red roses red, to say nothing of the fact that there are several thousand different varieties of roses in a wide range of colors and in many differing flowering types.

Shape constancy is often tied to orientation. A shape consistently recognized in one position may go totally unrecognized in a different position. This effect is so strong, for example, that we have even given a different name, a diamond, to a square when it sits on a point (Fig. 3.32 **a**). Both shapes seen in Figure 3.32 **b** are exactly alike; one is simply turned 90° to the other. Is the shape seen in Figure 3.32 **c** recognizable? If not, try turning it on its side and see if that helps.

A point: Although they stabilize our visual field, a necessity for existence, perceptual constancies often work against creativity and individuality in art.

Summary

We do not see what we think we do.

Any visual field is subject to ambiguity. Ambiguity may be reinforced or shaped by our perceptual constancies. We have constancies for all the elemental visual components such as line, shape, color, space, and movement, for example.

Caused by inadequate sensory information (ambiguity), visual illusions prove the existence of gaps in our sensory mechanisms. At the same time, they provide artists with three distinct advantages: (1) they tell us, in particular, the kind of two-dimensional spatial problems we must avoid; (2) they give us the conceptual means to create whatever degree of ambiguity in a design we wish to create; and (3) they tip us off about mechanisms through which we can expand or condense space or make things appear larger or smaller—whether a package or a person. Through visual illusions, we possess the means to create worlds of fantasy and imagination.

When we color grass green or a tomato red, we are responding to color constancy rather than to natural colors or to personal "feelings" about colors. Constancy is a stereotyping (model-making) process. It helps to stabilize our perceptions of our world and to make us more comfortable. Stereotypical things are familiar and pleasing. Perceptual constancy is necessary to our survival as a species. Yet the process focuses on similarities and tends to ignore or to disregard differences. It is differences in the visual field that attract our attention the most.

Artists must understand fully how perceptual constancies work and steer clear of the homogenization they bring to visual images. Creativity, uniqueness, and the development of a mature personal style may depend on it.

If attention-getting and compelling works of art are to be created, it is often necessary to break perceptual constancies.

Review of key terms

constancy *See* **perceptual constancy**.
equivocal Capable of being interpreted in more than one way; ambiguous.
figure-ground A perceptual characteristic wherein whatever circumscribed area we look at is interpreted as figure and advances while everything else in the field of vision becomes background and recedes.

illusion A perception that fails to give the true character of the object perceived; an unreal or misleading image presented to our vision; a deceptive appearance.
perceptual constancy We understand certain things to remain the same regardless of the changing image sizes, shapes, and light qualities on our retina. It is part of the brain's mechanism to stabilize our environment. For example, we have no doubt that a person seen in the distance is of average height, five to six feet tall, even though the image on the retina appears smaller than a hand held up beside. This is size constancy, among others; we also have object, color, and shape constancy.
scale A visual relationship drawn between parts of a figure or between differing figures according to some easily recognized standard such as the human body.

The Premier
Computer Graphics Conference

July 25-29
Detroit, Michigan

The Tenth Annual Conference
on Computer Graphics
and Interactive Techniques

SIGGRAPH '83 is sponsored by the
Association for Computing Machinery's
Special Interest Group on Computer
Graphics in cooperation with the
Engineering Society of Detroit, the
IEEE Technical Committee on
Computer Graphics and Eurographics.

Plan now to attend
ACM/SIGGRAPH '83
SIGGRAPH '83 pulls together industry
experts to present this year's most
comprehensive computer graphics
conference. There will be ample
opportunity for graphics professionals
to exchange ideas and discuss
advanced techniques. There will also
be programs to introduce the graphics
novice to this expanding technology
and its practical applications.

A complete technical conference,
SIGGRAPH '83 offers:
● A wide range of courses on such
diverse topics as introductory computer
graphics, animation techniques,
CAD/CAM/CAE and specialized
graphics applications
● Technical sessions featuring the latest
in research and innovative uses of
computer graphics

● An equipment exhibition displaying a
broad range of state-of-the-art
computer graphics products
● Two evenings of computer-
generated film & video shows
● A public showing of computer-
generated art

The full spectrum of graphics
SIGGRAPH '83 attendance is
mandatory for professionals striving to
keep their computer graphics
knowledge sharp. For registration
information, contact the SIGGRAPH '83
Conference Office, 111 East Wacker
Drive, Chicago, Illinois 60601; (312)
644-6610. Or, plan to register on site in
Detroit on Sunday, July 24, between
1 p.m. and 11 p.m.

acm

CHAPTER FOUR

Rhythm and proportional relationships

Connections of the narrow kind

In this chapter we will look at a number of organizing devices that join differing structural parts of a composition together, that is, techniques that help reinforce compositional coherency. Collectively, let us call these *connections of the narrow kind*, ''narrow'' because they relate only to the *internal systems of pattern relationships* — composition. We have already looked at a few of these in Chapter 2 — proximity, similarity, continuity, and closure, which are principles of Gestalt psychology. In this chapter we will examine two more broad groups: one is *graphic, or pictorial, geometry*, and another, which we will describe as *melds*.

In virtually all weak compositions, primary faults are the failure to relate one part of a composition to another and to break up the surface into interesting proportional relationships.

One answer to these problems, simple graphic geometry, provides a sound technological basis for creating a satisfactory variety of spatial divisions. Used as a basis for grids, ''proportional intervals'' may be established, which set up automatic rhythms that extend both the aesthetic and emotional qualities of any work. Grids are useful tools for enlarging or reducing the size of shapes, for creating anamorphic

4.1 Guenther Tetz (Artist) and the Association for Computing Machinery's special interest group in cooperation with the Engineering Society of Detroit, the IEEE Technical Committee on Computer Graphics, and Eurographics (Sponsor). This announcement for a computer graphics trade show, *Siggraph '83*, uses the title (composed of dots) as a motif, which serially decomposes from top to bottom. The design structure is a grid that is established by the width and height of the letters themselves.

4.2 Types of *rhythm* — repetition, alternation, and progression — as applied to interval and to figure: **a** The figure remains the same in this set, but the *interval varies*, the spacing between figures is changed. **b** In this set, the interval remains the same throughout, but the *figures vary*. Both of these techniques may be combined, altering both interval and figure simultaneously.

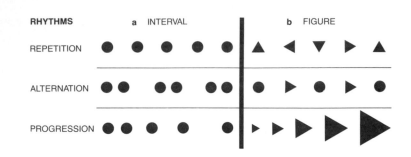

shapes and shape distortions, and for developing internal compositional relationships.

An introduction to the uses of interval

The term *interval* refers to the spacing between elements. It includes not only spaces across a flat, two-dimensional surface, which we will discuss in this chapter, but also distances across three-dimensional space (a relationship between movement and time), which we will look at later. When an element, like a line, is repeated as a pattern of equally spaced divisions across a surface, the result is called a *periodic pattern*. *Periodic* means recurring at regular intervals. A *grid* is two periodic patterns overlaid on one another, often at right angles (90°), like a checkerboard.

Repetition

Repetition is inherently rhythmic like drum beats in music. However, like beats on a drum, the repetition of the same motif or interval may become boring and irritating. Rhythms are more exciting and interesting if the beat is varied according to a pattern. When the patterns are repeated, with variation or change, it not only unites the work by providing an underlying structure for the subject of a composition but also adds a measure of variety that arouses and sustains interest.

Repetition is not limited to lines or spaces but can be applied to shape (a figure or motif) or to color or, in fact, to any of the elemental visual components, individually or collectively.

Rhythm

Pictorial rhythm is the repetition (similarity) in whole or in part, of any line, shape, or figure. The similarity may appear in the same size or in a reduced or an enlarged size, or it may be expanded or compressed in shape — in any subtle, but obvious variation — or any combination of these whether drawn strictly to scale or in any arbitrary fashion.

There are several basic rhythmic devices, all open to wide variation. Rhythmic progression may be determined in any of a number of ways, but it is always in natural order even though the direction of any progression may be reversed at regular or at arbitrary points. Though the term *interval* is used it could be read interchangeably with *figure* or *motif*.

1. The simple repetitive sequence (each interval is the same): o o o o o o o o o

2. Alternation (two differing intervals repeated one after the other): oo   oo   oo   oo   oo

3. Progression:

   a. Intervals grow larger or smaller in even steps: oo o o   o   o   o

   b. The geometric ratio (intervals grow larger or smaller based mathematical formulas): oo o o   o   o

Both figures and intervals may be varied — or one held constant while the other is varied (Fig. 4.2).

Periodic patterns: A basic rhythmic structure

A very simple periodic pattern is shown in Figure 4.3. Overlapping periodic patterns behave like wave forms in physics: light, sounds, or fluids. Superimposed patterns, slightly out of alignment, exhibit a form of *interference* more commonly referred to as *moiré* by graphic artists (Fig. 4.4). When printing photographs in a book or magazine, a moiré is a very undesirable characteristic, but as an artistic device, it offers exciting possibilities. Figure 4.5 **a** and **b** are some student studies. A similar concept was used by designer Jean Widmer for a poster (Fig. 4.6). A moiré attracts attention because it produces differences (changes) in the pictorial field. Something that is different always attracts.

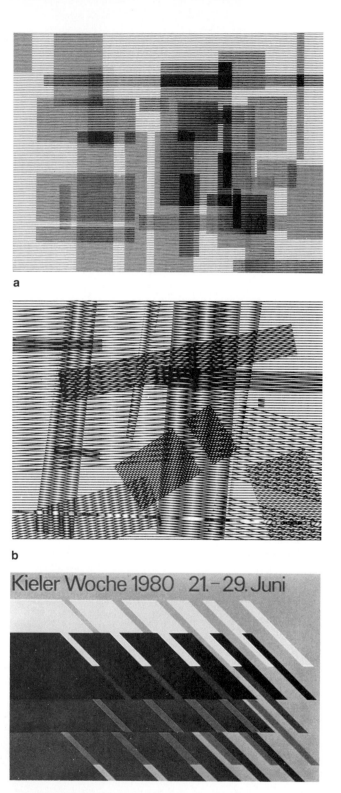

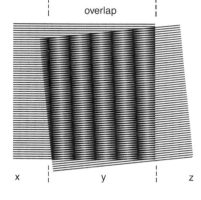

top: **4.3** A typical periodic pattern: a field of straight, equally spaced lines.

above: **4.4** The same periodic pattern, *x* (seen in Fig. 4.3) superimposed on itself at a very slight angle, *z.* In between, *y,* we can see a pattern of *beats* (dark lines) and *nulls* (light lines) created by *interference* between the two wavelike patterns. The result is called a *moiré.*

above right: **4.5** A project for students. Two experiments with rhythms developed from overlaying sheets of transparent shading films (periodic patterns): an exercise in moirés. In **a,** the variations in shape, luminance, and spacing (interval) are mostly interesting. Study **b,** perhaps, is less successful, but it is nevertheless more daring and exciting because the artist has attempted a greater variety of effects. In the long run, persons willing to experiment — to risk failure — are likely to be more successful in their profession.

4.6 Jean Widmer (Designer). *Kieler Woche,* 1980. Example of a professional application of periodic patterns to solve applied design problems. The result is crisp, clean, and effective. This poster suggests movement and excitement.

Proportion: Relative interval

Proportion is always relative. It may refer to ratios of one part to another part or of one part to a whole or of wholes to one another. The relationship may be based on linear measure (width or length) or on mass (surface area), but it must be consistent. We may compare length of one shape to the length of a different shape, but not the length of one to the width of another. We may compare length to width only of a single shape. The proportional relationship of a series of things to another is called a *geometric progression*.

Geometric progressions (or *proportional ratios*) may be used to divide a space rather than using equal spacing. No unusually difficult mathematics need be involved; ratios created simply by measure may be easily constructed with a compass, T-square, triangle, and drawing board. Geometric progressions are nearly always more interesting even when they continue only in one direction. If they stop and reverse or repeat, it adds variety without destroying their essential rhythm.

The Fibonacci numbers and the Golden Section

Canons of Western art aesthetics are based on the prominence of the square as a basis for design. Beginning with the Greeks, the square has been projected within itself and outside of itself to create proportional relationships considered "beautiful." These ideas were applied by the Greeks to their crafts, their art, and their architecture, such as the Parthenon (Fig. 3.20). The Parthenon represents an ultimate achievement of classic Greek—and subsequently all Western—ideas of beauty.

What the Greeks discovered we call "the Golden Section" and the "Golden Rectangle." Based on geometric ratios, these proportional relationships established not only Greek concepts of harmonious spatial divisions but also those that we have inherited from Renaissance traditions.

The ratio called the *Golden Section* was first published as a numerical set by a medieval mathematician, Leonardo Fibonacci, in a book called *Liber Abaci* (Book of the Abacus), 1202. The series, called *Fibonacci numbers*, looks like this: 1, 1, 2, 3, 5, 8, 21, 34, 55, 89, and so on. Note that each new number in the sequence is found by adding together the two previous numbers. As the numbers progress, they closely approach an exact ratio of 1:1.618 (the Golden Section), used by classical Greek artists to divide two or three dimensional spaces into pleasing proportions.

Much later, botanists were astonished to discover Fibonacci numbers occurred throughout nature. They were most clearly seen in the phenomenon of phyllotaxis, which is the spiral arrangement of leaves, scales, and flowers. The average-size sunflower head (Fig. 4.7), for instance, displays opposing spirals, exactly 55 rows in one direction and 89 in the other. Smaller or larger heads show exactly the same ratio but decreased or increased numbers of rows, 34:55 or 89:144, for instance. Such ratios are seen in other natural growth patterns like pine cones and the nautilus shell (Fig. 4.8).

This ratio never fails to provide good divisions of space. It was widely used during the Renaissance and continues to be used by contemporary artists, both fine and applied, either as a deliberately constructed framework for their art or as an intuitive division of

4.7 The opposing spirals seen in the arrangement of seed in the head of a sunflower adhere to rigid numerical rules, the Fibonacci numbers. So do many other plants and living things like the nautilus shell.

4.8 The patterns of growth in the chambers in this nautilus shell also adhere to Fibonacci numbers, which is the proportional ratio of the Golden Section, 1:1.618.

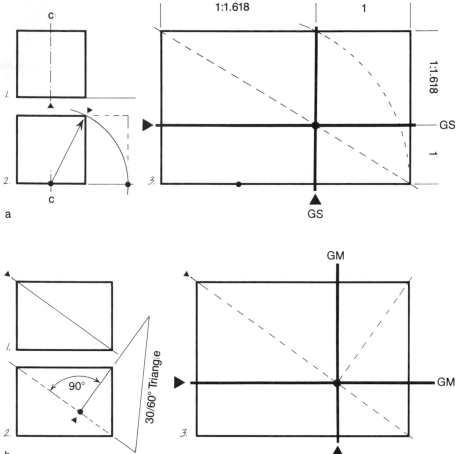

4.9 a The *Golden Rectangle* is constructed from a square projected outside of itself. Its proportions allow it to be subdivided into exact ratios of 1:1.618 to infinity. *To construct it:* 1. Draw a square with an extended base line, and locate the center of the bottom edge of the square. 2. Using that point as the center of a circle, and the distance from it to the opposite upper right corner as a radius, inscribe an arc to intersect the base line. 3. From that intersection, draw a vertical line. Then extend the top edge of the square until it intersects the new vertical. Eliminate the center line of the square, which was only used for construction. Draw a diagonal through the new rectangle. Where the diagonal intersects the right edge of the square, draw a horizontal line **GS**. **b** The method illustrated here shows how any rectilinear shape may be divided into pleasing proportions. 1. Simply draw a diagonal. 2. Drop a perpendicular line (90°) from any opposite corner. 3. Draw a horizontal and a vertical line at the point of intersection. The resulting division of space, indicated by letters **GM**, we will call the *Golden Mean*. Divisions of space approximate but do not precisely conform to the ratio 1:1.618.

space. Our sense of what is good or not so good may be improved by application of the Golden Section until the proportional relationships become intuitive.

As ancient Greek artists probably did, Figure 4.9 **a** shows how to construct the *Golden Rectangle* graphically. A drawing board, T-square, triangle, and a good compass are needed to do this accurately.

The Golden Section lines (**GS**) in a Golden Rectangle establish exact 1:1.618 proportional divisions. This rectangle may be subdivided into proportional spaces, 1:1.618, all the way to infinity. Sometimes this division of space is also called "The Golden Mean," using the terms *section* and *mean* interchangeably. However, *we will use these two terms to indicate different things.* The term *Golden Section* (**GS**) will be used to identify proportions that are *exactly* in a ratio of 1 to 1.618 and the term *Golden Mean* (**GM**) will be used to identify proportions that only *approximate* that ratio. How to locate *Golden Mean* proportions graphically in a rectangle of any arbitrary shape is illustrated in Figure 4.9 **b.**

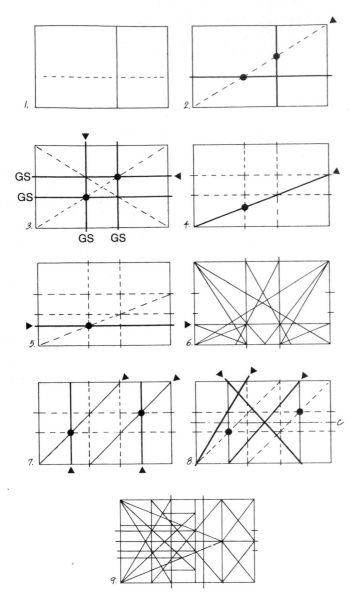

4.10 This step-by-step sequence shows how to create a *harmonic decomposition* of the Golden Rectangle, that is, how to divide the shape into smaller spaces that are all harmonically related.

Step 1. As a result of the construction shown in Figure 4.9 **a**, a Golden Rectangle is divided by one horizontal and one vertical line. One diagonal line will intersect the point where both lines cross.

2. It should be easy to understand that if the other diagonal is drawn, it will intersect the original **GS** lines at two new points.

3. Drawing a vertical and a horizontal line through these two new points produces a simple grid composed of nine spaces.

4. To "decompose" the shape further, draw diagonals connecting *any two points* of intersection either with the frame lines or the Golden Section (**GS**) lines. This is one example.

5. As such diagonals may produce one or more additional points of intersection, we can now add another line (or lines), either horizontal or vertical, through those points of intersection. At this stage, the choice of intersections (points) to connect is arbitrary.

6. If the process begun in step 5 is continued, more diagonals may be drawn between newly created points of intersection. Note that some lines have been eliminated or disregarded. This method produces a great variety of patterns like this example, and another one shown in step 9.

7. Steps seven and eight show how some of the lines in step 9 were located. Draw two diagonals and two verticals through the points of intersection with **GS** lines as shown in step 4.

8. The new verticals intersect the edges of the rectangle at four points. With theses, draw three new diagonals producing more points of intersection.

9. A few more diagonals, verticals, and horizontals have been drawn. This pattern of lines can be used as a basis for a design or to describe the general contours of figure-objects or masses to locate their position in any composition.

The basic divisions in each of these cases, formed by horizontal and vertical lines, may be further "broken down," *harmonically decomposed*, to provide smaller and smaller spaces with an increased number of optional construction lines. Figure 4.10 shows how to do that for the Golden Rectangle.

Harmonic decompositions serve as *guide lines* (structures) for good patternmaking and are ordinarily removed once a work reaches its final stages. The lines or spaces help to locate the dominant and sub-dominant figures in a composition; other divisions may be used to provide the general outlines of figures and figure parts in a composition. The divisions of pictorial

space may also be used to establish the proportional relationship of the major mass to the minor mass. The key to effective management of this grid is to place some limit on the number of lines actually used in any single work, that is, to use them "economically." For example, in *The Jar of Olives* (Fig. 4.11 **a**) the painter Chardin used such guide lines in exactly that manner. Figure 4.11 **b** shows how a harmonic decomposition of the Golden Mean was used to locate the edge of the table and the jar of olives as well as to define general triangular shape and position of all other objects in the still life.

The Golden Rectangle is created by projecting a

a

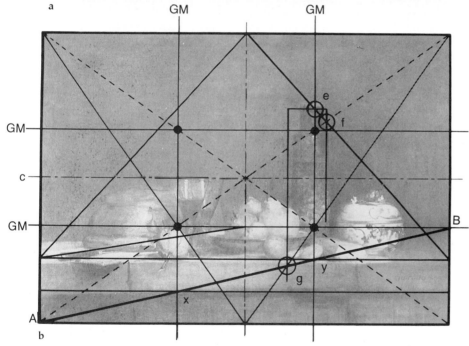

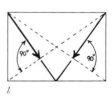

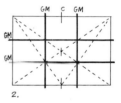

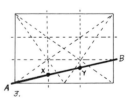

b

4.11 **a** Jean-Baptiste Siméon Chardin. *The Jar of Olives.* 1760. Oil on canvas, 28″ × 38½″ (71 × 98 cm). Louvre, Paris.

b Chardin's still-life paintings provide an excellent example of how geometry was employed to establish placement or shapes of the primary masses in works of the 15th to 19th centuries. In this diagram, diagonals were drawn first; then perpendiculars were dropped from the opposing corners to the diagonals (1). The points of intersection establish the Golden Mean (**GM**) divisions (2). In this case, they are almost perfect thirds! The next major construction line was **AB** (3). At the points, X and Y, where diagonal **AB** intersects the **GM** lines, horizontals were drawn to establish the edges of the table (4). Note how the intersections of other lines (circled), *e, f,* and *g,* establish both the size and shape of the jar of olives. Are there any other points of coincidence?

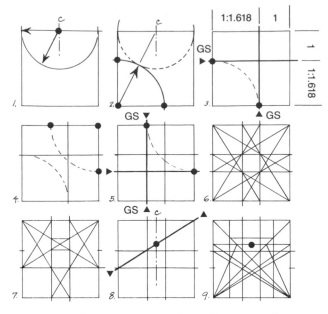

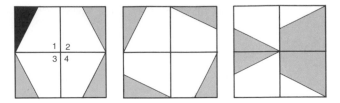

4.13 A simple motif (solid black shape in a square) is organized in a block of four and is taken apart and reassembled in differing positions (orientations) to create new overall patterns. This concept provides another means of creating interesting and harmonically related designs.

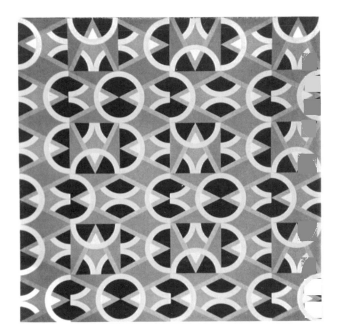

above: **4.14** Karl Benjamin. *#14, 1985.* 1985. Oil on canvas, 60″ × 60″ (152.4 × 152.4 cm). Collection of the artist. Benjamin utilizes the process described in Figure 4.13 as a compositional device for an abstract geometric painting.

4.12 Remember Figure 4.9 **a**? The Golden Rectangle was constructed by projecting a square *outside* of itself. There are a number of ways in which a square can be projected *inside* itself. One method produces Golden Section divisions.

Step 1. Draw a square and find the center of the top edge. Using the distance from the center to the corner as a radius, draw an arc from corner to corner.

2. Draw a diagonal from the center point (top) to a lower corner. Using this corner as the center of a circle, and the distance from it to the point of intersection with the first arc as a radius, draw a new arc that interesects the bottom and vertical edge of the square.

3. Draw a horizontal and a vertical through these points of intersection and two sides of the square are divided into divisions of 1 : 1.618 (two squares and two **GS** rectangles).

4. As with Figure 4.10 (steps 2 and 3), construction may be reversed to produce two vertical and two horizontal Golden Section divisions (**GS**). Using the same radius as in 3, draw an arc from the opposite corner to intersect opposite sides.

5. A horizontal and a vertical through these new points produces a grid of nine spaces (five squares and four **GS** rectangles).

6. This star pattern was created simply by drawing diagonals on the grid constructed in step 5.

7. Another pattern or "decomposition" based on step 5 above. Note one **GS** line is not used.

8. As seen in Figure 4.10, step 5, a new point may be located at the intersection of a diagonal and a vertical center line.

9. The square can be decomposed to provide an almost unlimited variety of patterns to use as basis for design or composition. This alternative pattern has one horizontal line derived from the construction in step 8.

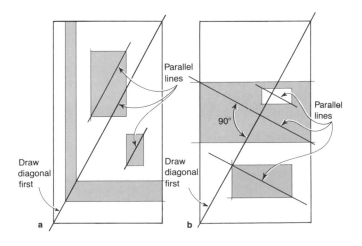

square outside of itself. Similar spatial divisions can be created by projecting a square inside itself. Figure 4.12 shows how that is accomplished.

Proportional divisions of space achieved by any of these methods tend to produce a sense of grace and elegance symbiotic with living things: human beings and nature, physically and physiologically.

Alternative approaches to compositional structure using grids. There are several other methods artists use to develop harmonious relationships. A simple motif arranged in a block of four is disassembled and reassembled in various ways (Fig. 4.13). Painter Karl

Benjamin uses a similar concept to create the stunning painting in Figure 4.14.

Another approach is illustrated in Figure 4.15 **a** and **b** where proportional relationships of the frame, width to height, are reflected in the proportional ratio of objects or divisions of space within the composition. It is fairly obvious that Vermeer's *A Lady and a Gentleman at the Vinginals* (Fig. 4.16 **a**) is an exercise in rectangles. What is not so obvious is that, like diagrams in 4.15, all the basic compositional divisions, as well as locations of figure-objects, result from repetitions of frame proportions. The underlying structural lines for the composition are shown in Figure 4.16 **b**.

below: **4.16 a** Jan Vermeer. *A Lady and a Gentleman at the Virginals.* ca. 1660. Oil on canvas, 28½″ × 24½″. (72.39 × 62.23 cm). Copyright reserved to Her Majesty the Queen.
right: **b** Vermeer's fondness for geometric patterns is evident both in the finished work as well as in the major construction lines, all of which are repetitions of the frame proportions (see Figs. 4.15 **a** and **b**). Notice how Vermeer has used certain lines as a central axis about which to construct both major and minor figure-objects.

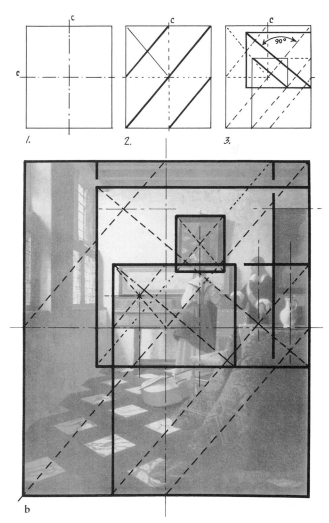

a

b

left: **4.15** These examples show how to use the diagonal to create repetitions of the frame proportions of a rectangle as a compositional device.
a Draw a diagonal. When perfect vertical and horizontal lines are drawn from any point on the diagonal, the resulting space is exactly proportional to the first because the same

diagonal passes through each shape. Rectangles may be placed anywhere in the space by drawing parallel lines to the original diagonal. Divisions of space shown here are arbitrary.
b When desired, shapes may be turned 90° simply by creating a perpendicular to the original diagonal.

Rhythm and proportional relationships

below: **4.17** A few representative grid structures based on regular periodic patterns.

right: **4.18** A student project in repetition. Here a motif has been worked on a regular grid pattern of squares, a checkerboard.

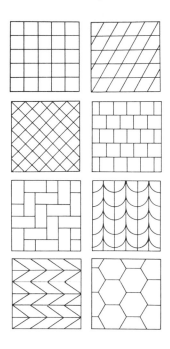

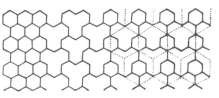

The motif

The motif with luminances (lights and darks) reversed

right: **4.19** The agreeable way in which triangles, hexagons, stars, and other shapes derived from a triangle grid combine to form an ingenious variety of complex patterns may account for its persistent use in Indian lattice design, Byzantine floor patterns, and Moresque tile work. These ideas are commonly picked up for contemporary applied design.

The grid

A structural basis for organization

A *grid* consists of two (or more) periodic patterns overlaid (usually at right angles, 90 degrees, but sometimes at 30, 45, or 60 degrees). Figure 4.17 displays just eight possible variations in grid arrangement out of an almost infinite number of possibilities. A design project based on a simple grid is shown in Figure 4.18.

Using another one of these possibilities, the hexagonal grid, (Fig. 4.19) shows several ways it has been developed in Byzantine, Arab, and Indian ornament to produce interlocking forms. This type of grid construction is a basis for textile, wallpaper, and many other forms of pattern design.

Communication artists should be aware that grids are used to establish a family resemblance between pages in the vast majority of books, newspapers, magazines, and collateral folders and booklets. Designers of advertisements for magazines also often use grids for the same reason, particularly when creating a series of ads or a promotional campaign. Figure 4.20 shows one such grid developed by designer Massimo Vignelli for a series of advertisements.

Grids form the basis of many works of fine art. Russell and Joan Kirsch, who are doing basic research on methods to analyze complex visuals systems, have attempted to write a grammar for painting. They are using formal descriptions and computer models to describe what painters do. For their task, they chose the "Ocean Park" series of paintings by contemporary painter Richard Diebenkorn. Diebenkorn's *Ocean Park No. 111* (Fig. 4.21) formed the basis for their analysis,

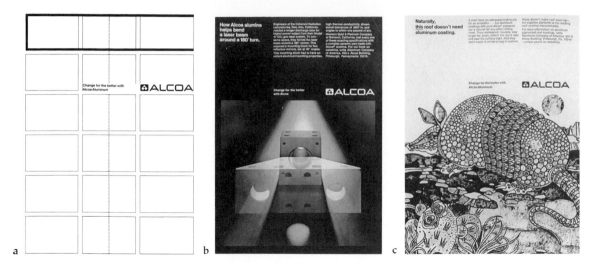

a   b   c

above: **4.20** Massimo Vignelli. Advertisement for ALCOA. The grid, **a**, was designed by Vignelli for a series of advertisements. Parts **b** and **c** are two of the ads created using the grid. Virtually every magazine, newspaper, brochure, or book employs some form of grid as a means of giving all pages a "family resemblance." That unifies the general appearance of the publication as a whole.

right: **4.21** Richard Diebenkorn. *Ocean Park No. 111.* 1978. Oil and charcoal on canvas, 93⅛ × 93¼" (336.2 × 336.7 cm.) Hirshhorn Museum and Sculpture Garden. Smithsonian Institution, Washington. Museum purchase, 1979. A work selected by Joan and Russell Kirsch for their basic research on how computers might be used to analyze complex visual systems.

below right: **4.22** A result of the Kirsches' initial studies: a computer program based on the Kirsch grammar generates a step-by-step sequence of rules duplicating the "deep structure" underlying a typical Diebenkorn *Ocean Park* painting.

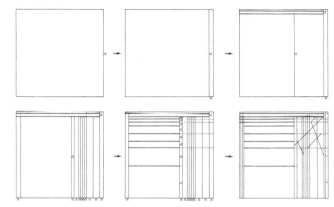

although they studied dozens of other paintings. The rules they developed produced the step-by-step sequence shown in Figure 4.22, a convincing simulation of the underlying structure of the artist's work. Of course, a computer cannot capture the subtleties of paint application, the expressiveness in the individual line and brushwork, which may differ in each part of a single work as well as between works of the same artist. Such analysis can deal only with the past performance, not with how an artist's last work conceptually affects the next; nor can it simulate the unpredictability of the creative human mind—make inferences. However, Russell Kirsch contends that "criticizing art can now begin to have some of the benefits of scientific discourse . . . "[9]

The function of all these alternative possibilities using grids is to provide an *invisible structure* on which to "set" or "hang" elements of the composi-

4.23 The overall proportion of the facade of the Parthenon (Fig. 3.20) is a Golden Rectangle. As the component parts of the Golden Rectangle are a square plus another Golden Rectangle, we should not be surprised to find these components determine all the major divisions of space in the architecture of the building. Compare this diagram to the decompositions in Figure 4.10. Perhaps what makes the Parthenon so outstanding is that it exhibits the same proportional forms and organic rhythms of growth we see in nature. That is something humans sense subconsciously.

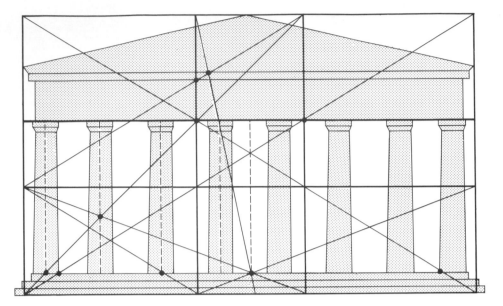

a

b

4.24   a   Marc Chagall. *I and the Village.* 1911. Oil on canvas, 75⅝" × 59⅝" (192 × 151.5 cm). Collection, the Museum of Modern Art, New York. Mrs. Simon Guggenheim Fund. **b**   Although grids are commonly thought of as rigid geometric devices, arbitrary grids consisting of straight, curved, or wavy lines are equally useful as a basis for composition. Here Chagall uses an arbitrary grid for a large oil painting. Most of the major grid lines are shown in the diagram. Note how some are discontinuous (lost and found), but perceptually closed.

tion. Figures or masses may touch or edges may coincide with the guide lines. Also, the central axis of any figure may be made to conform to a vertical or horizontal segment of such a line or the center of any small mass positioned at an intersection of the crisscrossed lines in the grid. These *narrow connections* or visual coincidences bring a sense of logical order to any work of art, drawing the composition together and unifying elements that are then perceived to be an integrated whole. They establish relationships between things and improve coherency.

The diagram of the Parthenon (Fig. 4.23) shows how its major proportional divisions all conform to the Golden Rectangle and the squares from which it is derived.

We noted how modular grids are used by periodicals and books. All of these employ "regular" grid forms, that is, those based on repetitive divisions by horizontals and verticals.

However, "freely formed" or arbitrary grids can also provide a basis for organization (Fig. 4.24 **a** and **b**). It should be obvious how many of the edges in Marc Chagall's painting fall on the same grid line.

Not so obvious is how this works in more complex relationships. Examine every work of art to determine how grids might have been used as a means of bringing coherency to the work—of unifying or harmonizing the design. Begin with Figures 4.11 and

4.16. Not only do edges sit on, or hang from, such construction lines, but the central axis of figures or masses often coincides with such lines.

Design by process

When we have arbitrarily decided on a particular grid structure, developed a motif, and selected a method by which we will apply the motif, a kind of structure has been created that will automatically produce a specific pattern. The character of the final design results from the *process*: a combination of chance (our arbitrary decisions) and order (following exactly the conditions that we have imposed on ourselves). If we alter any of the variables in any way, a different pattern will be produced.

The painting shown in Figure 4.25 is one example of this type of *design by process*. We may apply similar ideas to regular or "progressive" grids. A *progressive* grid is one in which intervals (spaces) vary sequentially in natural order according to some geometric formula.

Overlapping

For our first example, the progressive grid is produced with a straightforward "linear" numerical set, 4–3–2–1, horizontally; and the same, vertically. In other words, the smallest interval is "one," the next interval is double that, then triple, and so on.

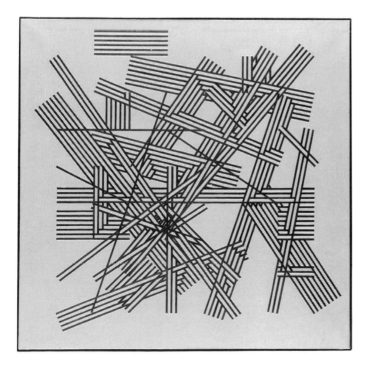

4.25   Kenneth Martin. *Chance and Order 10 (Monastral Blue)*. 1972. Oil on canvas, 36″ × 36″ (91.4 × 91.4 cm). Tate Gallery, London. Reproduced by courtesy of the Trustees. This painting is based on numerical sequences hit on by chance, and from these an order is produced by following a few self-imposed rules. The positions and lengths of the single lines and the bundles of lines are all arrived at by such a system or "game."

right: **4.26** A structure based on overlapping (imbrication or superimposition). Think of it as a series of identical cards like the upper left square, each one progressively tucked under the first an increasingly greater amount. The complete motif is seldom visible.

far right: **4.27** A structure based on compression or expansion of the original motif. The intervals are the same as shown in Figure 4.26, but here the motif has been compressed either vertically or horizontally to fit the space. The entire motif is always visible but frequently distorted.

right: **4.28** A student project. The "black pattern" was created on a progressive grid structure. Which of the two techniques was used? Here the weight is centrifugal (thrusting outward toward the corners). Compare this to a color version, Color Plate 2. What has happened in the color version? (Courtesy of Amy Taylor.)

far right: **4.29** Another "black pattern" created on a progressive grid. What type of structure is it?

right: **4.30** The Fibonacci numbers could be selected as one alternative to use to determine intervals for a progressive grid structure. Remember the series of figures looks like this: 1, 1, 2, 3, 5, 8, and so on.
a To begin, one needs to select an increment of measure; any one will do that will be appropriate to the size of the intended work. For example, ⅛th inch could be used. The first measure would be ⅛th inch also the second. The third is ⅔ths, then, in sequence, ⅜ths, ⅝ths, ⅛ths (or 1 inch) and so on in natural order.
b A completed grid, with the same divisions begun in **a**, drawn both vertically and horizontally. To make the grid more dynamic, the pattern has been moved off-center, and at axes *X* and *Y* the numerical sequence reverses direction.

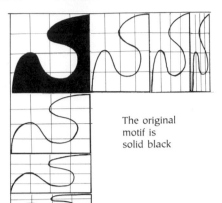

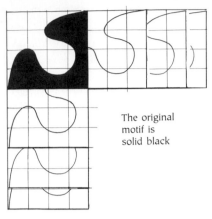

The original motif is solid black

The original motif is solid black

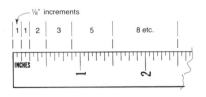

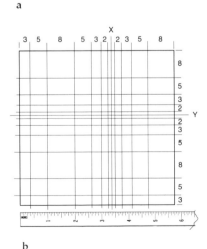

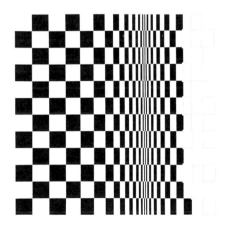

a

b

4.31 Bridget Riley. *Movement in Squares.* 1962. Tempera, 48½ × 47¾" (123.2 × 121.3 cm). Arts Council of Great Britain, London. A leader in the Op Art movement, Riley has employed a progressive pattern to suggest a change in dimension. It is both realistic and ambiguous at the same time. Does anyone *feel* it?

One of two methods used to develop the motif on a progressive grid is *overlapping* (imbrication) as shown in Figure 4.26. In this case, the motif is tucked under itself as if each were printed on a separate card. Each time the motif is applied to one of the spaces, one-quarter of the motif is sequentially covered (or uncovered). Though, in this case, the motif is treated as if it were opaque, we could have considered it to be transparent or treated the overlap as a luminance (light/dark) reversal. All of these would significantly alter the appearance of the resulting design.

In the example, only 4 steps were used. This is a *fast* progression. If we had used many more steps, say 16, that would be a comparatively *slow* progression.

Compression and expansion

Another approach is to compress or to expand the motif. An example is shown in Figure 4.27. For the grid, the same linear numerical set is used as in the first example, but the entire motif is progressively squeezed into the resulting space both vertically and horizontally. Observe how the result differs significantly from the first set.

Applying the concepts

Each design shown in Figures 4.28 and 4.29 uses a different method to create a progressive pattern. Although the selection of motif, numerical progression, and other factors is arbitrary, the choices made are components in a "formula," which is followed explicitly. It is usually impossible to preconceive how the pattern will ultimately appear, but the results are almost always good. Excellence, however, requires imagination and a willingness to make repeated attempts. These examples display some possibilities of design by process. Think of it as a kind of artist's game.

As an alternative to a simple numerical set, any numerical sequence that establishes a regular geometric ratio may be used, and each will produce a differing result. The Fibonacci series is one to consider. Figure 4.30 shows how the Fibonacci numbers might be used to develop a geometric progression for a grid structure such as those used for Figure 4.29.

The op artist Bridget Riley used compression as a device in 1962 for *Movement in Squares* (Fig. 4.31). Progressive grid structures imply both movement and spatial change because overlapping (imbrication) and density gradients provide us with perceptual spatial cues.

Photographers can duplicate some of these effects. In Figure 4.32, the image results from the reflection of natural surroundings in the corrugated stainless steel paneling on a food-vending truck. In the other example (Fig. 4.33), the photographer shifted the camera lens progressively during multiple exposures.

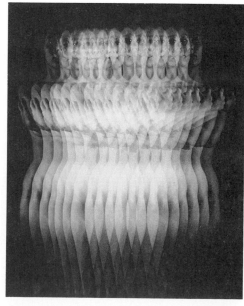

far left: **4.32** Jack Fredrick Myers. *Untitled* Photograph, 1978. The serial images were created by ordinary reflections of the surrounding landscape in the embossed aluminum sheets covering the sides of a food-vending truck. The pattern consisted o a regular periodic pattern of diamond shapes.

4.33 Charles Swedlund. *Untitled.* 1962. Photograph. An image created by shifting a view camera's lens one millimeter horizontally between multiple exposures. This technique automatically produces a periodic pattern of overlapping shapes.

4.34 Groucho Marx.

4.35 **a** A diagonal line is used to make a proportional shape identical to the original but larger. Of course, it could also be used to make a smaller shape. Remember Figure 4.14 **a**?

b To use the grid, both the original and the enlarged shape are divided into the same number parts—in this example, eight each way. Block for block, the contours are carefully copied. The greater the number of divisions, the more accurate the result will be.

c In this example one dimension is held while the other is doubled, providing a type of *anamorphosis*—a stretched out or distorted shape.

d, e, and **f.** By using the grid, any surface shape can be inscribed with whatever image is desired. Three possibilities are shown. (Courtesy of Rita Costigan.)

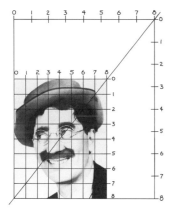

a

b

c

d

e

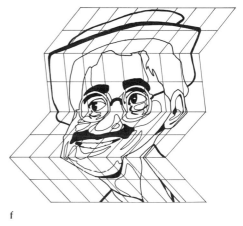

f

The grid as a tool

Sizing

An original of any size such as the photograph in Figure 4.34 may be reduced or enlarged by drawing its diagonal, then constructing horizontal and vertical lines at any desired point along the diagonal, 4.35 **a**. Enlargements may be made by extending the diagonal beyond the corner of the original rectangle. Although a different size, the shapes are proportional. Though not as precise as using a calculator or a photostat, if care is taken when constructing the shapes with T-square and triangle, this method produces very good accuracy.

Once the shapes used are the same proportion, simply divide each into the same number of divisions, and copy by eye what is seen in each corresponding small block. Eighths are good divisions for small pictures, but a much greater number for large pictures. An example is shown in Figure 4.35 **a** and **b**.

Anamorphosis and distortion

Now imagine what it would look like to have the width of the figure twice as wide while keeping the same height. Using the photograph inscribed with a grid as an original, Figure 4.35 **c** does this simply by doubling the width of the grid horizontally. This kind of stretching out of an image is called *anamorphosis* and can be extended to wrap an image around any surface form, such as a sphere, a box, or a folded paper, for example, Figures 4.35 **d**, **e**, and **f** and 4.36.

An outgrowth of the exciting discovery of Renaissance perspective, anamorphic art has varied in popularity over the centuries. See Figure 4.37. Artists often chose anamorphosis because of its covert nature or for its ability to mystify and amuse.

4.36 A student project. Completed studies in pen and ink with tones of gray (using commercial shading films) for **d**, **e**, and **f** in the preceding example, Figure 4.35. (Courtesy of Rita Costigan.)

a

b

4.37 William Scrots. *Portrait of Edward VI.* 1546. Oil on panel, 16¾ × 63″ (42.5 × 160 cm). National Portrait Gallery, London. In **a**, the painting is shown as it ordinarily appears. In **b**, the work is shown from its correct viewpoint—a hollow in the frame.

4.38 John Martin. *Another Day at the Office.* 1980. Illustration for *Financial Post* magazine cover. Anamorphosis is used here to distort the figure of a man. The subject is office stress. Does the image affect us emotionally? How can we say ''stress'' visually?

Anamorphic distortions can be used to convey many differing forms of visual messages. Of course, distortion is common in cartoons and satire, but it is also employed to suggest mental disorders, intoxication, the effects of drugs, dizziness, emotional disorientation, and pain, for example. What sort of emotional impact does the illustration shown in Figure 4.38 have?

Melds: Merging figure and ground

Closed, hard-edged forms, like cardboard cutouts, tend to flatten figure dimension although they advance over ground. They also retain their inherent integrity of shape, resisting integration into a design. Even when working in a decorative fashion, care must be taken to prevent a breakdown of unity. Gestalt principles of similarity, natural order, overlap, proximity, and the like can help.

As we have seen, when grids are used as invisible structures on which to build a composition, coherency is improved. The implied continuity established by coincidences of figure-mass contour or axis joins disparate elements together, unifying them.

Holding things together (unification) is always a primary aesthetic goal in any work of art. Another

method is to permit some of the construction lines, normally eliminated or covered as the work is completed, to be seen. Shadowy traces of the underlying drawing (structure) can be seen in Richard Diebenkorn's work (Fig. 4.21). In Figure 4.39, the artist uses a number of devices to allow one part of the work to merge with another, including extending contour lines and tonal masses beyond the edges of figures. Two of these ideas are diagrammed in Figure 4.40 **a** and **b**.

All these techniques create *melds*, which permit a fusing or blending of figure and ground and form passages or transitions between figures and grounds—''open'' not ''closed'' shape relationships. Melding is a concept that grows out of Gestalt continuation and it facilitates directional eye movements because it creates visual passages perceived to be in natural order. Like periodic patterns and grids, these are connections of the narrow kind.

If the edge of a figure is a hue (blue, for example) that is similar to the hue of the ground (violet), the eye flows easily between them. If the edge of a figure is nearly the same luminance (gray tone) as the ground, the edge between them may almost disappear. When edges are fuzzy, figures blend with ground.

4.39 In this illustration Jack Unruh has used a number of melding techniques. Some contour lines have been omitted—note the top of the leopard's head between the ears and the belly and foreleg, bottom, allowing these places to blend with the surroundings (ground). A contour line following the backbone jumps past the animal and continues all the way to the left edge of the picture plane. In other areas, lines or tones drift past expected termination points or lose solidity, creating shapes that interlock like a jigsaw puzzle. These techniques help to unify the work and hold it together. They also give it a mysterious, fluctuating quality appropriate to the subject.

4.40 Shown in diagrams **a** and **b** are two of the many kinds of *melding techniques* that help to merge figure and ground. Compare these effects with that of **c**, in which the hard-edged closed shape (a square) retains its integrity and is distinctly separate from the ground.

4.41 Charles Demuth. *I Saw the Figure Five in Gold.* 1928. Oil on composition board, 36″ × 29-¾″ (91.4 × 75.6 cm). The Metropolitan Museum of Art, New York (The Alfred Stieglitz Collection, 1949). Do the extended construction lines help unify this work? Note the feeling of "transparency."

When lines from the interior of a figure extend beyond the figure's edge, the result is the same as a fuzzy edge. Melding techniques cause figures to merge with the ground because they reduce edge contrast. They camouflage edges.

Melds are bridges from element to element that tend to destabilize the spatial visual field, flatten it out. Figure and ground cohabit the same space at the same time! Thus, all types of melds cause figures to recede, more or less, depending on choices. Melds are one of our most formidable unifying devices.

In *I Saw the Figure Five in Gold* by Charles Demuth (Fig. 4.41), construction lines are clearly made prominent parts of the composition not only by extending them into the ground but across the entire composition. In this case, these melds "flatten" the work and make it more decorative. Because the edges of one shape seem to penetrate and be visible through an overlapping one, shapes lose solidity, becoming filmy, transparent, and translucent.

Transparency is a field-merging quality like other melds we have mentioned. So are similarity and repetition of shape, color, line, interval, and so on, as they add cohesiveness to any work.

Rhythm and proportional relationships   **71**

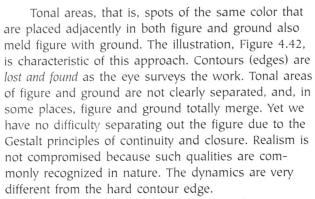

4.42 C. Michael Dudash (Illustrator) and Gary Gretter (Art Director). The perceptual mechanisms of "closure," together with "continuity," allow us to follow a figure's contours where there are none at all to be seen. In this illustration, the "lost and found" contours are obvious. They add interest to the work both aesthetically and naturalistically.

Tonal areas, that is, spots of the same color that are placed adjacently in both figure and ground also meld figure with ground. The illustration, Figure 4.42, is characteristic of this approach. Contours (edges) are *lost and found* as the eye surveys the work. Tonal areas of figure and ground are not clearly separated, and, in some places, figure and ground totally merge. Yet we have no difficulty separating out the figure due to the Gestalt principles of continuity and closure. Realism is not compromised because such qualities are commonly recognized in nature. The dynamics are very different from the hard contour edge.

In *Mont Sainte-Victoire* (Fig. 4.43), Paul Cézanne used very little outline. He worked with planes by applying masses of color. The solidity of shape and contour were allowed to develop perceptually in the viewer's mind. This type of vague contour has come to be known as the *Cézanne edge*.

Whenever we look at a work of art of any sort, we should analyze it to see what makes it work.

Summary

The group of artistic techniques we have joined under the term *connections of the narrow kind* are fundamental to the development of structure, which is the foundation of any work.

No adequate structure is ever developed by chance although chance is always an element in any structure. One makes choices every waking moment. Differing choices produce differing results.

Periodic patterns, both regular and progressive, and the grid structures made from them are inherently rhythmic and harmonic; so are any other components perceived to be in natural order.

Invisible construction lines, the structure on which we build a viable composition, bring coherency and unity (cohesiveness) to works of art. Compositions may fail or succeed on this point alone.

Artists have frequently used geometric divisions as one alternative method for determining where to place figures within a composition. The most common of these is the Golden Section, a mathematical ratio (1:1.618) described by the Fibonacci numbers.

We have seen, for example, how painters such as Benjamin, Chardin, Vermeer, and Chagall as well as Greek architects Ictinus and Callicrates have used grids as a basis for design. A majority of painters from the Renaissance to the 19th century used some kind of grid structure to develop proportional relationships in their work. So do many contemporary architects, painters, and designers of all sorts.

Grids are not rigid, shackling devices as might be concluded from a casual exposure. In creative hands, grids permit complex rhythms to be developed in more than one direction simultaneously. Rhythms can follow regular or irregular geometric construction, can be developed along curves of any sort—radial or parabolic, or may be constructed on freely chosen (arbitrary) straight or curved grid lines, or conversely employ mathematics or geometry as a precision-

4.43 Paul Cézanne. *Mont Sainte-Victoire from Les Laures.* 1902–1906. Oil on canvas, 25″ × 32¾″ (63.5 × 83.2 cm). Kunsthaus, Zurich. Cézanne was not interested in defining a figure-object by emphasizing its contour. He developed shape relationships by laying in masses of tone and color. Contours emerge when the brain perceptually joins together the edges of masses that have similarities in color (hues, luminances, and purities) just as happens in natural visual fields.

governing factor. All these approaches permit motifs to be subjected to fractionalization, compression or expansion, imbrication (overlapping), and interlacement. They produce coherent patterns and permit family resemblances (narrow connections) even between separate, but integral, parts of one work or between discrete but associated works in a series.

In addition, no matter what type of artwork we do or stylistic approach we take, the merging of figure and ground through techniques we have called *melds* allows infinite control over the advancing and receding characteristics of figure-objects.

This chapter has pointed out just a few of the many compositional alternatives available to the intelligent image manager.

Review of key terms

anamorphosis Optical magnification ordinarily in one direction or along only one axis. Anamorphic drawings or paintings are distorted images that may be viewed undistorted from a particular angle of view or with the use of a special instrument.

connection Something that connects. To *connect* means to join, fasten, link, unite, or consider as related. *Connections* may provide a logical ordering of ideas, establish common interests, conjunction, or coincidence. **Connections of the narrow kind** establish visual relationships between internal pictorial elements within a composition, or establish associational pattern similarities between works in a series. **Connections of the broad kind** are specific references that join a work of

art together with elements in the world at large: typically, the environment, society, culture, politics, or the sciences. These stimulate more creative solutions to visual problems and also enhance communication.

Fibonacci numbers A geometric progression in which the Golden Section ratio 1:1.618 is a constant factor. Each subsequent number in the series is obtained by adding together the two that precede it, for example, 1, 1, 2, 3, 5, 8, 13, 21, 34, 55, 89, and so on.

Golden Mean A term often used as a synonym for the Golden Section. In this text, the term *mean* is used more specifically to identify a method of dividing any rectangle into proportions that approximate the Golden Section.

Golden Section A ratio of 1 to 1.618, and the geometric progression or proportions associated with this ratio.

See **Fibonacci numbers.**

melds A variety of artistic devices that merge figure with ground by exploiting Gestalt "continuity"—for example, extending figure contours, colors, or textures, into the negative space or ground (particularly at sharp changes in contour); softening or "blurring" edges; retention of normally invisible construction (compositional) lines; and so on. A leveling procedure, melds add homogeneity and unity to works.

open-closed shape relationships A *closed shape* (or form) is one isolated from the ground or other shapes, usually by a hard, continuous, contrasty edge or contour line. An *open shape* (or form) will not ordinarily have a closed outline, but a broken one that exhibits points of entry and exit like lost and found edges and other forms of figure-ground melds.

5.1 Wassily Kandinsky. *Painting No. 200.* 1914. Oil on canvas, 5′4″ × 2′7½″ (1.63 × 0.8 m). Collection, The Museum of Modern Art, New York, Mrs. Simon Guggenheim Fund. In works like this, Kandinsky eliminated representational objects and focused on line, color, and shape as the subject matter. Forty years after they were painted, such works provided the inspiration for the Abstract Expressionists of the 1950s.

CHAPTER FIVE

Identifying visual problems

Picture making is patternmaking

Picture making is patternmaking. It satisfies our primeval perceptual imperative to identify figures (find patterns) in nature from which we can derive meaning about our environment.

Novice artists have trouble making coherent patterns. They are often unable to distinguish between what makes a good pattern as opposed to one that is not so good. When we try to analyze a work of our own creation, perceptions can get in the way. The difficulty is the fact that we commonly become emotionally attached to it. This produces a state of mind in which any criticism may be viewed unfavorably as prejudiced and irrelevant, even threatening.

We confuse our intentions with what we observe. That is, what we wanted to do exerts a strong influence over what we believe we actually accomplished.

No persons can improve their creative skills under these conditions, for it is through criticism, constructive criticism, that we grow.

5.2 Philip Pearlstein. *Female Model on a Platform Rocker.* 1977–78. Oil on canvas 72¼″ × 96⅛″ (183.5 × 243.8 cm). Brooklyn Museum, New York. J. B. Woodward Memorial Fund, A. Augustus Healy Fund B., Dick S. Ramsay Fund, and other Restricted Income Funds. The artist is less interested in the rocker and the person than in the shapes and the pattern interrelationships that result from them and their interaction with the light flowing over and around them.

Over the centuries, artists have attempted to solve visual problems in a wide variety of ways. Some of these are answers that work consistently—those that were intuitively based on perceptual characteristics. These can be used as principles to help us overcome perceptual difficulties and to evaluate our work more objectively.

There is more to creating a good pattern than simply avoiding the polka-dot effect. Compacting these elements into a unit (or mass) by touching and over-lapping them does not necessarily solve the problem. A good pattern needs more than contiguity. It needs a sense of direction and movement. It needs a focal point. More than likely, it should also be a vehicle for effective communication.

Affective responses

One key to effective communications is to arouse an emotional response in the viewer. The goal of most art forms is to engage the viewer or participant *emotionally.* Elemental visual components inherently possess emotional qualities to which viewers respond.

What are "elemental visual components"? Artists have traditionally defined these as all the colors of the rainbow, all qualities of balance, spatial relation-ships (two- and three-dimensional), movements, lines, edges, shapes, textures, and so on. These are also elemental components of visual processing that are biologically necessary for survival.

As the human animal evolved, like the brain itself, emotions seemed to become more complex; but deep down, emotions are primitive responses to whatever particular circumstance it is in which we find our-selves. Our strongest emotions are those tied to our survival as a species. It is these that produce intrinsic reactions to fundamental things in our visual field. On the whole, at survival level, humans respond similarly to similar things. The more similar the background and environment of any particular group of persons, the more likely responses will be similar. Though they may differ by individual or may individually differ by degree, such responses are typical of average (mass) behavior because they originate in the physiological acts of perceptual processing.

5.3　Tomi Ungerer. A poster protesting U.S. interference in Vietnam. Does it arouse anger? Then it is effective!

Our emotional responses to such components vary in strength based on what else in the visual field may be associated with any one of them. For that reason they are called *affective responses*; that is, they influence, rather than produce, a given reaction. Yet when coupled together, not one but many things possessing similar affective characteristics, the total result is likely to produce a strong communication — clear and effective. When these are combined with creative insight and imagination, the work produced is often an unusually compelling image with a powerful, sustained visual impact.

Artists are image managers

We have already taken a look at some of the problems involved in bringing coherency to works of art. We have examined some methods that will help divide a pictorial surface into interesting proportions. In addition, we noted three common problems together with some solutions: monotonous shapes, the polka-dot effect, and the bull's-eye. All of these are examples of visual problems.

The question is always, "What is the visual problem?" Also, "Which of the almost infinite possibilities will solve it best?"

For the novice, for any artist, problem recognition is the greatest problem! If we cannot recognize a problem, we can never solve it. By whatever name they are called, basic principles (rules, laws, axioms) often help us to avoid problems. Most important, such principles help us to *recognize* visual problems.

When we understand a problem thoroughly because we have consistently applied good principles, we can break the rules because we understand the consequences. When we break a rule, we must solve the visual problem as well as, or better than, the rule does. Be wary of breaking rules simply to break rules.

Principles based on style or on concept are continually overturned by succeeding styles, succeeding concepts, or succeeding generations of artists who, influenced by their own times and concerns, view things differently from artists who preceded them.

Visual principles that grow out of the way that we process visual information, perception, have never become outmoded, nor are they likely to do so because they are rooted in physiological reactions. Such general principles can form a foundation that all artists, no matter of what style or of what time, can use as a starting point for managing and evaluating their works.

To maintain control of all figures in a composition, artists must give careful and thoughtful attention to all the possible configurations in gradation from nonobjective to representational, from arbitrary color to natural color, from decorative flatness (2-D picture

plane) to volumetric rendering (chiaroscuro), from the almost mute sign to the elaborate message. It is a superabundance of alternatives from which artists must select just those things that best express their individual intentions. It is through such a balancing act that a good composition and a good communication are forged from disparate (unrelated) figures. That is *image management*.

For the purposes of expression and communication, artists heighten reality through exaggeration (overstatement), through image distortion, and through compression or expansion of space; and they create new worlds of worlds of fantasy, imagination, or expression out of fragments of our own or from constructions of arbitrary color, line, form, or space. Most of such processes depend on a psychological technique referred to as *leveling and sharpening*. This is a technique for managing contrast by making things more alike (conforming to expectations) or, conversely, making things less alike (confounding expectations). That is image management.

Leveling and sharpening

Leveling and sharpening are one of artists' most flexible, and most necessary, tools for creating effective works of art in any media, in any style, or in any form. (See Figs. 5.4, 5.5, and 5.6.)

above left: **5.4** Mick Haggerty, *Reds,* 1983. Poster; airbrush including spatter work. Although actor Warren Beatty remains identifiable, realistic shading and detail have been subordinated to simple, bold shapes and masses — a leveling process. Note deliberate evocation of Russian Constructivism, an art style contemporary with the action in the film *Reds* (1917).

top right: **5.5** Joan Arbeiter. Postcard announcement for her exhibit, *CAA Job Search Documentation,* April 16–May 4, 1985. Detail of actual letter of rejection plus hand-stamped exhibition logo. Sponsored by the Ceres Gallery, New York. Courtesy the artist. The artist interpreted the activities involved in seeking a teaching position as another form of art work. Various documents, including the postcard, became recorded evidence of that idea or *concept.* This approach is a sharpening procedure.

above: **5.6** Meret Oppenheim. *Object.* 1936. Fur Covered Cup, Saucer, and Spoon. Cup diameter 4⅜″ (11.1 cm); saucer diameter 9⅜″ (23.9 cm); spoon length 9⅜″ (23.9 cm). Collection, The Museum of Modern Art, New York. Purchase. Have these common utensils been so transformed that they defy utility? What does this do to a viewer emotionally? Would anyone like to use these to eat the next meal? Consider a person's reaction to a mouthful of fur. Transformation of familiar objects is a sharpening procedure.

Donis A. Donis tells us that in the visual language, opposites repel but similars attract. Harmony, a leveled state, is an almost foolproof method for the solution of visual problems because nothing is left visually unresolved.

Conversely, we can use contrast to sharpen meaning, to excite and attract as well as to dramatize that meaning and make it more important and more dynamic. There are contrasts of color, of change (movement and metamorphosis), of space and orientation, for example. There are psychological contrasts that have to do with symbolism and political or social status. Contrast, in these contexts, provides artists with one of the primary ways to solve visual problems. As a strategy, contrast intensifies meaning. It goes even further than that by eliminating the superficial and unnecessary. It leads to a natural spotlighting of the essential. Contrast is a technique, a tool, and a concept. By comparing the unlike, we sharpen the meaning of both.[10]

Herewood Lester Cooke puts it another way: Never forget the power of contrast, he warns. "If you want to make a shape seem soft and rounded, place it next to a shape which is hard and jagged. If you want to make a certain color stand out, surround it with its opposite. If you want to make something seem beautiful, surround it with ugly objects. If you want to make something seem bright, surround it with darkness. If you want to make something come alive, surround it with dead, inanimate objects. The unusual always stands out, and an artist should never lose sight of this fact."[11]

As a process, leveling and sharpening define visual elements clearly in terms of the artist's intentions. Elements are best presented as definitely one thing, not another. That avoids the neutralizing effect of ambiguity.

Leveling and sharpening are easy techniques to use and to understand, but they must be consciously and conscientiously applied until they become intuitive. A line drawn vertically, almost but not quite, in the center of a rectangle (perhaps slightly angled), as in Figure 5.7 **a**, appears to most viewers as an error, indicative of a lack of skill or interest—a casual mark of little consequence. The stimulus is weak and lacks sustained interest. Such a line may be made much more positive and stronger when leveled (placed perfectly in the center) or sharpened (clearly off-center and more sharply angled), as shown in Figure 5.7 **b** and **c**.

Any viewer finds such clearly *intentional* placement is perceptually significant. Like a written word, the line has been transformed into a strong, positive sign of the artist's intent.

Visual weight

What is visual weight?

Visual weight is the degree to which a figure in the visual field commands our attention and sustains our interest. Something we casually notice is "light" weight; something that inspires strong emotions—such as love, hate, anger, disgust, or fear—is "heavy" weight. Visual weight is the glue, the cement, the nuts and bolts that hold compositions together and makes them effective vehicles of communication for whatever purpose the artist has in mind. It is the pragmatics of the visual language. Visual weight is the primary tool we manage in order to accomplish four essential objectives:

1. To create a focal point or center of interest that will attract and hold the viewer's attention. Effective compositions will also provide a secondary center of interest—and a third—in other words, a hierarchy of dominances and subdominances.

2. To create a sense of order (coherency) to satisfy our craving for patterns and to construct a "whole entity," a cohesive work of art, rather than simply an array of disassociated parts.

3. To create a sense of physiological and psychological balance. Physiological balance involves *equilibrium*—our perception of natural forces like gravity, for instance, which we bring unconsciously to our viewing of pictures. Psychological forces have to do with emotional responses and meaning—*recognition*, *association*, and *symbolism*, which are primary characteristics of visual communication.

4. To establish a pattern of movement within the composition that will direct the viewer's eyes throughout the work.

Ordinarily, if we have successfully completed the first three objectives, we will also have accomplished the fourth one.

If we expressed these objectives in negative terms rather than in positive ones, it would be a list of the four most difficult compositional problems associated with works of visual art. They are problems that give pause to experienced professionals. Together with monotonous shapes, the polka-dot effect, and the

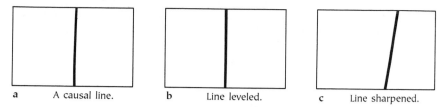

a   A causal line.   b   Line leveled.   c   Line sharpened.

5.7   **a**   An ambiguous line—not exactly in the center or off-center and neither vertical nor clearly slanted. In our perceptions, such a line is commonly interpreted as a ''mistake'' or, at best, is understood as a casual line of little consequence or significance.
b   The line leveled: perfectly centered and straight.
c   The line sharpened: clearly placed off-center and angled. Both leveling and sharpening procedures clarify an artist's intentions by creating stronger and more positive visuals.

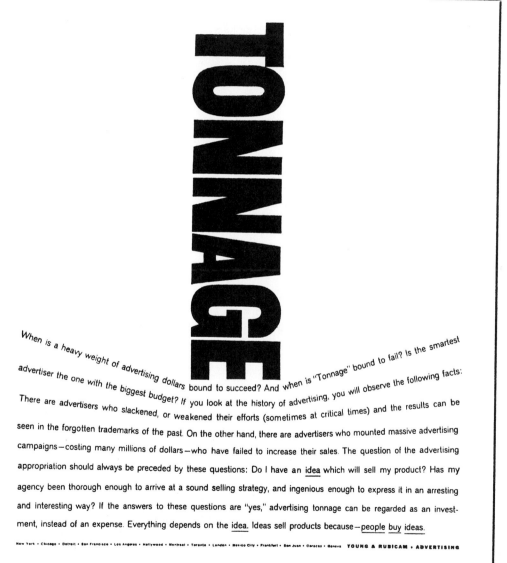

5.8   Donald Egensteiner (Designer), *Tonnage,* Self-promotion for Young & Rubicam, Inc. In this advertisement, visual weight is graphically portrayed.

5.9 The focal point in this student work was obvious to all viewers but the creator. Why is our attention riveted on the moon? Is that where we should be looking? How many alternative possibilities are there to improve the situation?

bull's-eye effect, they constitute the seven most significant problems that any visual artist must face. Beginning artists often are completely unable to recognize these deficiencies in their own work.

In order for pattern recognition to occur, components must be organized into a specific configuration. This type of association is clearly evident in the written language. Recall the introduction to this book. In these examples, the letterforms are identical shapes, yet word recognition does not occur. A specific, understood order of both letterforms and words is required for meaning. Consider the sentences below:

1. The quick brown fox jumps over the lazy dog.
2. Jumps lazy the over brown quick dog fox the.
3. T hequ i ckbrow nf oxju mpsov erth elazyd og.

The last sentence is the most difficult to read since the series of letters is broken in a random fashion rather than between words. This is because we recognize words by their overall silhouette not by the individual sequence of letters. It is easier to compre-

hend the second sentence where the words are simply out of order though the meaning can never be fully clarified. A word is a kind of picture, a Gestalt "whole"; it is not a sum of individual letters. The written language must follow certain prescribed rules if communication is to take place. The same is true of the visual language.

The distribution of visual weight tells the viewer where to begin and what is next in order; the affective responses establish the emotional context (mood) appropriate to the "message."

When novice artists are asked to identify the spot in their work where a viewer looks first, second, and so on, they ordinarily point out where *they want* a viewer to look, not where a viewer actually does look. (See Fig. 5.9.) Encumbered by their own perceptual baggage, they make emotional decisions often based on perceptual constancies, not knowledgeable, intelligent decisions. When success occurs, it is a matter of guesswork rather than knowledge. They relinquish control of their image. Other persons, even laypersons, can usually identify the focal point—where the eye goes—in an instant because their attention goes directly to the dominant visual area. For example, all other things being equal, the largest figure in our visual field is likely to draw attention first. Although size is one means of attracting attention, it is neither the most common nor the most effective.

How do we achieve dominance visually?

Remember the dominance principle? Dominance is created by increasing or decreasing the visual weight of every element in a composition (design) until one subject (one area, one figure, and so on) stands out. Adjusting visual weight places emphasis where we want it or de-emphasizes elements we wish to subordinate. Establishing dominance in a visual field simultaneously establishes a center of interest.

Varieties of basic visual elements—line, shape (or form), color, space, motion, texture, interval (distance and time)—possess differing weights depending on how they are associated or contrasted with other elements in any single composition or design.

It is very much like using a physical balancing scale in which an unknown quantity is balanced by a known quantity (a selection of differing weights) on the other side. It is like a seesaw.

Visual weight is the driving force behind our understanding of any visual field and our ability to derive meaning from it.

The manipulation of visual weight is a component of image management as are all leveling and sharpening procedures.

Because understanding and applying principles of visual weight are so important to the visual artist, we will separate essential categories for closer study.

Chapter 6 will deal with the qualities of visual weight that are associated with our understanding of physical weight and physical forces like balance and figure orientation.

Chapter 7 deals with the qualities of uniqueness or novelty; that is, with what is *different* in the visual field. That attracts attention. We bring to visual fields our understanding of the real world, and we interpret most, if not all, visual elements in such terms. Any visual configuration seen as different in a visual field tends to advance (gain weight). Unexpectedly found, a four-leaf clover may produce a considerable, if momentary, reaction (gain weight). We are always attracted by what is most unique in our visual field.

Chapter 8 deals with our brain's preoccupation with establishing spatial relationships of objects in the visual field. Things that advance attract attention first; those that recede usually do not.

Chapter 9 concerns the effects of change in our visual field. Change involves both the immediate: motion; the evolutionary: time; and interval in a spatial sense: increments of movement through space and time. Figures that exhibit change attract our attention. The more extensive the perceived change and the shorter the interval, the greater the attraction. We are primarily aware of change.

Chapter 10 discusses psychological weight, that is, the degree of emphasis that our brain gives to figures based on our past experience or knowledge, Gestalt *assimilation*. It is an area of intellectual and emotional contrast. Those figures that arouse strong emotions—like love, hate, fear, or anxiety—attract our attention most.

As we go along looking at all those things that affect visual weight, we will also look at many of their affective (emotional) response characteristics. Be sure to mark them with a distinctive color highlighting marker. Additionally, Chapter 11, "Communicating Visually," deals specifically with this subject.

What is important to understand at this time is that we do not ordinarily limit choices to any one of these things. It is generally not a matter of one or the other. A good work of art uses everything in exactly the right proportion and balance required to solve that particular work's special visual problems.

Understanding how to manage visual weight may be one of the most important things an artist ever learns.

Review of key terms

affect To influence or bring about a change in. To touch or to move the emotions. Also, a strong feeling that has active consequences.

contrast Opposing qualities of things when compared or set side by side; or the accentuation or sharpening of such differences.

focal point The dominant point or area in any visual or pictorial field wherever the eye is directed or impelled to look.

hierarchy A clearly defined relationship between things that establishes differing levels of dominance, emphasis, or influence, with each level subordinate to the one above it. Overall patterns with equally emphasized figures are sometimes called "nonhierarchical" designs.

leveling Making things more alike; emphasizing similarities.

sharpening Making things less alike; emphasizing differences between things—contrast.

Visual weight: The anatomy of organization

Mischa Richter. "Decisions, decisions, decisions." Drawing by Richter; © 1983 The New Yorker Magazine, Inc.

CHAPTER SIX

Balance and orientation

Physical forces affect pictorial balance

Pictorial balance (Gestalt equilibrium) is dependent on the relative eye attraction of all elements in a composition. It is influenced by the distribution of visual weight in accordance with an understanding of gravity and other physical forces.

Psychologically we cannot stand a state of imbalance for very long. As time passes, we become increasingly fearful, uncomfortable, and disoriented, even nauseated. Physiological imbalance has presented problems for our astronauts, for instance. Their sense of balance is frustrated by a lack of vertical orientation, a very unfamiliar experience.

If we are to achieve physical balance and stability, we must not only balance weight (gravitational equilibrium) but also balance physical forces. That also applies to pictures.

The affective responses associated with balance

Remember, every perception affects every subsequent perception. Essentially, we "expect" that pic- tured figure-objects will behave according to the same physical laws that govern natural figure-objects. When they do, the affective emotional responses are pleas ing, comfortable, nonthreatening; when they do not, affective emotional responses are uncomfortable, unpleasing, threatening, sometimes even frightening because they defy perceptual constancies. Theater, television, and motion pictures commonly use the latter to excite and thrill us with magic, fantasy, and the supernatural. Such ideas are easily applied to all forms of art. A rock *floats* suspended in the air (Fig. 6.1). A man stands *beside* his leg (Fig. 6.2). Such concepts command our attention. They possess a heavy visual weight.

left: **6.1** René Magritte. *The Castle of the Pyrenees.* 1959. Oil on canvas, 78¾" × 57⅛" (200 × 140 cm). Israel Museum, Jerusalem, Gift of Harry Torczyner, New York, to the American Friends of the Israel Museum. A rock floats in the air! Does that confound expectations?

right: **6.2** Bruno Ruegg; (Designer), François Robert (Photographer), and Sieber and McIntyre (Agency). Cover for *Current Concepts in Pain.* 1984. How can we say "pain" visually?

85

Balance in a pictorial sense involves all the ordinary meanings the word holds for us. It is the placing of equal weights on either side of a balancing scale; it is psychological balance (homeostasis) and the sense of "position" that each living thing possesses. Pictorial balance demands that all such forces conceptually neutralize each other, ultimately bringing the work to a state of rest. Works of art are satisfying in direct proportion to the degree of such achievement. This quality, *dynamic equilibrium,* is characteristic of all of nature. It is physically and physiologically necessary.

There are two basic types of balance. Formal balance, or symmetry, has a tendency to be static. Informal balance, or asymmetry, has a tendency to be dynamic.

1. Symmetrical balance

Bilateral symmetry

Bilateral symmetry is often called axial balance or axial symmetry. See Figure 6.3 **a** and **c**. In these, visual elements are repeated as mirror images on each side of a vertical or horizontal axis. Of all types of balance, perfect symmetry is the most obvious and also the most lacking in variety.

We see bilateral symmetry exhibited in living creatures, a butterfly for instance. We have the impression that the right and left halves of all living creatures, including the human body, are symmetrical. Whether they are or not is beside the point; we *perceive* them to be. Symmetry is an important aspect of many manufactured objects. Would anyone want an asymmetrical automobile wheel?

Approximate bilateral symmetry is more interesting and dynamic because it softens the rigidity of the pure state. Actually, it is more natural. Few creatures or objects we believe to be are perfectly symmetrical.

One way to make bilateral symmetry approximate is to employ the exact same contours, but redistribute the visual weight. In Figure 6.3 **b** the gray elements on the left side are white on the right and vice versa, a common approach seen in decorative patterns. Compare it to 6.3 **a**. Another way to achieve this effect is to vary each side so that each is obviously different, but also obviously similar. That has also been done.

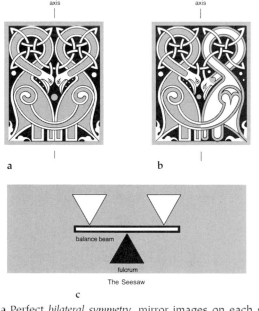

a   b

c

6.3   **a** Perfect *bilateral symmetry,* mirror images on each side of a single axis.
b Approximate bilateral symmetry. The design for both **a** and **b** is based on a medieval Celtic ornament.
c The seesaw.

6.4   Raphael. *Sistine Madonna.* Ca. 1515. Oil on canvas, 8′8″ × 6′5⅗″ (2.64 × 1.97 m). State Museums, Dresden. A classic example of approximate bilateral symmetry.

6.5 Frank Frazetta. *The Mammoth*. 1974. Oil on canvas panel, 30″ × 24″ (76 × 61 cm). As in the previous example, the composition for this poster is based on approximate bilateral symmetry.

6.6 *Radial symmetry*, or radial balance, mirror images on each side of both a horizontal and a vertical axis or on each side of an even number of equally spaced radii. Design based on a French Romanesque ornament.

Note the subtle changes. Observe how Raphael has "broken" the symmetry in *The Sistine Madonna* (Fig. 6.4) with wonderful results. The variations are different enough to be seen as "intentional," not mistakes, yet close enough to a formal bilateral balance that the integrity of the compositional idea is not compromised—balance not only in design but also balance in judgment. Observe a similar structure in Frank Frazetta's poster (Fig. 6.5).

Radial symmetry

Radial symmetry (Fig. 6.6) in its formal expression may be seen to be a type of balance with images mirrored along both a horizontal and a vertical axis. Actually, any number of axes may be employed so long as they represent an even number of equally spaced radii that originate at a single central point. As in bilateral symmetry, approximate radial symmetry may be achieved through tonal reversal as well as shape modification. It can also be created through unequally spaced radii or odd numbers of radii, or by moving the radiating point off-center. The result may seem merely grotesque and distorted on the one hand or, on the other, may appear more interesting and dynamic. Psychological factors usually determine which one of these responses dominates. Radiating designs tend to make objects look larger. Radial symmetry is commonly used in all sorts of design work from Japanese crests to modern logotypes or trademarks (Fig. 6.7 **a**, **b**, and **c**). There are three types of radial balance: centrifugal (Fig. 6.8), centripetal (Fig. 6.9), and concentric (Fig. 6.10).

Centrifugal balance

In centrifugal balance, forces are moving outward. The affective emotional responses are those of dispersion and expansion: flying apart, explosion, a spinning top, and effervescence (liveliness-vivaciousness).

Centripetal balance

In centripetal balance, forces are moving inward. The affective responses are those of concentration and compression: whirlpool, tornado, draining, assembly, gathering together, coming together, association.

Concentric balance

Concentricity moves attention from frame perimeters to focus strongly on the center of the composition. In perfectly concentric balance, all shapes or forms have a common center.

The bull's-eye effect created by any form of concentric division of space, including the spiral, form swift paths for the eye to follow, but bring all action quickly to rest in the center where the eye is trapped. Involvement (emotional or otherwise) is over almost instantly because the action is truncated — the climax revealed before interest has been built.

In concentric balance the eye is drawn irresistibly inward. The effect suggests concentration, confinement, squeezing, singularity. Through careful application of visual weights, these affective responses of enclosure and drawing inward may be reversed to

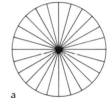

6.7 **a** Don Irwin (Designer). Trademark for Metropolitan Life Insurance. 1964. This design is an example of perfect radial symmetry.
b Lippincott and Margulies (Designers). Trademark for the Chrysler Corporation. 1963. Courtesy Chrysler Motors Corp. This is also an example of perfect radial symmetry.
c Japanese crests (family symbols) in a circular design. In these three examples, the artists have used approximate radial symmetry.

Types of radial balance or symmetry

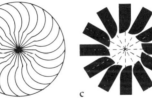

6.8   Centrifugal: forces moving outward.

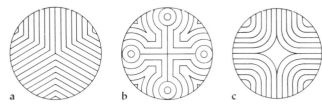

6.9   Centripetal: forces moving inward.

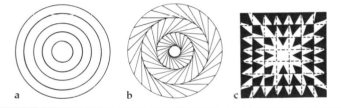

6.10   Concentric: the "bull's-eye."

produce responses of expansion and release. Usually, it is a poor compositional choice unless an artist is equal to the task.

The spiral

The spiral is associated with forms of radial balance. As a compositional device, it is best "broken," that is, not seen to be a perfectly continuous line of movement throughout the work. A broken spiral was a favorite compositional device of the 17th-century painter Peter Paul Rubens. The subtle broken spiral creates an easy undulating movement whose pace can be controlled by image management: distributions of visual weight, connections of the narrow kind, and figure-ground melds. Observe the effect in *Tiger Hunt* (Fig. 6.11). Figure 6.12 diagrams the painting's spiral movement.

Important: Observe that the affective emotional responses for all forms of radial balance are consistent with dictionary definitions for their physical force counterparts.

Circular compositions

In *Madonna and Child with St. John* (Fig. 6.13), notice how Raphael used radial lines to section the circle into interesting divisions. The radial lines are curved, repeating arcs of the circular perimeter. Other compositional arcs reinforce such rhythms by counterpoint. Draw a line through the centers of the eyes of all three heads, for example, and discover another arc, a complementary one. Are the two arcs, like parentheses, enclosing the figures of Mary and Jesus obvious? Every artist should see them. One is created by Mary's hair covering and arm (left); the other touches the heads of Mary and Jesus, then runs down the back of

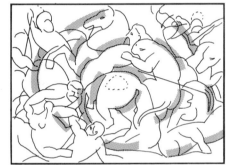

6.11 Workshop of Peter Paul Rubens. *Tiger Hunt*. ca. 1616. Oil on panel, 38⅞ × 48¼″ (98.8 × 125 cm). The Wadsworth Atheneum, Hartford. The Ella Gallup Sumner and Mary Catlin Sumner collection. A *broken spiral* has been used as a unifying compositional device. Rather than being a relatively continuous line, it has components offset one way or the other. The painting boils with movement.

6.12 Diagram of the broken spiral in *Tiger Hunt*. Although the spiral line is discontinuous and segments are offset, the mind "closes" the line of movement.

6.13 Raphael. *Madonna della Sedia* (*Madonna and Child with St. John*). Ca. 1514–1515. Oil on wood, 28″ (71 cm) diameter. Galleria Palatina, Palazzo Pitti, Florence. Observe the rhythms created by the many repeated arcs of all sizes and configurations in this example of approximate symmetry.

the infant. Everywhere, circles and fragments of circles spread harmonic rhythms throughout the work. Similar, but more dynamically expressive, is Orozco's *Earth, Air, Fire, and Water* (Fig. 6.14).

It is possible to increase the excitement and effectiveness of formal structures by fragmenting. One type of fragmentation may be produced by simply eliminating chunks of the structure. In another, an artist may design around only a few radial lines as Rockwell Kent has done in a book illustration (Fig. 6.16).

2. Asymmetrical balance

Asymmetrical balance is simply "off-center" balance. It is best understood as the principle of the seesaw (Fig. 6.17). Any large, "heavy" figure must be placed closer to the fulcrum in order to balance a smaller, "lighter" figure located on the opposite side. The *fulcrum* is the point of support for this balancing act. It is a physical principle transposed into a pictorial field. **The fulcrum is never seen,** *but its presence must be strongly felt.*

Asymmetry became a major force in 20th-century art. It is likely this came about through the influence of Oriental works on late 19th-century artists. In *Sumi*, Japanese watercolor, asymmetry is a matter of tradition. Examine the contemporary work *Bamboo* (Fig. 6.18); notice how the heavy weight of the bamboo stem (a simple shape) is balanced by the light, complex shape on the left. It has a perfect seesaw balance, also an obvious characteristic of *Person Throwing a Stone at a Bird,* a painting by Joan Miró (Fig. 6.19).

Figure 6.20 is a typical work by Piet Mondrian. The large neutral area provides stability for the smaller panels in primary (red, yellow, and blue) colors. Everything balances. Where is the fulcrum?

The architectural designs of Frank Lloyd Wright appear to spring from the same interests (Fig. 6.21). One should become sensitive to such relationships between artworks, art forms, and art concepts, which are connections of a broad kind.

Figure 6.22 **a** illustrates "visual topple." The heaviest weight, placed on the left edge, appears to be falling out of the picture. There is nothing on the right side, no counterpoint weight, to pull it back—to bal-

above left: **6.14** Jośe Clemente Orozco. *Earth, Air, Fire and Water.* 1938. Fresco. Museo José Clemente Orozco, Guadalajara, Mexico. Note the Chinese yin-yang symbol used here as a compositional device.

left: **6.15** The Chinese yin-yang symbol stands for the symmetry or balance of earthly forces, sun/moon, light/dark, male/female, active/passive, and the like.

above: **6.16** Rockwell Kent. *Bowsprite.* 1930. Wood engraving (maple) 4½" × 7⅞" (11.4 × 20 cm). Courtesy of the Rockwell Kent Legacies. In this design, Kent employs just a few lines, which radiate from the same point, as a major compositional device.

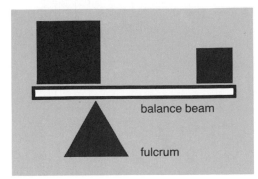

top: **6.17** The seesaw and asymmetry. In this diagram, the weights are different. Notice the positions of both the large and the small weights as related to the fulcrum. Is the fulcrum in the physical center of the space?

above: **6.18** Dee Gilson. *Bamboo.* 1972. Ink on rice paper, 13½″ × 18⅛″ (32 × 46 cm). Collection of the author. An example of traditional Japanese sumi painting, which employs asymmetry as an aesthetic principle.

left: **6.19** Joan Miró. *Person Throwing a Stone at a Bird.* 1926. Oil on canvas, 29″ × 36¼″ (73.6 × 92 cm). Collection, The Museum of Modern Art, New York. Purchase. This black and white reproduction fails to show the brilliant red of the "bird," left, which balances the large white "person," right. The ground is yellow, with the sky area painted a relatively pure green. Where is the fulcrum? The fulcrum is not seen, but it is always *felt.*

above: **6.20** Piet Mondrian. *Large Composition with Red, Yellow and Blue.* 1928. Oil on canvas, 48″ × 31¼″ (122 × 79.4 cm). Stefan T. Edlis Collection. Courtesy Sidney Janis Gallery, New York. Where is the fulcrum?

Balance and orientation **91**

a   Visual topple

b   An improved balance

6.21 Frank Lloyd Wright. *Robie House*. 1909. Chicago. Does anyone see conceptual and aesthetical connections that link this together with Figures 6.17, 6.18, 6.19, 6.20?

6.22 **a** "Visual topple." The large black mass is falling out of the picture. There is nothing on the other side to balance it.
b Moving the mass toward the center improves visual stability even though there still is nothing opposite to balance it.

ance it. If we move the weight toward the center (Fig. 6.22 **b**), observe that it holds its balance fairly well even without a counterforce, and is stabilized satisfactorily.

A **principle to remember: It is the *heaviest visual weight*, not the largest mass, which must be placed close to the fulcrum so that it is visually balanced in the same manner in which physical balance is achieved. Equal weights are placed on each side of the fulcrum, not equal masses. Heavy weights are placed close to the fulcrum, not necessarily close to the center of the pictorial field.**

Take another look at the Miró, Figure 6.19. Where is the fulcrum?

We are fearful of unsupported weights, of unbalanced weights, and of unstable weights (those which are moving or possess the "potential" to move); they are both dynamic and unsettling. Recall the thrill—and perhaps a little fright—created by apparent imbalances on a roller coaster ride. A good movie of a similar ride from a subjective point of view will bring back the same feelings and affect us much in the same way. We find it intolerable to be caught up for very long in an unbalanced visual field, whether real or synthesized. We are likely to experience empathic feelings when observing other persons caught up in these same circumstances.

During a high-wire act at a circus, performers seek to satisfy the audience's expectation of danger by

suggesting, through their actions, that they are about to lose their balance. None would ever take such a chance deliberately. They train rigorously. They are always in control. If balance were truly lost, the performer would fall. Making a good composition is like walking a tightrope!

In creative work, artists must never let the dynamic forces of balance and weight out of their knowing control. Remember the seesaw.

Orientation

Orientation means alignment or positioning with respect to a specific direction or reference system. There are two aspects to consider. *Position* is the placement or location of a figure relative to the picture frame or to the borders of the pictorial field. *Spatial attitude* is the relationship of a figure to its own vertical-horizontal axes, that is, its typical or atypical verticality.

Position

Wherever a figure is placed within a pictorial field affects its visual weight and creates differing affective (emotional) responses within us. A viewer's left-right, up-down expectations also affect the division of pictorial space into areas of interest. For most of us living in Western societies, entrance is upper left and movement proceeds to lower right.

Position

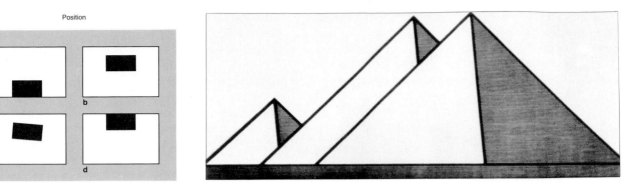

6.23 Placement of any shape or defined mass in the pictorial field produces differing affective (emotional) responses, as well as differing perceptions of space and movement: **a** secure and stable; **b** threatening (suspended in space); **c** unstable and dangerous; **d** insecure but stable.

6.24 Roy Lichtenstein. *Three Pyramids*. 1969. This is not as simple an organization as one might think at first glance.

A position close to the bottom of the picture frame and roughly parallel with the frame line suggests a body at rest. It is perceptually nonthreatening, calming, and quiet and possesses weak visual weight. It tends to suggest stability and ordinarily exhibits a lack of movement and energy (see Fig. 6.23 **a**).

Observe Roy Lichtenstein's *Three Pyramids* (Fig. 6.24). The idea of stability is increased in this work by placing the figures very close to the frame line and darkening portions for extra visual weight. Yet it has both rhythm and "dynamic" effects. How is all of this possible in so simple a composition? What would happen if we inverted the pyramids? Now, what observations can we make?

A point to remember: Like affective responses reinforce one another to produce effective results. Dissimilar, or opposing, affective responses cancel out one another.

A figure positioned in the upper half of the visual field near the top of the frame possesses a very strong visual weight (Fig. 6.23 **b**) because its position suggests the object is unstable.

When the separation is wide enough that the figure is perceived to be detached, like an object suspended in space, it is a model that defies the law of gravity (levitation, for now, is impossible). We know such a figure must fall. Given a slight angle, the figure is launched into motion (Fig. 6.23 **c**). We *feel* it. Downward movements are nearly always threatening and possess a potentially heavy weight, but if our

figure is very light in contrast with the ground, the model may be "cloud," and its weight will vanish accordingly.

It is less threatening (lowering its weight) if it can be seen to be attached to the upper frame line (Fig. 6.23 **d**). Visual weight is affected when closure occurs. In fact, all such attachments to any frame line modify visual weight; they provide entrances into, or exits from, a composition. They can help create open compositional shapes (especially if they penetrate rather than just touch the edge). Figures whose contours are unbroken produce closed shapes. Closed shapes are virtually always heavier than open ones but are also more divisive.

When shapes, particularly points on arcs or corners of triangular or rectilinear forms, just touch one another or touch the frame edge, they create a point of emphasis called a *tangent*. A tangent draws unusual attention to itself, ordinarily a very undesirable effect. As may be observed in many formal designs, sheer numbers of tangents will effectively neutralize their individual weight.

Spatial attitude

Our notions about the attitude of bodies in space are governed by our understanding of how figures physically behave according to gravity. All figures are stabilized (brought to rest) by the action of gravity unless a force is applied great enough to cancel out its effects.

All figure-objects have a center of gravity or point of equilibrium through which three axes pass. For a person, the most stable position, our natural spatial attitude, is when we are standing up straight with both feet, about a foot apart, planted firmly on solid ground. In this position, we are vertically oriented and have a vertical attitude. An axis passes through the center of our body mass, weight not shape, to the center of the earth. The other two axes, one directly forward and backward from us and another directly from side to side, pass through exactly that same point roughly located inside our bodies in front of the backbone and a little below the bellybutton. Every living thing has an innate "attitude."

In order to understand revolving movements of any figure-object about these three axes, perhaps it will help to look at an illustration from the NASA space program (see Fig. 6.25). *Roll* is a figure-object's rotation about a horizontal axis, any position in a 360°

circle. *Yaw* is the 360° rotation about a vertical axis. *Pitch* is a 360° rotation of the whole figure-object 360° forward or backward: a tumbling action. Of course, every two- or three-dimensional figure is affected by these concerns whether existing in real space or in illusionary space on a two-dimensional surface. Whether working realistically or abstractly, artists should question if their first choice of orientation for any figure is the best one. It may be wise to explore alternative attitudes—a different roll, pitch, or yaw.

Living creatures try to maintain their normal attitude even if the ground plane is uneven, curved, or slanted. This is because the effects of gravity establish our essential verticality. Think how the body must be positioned in order to maintain balance when walking uphill. How would we react to a person walking perpendicular to the angle of the mountainside as is sometimes seen in cartoons?

Any perceived deviation from a normal attitude

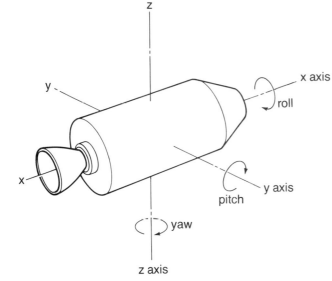

6.25 Suspended in space, all bodies have three axes about which they may revolve. Early in the space program, NASA adopted the terminology roll, pitch, and yaw to describe movement about each of these. Any one, specific configuration combining a single position of all three axes is that body's *spatial attitude.*

6.26 Three positions of a stool show how our emotional responses are affected by an innate understanding of the consequences of a figure-object's diagonal orientation.

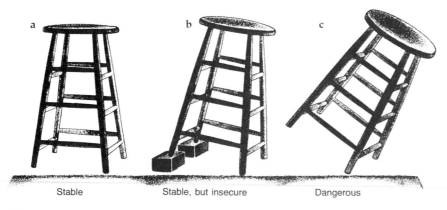

Stable   Stable, but insecure   Dangerous

suggests to us that the figure is in a state of motion. In any visual field this produces a diagonal figure, line, or line of movement. The visual weight increases dramatically. Diagonals are very dynamic.

Why should a diagonal be dynamic?

Perceptually, any figure-object in a diagonal attitude is inherently unstable. We have learned to fear this situation. We "expect" that a diagonally oriented figure will fall—sooner or later (Fig. 6.26). A diagonal acquires dynamics (movement) by virtue of this perception. Only those diagonals that are seen to be supported are perceptually stabilized.

Take another look at Figure 6.24. Is it possible to explain why these pyramidal forms, the most stable of all structures, should, in this case, somehow appear about to shift position? What could Lichtenstein have done that would have added stability to the composition? Would that have improved the work or made it less satisfactory?

Whenever diagonals are used as a compositional device, they add an element of movement and dynamism that simply is not present when forms are only oriented vertically and horizontally.

Examine Rembrandt's *Storm on the Sea of Galilee* (Fig. 6.27). Note the triangular composition and the attitude (angle) of the mast, a strong diagonal. These are unsupported, exciting, and dynamic. We feel the power of the storm at sea. Compare that work to one by an earlier painter, Jerome Bosch (Fig. 6.28). Bosch has also constructed a triangular composition with a mast at a slight diagonal. In this case, there are no wild dynamics at work as there is in the Rembrandt. Bosch's scene is essentially calm although the angle of the mast adds a rakish (reckless) quality appropriate to the subject of the work. It is exactly the correct touch to reinforce the argumentative nature of the participating characters.

6.27   Rembrandt. *Storm on the Sea of Galilee.* 1633. Isabella Stewart Gardner Museum. Trace the triangle formed by the tip of the mast and the front and rear of the ship. Where should it be placed among the examples in Figure 6.26? Would that orientation be appropriate to the story?

6.28   Jerome Bosch. *Ship of Fools.* ca. 1500. Louvre, Paris. How do the orientation and emotional qualities of this work vary from *Storm on the Sea of Galilee*? Observe that in both, a geometric form—the triangle—has been used as a means of organizing the major masses in the composition.

6.29 Theodore Géricault. *Study for the Raft of the Medusa.* 1818. Oil on canvas, 25½″ × 32¾″ (64.7 × 83.2 cm). Louvre, Paris. This is one of many studies for a large painting. It is another triangular composition. Carefully compare it to the finished work (Fig. 6.30) and to Rembrandt's use of the same compositional device.

A similar composition is shown in its formative stage (Fig. 6.29). This is a study by Theodore Géricault for a major painting called *The Raft of the Medusa.* Although the triangles are unsupported, like Rembrandt's, it is less dynamic and dramatic; and these, above all, are the qualities Géricault desired for this work.

The topical quality of the painting is lost on us today because we are unaware of the circumstances that motivated Géricault. In 1816 a French ship, the *Medusa,* filled with settlers and soldiers bound for Senegal, was wrecked. The captain's ineptitude, the lack of lifeboats, together with the large number of persons drowned became a *cause célèbre* (an issue that arouses heated debate). This painting, *The Raft of the Medusa,* was a kind of political poster—an act of social consciousness like those who protest against nuclear armaments today. Knowing this adds another level, an intellectual one, to the masterpiece. It supplies us with a reason for its existence; more important, it establishes a reason for most of Géricault's artistic decisions, both compositionally and emotionally. This is especially significant to artists because it tells us *why.* When examining any work of art, we should always be asking ourselves, "What motivated the artist to make the decisions that were made?" Why did he or she choose to solve the visual problems in that particular way? Knowing what Géricault was trying to accomplish gives us the rationale for understanding the artistic decisions the artist made.

In the completed form (Fig. 6.30), many changes have occurred in the composition. A new—stronger—diagonal was added, shooting upward through the central mass of the persons grouped on the raft. The impact of the angled mast was reduced to second place. Contrast (of luminance) was increased. The shape of the cloud forms, upper left, now lead us back into the composition. Diagonals are everywhere. The light source is low, just skimming across the figures, who are otherwise wrapped in gloom (darkness). The rescue vessel is smaller—further away! Is it theatrical? Yes, it is exactly what was called for.

Compare these aspects to the early study. Observe how the diagonal thrust moves swiftly from lower left to upper right, focusing attention on a person who waves frantically to the passing vessel, so small, and so far away on the horizon. Rescue is now more in doubt. Did Géricault make improved decisions on both artistic and conceptual grounds?

6.30 Theodore Géricault. *The Raft of the Medusa.* 1818–1819. Oil on canvas 16′ × 18′ (4.9 × 5.5 m). Louvre, Paris. How has the completed work changed aesthetically and emotionally from the study?

Summary

Everyone's understanding of physical weight and of the way in which the physical forces of gravity and motion (centrifugal and centripetal forces) work is brought to bear on the perception of pictures. It is necessary to balance pictorial elements as we perceive natural elements would have to be balanced. Imbalance is uncomfortable and disturbing to us. Clever artists realize that physical balance on a two-dimensional surface is illusionary. Pictorial balance may be achieved through the management of the characteristics of visual weight and yet give viewers, through an asymmetrical arrangement, an illusion of physical imbalance, which adds dynamism and excitement to any composition.

Everyone's understanding of balance is related to the physical balancing of a seesaw, where the fulcrum is the point of equilibrium, not necessarily the center of a visual field or of a picture. We are all greatly affected emotionally by changes in our physical attitude and position—our orientation in space. These feelings are brought, perceptually, to the viewing of pictures. Such understandings provide artists with a vast array of tools with which to construct more effective compositions or designs, as well as to create more compelling communications.

Review of key terms

asymmetry The principle of the seesaw transposed into pictorial form. Parts of a composition, unequal in area (size), are balanced in visual weight on either side of an imaginary fulcrum. The fulcrum is the center of visual balance, not the center of the picture.

balance Equilibrium of opposing visual weights, hues, or psychological and physical forces.

bilateral symmetry A form of design in which elements repeat themselves as perfect mirror images along a vertical (or horizontal) axis or bisector.

orientation Alignment or positioning of anything with respect to a specific direction, reference system, or axis; also, familiarizing oneself or adjusting to any situation.

physical Pertaining to the body as distinguished from the mind; pertaining to matter and energy.

physiological Pertaining to the biological science of life processes, activities, and functions.

radial symmetry, or balance Mirror images on either side of both a vertical and a horizontal axes or along any even number of equally spaced radii.

spatial attitude The position of any body relative to its normal or innate vertical axis, usually a position that takes the physical effects of gravity into account. Every figure-object possesses three axes about which it may rotate.

symmetry, or symmetrical balance Exact repetition or correspondence of shapes on opposite sides of an axis or a point. When correspondence is not exact, but still similar, it is called "approximate" symmetry.

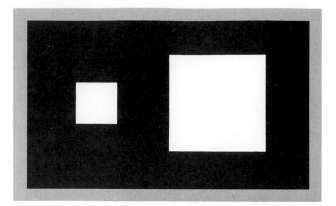

CHAPTER SEVEN

Relative visual attraction

What attracts?

In any visual field, perceptual studies show that it is what is most different in some way from customary that first attracts our attention. Therefore, *visual attraction* pertains to uniqueness or novelty (the quality of difference) in the visual field. Differences may be related to a figure's size, color (all three dimensions: hue, luminance, and purity), movement, distance (space from us), shape, and so on. What makes anything different is its contrast with associated figures or with its environment. Mechanisms of attraction are a relative phenomenon.

Our very survival as a species required our brain to reject certain kinds of sensory information but to pay attention to other kinds. It is these things that attract our attention first even if such attraction may be only momentary.

Attraction is one determining factor in establishing spatial relationships in the perceptual field. This has little to do with three-dimensional representation but a lot to do with how the brain functions. Figures that attract our attention advance (possess a heavier visual weight, *pull*). Those that do not recede (*push*). Perceptual attraction, therefore, is one means of pushing-pulling the two-dimensional surface.

The significance of scale

Large and small. When we are dealing with scale, there are two aspects that concern us. One is sheer area or mass (largeness as opposed to smallness). Any figure may gain or lose weight based on its size. In a field of things that are all about the same size, something large usually stands out (Fig. 7.1).

However, things are not always equal in size or significance. Human beings are generally more concerned with importance than size. A small object may be moving or more brightly colored, or it may be more distinctly defined, contrasty, or alluring in shape. These qualities make a small figure as likely as a large one without such qualities to attract our attention.

Relative size. Size constancy refers to our understanding of the ordinary and functional sizes of familiar figure-objects. Our brain continually makes comparisons between figures that come into view and our assimilated knowledge of them. Though there may be any number of reasons why we might be attracted to

7.1 In a visual field consisting of two shapes or in a field in which all shapes are a similar size, a large figure stands out because it is *different*.

7.2 Basketball player Manute Bol is seven feet, seven inches tall — *a real giant*. Whenever we encounter a person who is nearly a foot and a half taller than the average male, that person is a subject of consternation and awe.

7.3 An ersatz giant. Our brain is playing tricks on us. The room is not a rectangle but a trapezoid. From just one point of view the room looks normal, but persons of normal size do not. The illusion occurs not only in a photograph but also when viewing the actual room! Perceptual constancies are confounded. The room was devised by artist Adelbert Ames.

a particular person or thing, size becomes important only when it is perceived to be different or unusual; that is, when it does not conform to expectations (defies constancies).

The greater the size deviation from perceived normality, the greater the visual weight. Giants and dwarfs, for example, have potentially heavy weight (Figs. 7.2, 7.3). It may be worthwhile to review the discussion of size constancy presented in Chapter 3.

The attraction of color

When we use the term *color*, we should always mean to include more than one of the color dimensions. If only one dimension is meant, then we should specifically identify it as a hue (red, for example), as luminance (lightness-darkness), or as purity (the relative vividness-intensity-saturation versus grayness).

The following principles are tools that enable artists to manage the relative attraction of figures when using color. They are easy to understand and should be incorporated into every artist's intuitive operating procedure.

Please place a marker by Color Plate 1 (p. 257), so that it is possible to flip back and forth easily.

In a black and white pictorial field, color is unique and possesses a heavy visual weight. Observe that effect in Color Plate 1**a**, where the red square stands out brightly against the white and the gray. Attention can be directed to any particular figure-object by making everything else in the picture black, white, and shades of gray.

Colors advance (*pull*); black and white (grays) recede (*push*).

It is not always desirable to eliminate all but one color from a picture, nor is it necessary. A very similar effect may be obtained by simply reducing the purity of all colors (graying them) except for that of the figure that must stand out.

Relative attraction in the color field

In a color pictorial field, if a change in hue, luminance, or purity of a color confers some unique quality on one figure that others do not possess, that one figure will stand out.

In Color Plate 1**b** (p. 257), even though both hues are pure (saturated or intense), the orange stands out because it exhibits the most difference. Orange provides both higher luminance contrast with the blue ground and greater hue contrast. Why? On the Prang hue circle (Fig. 7.4), orange and blue are *complementary*

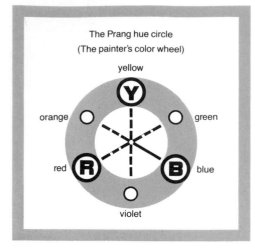

above: 7.4 In the Prang hue circle, primary hues are red, yellow, and blue. Secondary hues are orange, green, and violet. Complementary hues are at opposite ends of the dashed lines. Louis Prang published *The Theory of Color* in 1876. His ideas were subsequently adopted by many American educational institutions for primary and secondary levels but are commonly taught at all levels, including junior and senior high school.

above right: 7.5 In **a**, a hard-edge geometric shape will attract most persons' attention first when compared to an amorphous (poorly defined and fuzzy) shape, which does not usually have strong meaning for us. In **b**, the more intricate design attracts or tends to hold a person's attention more than the simple geometric shape because it inherently possesses more significance (meaning).

right: 7.6 Differing types of edges: **a**, a "hard" edge; **c**, a "soft" edge; and **b**, an intermediary edge.

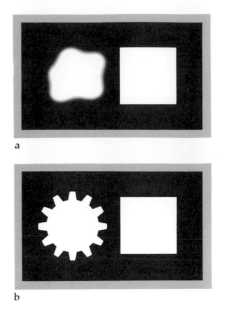

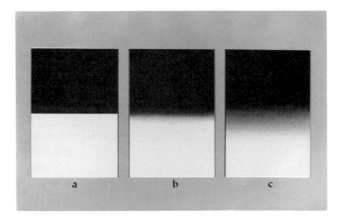

(opposite) hues. **A figure whose hue is complementary to the perceived ground will draw our attention first**. Because the purple-red is much closer to blue than orange, the orange advances (*pulls*) and the purple-red recedes (*pushes*) relative to the blue ground. The orange, in this case, demonstrates greater visual weight even though the figures are the same shape and the same size. In fact, the violet figure would have to be much larger for it to compete successfully with the orange.

The luminance contrast of a hue with the ground will cause a figure to advance or recede, (Color Plate 1 **c** (p. 257). In this example, even though the figures are the same size, shape, and hue, the light red stands out while the dark red fades away.

In Color Plate 1 **d** (p. 257), figures are the same size and the same shape and are seen against the same ground hue, yet the square on the right advances. It attracts our attention because we sense that it is a purer, more vivid hue than the one next to it. Obviously, **pure hues advance, and grayed, or impure, hues recede.**

These separate approaches may be combined to heighten attraction or, conversely, to diminish it. Only in the most simple applications do such things work alone. Each is one more "tool" to use in solving a visual problem, for example, how to make a figure stay in its place.

The attraction of shape (or form)

We all possess certain perceptual expectations with regard to the shape of recognizable figure-objects. These are aspects of perceptual constancy that

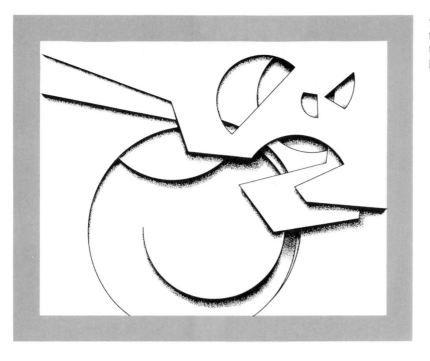

7.7 A project for students in which all spatial dimension is indicated through the use of the "forced edge," a graphic replication of a perceptual brain activity (irradiation).

have an effect on the degree of interest any shape holds for us.

Abstracted shapes, like representative ones, gain or lose weight depending on our response not only to color but also to shape or contour. The significance of contour is dependent on a contrast gradation scale from amorphous and soft-edged (light weight) on the one side, to intricate and hard-edged (heavy weight) on the other.

Our sensibilities tell us that a simple geometric shape indicates the presence of humankind, since we have learned to associate such shapes with objects made by human beings. A geometric figure-object or "sign" may have once indicated the presence of a friend or a foe. **When directly compared against an amorphous shape, a simple, strong geometric shape draws our attention** because it appears it must have been fashioned by an intelligent being like ourselves (Fig. 7.5 **a**).

When we look at the mechanism of a watch, we understand that its intricacy required a higher degree of intelligence than fashioning a simple geometric form. Such a shape, particularly when symmetrical, may suggest that it is a component of an instrument or a machine (an associational meaning). Perhaps we may simply react to our sense of the beautiful (the decorative character of the figure). Or we may react to both of these at once. **When directly compared to a** geometric form (simplicity), an intricate shape (complexity) ordinarily attracts greater attention (Fig. 7.5 **b**).

The significance of edges

Throughout this book, there is a conscious attempt to emphasize the point that edges are a significant perceptual characteristic. Consequently, they are also an artist's tool of major importance. This is a fact that is often overlooked in the studies of composition and design. Understanding edges will always lead to the creation of improved or superior works.

The distinctness of edges, that is, the degree of their perceived sharpness, has a strong attraction. Sharp edges that flow as unbroken contours around the perimeter of a shape create a closed form with enormous integrity. They advance. Soft edges recede because of their tendency to blend with, or meld into, the ground. Soft edges are analogous to open forms. Edge definition is one of the perceptual characteristics of aerial perspective.

Figure 7.6 shows a range of edges from hard to soft. Edges may be "forced," that is, made hard on one side of line and made soft on the other. This reinforces a perceptual phenomenon called *simultaneous contrast*, of which irradiation is one characteristic. Hard edges advance (pull). Figure 7.7 is one example from a project for students that uses the forced edge as the

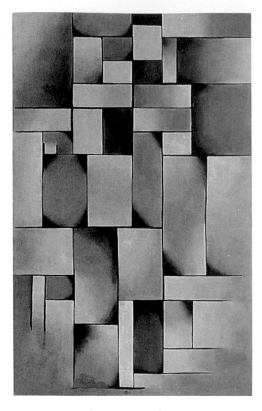

a

b

7.8 Theo van Doesburg. *Composition in Gray (Rag Time)*. 1919. Oil on canvas, 38 × 23⅜″ (96.5 × 59.3 cm). The Peggy Guggenheim Collection, Venice; Solomon R. Guggenheim Foundation, New York. Van Doesburg uses the forced edge to warp the two-dimensional surface in this abstract pattern of rectilinear shapes.

7.9 **a** Paul Signac. *Breakfast*. 1886–1887. Oil on canvas, 35 × 45¼″ (89 × 115 cm). State Museum, Kröller Müller, Otterlo, The Netherlands. Signac forces all the edges in his painting, working light against dark in order to extend perceptually the apparent luminance range on his canvas—a very common painting technique.
b Signac's *Breakfast*, detail. This detail of the painting shows more clearly how Signac used the forced edge. In particular, note the edges of the plate against its cast shadow.

7.10 George Green. *Untitled.* 1981. Acrylic on canvas, 66 × 54″ (167.6 × 137.16 cm). Courtesy Hokin/Kaufman Gallery, Chicago. Shapes curl and twist above the surface, projecting into the viewer's space. It is all an illusion; the surface of the canvas is perfectly flat. Note how Green has used many of the spatial cues discussed in this chapter, particularly cast shadows and the forced edge.

only means to suggest spatial relationships.

Theo van Doesburg used the idea to modulate the surface of his painting *Composition in Gray* (Fig. 7.8), completed in 1919 after he and Piet Mondrian founded *De Stijl*, a magazine designed to promote their aesthetic ideas.

In Figure 7.9 **a** and **b**, the use of the forced edge as a means to extend the luminance range of a reflective surface may be seen. Both Signac and Seurat were masters of the technique. In the contemporary painting by George Green, (Fig. 7.10), forms seem to rise up, curl, and twist above the surface — to levitate. Yet the surface is perfectly smooth and flat.

We should learn to sensitize ourselves to the qualities of edges. A soft edge, a blur, can be an indicator of motion or of roundness or of softness. The affective emotional responses of such soft edges together with their opposite, the razor-sharp cutting edge, can give to any artist a range of emotion and mood on which to play, like a musical instrument: sweetness, stridency, passion, detachment, merriment, or gloom — whatever one has in mind.

Abstract and representational figures

Representational figure-objects virtually always possess a heavier weight when directly compared to nonobjective figures in the same field. This is because recognizable shapes hold meaning for us. A nonobjective shape is one that we do not recognize as having any distinctive representational features.

When even slight representative features are given to nonobjective shapes, these will usually have greater attraction (more weight) than those shapes perceived to bear no such association or meaning. For example, consider our compulsion to find figures or faces in clouds or rocks. Understanding this characteristic of perception should help a nonobjective artist avoid focusing attention on a minor part of a composition through inadvertent suggestions of representative images. It can turn a composition topsy-turvy.

7.11 Forms of *isolation*. **a** Isolation by *interval* (physical separation). **b** Isolation by *anomaly* (differentiation or change). This requires an established "norm" or regularity against which to determine what is anomalous.

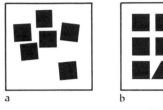

a   b

7.12 An example of isolation by interval. Where is the focus of attention?

7.13 Lord, Geller, Frederico, Einstein (Agency) and Isadore Seltzer (Illustrator). Double-page spread, advertisement for IBM Corporation. Used by permission. An example of isolation by anomaly. The headline reads, "If your failure rate is one in a million, what do you tell that one customer?" Are there other symbols as good as clouds? Could the ad be effectively redesigned using chocolate chip cookies? How? Where is the focus of attention?

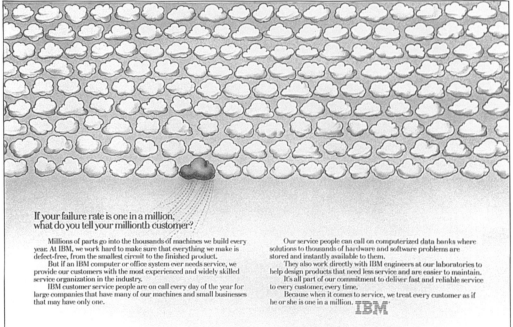

Isolation: The relative proximity of figures

A figure will gain weight by virtue of its isolation from a group of figures in a composition. Something that stands off by itself always attracts attention. Remember, it is what is different in the visual field which stands out.

A figure may be isolated from others by one of two methods: *interval* or *anomaly* (Fig. 7.11).

Isolation by interval

In Figure 7.12, the isolation is accomplished by physical separation, that is, the distance that the figures stand apart, the *interval*. Observe that there are three spatial planes established in this simple design. The group of penguins advances over the ground (white field), and the isolated, single penguin advances over the group.

Isolation by anomaly

In Figure 7.13, the isolation is accomplished through differentiation or, more to the point, anomaly.

An anomaly is a deviation from the normal order, form, or rule—something that, on the basis of precedent, is irregular or abnormal. An important point to remember is that there can be no anomaly unless the normal order is clearly established. In the advertisement, there is a regular field of little white clouds (the precedent or normal order). The one, single black cloud is an anomaly. This abnormal figure draws our attention just as it is supposed to do. Consider the psychological implications of a black cloud.

Because anomalies attract attention, we must be wary of creating anomalies where they are not appropriate. They can disrupt or destroy our entire composition. Such a possibility is not a rare occurrence.

When we draw a portrait, for instance, a misplaced eye or a poorly drawn one is an anomaly. Everybody "knows" where the eyes belong in relationship to the skull and how they appear from whatever viewing angle they are observed. Acceptable deviations from normal fall within a very narrow range. Otherwise, the head will be viewed as ugly, distorted, grotesque, and unreal.

Yet, interestingly enough, it is these very things that attract attention.

How contrast attracts

Perceptually, any change in our environment is significant to our survival. Our brain, therefore, makes all of us extraordinarily aware of change. *Contrast,* a form of change, is characterized by the quality of *transition,* the process or act of something changing from one form, shape, state, activity, or place to another.

Transition inevitably links opposites to one another even when the intervening stages are not shown. We understand that frozen water (ice) will melt at normal room temperatures and become the fluid that we drink and use in so many ways. We do not necessarily have to witness its transformation from a solid into a liquid. The transformation provides an infinite number of gradations, each representing one stage in the process of change from one state to the other. Opposite stages provide the strongest contrast, though the midpoint is neutral, neither wholly one or the other. The midpoint is usually a leveled state, but the opposite poles represent sharpened states. Thus figure-objects included in compositions may be leveled or sharpened in order to emphasize or de-emphasize the degree of observed difference.

Contrast is one of the primary ways we attract attention.

All the dimensions of color (hue, luminance, and purity) exhibit types of contrast gradation; so do shapes and forms—every one of these basic visual elements. We can also have forms of intellectual contrast, which are contrasts of concept, of theory, of language, and so on.

The following list provides a very few examples to start the thinking process.

Sample contrast gradation list

Color (hue and purity)

Black and white . . . to . . color
Grayed (weak) . . . . to . . pure (vivid)
Dark hue . . . . to . . light (bright) hue
Analogous hue . . . . to . . complementary hue
Warm/hot . . . . to . . cool/cold

Luminance

Light . . . . to . . dark
Strong contrast . . . . to . . little or no contrast

Various: such as form, line, texture

Hard edge . . . . to . . soft edge
Intricate detail . . . . . to . . lack of detail (smooth)
Fuzzy . . . . to . . sharp
Coarse . . . . to . . fine (like line, or texture)
Close-up . . . . to . . full view
Opaque . . . . to . . transparent
Solid . . . . to . . disintegration (atomization-spots etc.)
Untouched (pristine) to . . encrusted (with dirt-rust-crud)
Flat (2-D) . . . . to . . solid volume (3-D)
Organic . . . . to . . inorganic (crystaline-petrified-etc.)
Parts . . . . to . . whole
Positive . . . . to . . negative
One . . . . to . . many
Random . . . . to . . direct
Horizontal . . . . to . . vertical
Convex . . . . to . . concave

Intellectual [conceptual]

Nature . . . . to . . a person, homo sapiens sapiens
Man . . . . to . . machine
Dumb . . . . to . . smart
Illiterate . . . . to . . educated
Love . . . . to . . hate
Poor . . . . to . . wealthy
Analog . . . . to . . digital

Many of these contrasts affect depth perception. As cues, they help create illusionary space because they *push-pull* the 2-D surface. So do some of those intellectual contrasts because they involve *psychological weight*.

Would there be contrast gradations specifically associated with a single profession, ethnic group, or contiguous geographic area? How long would any such list be?

Summary

When comparisons are made between elements in a visual field, there is a hierarchy of visual attraction that is common to the majority of viewers. This has been determined by physiological characteristics necessary for our survival as a species. No figure-object, however, will possess *sustained* interest based on these simple characteristics. In spite of this, they are very useful tools that can help artists construct effective compositions for whatever purposes they have in mind. To become truly effective these characteristics must be coupled to other factors that possess appropriate associational or symbolic relationships. Of course, we must also *apply them creatively* to the solution of problems in visual design.

Any representational or nonrepresentational figure may be emphasized or de-emphasized (pushed or pulled) by controlling hue, luminance, and purity of colors in relationship to associated figures or grounds. Further management of such images may be made by adjusting other forms of visual weight.

A composition is an exercise in construction like building a building or engineering an automobile. Although the innumerable options or *alternatives* give us a great amount of flexibility, certain things must happen, or the end result will not be successful or appropriate for its purpose. Professional artists are purposeful builders and composers.

Review of key terms

abstraction   A type of painting that uses representational shapes or forms as a point of departure but freely adapts or subjugates these to the aesthetic purposes of the artist.

anomaly   Deviation from the common rule or form; in particular, an irregular, abnormal, contrary, or missing element (or motif) in an otherwise regular field or sequence of identical figures.

color   A property of light, not of bodies or pigments. As sensed by photoreceptors in the eye, our perception of color results from a certain bundle of wavelengths of electromagnetic energy bombarding the retina. Color has three "dimensions" or characteristics. *See* **hue, luminance; purity.**

complementary colors   Hues that are diametrically opposite one another on any hue circle (color wheel).

contrast   Opposing qualities of things when compared or set side by side; the accentuation or sharpening of such differences.

distinctness   The ability to resolve very fine detail in any visual field. Visual acuity, sharpness, or clarity; also, a relationship or ratio between such things as soft and hard edges, wide and narrow luminance ranges.

hue   The traditional color "name," such as "red," which is attached to a specific wavelength of visible light (electromagnetic energy).

interval   The amount of spatial separation between things such as lines, figures, colors, areas, spaces, and points in time. Intervals are *regular* when spacing is all the same and *progressive*, when the spaces change in natural order whether based on a simple numerical progression or on a geometric ratio.

luminance   An index of the amount of light reflected from a surface viewed from a particular direction. It relates to the lightness or the darkness of reflected colors and is compared to a gray scale.

purity   One of the dimensions of color that identifies the monochromatic quality of any hue, that is, its relationship to light of a single wavelength. This relationship establishes a scale ranging from the most vivid hue that is physically possible to a neutral gray.

scale   A visual relationship drawn between differing figures according to some easily recognized standard such as the human body.

shape   The overall outline or contour of any perceived unit, figure or ground, particularly when related to a two-dimensional surface. In this text, the more specific term *shape* is preferred to *form*, which has many broader meanings.

visual attraction   The quality of "difference" in a visual field, observed uniqueness or novelty of any kind. Differences may be related to any form of change such as motion or metamorphosis.

CHAPTER EIGHT

Spatial relationships

Important: Establishing spatial relationships is one of the *dominant* and *autonomic* perceptual characteristics. We cannot look at any visual field, natural or pictorial, without evaluating it in terms of spatial relationships.

There seems to be a widely held belief that the idea of depth is applicable only to realistic or representational works of art. There is also a corresponding belief that nonobjective works remain flat on a flat surface. Both are myths. As we have learned in Chap-

ter 2, pictures have a *dual reality;* they are always perceived as being flat and dimensional at the same time. Various cues to spatial depth that our brain automatically recognizes in actual scenes also apply to

8.1   Jan Vredeman de Vries. From *Perspective,* first published The Hague and Leiden, The Netherlands, 1604–1605. De Vries' knowledge of Renaissance perspective was based on Dürer. This plate depicts one-point perspective and includes a foreshortened human figure.

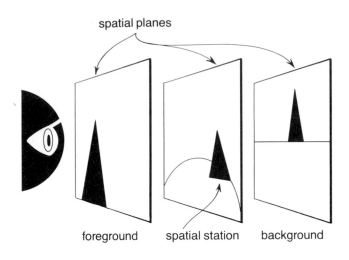

8.2 The concept of spatial planes and stations is not easy to picture graphically. Like windows we look through, think of planes as sheets of ultrathin glass that extend to infinity. A spatial station would be something fastened to one spot on one sheet.

spatial planes

foreground　　　spatial station　　　background

pictorial ones. Most of these are perceived by each eye acting alone. These *monocular* cues are especially appropriate to 2-D surfaces. True, many modern artists are little concerned with creating illusions of real space, particularly deep space. However, it is virtually impossible to produce a perceptually "flat" surface.

To persons influenced by Western cultural traditions, flatness is inherently decorative. It is one of the qualities that reinforces the 20th-century concept of a painting as an object rather than a window.

Depth cues: A means of encoding pictorial space

Each of the depth cues or signals may be thought of as a kind of cipher that the brain recognizes and decodes in order to determine spatial relationships in any kind of actual visual field. It then follows that if such codes exist naturally, artists may employ them, encoded, in works of art.

Spatial cues are imbedded within sensory data in two basic ways:

1. Through binocular vision. Our eyes receive two differing images that the brain merges into one. This process, called *stereopsis*, grows rapidly weaker as the distance increases. It is truly effective within about 12 to 15 feet and entirely ceases at about 1,200 feet, roughly three city blocks. Binocular vision originated as a survival characteristic neces-

sary to estimate precisely short-to-intermediary distances for activities close at hand.

2. Through many *monocular depth cues* that do not depend on having two eyes. Although these reinforce and confirm the sensory information developed through binocular vision, they also work by themselves. Monocular cues are our primary means of evaluating intermediary-to-far distances. As two-dimensional pictorial space exists in one spatial plane, monocular depth cues provide artists with major tools for triggering a viewer's spatial perceptions.

We will begin our study of depth cues by looking at a variety of monocular cues.

Defining spatial points, stations, and planes

Theoretically, a spatial plane is a flat visual field oriented (positioned) with absolute frontality to our line of sight, having no spatial dimension whatsoever. See Figure 8.2. Because each plane has no thickness, an infinite number of such planes exist, beginning at our nose and continuing into space to the end of the universe. Typically, we think of these planes in much simpler terms. A background plane exists at the furthest point we can see; a foreground plane is immediately in front of us, not necessarily as close as our nose; and we establish a middle ground somewhere in between. Sometimes, for purposes of discussion, intermediary planes are placed between these. We may

8.3 In this photograph taken in one of the tunnels inside the Glen Canyon Dam at Lake Powell, the converging lines of one-point perspective are clearly recorded.

have oblique and curved planes, which may intersect the vertical spatial planes at many points, and flat planes rising from the ground to the sky—in other words, a kind of three-dimensional grid or matrix.

Artists are limited in every direction by the edges (the physical dimensions) of the canvas, paper, or board on which they work. This limitation of the visual field is called the *picture plane*, but that term does not refer to spatial depth; it establishes boundaries. The boundaries of a picture plane do not limit the expanse of the pictorial field in any way. Our picture may take in a very broad field of view if a landscape (like a wide-angle camera lens) or a quite narrow angle of view if a still life (a "close-up"), or it may be transposed into a wholly arbitrary angle of view if a nonobjective work, a layout, or a work of decorative design.

A spatial station is the location of any defined shape or object on a spatial plane, and a spatial point is any single point within that figure-object.

The moment so little as a single dot (a spatial point) is placed on a piece of paper, a spatial station and a spatial plane are established. The dot is perceptually seen as a "figure" and appears to float slightly above the surface. Therefore, any mark on a surface immediately establishes a spatial reference.

The manner in which we draw or paint a figure or a ground establishes the relationship between them, and the degree of spatial dimension perceived. Take another look at Figure 2.6.

Linear perspectives: Two distinctly different types

We will not be much concerned with details here because this subject is more appropriate to drawing studies rather than design. Our primary interest is in how Renaissance perspective fits into the scheme of things. Essentially the same is true for parallel line perspectives, although these are probably not as familiar unless one has studied mechanical drawing or drafting.

Renaissance (vanishing-point) perspective

As we observe in photographs, lines like roads or railroad tracks grow closer together as they recede into the distance and appear to meet on the horizon.

Figure 8.3 shows how a photograph records one point perspective. Cameras give a one-eyed cyclopean view of any visual field that generally conforms to the principles of Renaissance perspective.

In *Renaissance perspective*, lines converge not only on the horizon but also up into space and down into the depths of the earth as figure-objects recede into the distance. Renaissance perspective is characterized by increasing textural density, decreasing figure sizes, and decreasing luminance contrast.

The general principles for Renaissance perspective were laid down at the beginning of the 15th century. It dominated European art until the 20th century. Its

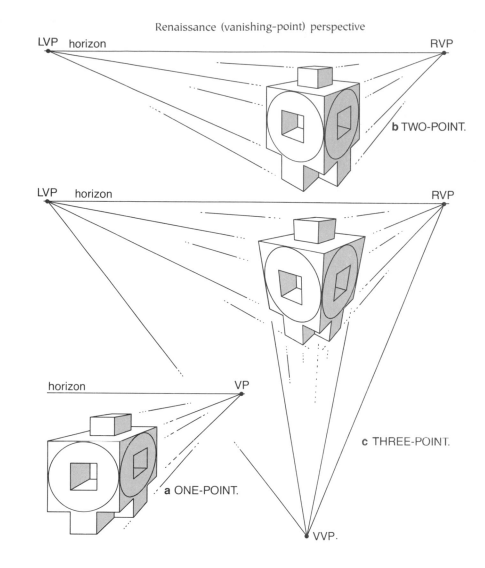

Renaissance (vanishing-point) perspective

LVP horizon   RVP

b TWO-POINT.

LVP horizon   RVP

c THREE-POINT.

horizon   VP

a ONE-POINT.

VVP.

8.4 **a** One-point perspective. Verticals are perpendicular, and horizontals parallel, to the horizon line.
b Two-point perspective. Verticals are perpendicular to the horizon line.
c Three-point perspective. No lines are perpendicular or parallel to the horizon line.

Note: For any object observed, its vanishing points are located on the horizon and form a 90° angle to the eye. Stretch out your arms, 90° apart, to find them.

Key to abbreviations:
  C = center
  H = horizon line
LVP = left vanishing point
RVP = right vanishing point
 VP = vanishing point
VVP = vertical vanishing point

principles were discovered through the use of devices such as grids ruled on glass "windows" and the camera obscura, a device (a predecessor of today's camera) that contained no film and was used simply for viewing or tracing. It is important to separate the European Renaissance perspective of converging lines from other cultures and peoples because none of them used this type of perspective as a means of indicating spatial relationships until modern times. Point of fact: It was not even an absolutely consistent feature of European art before or after the Renaissance.

There are three versions of Renaissance perspective, each referred to by the number of primary vanishing points used in their construction: one point, two point, and three point. Examples of each of these are shown in Figure 8.4 **a–c**. When any of these is constructed architecturally using drafting instruments and true measures (to scale), it is called "measured perspective."

Parallel line perspectives

Parallel line perspectives often appear ambiguous to us; they suggest dimension while, at the same time, they seem to flatten objects out. For persons brought up under the influence of Western culture and inundated with photographs, parallel line perspectives appear inherently decorative. For this reason, they are of special interest to designers.

There are three versions of perspective using parallel lines.

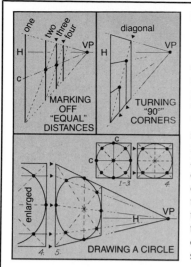

Some tips for working in perspective: *MARKING OFF "EQUAL" DISTANCES.* For telephone poles, rows of the same size boxes, and so on. Establish first line by measure or by observation, or draw what "feels" or appears correct. Run guide lines from tip, bottom, and center (c) to VP. Establish second line in the same way as the first but within guide lines just drawn. Position of next line is found by running a diagonal from the bottom of the first through the center of the second to intersect the upper guideline. Drop a vertical from this point to establish line three. Line four is found the same way. *TURNING 90° CORNERS.* Draw a diagonal. Wherever the first lines intersect, create a "perpendicular" following the rules for the type of perspective used. This is exactly the same thing done in Figure 4.14 a. *DRAWING A CIRCLE.* Step 1: draw a square. Step 2: using crossed diagonals to locate the center, inscribe a circle in the square. Step 3: draw a horizontal and a perpendicular through the center. Note that together with the diagonals, these lines intersect the circle at eight points. Step 4: at the points where the circle intersects the diagonals, draw a horizontal to bring the spacing out to the edge. In the example, the left side measures of step 4 are used to construct a square in perspective and divide it exactly as we did in steps 1, 2, 3, and 4. Mark the eight points where the circle should meet the inscribed guidelines. Using french curves or ellipse guides; connect these points with arcs. The original circle can be divided into more parts than shown in step 1. The more points, the more accurate the circle in perspective will be.

Linear perspectives using parallel lines

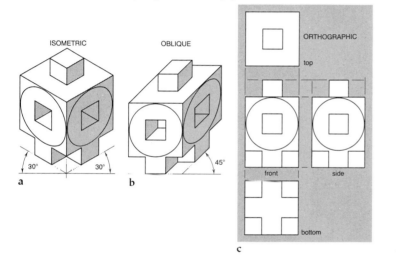

8.5 **a** Isometric: All construction lines either depart at an angle of 30° from the base line of the picture plane or are perpendicular to the base line.
b Oblique: One set of construction lines departs at an angle (usually 45°) from the base line. Other lines are perpendicular or parallel to the base line.
c Orthographic: All construction lines are parallel to the picture plane, vertical and horizontal. No lines are angled unless the object itself possesses an angular shape.

Note: So that we may observe the differences between them, all measures for these drawings are to the same scale.

Isometric perspective

The term *isometric,* meaning of equal measure, is often applied to all forms of parallel line perspective. These differ from Renaissance perspective in that lines do not converge and therefore do not meet at a point on the horizon line. Technically, *isometric perspective* is one form of many differing types used in drafting and technical illustration although, as we shall soon see, it is not limited to these applications. An Isometric drawing begins with a vertical axis from which all sides of a figure depart at an angle (normally 30°). Usually, the same scale of measurement is used for all three dimensions of an object.

No side of an object in isometric perspective is parallel to the picture plane. Three faces of an object can be displayed at the same time (Fig. 8.5 **a**). Isometric perspective may be used in fine art, illustration, or design whether abstract of representional. It is especially valuable for suggesting architectural, or *architectonic* (architecturelike) forms (Fig. 8.6).

Oblique perspective

Oblique perspectives are similar to isometric ones, but they differ because *one side of the object is always parallel to the picture plane.* An angle of any degree may be used, although 45° is the most common. An example of an oblique drawing may be seen in Figure 8.5 **b.** Full scale is always used for the front face although the scale of the angled line sometimes varies. Oblique perspective is the type of perspective most commonly associated with Oriental art.

GRAPHIS 245

8.6 Takenobu Igarashi, Cover for *Graphis* 245, 1986. Courtesy Igarashi Studio, Tokyo. Design using isometric construction. Note *melding:* construction lines have been deliberately retained and even extended considerably into the ground/space as part of the design concept.

Orthographic perspective

Orthographic perspective (Fig. 8.5 **c**) is less acceptable pictorially to Western eyes than the previous two. Its form is commonly seen in electrical and electronic schematics and architectural plans. This is the so-called "plan view" typical of blueprints. In an orthographic drawing *all sides of a rectilinear object are parallel to the picture plane,* and all measures are usually actual ones or measured to a precise scale. The form is used by architects, engineers, and industrial designers as well as artists.

The relationship to constancy

Parallel line perspectives are consistent with perceptual constancies. For example, a table is the same dimension on one end as on another, yet in Renaissance perspective, one end of the table is shown smaller than the other. Early Chinese artists would likely have laughed at such a distortion of "reality." They used oblique perspective in which both ends of the table are measurably the same size. Because "reality" is in the mind of the beholder, other cultures found parallel line perspective more natural (perceptually constant) than Renaissance perspective. See Figures 8.7 and 8.8. Is oblique perspective, therefore, more true to life?

Orthographic perspectives also meet constancy expectations. Everything is shown in its actual or exactly proportional size relationships. Because of this, the road map (Fig. 8.9) is easily understood and read; so are architectural plans (Fig. 8.10) and blueprints of many types. When we apply these ideas to the human form itself, we find the result distinctly uncomfortable and disconcerting (Fig. 8.11).

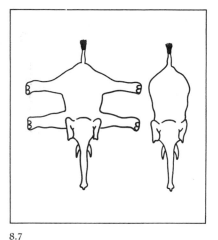

8.7

8.8

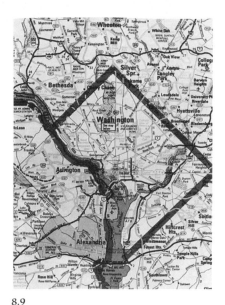

8.9

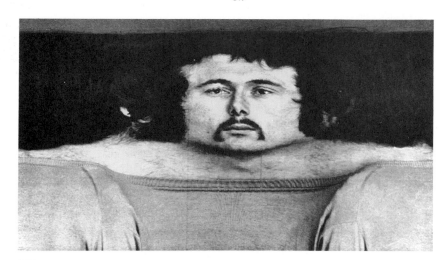

8.10

8.11

8.7 In psychological research studies, the split-elephant drawing (left) was generally preferred by African children and adults to the top-view perspective (right). This is a form of perceptual constancy. One person, however, did not like the split drawing because he thought the elephant was jumping around in a dangerous manner. Note that the preferred image (left) combines two orthographic views, top and sides. After all, the elephant on the right does not appear to have any legs at all.

8.8 Haida motif representing a bear. From Franz Boas, *Primitive Art* 1927. In this drawing, the artist has combined a left and a right side view with a front view. Outside of Western cultural traditions, no art from other cultures used Renaissance (vanishing point) perspective until comparatively modern times.

8.9 A common road map is one form of orthographic perspective although maps have their own special projections. Each type has certain advantages and disadvantages when dealing with the effects of the curvature of the earth.

8.10 Westminster Abbey, London, section and plan. Banister Fletcher. *A History of Architecture . . .* (New York: Scribner's, 1963), p. 424. Architectural plans and blueprints of all types commonly use orthographic projections because measurements may be taken directly from them.

8.11 This is a periphotograph, or "wraparound" picture. The subject sits on a turntable while a changing image is recorded on moving film. Both the speed of the turntable and the film movement are synchronized. The result is an orthographic view of human features, which is disturbing to most viewers.

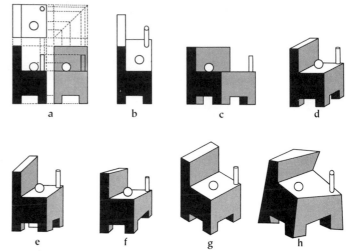

8.12 These illustrations show various ways in which perspective is utilized by contemporary artists, by artists of the past, and by artists from different cultures. The figure is a chair with a ball and a cylinder on the seat.

a Strict plan—side, top and front elevation—gives us accurate information about dimensions, but only the side elevation shows very much about the appearance of the objects.

b A side and top elevation fitted together has about the same degree of accuracy as before though the visual appearance of the structure is shown more effectively.

c Another combination of orthographic views: side and front. It looks more like the chair, though to be strictly accurate, the ball and cylinder should appear twice.

d In this oblique perspective, the side view is the same. Lines that construct the front panel are parallel. This, in a sense, gives a truer representation of the shape than Renaissance perspective.

e Side and front planes are combined in a way that contradicts normal perspective by employing diverging lines. This improbable convention is often used in pre-Renaissance, modern, and non-European art.

f An inversion of the preceding system. Though the lines appear to converge, they do not meet at a point on the horizon. Their placement is arbitrary.

g The same object as seen in isometric projection. This provides a high level of visual information with good spatial representation.

h The perspective is deliberately arbitrary and inconsistent though it is still seen as a chairlike object. Similar distortions are common in 20th-century art.

Figure 8.12 displays varieties of perspectives as used in art by other cultures and by modern artists who found these different forms fresh and exciting.

Though some of these perspectives are partly arbitrary, most are derived from various combinations of parallel line perspective views. Their applications to fine art are not often acknowledged. A Mogul painting employs oblique perspective to suggest placement in three-dimensional space (Fig. 8.13). Not much interested in depicting spatial dimension, Pablo Picasso combines several orthographic views to create an unforgettable image of a multifaceted personality (Fig. 8.14).

Aerial perspective cues

Aerial perspective is based on our understanding of the effects of atmosphere on vision and color. This understanding results from our experiences with natural physical conditions as well as some genetic predispositions. Our sense of spatial dimension is highly influenced by perceptual constancies (a psychological response) and by the biological peculiarities of our visual apparatus. There are three fundamental cues.

Distinctness: Edge definition

Unlike a photograph, it is impossible for us to see a sharp overall visual field. It is easy to test this out for ourselves. Close one eye; then focus the other on the tip of a finger held out at arm's length. Notice that the tip of the finger is sharpest in focus, with objects in the background exhibiting greater or lesser sharpness—rather like the depth of field characteristics of

8.13 Anonymous. *Rukmini and Her Maids Watched By Krishna and Balaran,* illustration to the *Bahagavata Purana, Kishangarh.* ca. 1760. Victoria and Albert Museum, London.

8.14 Pablo Picasso. *Girl Before a Mirror.* 1932. Oil on canvas, 64″ × 51¼″ (162.5 × 130.2 cm). Collection, The Museum of Modern Art, New York. Gift of Mrs. Simon Guggenheim. Analyze how Picasso has used orthographic perspective to create a unique image. What is different (or uncommon) will always appear unique and stand out although uniqueness may not always be received in a positive manner.

photographs. Now open the other eye. Observe that absolutely nothing is sharp but the fingertip.

Edge sharpness of distant scenes is degraded by intervening layers of atmosphere containing such things as dust, smoke, water droplets, rain, sleet, and snow. These features make *distinctness* a primary cue our brain uses to separate things that are close from things that are distant. What has sharp and distinct (hard) edges advances (*pulls*); what has soft, or fuzzy, edges recedes (*pushes*).

Atmospheric blueness

Purple-blue is the perceived color of the atmosphere; the hue veils or covers over everything in the landscape. Warm colors appear to advance because they are strongly affected by the cooling effect of

purple-blue. In theory, it is like adding a tiny bit of blue to every color starting with that of an intermediary foreground plane. The amount of blue added is increased for each succeeding plane until in the background (distant hills) the blue virtually eliminates every other color. Cool colors—purples, greens, and blues—are closer to matching the hue of the distant landscape (the background). Because of this, our brain recognizes another depth cue: **In nature, pure (intense) warm colors must be relatively close to us (advance).** That ordinarily causes cool colors to recede. See Color Plate 2 (p. 257).

If we examine this phenomenon carefully, we will see that we are responding to the purer warm hues. Another principle easily follows: **Pure hues advance; impure hues recede.** Pure blues and greens (cool

8.15 a Pat O'Hara. *Western Hemlocks Surrounded by Fog,* detail. In this photograph, the effects of atmosphere on the luminance contrast range of trees can easily be observed. Textures of close trees exhibit a wide range from light to dark and strong contrast with their ground. Distant trees have little or no surface detail. Their contrast with the ground also diminishes as the distance increases.
b The aerial perspective principle of luminance contrast as seen in photograph **a** is demonstrated in this diagram. A wide luminance range advances (right) while a narrow range recedes (left). Contrast with the ground must always be considered.

a

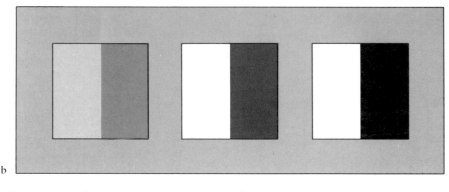

b

hues) will advance over dull or grayed oranges and reds (warm hues).

Luminance contrast

Remember that our brain accentuates the contrast between areas of differing luminances (irradiation). The strongest possible contrast is a sharp edge with black on one side and white on the other. This is perceived to advance (*pull*) while areas with less contrast, a gray next to white, are seen to recede (*push*) when present in the same visual field. The interposition of any atmospheric particles—such as haze, dust, or water vapor—will convert white versus black contrast into a light gray versus dark gray contrast. As a result, the *contrast range* between the lightest and the darkest parts of any figure is greatly altered.

A wide range between light and dark luminances (strong contrast) is seen to advance (*pull*). Conversely, a narrow range of luminances (weak contrast) recedes (Fig. 8.15). Both of these cues hold true (1) within the makeup of any figure (contrast of texture), as well as (2) in the relationships between figure and ground.

Perceptual constancies: Cues to spatial relationships

We have already learned that perceptual constancy is the ability of the brain to maintain, more or less, unchanging ideas about the physical nature of figure-objects regardless of continual variations in their retinal images.

In the establishment of a figure's spatial position, many cues may be recognized, but no single one is in control except at very close distances when binocular vision dominates. Of all such cues, recent studies suggest that perceptual constancies play a far greater role than once thought.

Relative size

Many depth cues are related to constancies. One is *relative size*. We understand familiar figure-objects exist naturally within certain size perimeters. A human being, for instance, averages around 5 feet 10 inches

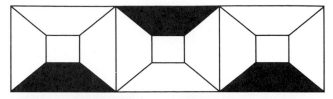

8.16 The perceptual constancy that tells us light is always overhead clearly adds a dimensional quality to this simple diagram consisting of three configurations identical except for the placement of one black panel.

8.17 Perceptual constancy tells us that people's faces always come out toward us—they are convex not concave. This constancy is so strong that our brain spatially inverts the concave face seen in this photograph to convex. Our brain will do this even when viewing such a thing three dimensionally with both eyes! In other words, the brain will totally ignore binocular stereopsis to fabricate its own space if it senses that incoming visual data are inconsistent with a preconceived view of reality.

in height. In spite of a relatively small retinal image of a person in the distance, we do not perceive a human being seen at a distance to differ from normal. Indeed, if the person approached, we would be surprised to find the height unusual. Ordinarily, we determine the size of objects in that person's environment by the same 5- to 6-foot scale. If a person is standing by a tree that is three times his or her height, we assume the tree is around 15 to 18 feet tall. Using this kind of a scale or spatial cue, we are able to estimate the size of objects in the distance with a high degree of accuracy. It happens so automatically that we are not ordinarily aware of it.

Of course, there are many objects for which we have no size constancy. We are usually surprised when any object is discovered that varies significantly from our expectations. This is one reason why unusually large animals or persons attract our attention; they are both fascinating and awesome. So are unusually small things. Such figures possess a heavy visual weight. Perhaps we should also be aware of the fact that children often find normal size adults awesome.

Overhead light

Constancy tells us that light sources are overhead. Remember the moon craters in Figure 3.2? Though this is primarily attributable to our understanding of sunlight, most artificial light sources are also placed overhead. We prefer it that way. Note how spatial qualities result from placement of black shading in otherwise identical drawings (Fig. 8.16). This phenomenon is used to help establish the orientation of oblique spatial planes and the relationship of objects to these planes. We find light sources at eye level disturbing. Light from underneath an object may actually cause a spatial inversion. The aspect of the brain's mechanisms that we call perceptual constancy is so strong that a concave face is very difficult to see. The brain ignores binocular vision and all other spatial cues to normalize our perception (Fig. 8.17). This is why a person's face looks so eerie and frightening when we hold a flashlight underneath the chin. It's a ghastly sight to us—the face appears to be turned wrong-side out.

Spatial relationships   117

8.18 Victor Vasarely. *Manipur.* 1952–1960. Oil on canvas, 5'3¾" × 4'11¾" (1.62 × 1.52 m). Vasarely Center, New York. Vasarely has suggested believable spatial dimension simply by employing the spatial cue of curving and bending lines.

Brightness constancy

Brightness constancy tells us that all prime light sources are small, and intensities (amounts of light) vary with the distance from us. This perceptual concept can be encoded on a two-dimensional surface if the artist is very careful how the luminances are managed. Only luminance and purity are of significance; choice of hue is virtually unimportant in establishing distal relationships of light sources. The purity principle (atmospheric blueness) of aerial perspective, however, always applies. Methods and formulas for creating convincing effects of prime light sources contained *within* the work of art are described in Chapter 17.

Curving and bending

We are aware of the absolute frontality of objects viewed head on—their flat contour. We are inherently aware that, when lines curve or bend away from this frontality, we are observing a spatial phenomenon. Any such movement is interpreted by the brain as an indication of depth. In the painting by Victor Vasarely (Fig. 8.18), an awareness of spatial dimension— convexity and concavity—is created just by curving or bending lines. It is a form of *contour map*. Figure 8.19 is a geographical contour map of a Norwegian valley scanned, processed, and plotted by the SysScan system. Figure 8.20 is a student project, and Figure 8.21, shows the concept of a contour map applied to

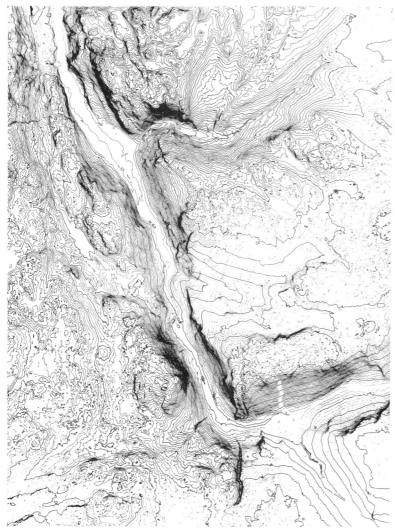

8.19 Contours of a Norwegian valley scanned, processed, and plotted by SysScan, an earth satellite system. Reproduced by permission of *Computer Graphics World*. In this contour map, a computer defines boundaries between differing ground levels (elevations) according to specifications designated in its program.

8.20 A student project. Simply by curving and bending the black and white bars in this contour map, a student has given a strong dimensional quality to the image of a child. (Courtesy of Dee Mustafa.)

8.21 Klara Tamas-Blaier. Poster for *The Fruits of the Forest*. The same idea as seen in the previous student project was used a basis for this film poster.

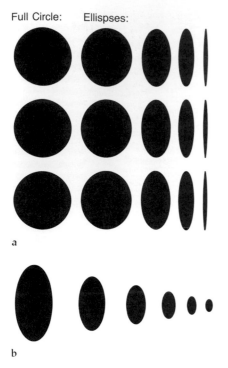

Full Circle: Ellispses:

a

b

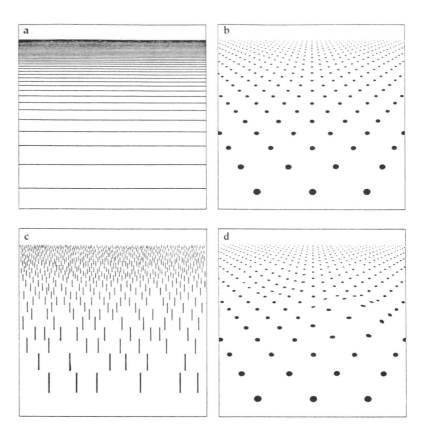

8.22 Scientists are not certain why we see ellipses as circles in perspective. Perhaps it is because there are few natural ellipses in our environment. In **a**, the ellipses seem to curve around an object because the height does not vary, but their degree (the angle of view) differs in natural order—a situation similar to a design on a soft-drink can. In **b**, the ellipses appear to be lying on a flat surface extending into the distance because, although they vary in size, the degree remains the same and the top and bottom edges form converging lines.

8.23 Like the examples shown, the textured surfaces of the visual world convey information concerning the orientation of surfaces because they structure the light that falls on the retina of the eyes. These *density gradients* (or texture gradients) convey an impression of depth. Depending on the size, shape, and spacing of elements of the texture, the gradient may create the impression of a smooth flat surface **a**, **b**; a rough, flat surface **c**; or a surface broken by a bulge and a depression **d**.

poster design by the Rumanian artist Klara Tamas-Blaier. Spatial volumes can be visually described through changes in line direction alone.

Ellipses: Cues to circles in space

Our brain insists on perceiving a series of ellipses as shown in Figure 8.22 **a** as circles on a curved surface, such as a design on a can of pop, for instance. When these ellipses grow smaller in one direction, we see them as lying on a flat plane that extends into the distance (Fig. 8.22 **b**).

These perceptions are the consequences of shape and size constancy. A probable explanation is that there are few natural ellipses in our real world. Seen from above, a pond may be roughly circular or com-

posed of overlapping circular forms. We "know" this and perceive the elliptical shape of a pond seen from ground level to be an indication of an approximately circular configuration. Another example would be wheels observed in perspective. We never have any doubt that they are all perfectly round because, otherwise, they would not be functional.

The same general phenomena exist for rectilinear forms, especially trapezoidal shapes. We expect that such shapes will prove to be perfect squares or rectangles when viewed from above in absolute frontality, that is, if we viewed them orthographically.

Any perceived combinations of such curvilinear or rectilinear shapes are more likely than not to be viewed in the same manner.

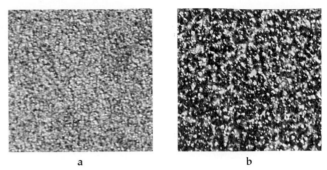

a   b

left: **8.24** Density gradients occur everywhere around us. They are strong cues to space and distance. In this photograph note how the texture of windblown sand helps to define space. **In the natural world everything is gradated.**

above: **8.25** Spatial dimension in these photographs is *inferred* by the brain as both were taken at exactly the same distance from the camera. Photo **a** is fine sandpaper and **b** is coarse sandpaper.

The density (or texture) gradient cue

The characteristic of the *density gradient cue* is the increasing or decreasing density of surface patterns—textures. Take a look at Figure 8.23 **a–d**. Up close, large elements are widely spaced (*pull*); in the far distance very small elements are packed together—smooth or virtually smooth in appearance (*push*). Consider the appearance of a stone driveway or a brick walk. Observe the texture gradient created by ripples of windblown sand in Figure 8.24; does Figure 8.25 **a** show this same sand at a distance, and Figure 8.25 **b** show the sand close up?

Pattern density is a significant element in Renaissance linear perspective because that system produces pattern density gradations. Forms of linear perspective employing parallel lines *do not* produce increasing textural densities and, therefore, tend to "flatten" space (*push*). To Western eyes, this fact makes them inherently more decorative (less naturalistic).

The greater the textural diversity of elements within an environment, the more difficult it becomes to separate figure from ground. Under this condition, a person must use a greater number of spatial cues, occupying the brain more fully by greatly increasing sensory data processing. This tends to make us uncomfortable, even fearful, because we must focus attention on one area at a time, leaving other areas unattended. We are at risk.

When there is great textural density *within observed figures,* we understand those figures to be close. Figures with little textural indication, that is, smooth figures, tend to recede.

When we use a shape with a coarse texture as a background, it is very important to recognize these facts and to use principles of aerial perspective to keep the background in its place; otherwise, it may advance and invert the entire composition.

Let us summarize the characteristics of the density (or texture) gradient cues:

1. In a visual field, coarse texture advances while fine texture (increased density or smoothness) recedes.

2. Within figure contours, strong textures advance (*pull*) while smooth or fine textures recede (*push*).

8.26 Vincent van Gogh. *The Night Cafe.* 1888. Oil on canvas, 28½ × 36¼" (72.4 × 92.1 cm). Yale University Art Gallery, New Haven, Connecticut. Bequest of Stephen Carlton Clark, B.A., 1903. Although differing sizes of objects and the converging lines of perspective add a sense of depth to this work, it is the systematic overlapping of visual elements that most conveys the sense of spatial separation.

8.27 In this detail of a wall fresco from an Egyptian tomb, the Vizier Ramose, at Thebes, overlapped persons indicate numbers in a row — not a spatial illusion. The same physical size as the front figures, those in the rear appear larger in size, a result of the Ponzo illusion (Fig. 3.8). They look like thin sheets of cardboard. Would they have appeared unusual to an ancient Egyptian?

The stronger the texture and the greater the luminance contrast, the greater the pull.

Overlap, or interposition

The brain assumes that whole, or perceptually complete, figures are in front of ("overlap") partial or fragmented figures that are grouped in a composition. In *The Night Café* (Fig. 8.26), notice how Vincent van Gogh has used *overlap* as a technique to indicate relative spatial stations.

Overlap is the means that Egyptian artists used to suggest spatial relationships (Fig. 8.27). Like other African and Pacific island peoples, they also used elements of orthographic projection.

Often estimates of size may be based on overlap. In Figure 8.28 **a**, the small square overlapping the larger one is not only perceived to be in front of, but smaller than, the square it overlaps. This idea, relative to shape constancy, should be easily understandable. However, observe the psychological effect of Figure 8.29 **b**. Because both house shapes appear to be drawn to the same scale, the foreground house is assumed to be a playhouse or a model — the "real" house sits behind because it is perceptually larger.

The angle of regard cue

The *angle of regard* cue is a response to our understanding of the relationship of all figures to a line that runs from beneath our feet to the horizon. The bases of all figures rise toward the horizon in any natural visual field in direct proportion to their distance from us. (The brain assumes one is level with, or above, the figure being viewed.) Note Figure 8.29 **a–c**, where our perception of the size of figures differs by virtue of the position of their bases related to one another and the horizon line. Figures set low in the visual field are presumed (perceptually) to be close (*pull*); those high in the visual plane, further away (*push*). A figure high in the visual field but not attached to the ground is presumed to be suspended in some precarious fashion or in a state of motion.

Although more characteristic of the Middle Ages, the 15th century artist Giovanni di Paolo used both overlap and the angle of regard to indicate spatial positions (Fig. 8.30). Neither technique distorted the scale between foreground and background figures whose importance (worth) is thereby rendered equal. Note the similarities (connections) between Paolo's work and a traditional Chinese landscape (Fig. 8.31).

8.28 The small square in **a** appears to be in front of a larger square behind it. The size differential does not challenge our expectations as we have none related to square shapes. When we observe the same situation using house symbols in **b**, a very different perceptual effect occurs. Our brain is confused by what appears to be a tiny house for little people. Can this be explained in terms of constancy?

a   b   c

8.29 All the figures in these three illustrations are identical in size and shape. They differ only in their position relative to the picture frame. In each case, judgment of the size of the objects is based on the perceived human scale. We are hardly ever aware of how significant placement in pictorial space is to a viewer's understanding of size and distance.

8.30 Giovanni di Paolo. Detail: *Paradise*, predella panel. Possibly from the Guelfi altarpiece. Tempera and gold on canvas, transferred from wood panel; 18½ × 16″ (47 ×

40.6 cm), overall. The Metropolitan Museum of Art, New York. Rogers Fund, 1906. In this painting, space is suggested primarily by the differing positions of the ground lines on which each figure stands. The figures themselves are all the same height. This type of spatial cue is called the *angle of regard*—a type of isometric perspective.

8.31 Anonymous. China, late Ch'ing Dynasty. A traditional landscape. Can comparisons be made between this painting and the Paolo work? What sort of perspective is dominant?

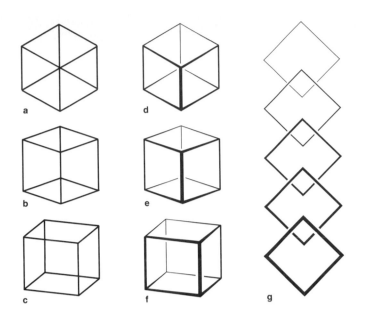

left: **8.32** Ken Raney. *Self Portrait.* Technical pen on illustration board; 9 × 3″ (22.86 × 7.62 cm). Courtesy the artist. In this drawing, volumes are represented by light and shadow (*chiaroscuro*) rather than with contour lines. Notice that some missing parts of the figure are "filled in" by the brain, like those seen in Figure 3.17.

Chiaroscuro as a cue to spatial volume

Rays of light flowing over a three-dimensional shape define volumes through luminance gradations. Shading two-dimensional shapes in accordance with this gradation is called *chiaroscuro*.

All lighting produces luminance gradations on surfaces. Any artist working realistically must take this fact into account. Painting a flat layer of paint on a 2-D surface is inherently decorative. A gradated line or surface advances. An evenly weighted line or a smooth (undifferentiated or unmodulated) surface recedes. Ken Raney's *Self Portrait* uses only the interplay of light and shadow to describe his shape (Fig. 8.32). There is no contour line except that produced by a shadowed edge as observed against the ground. Note that light edges of the figure are inferred (perceptually closed).

A gradated line, one that varies in width or lightness/darkness, is called a "weighted" line. Like the density gradient, a weighted line alone can describe objects in space. Each spatial plane displays different line thicknesses with thickest lines at the front and thinnest at the rear. Observe that the ambiguous qualities of the wire frame cube (Fig. 8.33 **a, b,** and **c**)

disappear when the same figures are rendered with weighted lines (Fig. 8.33 **d, e,** and **f**). Fig. 8.34 is an "isometric landscape," a project for students that experiments with weighted lines as the sole means of creating spatial relationships.

Cues to the orientation of ground planes

Cast shadows define a figure's position in space and also the ground's relationship to that figure. Carefully observe all the effects in Figure 8.35. Note that in every example the shadows tell us from which direction the light is coming.

When we work with cast shadows, it is important to understand that perceptual constancy requires that the contour of a figure (its edge) must be more sharply defined than the edge of the shadow it casts. To put it another way, the shadow must have a softer edge. Cast shadows with hard edges are decorative; they *pull* space, causing figure and ground to occupy the same plane. That is a decided advantage for an abstract or stylized work, but a sharp edged shadow in a realistic painting may totally destroy any illusion of spatial dimension.

As most 2-D surfaces have no binocular depth,

a, b, c A series of
outline drawings of a transparent
cube, shown from differing
angles. Like other equivocal figures we have studied, they can be
perceived as flat or dimensional
shapes.

d, e, f A *weighted line* helps
remove ambiguity from the same
line drawings. Note the tiny white
breaks in **f**, where foreground
lines pass over the background
lines, an artist's trick to reinforce
the illusion of space.

g Simple spatial sequence of
weighted lines for comparison.

8.34 A project for students. This is an "isometric landscape." The spatial effects seen
in this work are developed primarily with the weighted line.

sometimes an artist can play around with the position
of cast shadows without seriously disturbing spatial
effects. Often angles of shadows may be arbitrarily
altered to improve composition, particularly when
shadows are cast by a cutoff or by partially hidden
objects. Cast shadows not only indicate spatial positions of figures but can also be used to contribute to
the overall unity and quality of design.

Physiological depth cues

Stereoscopic or binocular depth cues are based
on the differences, *the image disparity,* between the
visual data received by the left and right eyes independently. The brain is able to use the sensory data to
define points anywhere on a figure-object or ground
as precise locations in space.

Binocular vision is most effective at distances
closer than 12 feet and relatively weak at 100 feet. Its
effectiveness declines rapidly thereafter. There is no
difference between retinal images received by the left
and the right eyes at distances greater than 1,200 feet;
that's about the length of four football fields placed
end to end.

However, our visual mechanisms for determining

How cast shadows define space

8.35 **a** A spherical object rests on a flat plane.
b A spherical object floats in front of a vertical plane.
c A spherical object floats above a flat plane.
d A spherical object suspended in open space.
e A flat plane described by the position of shadows cast by
objects sitting on it. Note that the object nearest the horizon
looks larger than the one at the bottom of the diagram even
though their size is identical. What perceptual cues are at
work here?

Spatial relationships 125

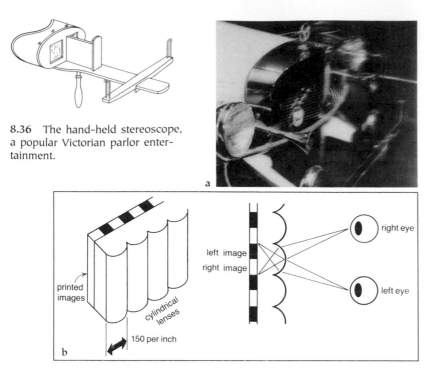

8.36 The hand-held stereoscope, a popular Victorian parlor entertainment.

8.37 a A photograph taken with a Nimslo 3-D camera. This ordinary black and white reproduction cannot duplicate the stereoptic effect, which is created by viewing the original color picture through a lenticular screen composed of hundreds of almost microscopic cylindrical lenses. This consumer product is similar to the commercial Xograph.
b The diagrams show how lenticular devices such as the Nimslo 3-D camera and the Xograph work. The sharp curvature of each lens permits each eye to see only half of the material printed under the lens. Alternating vertical stripes of the right eye and left eye images are printed so that one pair is exactly aligned under each lens. The lenticular screen is usually molded from clear plastic.

a figure-object's position in space are much more complex than that. If we were to capture and kill an animal for food, defend ourselves from attack, or invent and use precision tools, we had to be able to judge close spatial positions with extreme speed and precision. Natural selection ultimately equipped each of us with four basic mechanisms for this purpose.

Binocular cues

We mentioned image disparity earlier. That is one binocular cue. Studies tend to confirm that a genetic component is significant in the recognition of spatial volumes and distances although learning greatly develops and improves our skills.

In addition to the difference between images, the brain recognizes the degree of image sharpness (distinctness) as a second indicator. When the eyes are focused on the far distance, images in that range seem fairly sharp across entire visual planes. When we focus on an object close at hand, everything but that object (or a part of that object) is fuzzy.

Ocular motor cues

Ocular motor cues are ones that our brain derives or calculates from the motion of the muscles that control our eye movements. The third and fourth mechanisms are two types of such cues.

Convergence

Convergence is a kind of range-finder effect. The brain senses how much inward turning of each eye is required to bring the separate images together at the same point (the figure-object), and it draws a conclusion about the distance of that point from where we stand according to the degree or angle of inward movement required. This system is very efficient up to about 25 feet and functions rather like triangulation in navigation.

Accommodation

The lens in our eye is flexible. Objects are brought into focus by deforming the shape of the lens, a function of certain muscles. Whenever we move our gaze to a new figure-object, the brain senses the amount of muscle effort required to draw the lens into shape and focus the image clearly. This action is called *accommodation*. It is quite unlike the camera lens, which is focused by moving elements forward and backward, increasing or decreasing the distance from the lens to the film plane. In the eye, the distance between the lens and the retina remains essentially the same.

"Real" binocular 3-D from just two dimensions

We seem to have always been fascinated by the possibility of representing true spatial three-dimen-

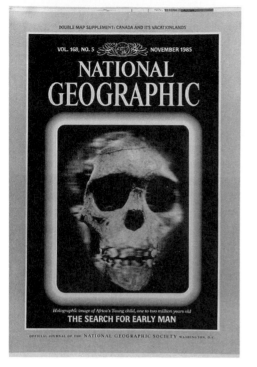

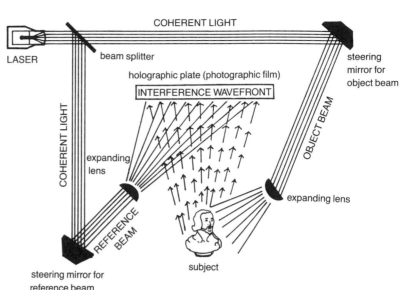

sionality, *stereopsis,* in a two-dimensional picture. That fascination, in all probability, led the archaic Greek artists toward more and more realistic representation both in surface decoration and sculpture. It was the motivation for the development of Renaissance perspective. In the Victorian era, the favorite parlor toy was the stereoscope (Fig. 8.36), which created three dimensions from two by offering a different photograph for each eye, each one separated by the interocular distance, about 2-5/8", from one another. A modern version of this device is the Viewmaster. There were other devices that used mirrors. Cardboard glasses with red and green lenses of the late 1930s, as well as glasses with polarizing filters as lenses (early 1950s), have been used for both still and motion picture presentations.[12]

All the techniques described here make use of physiological cues because they involve both eyes, a different image being presented to each eye. Of course, monocular cues may also be involved.

Lenticular devices represent another form of 3-D reconstruction. Figure 8.37 **a** is a photograph taken with a Nimslo 3-D camera, which uses four lenses to take four pictures on regular 35mm print film. A computerized printer combines the four into one picture of alternating stripes of left-eye and right-eye images. When laminated to a sheet of tiny plastic cylindrical lenses in precise alignment (Fig. 8.37 **b**), a

above left: **8.38** In November 1985, the *National Geographic* used a white light transmission hologram for the cover illustration, the second time in less than two years. This black and white reproduction cannot convey the spatial qualities or the prismatic color effects, but most libraries will have a copy that can be examined in its original form.

above: **8.39** A typical arrangement of laser equipment required to make a hologram: In a dark room, a laser beam is split into two parts. By using mirrors, one beam is reflected directly onto photographic film. The other beam is focused on the object in such a way that the beam is reflected from the object onto the photographic film. The two beams of light form an interference wavefront at the film's surface, rather like the overlapping of two periodic patterns. When the film is processed and viewed in the same laser light, the object is visually reconstructed. White light transmission holograms, such as the *National Geographic* cover, are made by reholographing the master hologram masked to a narrow slit. The resulting plate can be viewed with ordinary light (though it lacks the breathtaking realism of a master hologram).

8.40 Free-Vision Instructions. It is easy for most persons to develop the ability to concentrate on a point in space without a physical aid. Practice by sitting comfortably at normal reading distance in front of two identical coins about three to four inches apart. Use the photos reproduced here as a substitute. Place the point of a pencil in the center between the two coins as a focal point. Keep the eyes focused on the pencil point and slowly raise it toward the nose. At one place become aware of three coins behind the pencil point—one left, one in the center, and one to the right. Allow the eyes to concentrate on the *center image* until it becomes sharp and clear. Hold the concentrated gaze, allowing the pencil point to drop out of sight. It takes a little practice. Once the technique is mastered, a center image composed of a combination of the two coins can be made to pop into view instantly (without using a pencil) and can be held as long as desired.

8.41   After learning to concentrate on a point in space (Fig. 8.40), try the technique with these computer drawings. A fully three-dimensional image with height, width, and depth will pop into view!

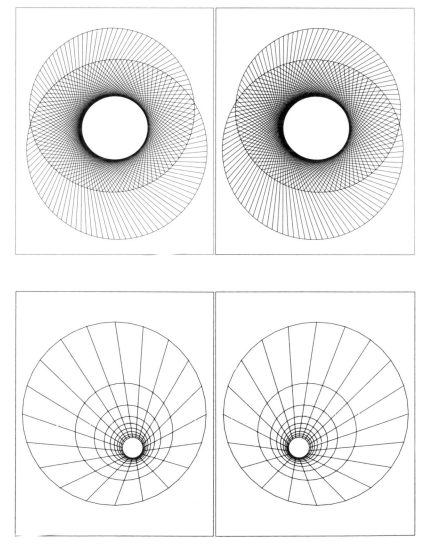

8.42 Jack Fredrick Myers. *Does the Cool Come Forward?*, Experiments in Free-Vision No. 4. 1982. Acrylic on canvas, two canvas panels, 48″ × 78″ (122 × 198 cm). This is a FREE-VISION STEREOGRAM ©. The black dots above the picture are there to help with concentration. Follow the same procedure as for Figures 8.41 and 8.42. Be sure to hold the page level.

three-dimensional image is seen. A commercial product based on similar technology is the *Xograph* (pronounced zo' graph). The same idea has been applied to greeting cards, religious photographs, and some types of winking or moving images on sports cards, badges, and toys.

Perhaps the most currently exciting technological development is the *hologram*. Although holograms have practical industrial uses (the scanning price checker at the supermarket is one), their pictorial potential has never been fulfilled. Though they offer certain advantages, their limitations usually far outweigh such considerations. They are restricted by size, extreme cost, and a lack of naturalism. The images tend to look like little carved miniatures unless the photographic plate is very large. Though often startling on printed surfaces like the cover of the *National Geographic* (Fig. 8.38), for now, hologram reproductions are essentially a curiosity rather than a serious communication medium. For scientists and artists, however, interest in holograms remains high. A diagram of the setup for making a hologram is shown in Figure 8.39.[13]

Another method for perceiving three dimensions from two is the FREE-VISION STEREOGRAM ©. This method does not require any equipment and is an easy one for graphic experimentation once the technique is learned. The directions for viewing and a few examples are shown in Figures 8.40 through 8.42.

Summary

When an artist works realistically or naturalistically, vanishing point (Renaissance) perspective, aerial perspective, and psychological depth cues must be used to achieve maximum spatial effects. Linear perspectives employing parallel lines, in this case, should be avoided because these appear inherently decorative to persons with a Western cultural background.

Yet all forms of perceptual depth cues are conceptually abstract and can be applied without prejudice to every form of two-dimensional composition and design and in whatever context the artist feels they are appropriate.

Pushing and pulling the two-dimensional surface helps create dominances through emphasis/de-emphasis. That is, an element perceived to advance in space has more visual weight; it is emphasized, and one perceived to recede is de-emphasized.

We should observe that our depth perception is an enormously complex mechanism involving both psychological and physiological systems, which work in concert. Our brain handles all of these, as effortlessly as we do breathing, at the subconscious (autonomic) level.

Binocular depth cues are always allied with monocular cues in this process, but binocular cues are limited to close and intermediate distances. Each type of cue reinforces the other.

Monocular depth cues are effective at any given distance from the viewer. Because they work with only one eye, they are especially appropriate to two-dimensional surfaces. Monocular depth cues are applicable to all forms of art: decorative, nonobjective, abstract, color field, and flat field design work as well as to realistic paintings or illustrations.

Both differing cues and types of space arouse a variety of emotional responses in viewers. These qualities are useful tools for the image manager who wishes to refine and direct communication.

Review of key terms

accommodation The ability of our eye's flexible lens to change shape in order to adjust focus between far and near figures. The muscle movements required are detected by the brain as an indicator of a spatial station.

aerial perspective Our understanding of the effects of the atmosphere on the distinctness, contrast, range, and the hue and purity of colors.

isometric perspective A form of parallel line perspective in which no construction lines are parallel to the picture plane. Three faces of an object are viewed simultaneously.

linear perspective A method of encoding a two-dimensional surface to create an illusion of three-dimensional figure-objects. The term is usually meant to describe Renaissance perspective (vanishing point perspective) wherein parallel straight lines appear to converge on the distant horizon. However, there are other types of linear perspectives, including isometric, oblique, and orthographic, in which parallel lines remain parallel. The latter forms have been commonly employed by cultures other than our own and are especially important in 20th-century art.

monocular depth cues A set of perceptual cues that our brain recognizes as indicative of spatial relationships in any visual field. These are especially important to two-dimensional design because they may be recognized by one eye acting alone and do not require binocular (two-eyed) vision. Most monocular depth cues are related to perceptual constancy.

oblique Inclined, slanting, or sloping. Also, a form of linear perspective drawn with parallel lines in which one face of an object is always parallel to the picture plane, characterized by horizontal and perpendicular lines and right angles. The other two faces are constructed from the first at any convenient angle.

orthographic Characterized by perpendicular lines and right angles. A form of linear perspective in which multiple views of a solid object are presented as if they were all in the same plane — the "plan" view used by engineers and architects.

pictorial space Illusionary three-dimensional space as observed from depth cues encoded on a two-dimensional surface.

Renaissance A period of revived intellectual and artistic enthusiasm from roughly the 14th century to the 16th century; pertaining to the styles, characteristics, and attitudes of that period.

Study list of spatial terms explained in the text:

1. Spatial plane, spatial station, spatial point

2. Linear perspectives:
   a. Renaissance: one-point, two-point, three-point
   b. Parallel line perspectives: isometric, oblique, orthographic

3. Aerial perspective: distinctness, atmospheric blueness, luminance contrast

4. Other monocular depth cues also related to constancy:
   angle of regard
   brightness constancy
   cast shadows
   chiaroscuro
   curving and bending
   density gradient cues (two aspects)
   ellipses
   overhead light
   overlap or interposition
   relative size

5. Physiological depth cues:
   a. Binocular cues: image disparity and distinctness
   b. Ocular motor cues: accommodation and convergence
   c. General terms: stereopsis, free-vision, hologram, Xograph

CHAPTER NINE

Change, sequences, and movement

Change may be best understood if we visualize a pictorial field filled with identical figures. If just one of them moves or changes color or displays a visible difference of any kind, it will stand out. Differences could be related to a figure's shape, size, color, texture, contrast, spatial position or interval, or state of mobility. Through any of these means, a figure may undergo a transformation, that is, change its appearance or location.

We are primarily aware of change. What is unique or novel in our natural environment attracts attention. The same is true for pictorial fields.

Morning, noon, evening, and night: The transformation from lightness to darkness every day is change. Growth of living things is change. Metamorphosis (sequential transformation in shape or form) is change. Motion is change.

Ultimately, *change* involves a transition from one state to another altered state, a movement from one place to another place, or a passage from one period of time to another in the continuum. Any single stage in the transformation represents one frozen instant in a rolling succession of events.

Motion

Motion is the visible displacement of an object in space.

When we can observe movement in process (as it happens), it is called *direct* or simultaneous movement.

9.1 Umberto Boccioni. *Elasticity*. 1912. Private collection. A futurist attempt to depict the dynamism of motion on a two-dimensional surface. Though the connections are obvious, futurists rejected cubism as static.

131

9.2 Umberto Boccioni. *Unique Forms of Continuity in Space.* 1913 (cast 1931). Bronze, 43⅞ × 34⅞ × 15¾" (111.4 × 88.6 × 40 cm). Collection, The Museum of Modern Art, New York. Acquired through the Lilly P. Bliss Bequest. Futurist Boccioni attempted to translate his ideas developed in painting into concrete form, a bronze sculpture. It is less successful, producing grotesque distortions.

When it is happening too slow or too fast to be observed directly, it is called *inferred* motion.

Never forget that lines of movement (paths the viewer's eye follows throughout a composition) are part of every work of art. Without movement, a work of art is static, usually less interesting and less effective. Relative eye movement in two-dimensional compositions is principally established by application of the dominance principle to the distribution of visual weight.

There are also lines of movement created by any fixed point on an object or on a body that moves across a surface or through space. Movements always leave linear trails.

Let us take a closer look at some of these states of motion.

Direct, or simultaneous, motion

Direct motion is what we observe when we watch a person walking or running. It is movement viewed in real time and space.

It is not only what we see, *but what we feel* when riding in an automobile or an airplane. Fluids in the inner ear send sensory data to the brain to provide information on our orientation in space relative to gravity. Such data provide information on the qualities

of acceleration or deacceleration, a combination of the effects of gravity and centrifugal and centripetal forces. Once we are launched into motion and continue at a relatively steady rate, all feelings of movement may cease. Physiological studies suggest that vision plays a large role in our sense of motion—so much so that physiological reactions, which recall real experiences, can be created with moving visual images alone. One key to such effects is to engage the peripheral vision of the viewer. In motion pictures, that may require a screen large enough to encompass a high percentage of the viewer's entire visual field.

Inferred motion

Some motion is observable only by its effects on things. Motion that is too fast or too slow to be directly observed may be implied through *displacement,* that is, a change in the position, in the size, or in some other characteristic of a figure-object. We may hear a bullet fired, for example, and see the evidence that the bullet has entered a wooden target: the hole and splintered surface. We have not seen the bullet. We observe that a germinating vegetable seed, just breaking the surface of the ground one day, has grown into a bushy plant with many leaves a month later. We have not seen the plant grow. Yet, in both

9.3 Giacomo Balla. *Dynamism of a Dog on a Leash.* 1912. Oil on canvas, 35-⅛″ × 43-¼″ (90.17 × 110.49 cm). Albright-Knox Gallery, Buffalo. Bequest of A. Conger Goodyear and gift of George F. Goodyear, 1964. Futurist Balla was greatly influenced by the work of photographer E.-J. Marey.

examples, we know movement has occurred because figure-objects were displaced in the visual field.

Observed effects of displacement are so common that we have created words to describe various types of slow change. *Evolution* describes imperceptibly slow change over many years or centuries. The term *metamorphosis* describes a slow change in physical shape or condition. Changes in the development of living things we call *growth*.

Perhaps the urge of artists to depict motion in art is as old as that of the cave dwellers who sometimes drew animals with multiple legs. Several medieval works could be interpreted as an interest in depicting motion by presenting multiple images or *sequences*, but it was not until comparatively recent times that the idea of motion in art captured the imagination of both artists and the general public.

Movement as an artistic concept

Until the development of *cubism* and *futurism*, painters had not deliberately used time as a conceptual tool. Cubists like Picasso and Braque often portrayed objects as if seen from more than a single point of view. This implied that the viewer had changed position—*moved*. Considering that movement can occur only through time, both a sense of motion and

time were suggested by the nature of the images. To convey motion and time on a two-dimensional surface required graphic approaches, which varied greatly from those of the past; some of many may be observed in Figures 9.1, 9.2, and 9.3. The methods that Boccioni and Balla used do not look very strange to us today, but they were revolutionary concepts in the early years of the 20th century.

In some ways similar to the cubism of Picasso and Braque, which they found static, futurists declared in their 1910 manifesto "[t]hat all subjects previously used must be swept aside in order to express our whirling life of steel, of pride, of fever and of speed."[14] They wished to capture the dynamism of the industrial age in paint.

Of Umberto Boccioni's *Elasticity,* Werner Haftmann writes, "Futurists distinguished between 'relative movement'—that is, the movement of an object from one point to another—and 'absolute movement' or the potential movements inherent in an inert object . . . "[15] A sculpture, *Unique Forms of Continuity in Space,* also by Boccioni is far less successful in translating such concepts into three-dimensional form.

Many of Giacomo Balla's works, like *Dynamics of a Dog on a Leash,* employ multiple images in a clearly direct fashion. Balla was influenced by the photo-

Change, sequences, and movement 133

graphs of Eadweard Muybridge and E.-J. Marey.

Motion pictures as we know them probably began with the work of Muybridge, who set out in 1872 to solve a 19th-century debate among artists and scientists over whether all of a horse's hooves were ever off the ground at the same time. (They were but drawn up underneath rather than outstretched as generally believed.) Eventually, his studies were extended to all sorts of animal and human locomotion, involving as many as 40 cameras simultaneously and tens of thousands of photographs. One sequence of plates is shown in Figure 9.4. For the first time, scientists and artists could see how living creatures actually moved.

E.-J. Marey, a person who followed in the footsteps of Muybridge, created multiple exposures on a single plate and drew simplified diagrams of the principal position points of a body in the execution of specific movements as seen in Figure 9.5.

Interested in the work of both Muybridge and Marey, the French artist Marcel Duchamp expressed the idea of movement in a diagrammatical way, reducing body forms to abstractions of energy. Perhaps one of the best-known works of modern art, *Nude Descending a Staircase No. 2* (Fig. 9.6), was one of the artworks that created a public scandal at an exhibition in the New York Armory in 1913.

Though both of these examples look suspiciously like modern stroboscopic photographs, the strobe light did not exist as a laboratory process until 1927. Figure 9.7 is a reproduction of one of the early multiple-image photographs taken by the inventor, Dr. Harold E. Edgerton.

9.4 Eadweard Muybridge. Plate 49 from *The Human Figure in Motion* (1878). Photograph. International Museum of Photography at George Eastman House.

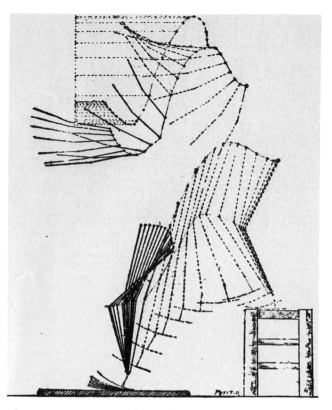

above: **9.5** E.-J. Marey, "Jump from a height with stiffened legs," from his book, *Movement.* 1895. A diagram of serial movement made from photographs. A similar idea is currently being used by contemporary researchers to create software capable of naturalistic computer animation.

above right: **9.6** Marcel Duchamp. *Nude Descending a Staircase No 2.* 1912. Oil on canvas, 58 × 35" (147 × 89 cm). Philadelphia Museum of Art (Louise and Walter Arensberg Collection). Like Balla, Duchamp was also influenced by Marey although Duchamp emphasized the abstract qualities of serial movement.

right: **9.7** Harold E. Edgerton. *Densmore Shute Bends the Shaft.* 1938. Photograph. One of the early multiple-exposure photographs taken with a strobe light by inventor Edgerton. Approximately 50 separate images were recorded on one negative. Exposures were $1/100,000$ second each, taken $1/100$ second apart.

Change, sequences, and movement   **135**

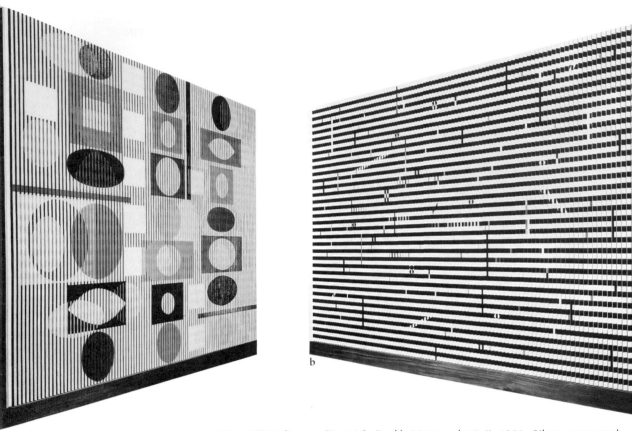

a

b

9.8   AGAM (Jaacov Gipstein). *Double Metamorphosis II.* 1964. Oil on corrugated aluminum, in 11 sections; 8'10" × 13'2¼" (2.69 × 4.93 m). Collection, The Museum of Modern Art, New York. Gift of Mr. and Mrs. George M. Jaffin. A multi-plane painting with different designs painted on differing faces of aluminum slats. In **a**, the view from the left side reveals one pattern of hard-edge forms. Another pattern is visible from the right side, **b**. From the front, aspects of both of these may be observed. As a person walks from one side to the other, the patterns shimmer and change. Sharp contours of figures are broken by the overall activity of the various surfaces.

Direct motion (change) on 2-D surfaces

Nothing attracts attention like movement. There are two principles to remember: (1) Any moving figure possesses more weight than a static figure; and (2) in a field of moving figures, the one moving the fastest will ordinarily have the greater visual weight.

There are a number of methods that produce the effect of motion in pictures. For two-dimensional art, direct motion does not always depend on having the work or any of its parts in action. Instead, motion may be achieved through viewer engagement like shifting gaze, shifting position, or using a viewing device. It may oblige the viewer to pass by or around the work,

or physically to alter the position or status of the work. Some basic techniques follow.

1. Dimensional grids. Works may be constructed using slats, grooves, or "V" configurations in which a different set of elements or pictures are applied to each side. As the viewer walks from one side of the work to the other, new elements are revealed with each step, creating a *metamorphosis* or sequential change in the work. One such work, *Double Meta-morphoses II,* by AGAM, is shown in Figure 9.8 **a–b**. For experimental purposes, Figure 9.9 **a–b** shows two relatively simple methods, using ordinary card-board, to create multiplane works similar in concept to those of AGAM.

9.9 DIAGRAMS FOR CONSTRUCTION OF MULTIPLANE PAINTINGS

a FOR TWO IMAGES

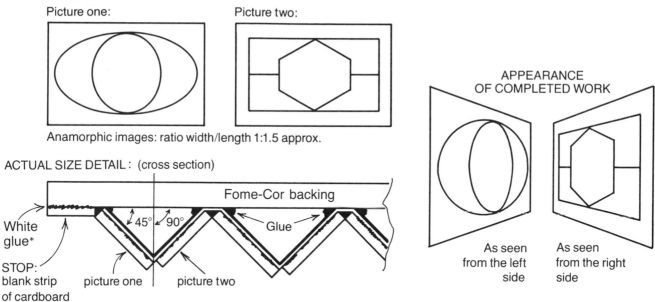

Picture one:

Picture two:

Anamorphic images: ratio width/length 1:1.5 approx.

ACTUAL SIZE DETAIL : (cross section)

Fome-Cor backing

White glue*

45°   90°

Glue

STOP:
blank strip
of cardboard

picture one   picture two

APPEARANCE
OF COMPLETED WORK

As seen
from the left
side

As seen
from the right
side

Instructions: For two-image works, make two paintings the same size on any lightweight cardboard such as railroad board (ordinary illustration board is too thick). When this is done, carefully cut each into vertical strips ¾" (1.9 cm) to 1" (2.54 cm) wide. Be as uniform and precise as possible. Glue* strips from one, then the other, alternately, on a sheet of one-ply cold-pressed bristol board (or heavy drawing paper), which will act as a carrier. Fold in accordion fashion and glue to a Fome-Cor ® backing as shown in the diagrams.

b FOR THREE IMAGES:

picture three:

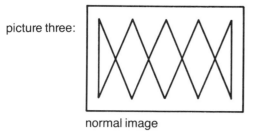

normal image

Instructions: For three-image works, complete images one and two in the same manner described in **a**. This time, however, glue* them back to back before cutting them in strips. Make sure to glue top to top. Complete the third painting and cut it into strips likewise. Assemble all the strips on a Fome-Cor ® backing as shown in the diagrams. It is a bit tricky; expect to take some time. It is easier if all the strips of painting three are glued in place first. Allow them to dry under a weight. Use a dummy strip of the sandwich of paintings 1 and 2 in order to get exact spacing. Later, glue* the 1 and 2 sandwich strips into place, one at a time.

ACTUAL SIZE DETAILS : (cross sections)

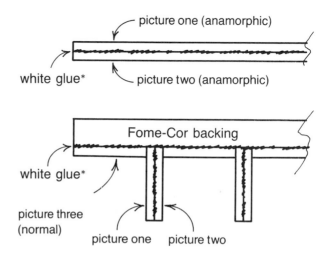

picture one (anamorphic)

white glue*

picture two (anamorphic)

Fome-Cor backing

white glue*

picture three
(normal)

picture one   picture two

*Do not use rubber cement; it is not strong enough.

Change, sequences, and movement   137

left: **9.10** *Motograph Moving Picture Book.* Originally published by Bliss, Sands and Company, London, 1898. Illusions of movement were produced by creating moirés (beats and nulls) when a linear periodic pattern printed on a transparent sheet was moved up and down over them.

A viewing screen for these examples can be made by purchasing any shading film with a 65 lines-per-inch linear screen (such as Letratone LT222) at an art supply store. Apply a piece about 4½" (11 cm) wide × 6" (15 cm) deep to a sheet of clear acetate, which is about 1" (2.54 cm) larger all around. Be sure the lines run horizontally, not up and down.

right: **9.11** *Motograph Moving Picture Book.* Steel engraving. When the linear screen pattern is placed over The Traction Engine, tilted slightly up to the right, and moved slowly up and down, smoke pours out of the smokestack funnel and the wheels revolve. The possibilities of using this idea to animate two-dimensional works of art should not be lost on contemporary artists.

2. Glass or plastic cylindrical lenses. If a different image appears under each half of a cylindrical lens, an effect similar to that described in the first example will be produced. Best results are obtained when the lenses are very small. One commercial system designed to produce 3-D effects (see Fig. 8.37) can be used to produce motion instead. The periodic pattern used to create motion in the *Motograph Moving Picture Book* (Figs. 9.10 and 9.11) is also a form of "lenticular screen." *Lenticular* means pertaining to lenses or functioning like a lens. Under this definition, dimensional slats or grooves as noted earlier in item 1 could also fit this broad category. Though glass or plastic lenses are difficult to use, other lenticular devices provide an easy means for experimentation.

9.12 Marcel Duchamp. *Rotoreliefs*. 1935. Color lithograph on six cardboard discs; app. 8″ (20.3 cm) diameter, each. Philadelphia Museum of Art. Louise and Walter Arensberg Collection. These cardboard discs were designed to be played in a phonograph turntable. Fish swam around, balls rolled, and balloons spun.

9.13 Thomas Wilfred. *Lumia Suite, Op. 158*, one stage. 1963–1964. Lumia composition (projected light on translucent screen). Three movements, lasting 12 minutes, repeated continuously with almost endless variations. Duration of entire composition not calculated. Screen, 6 × 8′ (1.83 × 2.44 m). Commission by the Museum of Modern Art through The Mrs. Simon Guggenheim Fund. Collection, The Museum of Modern Art, New York. Like a moving picture, fine art designs composed of moving lights are kinetic art works.

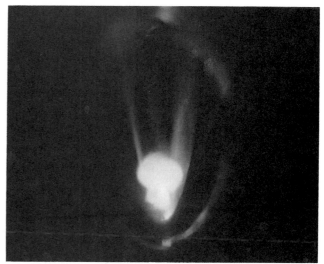

3. Pop-up sculpture. Pop-up works are usually constructed of single or multiple pieces of paper or cardboard which, unfolded, change from a flat form into a dimensional form. These exhibit both dimensional change and movement. They provide easy and inexpensive experimental potential. Examples can be found in most book stores.[16]

4. *Kinetic art.* Kinetic artworks actually move. There are two types: active and passive.

Active and passive kinetic art

Active forms of kinetic art involve the use of motors. Although more common in fine art sculpture, two-dimensional paintings and designs as well as advertising displays may have portions attached to electric rotary, pendulum-action, or vibration motors to create various movement effects. This technique is commonly used for trade-show exhibits and point-of-purchase (P.O.P.) displays.

In 1935, Marcel Duchamp created a number of phonograph discs that he called *Rotoreliefs* (Fig. 9.12). This idea is also an easy one to use for experimentation. Discs rendered with markers on thin cardboard can be hooked on a bent paper clip and spun by hand as well as "played" on a phonograph turntable.

Two-dimensional kinetic works would also include any artworks using light as a medium such as Wilfred's *Lumia Suite, Op. 158* (Fig. 9.13) and multimedia slide presentations, whether works of fine art, advertising, promotion, or entertainment.

Passive forms of kinetic art are those that depend on some outside energy source rather than motors to move them. In the past, works have been designed for

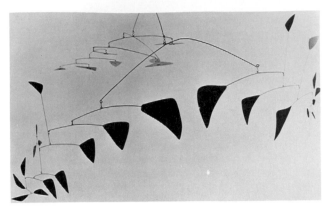

9.14 Alexander Calder. *Sumac.* 1961. Hanging mobile, sheet metal, and steel wire; 4'1¾" × 7'10" (1.26 × 2.39 m) Courtesy Perls Galleries, New York. This *mobile* is a passive kinetic energy device.

9.15 C. M. Russell. *Indian Hunting Buffalo (Wild Men's Meat).* 1894. Oil on canvas, 24⅛ × 36⅛" (61.3 × 31.75 cm). Sid Richardson Collection of Western Art, Ft. Worth, Texas. Here is a "pregnant moment" depicted in art—an inferred motion cue. Compare its effect with that of serial development (Fig. 9.4) and with stroboscopic repetition (Fig. 9.7).

wind, light, and touch. When we imitate a Duchamp Rotorelief disc and spin it by hand rather than on a turntable, it becomes a passive, not an active, work. A Calder *mobile* (Fig. 9.14) is a passive device depending on touch or the wind to launch into motion.

Innate and metaphorical cues to motion

In a static pictorial field, such as a painting or an illustration, motion must be inferred or implied. Because pictures are partly interpreted as if they were real scenes, in a pictorial field some types of inferred motion are likely to possess a relative visual weight that corresponds to a moving object.

There are *motion cues* that can be embedded in a work of art to convey a sense of action and direction. Like depth cues, some motion cues are *innate* (of genetic origin), buried deep in the most primitive part of our brain's subconscious processing of sensory data. Other cues have been learned; they are conventions or *metaphors* that we have come to accept as indicative of motion.

The blur

An example of an innate cue is the blur. Our perceptual processes, despite fuzzy retinal images, are designed to synthesize a sharp and complete visual field. Fast movements do not provide enough time for these brain mechanisms to clarify shapes and resolve detail. The brain is aware of the blur created by fast movements as well as blurs created by rounded three-dimensional forms. A blur is an early warning system of impending danger and carries a heavy visual weight. Although we may be totally unaware of such a response at a conscious level, it governs responses to an array of circumstances.

Frozen motion

Multiple images as revealed in paintings and stroboscopic photographs are now accepted conventions or metaphors for motion. These are culturally learned cues. Overlapping images, however, are just another manifestation of the blur.

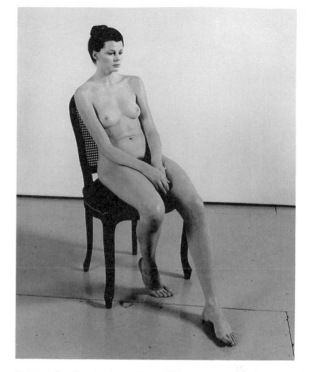

9.16 *Myrm Discobolus (Discus Thrower)*. Roman copy after Greek original of ca. 450 B.C. Marble, life size. National Museum, Rome. This example of "frozen motion" is very different from De Andrea's *Seated Woman* (Fig. 9.17). Why? Compare the *Discobolus* to Muybridge's serial photographs of the same subject (Fig. 9.4).

9.17 John De Andrea. *Seated Woman*. 1978. Life-size polyvinyl, polychromed in oil, life size. Courtesy of Carlo Lamagna Gallery. Note that the figure is "at rest," a position in which little movement is anticipated. How does that fact contribute to our expectations and make the figure more lifelike than the discus thrower (Fig. 9.16)?

The photograph that freezes a split second of the action of a body suggests motion to us only by implication—that is, the orientation of the object or parts of the object relative to its environment: space and ground in the picture plane. Because these are commonplace, we have come to accept them as reasonable and accurate. We do not accept fuzzy images as natural; who ever "saw" a person blur? Perceptual constancy places such an idea beyond conscious belief.

Cues like these provide artists with the ability to stimulate a sense of action and movement in the eye of the beholder. Perhaps it is worth emphasizing that many of these cues will work in exactly the same way for abstract or nonobjective compositions as they do for realistic works of art.

Inferring motion on 2-D surfaces

Dynamic tension (a pregnant moment)

If action in a painting is frozen a few moments before its point of climax, the viewer's mind fills in, *closes*, the action needed to complete the movement.

C. M. Russell's *Indian Hunting Buffalo* (Fig. 9.15) captures such a moment: a horse in midleap, the string of the bow drawn taut, and the weight of the buffalo clearly thrown forward, off-balance, as it lunges toward horse and rider to defend itself. The process involves the Gestalt concepts of closure, equilibrium, and assimilation.

Russell has isolated a moment in time. The figures are suspended in space. We know that they must move or fall, but somehow their clarity and sharpness rivet them to their background and seem to falsify their dynamics—draining the action of much of its immediacy and emotion. The excitement is not there.

This same fact presents problems when a figure is viewed in solid, three-dimensional form. At first, the discus thrower (Fig. 9.16) seems so lifelike that we almost expect him to move. Yet we always know it is a statue, not flesh and blood. It is not quite the same thing as encountering De Andrea's *Seated Woman* (Fig. 9.17), a figure, it should be noted, that is depicted as quietly seated. For a person at rest, we do not have the same expectations.

9.18 Motion only occurs through time. Here, captured on film is one moment, the blur created by an object traveling from one point in space to another during a two-second exposure. This kind of photograph is called a *time exposure*.

The blur (soft edges)

The ambiguity provided by the soft edge suggests phases of motion seen simultaneously. Fast movements are actually blurred because our sensory visual mechanisms were not designed to follow action exceeding a certain speed threshold. We are unable to sharply define any image that changes shape or position in less than one-fifth second. Since our brain cannot accept the concept of smeared natural figure-objects, we are usually not aware of the blur. We can see evidence of the manner in which our vision works by comparing it to photographs taken at slow shutter speeds.

The blur in the photograph (Fig. 9.18) was created by making a time exposure of a two-second duration, during which the amusement park ride revolved some distance. The sharp image of persons watching who stood still during the brief exposure accentuates the movement seen in the blur of the lights attached to the arms of the machine. An important point: We have not only glimpsed motion but also time. Motion always takes place through time.

Observe in the detail from Mary Cassatt's *Portrait of a Woman* (Fig. 9.19) that the artist has deliberately smeared (blurred) the woman's left hand. Though such an action reduces the visual weight, merging figure and ground (*melds push*), the simple gesture also adds the quality of life to the portrait. People are seldom still—movement is characteristic of living things. This apparently insignificant detail, which our brain recognizes subliminally as a motion cue, contributes immeasurably to transforming a potentially ordinary work into an extraordinary one. It is an artist's attention and sensitivity to such details (both of concept and execution) that always separates the masterpiece from pedestrian works.

In humorous illustration, all types of cartoons, and other forms of illustrations or diagrammatical material, the blur may either be reinforced or replaced entirely, as in line or hard-edge work, by drawing lines of movement, streaks, which extend from points within a figure-object into the field or ground. This type of meld simulates the blur.

Sequences: Serial transformation

Serial transformation is the basis for animation. Individual phases of motion are depicted individually, one after the other, in natural order like those shown in the photographic sequences first taken by Muy-

9.19 a Mary Cassatt. *Portrait of a Woman.* 1882. Oil on canvas, 39 × 28½" (99.1 × 72.4 cm). The Birmingham Museum and Art Gallery, England. Reproduced by permission.

b A detail from Mary Cassatt's *Portrait of a Woman.* We can only theorize why Cassatt felt impelled to smear the hard-edge contour lines that originally outlined the subject's left hand. Perhaps she felt they were too prominent or strong, attracting unnecessary attention. Perhaps it just seemed unlifelike, static, and harsh.

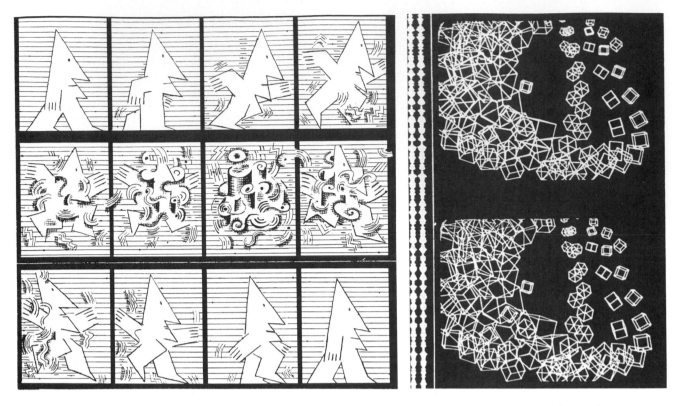

9.20 A serially developed work by Marciek Albrecht, who moved from film animation into fine art. What are the affective (emotional) implications of this sequence?

9.21 John Whitney. *Matrix*. 1971. Two frames from a computer animated film. A pioneer in the computer animated film, Whitney is now able to compose with shapes that are actually moving in real time rather than with painstaking individual drawings. Rapid technological developments are providing artists with an increasing variety of hardware and software for creating images, abstract or realistic. For another example, see Color Plate 34.

bridge. This concept lends itself to uncountable differing possibilities and forms. Figures 9.20 through 9.22 display some applications that include all forms of animation.

This flexible technique is not only adaptable to depictions of any sort of relative movement but also to transformations of one form into another, metamorphosis, as well.

Figure repetition

Figure repetition is observed in stroboscopic photographs in which we see many phases of motion depicted in the same frame or artwork, each one overlapping the other. The differing positions (serial development) and the quality of transparency (another form of the blur) create strong motion cues.

The illustration by Dom Lupo for an article in *Golf* magazine (Fig. 9.23) reflects Giacomo Balla's work completed over 70 years before it. In the photograph

for a Matsushita Electric ad (Fig. 9.24) an actual human silhouette is transformed into a robot by mechanically repeating the same image (rather than sequential ones), blurred and distorted by the light that defines the figure's contour. These effects suggest movement and change, and they may also amplify the affective responses of such images because time appears suspended.

Movement revealed: A record of action

We may recognize evidence of movement by the visual traces of creative acts such as painting or sculpting that remain after the act is completed—*the displacement record*—in the same way that we recognize a diagonal streak of black rubber on a highway as indicative of a skidding automobile. One aspect is "brushwork" or, more specifically, the calligraphic effects of brush, pen, pencil, or whatever tool artists

9.22 *The Return of the Jedi.* Three storyboard panels. © Lucasfilm Ltd. 1982. All rights reserved. Courtesy Lucasfilm Ltd. For animation, television, and motion pictures, storyboards created by artists help the director and producer visualize the film. Storyboards also help designers, craftspersons, costume designers, and others to create the physical objects needed to bring the film to life.

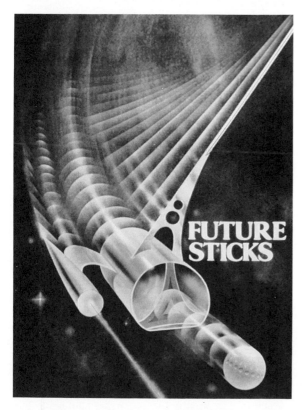

9.23 Dom Lupo. Illustration for *Golf* magazine. March 1980. Reproduced with permission. Compare this work to the stroboscopic photography by Dr. Edgerton in Figure 9.7 and to Balla and Duchamp (Figs. 9.3 and 9.6). These progressions are all in natural order.

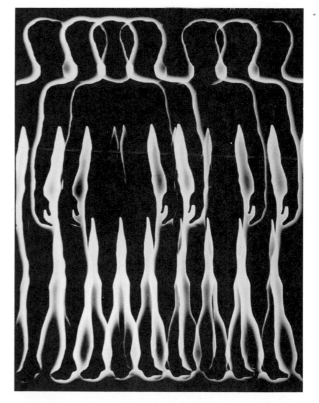

9.24 Peter Angelo Simon. Photograph. Repetition of a different sort, unnatural (random) order. Simon duplicates the same human figure six times to suggest "robotics" in this illustration used for an advertisement for Mitsushita Electric Company.

9.25 Jackson Pollock. *Number 1, 1948.* 1948. Oil on canvas, 68 × 104″ (1.7 × 2.6 m). Collection, The Museum of Modern Art, New York. Purchase. This work is something more than simply a lot of paint thrown on a flat surface. It is a record of a performance—*an act of painting.* It is, perhaps, the exemplar piece of the abstract expressionist movement.

9.26 Hans Namuth. *Jackson Pollock, 1950.* Photograph. Jackson Pollock in performance at his East Hampton, L.I., studio. This photograph documents the making of a very physical art.

may employ, including their own hands, fingers, even the whole body, as well as the force of hurtling materials, air, explosion, or gravity. The disposition and form of this texture as spontaneously applied take on specific characteristics that echo the artist's movements. A quality evident in most impressionistic and expressionistic works, "brushwork" in the abstract expressionist movement rises to the status of a major pictorial element in its own right.

Jackson Pollock's *Number 1* (Fig. 9.25) is a record of a very physical performance, a kind of dance, in which he poured, dripped, flicked, and threw paint across the surface of the canvas (Fig. 9.26).

Optical effects

All motion effects that capitalize on the physiological characteristics of the eye are included in this category. *Optical dazzle* (a fatigue illusion) is produced by creating a pattern of relatively small bars, lines, or shapes, about equally balanced between white and black. Such patterns produce illusions of motion because they are visually unstable—they vibrate (Fig. 9.27).

Bridget Riley uses the concept with stunning effect in her painting, *Fall* (Fig. 9.28). A work of this kind may be given an added dimension by employing the color effects of *vibration,* a term applied to a form of optical dazzle. *Color vibration* is created by juxtaposing complementary colors at equal luminance levels. It is a trick that can create pulsing, highly charged color qualities.

The interaction of elements

Interaction refers to a condition in which figure-objects look or point to one another or to some fixed center of interest (the focal point). The hierarchy of dominant and subdominant elements creates movement in a composition by providing a direction for the eye to follow when observing the works. Direction is a primary and indispensable part of any composition, and interaction is a means by which we achieve it. The weight shifts in the direction of the motion. Ideally, the elements should also interact or react with their pictorial environment. Interaction is a melding technique, one of the connections of a narrow kind.

9.27 These lines (static images) are not actually moving, yet it is impossible to view these without feeling the movement. This is another illusion perpetrated by our visual mechanism and the brain. The cause is generally thought to be associated with eye movements (saccades and tremors) and the "fatigue" of the photoreceptors in the retina.

9.28 Bridget Riley. *Fall.* 1963. Emulsion on board, 55½" × 55¼" (141 × 140.33 cm). The Tate Gallery, London. Reproduced by courtesy of the Trustees. Riley attributes her interest in applying optical effects to painting to Georges Seurat. The combination of black and white lines in Riley's painting not only produces a sensation of movement but also evokes impressions of pastel colors among the vibrating lines. In addition to lines, dazzling moiré effects can be created with dots and other geometric forms.

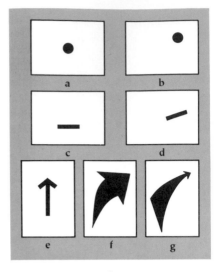

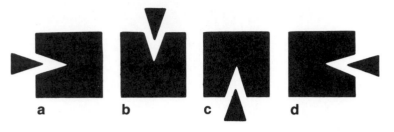

9.30 The square and the wedge graphically illustrate the sensation of movement induced when objects are placed in different orientations or positions relative to one another. In **a**, the wedge appears to be moving into the square; at **b**, it appears to be dropping into the square; in **c**, falling out; and in **d**, moving out.

9.29 Sensations of movement inferred from the placement of a figure in a static visual field. In **a**, a dot is imprisoned in the exact center of a space, a "bull's-eye" effect. In **c**, a short bar is similarly immobilized by being centered as well as oriented parallel to the picture plane. Note how these same figures "take off" when their position is changed, **b** and **d**. Diagrams **e**–**g** show variations in the distribution of visual weight on an arrowhead shape. What happens to the sense of movement in each case?

9.31 Katsushika Hokusai, *The Great Wave of the Kanagawa*. ca. 1823–1829. Woodcut. The Metropolitan Museum of Art, New York. Howard Mansfield Collection, Rogers Fund, 1936. How does the asymmetrical balance contribute to the feeling of motion? Where is the fulcrum? It is not seen but should always be felt.

Interaction may be achieved through interrelationships such as intersecting, through color similarity, and through all forms of grouping and organization (Gestalt). Even such simple elements as a dot or a line may imply movement and direction. Although a dot centered in a field (Fig. 9.29 **a**) is neutral, when it is moved to the right and up (Fig. 9.29 **b**), there is an implication of movement in that direction perceptually. A similar effect takes place with the line (Fig. 9.29 **c**), which is tied to the frame lines by virtue of its alignment. Shifted to the right and angled (Fig. 9.29 **d**), it takes off.

When we draw an arrowhead, the tip has more

contrast and is heavier than the shaft end. This can be strengthened by making the head darker. The thrust can be reversed by exactly the obverse procedure. Observe the effects in Figures 9.29 **e**–**g** and 9.30. We can use visual weight to move in or out, to move up or down, depending on how such weight is placed or distributed.

In the print by Hokusai, *The Great Wave of the Kanagawa* (Fig. 9.31), there is a strong left to right movement. The heaviest weight is suspended above and to the left. All the lines of movement within the composition point to that heavy form. The total effect is one of substantial force and movement even though

9.32 Ruth Orkin. *American Girl in Italy.*
© 1952, 1980 Ruth Orkin. In this photograph our attention is directed to the young woman, not only because of her central location but also because all other faces look at her. Subconsciously we want to see what they see. Test out this human characteristic by intently staring up at an object some distance away or just up into empty sky. Say nothing. In a little while, persons in the vicinity will be doing the same thing.

the work is relatively flat and stylized. Realism in emotional response does not necessarily require realism in a natural sense. Be sure to observe the qualities of rhythm in this work.

Take another look at Géricault's *The Raft of the Medusa*, Figure 6.30. Observe the strong movement from lower left to upper right. Notice the mast, which brings the eye down in a diagonal opposing the first. Opposing diagonals suggest conflict, struggle, and controversy. Are these ideas appropriate to the theme of the work?

One should never forget that there is always a horizontal/vertical component to any figure (its spatial attitude) and a corresponding affective response to that orientation. For example, an arrow pointing to the right suggests progress in time; pointing upward, an increase in magnitude. If the movement is both upward and to the right, it suggests increasing magnitude over time.

All sorts of "mechanical" devices can be used to point or direct the viewer's eyes throughout a composition. Such common clichés as pointing fingers, arrows, and "bullets," "flags," and check marks appear everywhere in all forms of literature. These pointing mechanisms set up lines of movement that direct attention from element to element. In a work of art, equivalents can be disguised or camouflaged and be equally as effective.

Another form of interaction refers to the gaze of the eye. The eyes of persons or animals portrayed in a painting can direct our eyes (the viewer's) to the most important figure in the composition. Like the eyes of all the men lining the street in the photograph (Fig. 9.32), our eyes are immediately directed toward the young woman passing by. When looking through books about art, notice how frequently painters of large figure compositions used this concept to help unify their work.

The customary visual flow

When we look at any visual materials, the initial eye movements are biased according to the way we read. The strongest point of entry for any communication is, therefore, upper left. Though such cultural biases are not shared by many non-English speaking peoples, it is a characteristic that should be exploited without embarrassment, especially in communication arts.

For the majority of persons living in Western societies, the movement proceeds from upper left to the lower right in a Z or reverse S pattern. This movement is easy, fast, "correct," and comfortable because it stems from the way that we read. Conversely, movements from right to left are difficult, slow, "wrong," and uncomfortable. Could these negative feelings be put to effective uses?

Summary

Nothing in a visual field attracts our attention like change. We are aware of every movement going on around us because movement is the most obvious change. The primary function of our peripheral vision is to detect motion. Moreover, we are also keenly aware of other forms of change: differences in the appearance or position of figure-objects over a period of time. These forms of change, which we call displacements, are caused by movements too fast or too slow to be observed, such as growth, weathering, and decomposition.

Phases of change in natural order are referred to as *sequences,* and each point in a sequence is a single "frozen moment" in time. Not only are we able to understand various types of movement through analyzing sequences, but sequences also provide a basis for a large part of our entertainment industry, motion pictures and television. Like painting, still photography, illustration, and design, these are two-dimensional art forms.

Movement may be created kinetically in any of these two-dimensional forms by attaching motors or by devising methods whereby outside energy forces can cause the work to move. A motion picture projector is an active kinetic energy device because it uses a motor. Though they may not be works of art, wind chimes are passive kinetic energy devices, and so are whirligigs and windmills.

Whenever visual motion cues appear in two-dimensional artworks, they trigger perceptual responses associated with our real world experiences.

Operating by inference, such cues conjure an illusion of motion within works that possess no kinetic energy of their own. Perceptual mechanisms (like optical dazzle) and lenticular devices (like fields of tiny cylindrical lenses and dimensional grids) create movement by requiring the viewer to interact with the art, willingly or unwillingly.

The concept of intervals as a component of time and motion is analogous to intervals of proportion and spacing on two-dimensional surfaces. Progressive grid structures infer both space and motion. Remember Bridget Riley's *Movement in Squares* (Fig. 4.31)?

What moves or is perceived to move (inferred motion) possesses a greater visual weight than static figure-objects. The greater the perceived motion, the greater the attraction will be up to the point where motion is too fast to be seen.

No artist may ignore the consequences of perceptual motion cues any more than depth cues. They are intrinsic components of every visual field whether we want them to be or not, part of the dual reality of pictures. The alternative possibilities for application are almost beyond comprehension. Direct motion or inferred, sequences, intervals of time, or metamorphosis—**the many faces of change** are creative tools of the highest order.

Review of key terms

change A transition from one state to another, altered state; a movement from one place to another place; a passage from one moment in time to another; any sort of transformation such as metamorphosis, growth, decay, and erosion.

cubism A style of art developed by Pablo Picasso and Georges Braque that is characterized by figure-ground ambiguity, flattened perspectives, and multiple points of view.

futurism An early 20th-century Italian art movement that focused on the violence, speed, force, and efficiency of modern society and on the mechanical energy exhibited by automobiles, trains, and industrial manufacturing.

interval The amount of spatial or chronological separation between things such as lines, figures, colors, areas, spaces, and movements. Intervals are *regular* when spacing is all the same and *progressive* when the spaces change in natural order whether based on a simple numerical progression or on a geometric ratio.

kinetic Moving; pertaining to motion; produced by motion.

movement The visual act or appearance of change. The progression of events through time and space or across a two-dimensional surface. Visible displacement in space. When we observe movement, it is called *direct* or simultaneous; when it is too fast or slow to be observed, it is called *inferred* or implied. *See* **kinetic.**

optical dazzle A type of pulsating, shimmering, and dazzling optical effect attributed to the fatigue of photoreceptor cells (rods and cones) in the retina. Generally, strong contrasts of black/white or complementary hues are required.

sequences Usually a series of images exhibiting serial development: discrete phases of motion depicted individually, one after another in natural order. However, sometimes these are depicted together on a single picture plane. *See* **serial.**

serial Arranging in or forming a series in natural order. Serial development is the process of engaging in such an activity. Animation is serial development, and picture stories (like comic strips) are serial presentations. *See* **sequences.**

CHAPTER TEN

Psychological weight

What is psychological weight?

Any shape or form identified as a "figure," separate from ground, acquires *meaning* simply by virtue of its existence in the visual field.

Psychological weight is dependent on the significance of meaning each of us attaches to a figure, that is, the relative importance of that figure to us. There is a wide gradation scale ranging from the most passionate emotions (love, hate) to virtually total disinterest.

Our reactions or responses to any visual stimuli are based on our lifetime experiences (assimilation). This represents a kind of "behavioral conditioning" acquired through our interaction with our environment, our parents, ethnic and national origins, and our own likes and dislikes whatever their origins. Psychologists use the term *behavioral conditioning* to refer to nurtured

or learned responses as opposed to genetic or instinctive reactions.

Communication begins with shared experiences

While responses to any specific figure or situation are unique and personal, perceptual studies indicate that human beings react in much the same way to a wide variety of figure-objects, environmental, and social events. The list of common responses would be relatively small if we use a global reference, mostly things related to basic emotions and physiological

10.1 Henri Cartier-Bresson. *Outside a Bistro, France.* 1968–1969. Photograph. Emotions reach a peak when we fall in love. The object of our affections may become so important that we are oblivious to everyone and everything else.

151

body functions and to similarities in environment. However, the more closely knit the body of persons, the more experiences they are likely to share.

Persons with close ties of any sort, such as political philosophy, religious belief, age, or social status or those engaged in the same profession, will have certain concepts, terminology, and understandings that they do not share in common with the general public as a whole. A visual communication addressing such a group must take into account ethnocentric views if real communication is ever to be established.

In fact, if any such group can be isolated (defined and separated), the majority of the group will share so many interests that they will also exhibit common motivational characteristics; characteristics that can be used as vehicles for communication. It is on this strategy that the entire fields of marketing and advertising are based.

The path to more effective communication

The general public's reaction to a product, a service, a subject, or a set of circumstances, called *consumer behavior* by marketing professionals, provides a means to improve communications in any work of visual art regardless of whether one is selling a product, a service, or an idea; expressing a point of view; or simply telling a good story.

Intuitively, artists have been employing such strategies from before the beginning of recorded history. The term *artists* is used here broadly to include writers, poets, dramatists, and so on, as well as visual artists. What worked and what did not was discovered strictly by trial and error. That is still true because the result is always a kind of "formula," a new combination of many possible alternatives. However, recent research in psychology, perception, and marketing is providing insights that make the task of communication easier and offers directions with greater potential for success.

Based on the likely responses to recognizable shapes, psychological weight provides an effective leveling and sharpening tool for visual artists. There are three levels of *meaning* related to psychological weight: recognition, association, and the symbol.

Recognition: Figure naming

A fundamental process of perception, figure *recognition* involves not only separating figure from ground but also attaching a name or identification tag. At the most basic level, recognition gives the figure its meaning. Deriving such meanings about our world is the primary and imperative function of all our sensory organs although it is vision that dominates such activity.

Once we have recognized a figure, we first respond to it at an emotional level. Like differing measures used on a balance scale, differing figures possess differing degrees of weight.

For normal adults, the strongest figure and the greatest weight are attached to one's own child or lover; then in declining order, a spouse (husband or wife), a parent, any other close or immediate family member, close acquaintances or friends, other acquaintances like persons with whom we work, more distant family, neighbors, persons of our own ethnic or nationality group, and finally all human beings in general. This list is composed of persons we like or love; but someone or something we hate could well consume most of our passion and energy, conferring on it, at least temporarily, weight greater than that given to persons we love.

We always look for familiar faces

A person we know has a greater impact on us than someone we have never seen before. Whenever we are in a crowd, we unconsciously search for any familiar face—anyone we might recognize—including television, film, and political personalities. Is there any face that is recognizable in Figure 10.2? How quickly was it found?

Some of the weight reserved for family is extended to celebrities because they often become members of an extended family that may include a circle of close friends, members of the clergy, the family doctor, the president (prime minister, king, or queen), sports heroes, and the like. Thus, the image of any such persons attracts extraordinary attention in a way no ordinary person can.

The heaviest weight of living things, after human beings, is usually a pet who also may be considered a member of the immediate family. Almost everyone reacts favorably to kittens and puppies.

Favorite things of any sort command our attention. We are prone to fads, which are manifestations of our need to be liked, to be approved of, and to belong. Such "topical" things may have enormous, if temporary, worth as vehicles for communication. *Topical* subjects are those that are currently in the news or in fashion.

Functional animals, such as horses or other beasts of burden—animals who share in the work of living—are important to a wide variety of persons

10.2 Faces fascinate. Looking into a crowd, our eyes automatically scan a scene rapidly, searching for a familiar face. If one is found, it quickly becomes the center of visual attention and the scene assumes new meaning. This is an occurrence that psychologists attribute to *emotional loading*, that is, our personal emphasis or emotional involvement with that figure-object or with our own species. This is one reason why we see faces in such things as clouds and rocks.

because they have an economic impact on individuals and on society. So do food animals like cattle, swine, sheep, and chickens. Obviously, this varies greatly depending on locale and culture. Many persons raised in an urban environment have no understanding of the significance that crops or cattle may have for farmers and would be completely oblivious to a farmer's concerns over stock feed or low rainfall. As a consequence, visuals designed for farmers, for example, may require a considerably different pictorial emphasis than those directed toward urban dwellers. Would a farmer necessarily relate to graffiti or rush-hour traffic?

After others of our own kind, the common preference order declines from humanlike primates (chimpanzees and monkeys); rare animals that arouse curiosity or awe; animals in general; birds; trees, flowers, and vegetables; fish; down to insects. Though this

hierarchy varies from person to person, the list represents an average sequence. A gardener may prefer flowers and vegetables, but a sportsperson may respond to fish before flowers. Positions are easily altered by circumstances. For persons who unexpectedly discover cockroaches in their kitchen or termites in their walls, insects may suddenly acquire a very heavy weight indeed.

Ice may immediately acquire enormous weight when we find that a sudden storm has coated streets with a glossy, extremely slick coat of it and we have to drive home. It may also gain weight for us if we are at home looking out the window. We may be struck by the "beauty of nature." In these cases, the reaction to the same stimuli is emotionally opposite: beauty and fear. Could these differing responses be recalled in a painting or illustration?

left: 10.3 Objects that are commonly used together in order to be functional may possess such a strong association that the appearance of one immediately recalls the others to mind.

right: 10.4 Raymond Savignac. Poster for Dunlop Tires. Courtesy Dunlop Holding Plc. The case of the invisible automobile. It is really there, isn't it?

Association

Many figures have some association with other figures in our perceptions. Generally, such recall occurs in the fraction of a second. Once a figure is recognized as a fork, we immediately associate it with food and with other eating utensils, a knife and a spoon (Fig. 10.3). There will be more remote associations with tables, stoves, kitchens, and perhaps restaurants. A pitchfork is likely to bring a very different set of associations to mind.

A figure tends to gain weight temporarily if it can be immediately associated with one or more other familiar objects. Familiarity makes us feel comfortable, at ease, unthreatened. Such associations can be effective problem solvers.

In the poster (Fig. 10.4) for Dunlop Tires, the automobile has been omitted. Yet perceptually it is clearly present in our minds. The position and the attitude of the driver (his orientation) reinforces our initial impression.

Association and creativity

Psychologists believe that the faculty of association may be one of the primary characteristics of creativity.

Without the concept of association, civilization as we know it could not exist. The only way we can make any advancement at all in knowledge and technology is through our ability to draw associations between apparently dissimilar objects, concepts, actions, or reactions, thereby arriving at new theories, systems, or products. That is, we make *inferences.* Inferences allow us to string together apparently unrelated facts in order to fashion a new theory, a new product, or a fresh idea. Association allows us to add to our store of knowledge. It is through knowledge that we are able to change our perceptions—to perceive our earth as a round globe that travels around the sun rather than as a world, flat as a pancake, which is the center of the universe.

A person in a football uniform with ball in hand,

10.5 A student comprehensive editorial layout. Blindness is symbolized by a doll without eyes. (Courtesy Helene Y. Redmond.)

a

b

10.6 a A landscape.
b The same landscape with a human figure added — *evidence of the presence of other human beings.* What attracts?

arm raised high, suggests the entire game, as well as that specific moment that is transpiring. In this way, one particular visual may imply a whole series of associated behaviors.

Because this type of association is "expected," confounding expectations will command attention. Rocks do not float (Fig. 6.1) and eating utensils are not ordinarily covered with fur (Fig. 5.6). Such images turn our understanding of the world in which we live — our expectations — upside down. Whether they frighten, amuse, or merely appear ridiculous, images of this kind possess a relatively heavy visual weight.

A distorted or incomplete figure gains weight. We can use this associative response to solve visual problems. How do we say "blind" visually? In Figure 10.5, a doll without eyes offers one provocative answer. It commands attention. Like the missing automobile in the Dunlop poster, the missing eyes dominate our

perceptual response. Implied, but unseen, figures may have a heavy visual weight.

In the landscape (Fig. 10.6 **a**), our attention tends to wander even though the distribution of visual weight establishes the old tree as a center of interest. Psychologically, the composition is passive. If we add a person (Fig. 10.6 **b**), our attention is immediately riveted on that person to the exclusion of everything else. We attach a very heavy visual weight to our own kind.

The more associations we can come up with, the more likely it is that we will find the best or most appropriate solution to any visual problem. One single percept should recall innumerable relationships or alternatives.

Take the number six, for example. It should bring to mind its Arabic form, its Roman numeral form, half a dozen, a hexagon, insects (class Hexapoda, six legs), the face of a die, six-gun (a six-shooter), a six-pack,

Psychological weight   **155**

a

b

c

10.7 **a** Original art work. What attracts?
b Original with a symbol added. Where is the focal point?
c Original with words added. Has the focal point changed?

sixpence, five plus one, two times three, a six-footer (person), sixfold, sixth (in order), sixth sense, and so on. How many more "sixes" could be added? What about other numbers like one, two, or three? Where could we look for more ideas?

Symbols

A *symbol* (a figure or a sign) "stands in" for an entire idea or concept—a kind of shorthand. One writer defines symbol as "information content infused with form." A familiar symbol (heavy weight) possesses meanings of cultural, political, or religious significance.

Of course, symbols are used in far more limited ways (light weight): for example, in mathematics, physics, electrical schematic diagrams, and computer science or for common directional signs for traffic. Their use simplifies both the recording and understanding of information. In typography, the symbol *ℓ* always means "delete." Symbols can be as broadly recognized as the Red Cross or Mickey Mouse or as private and personal as a birth date. Symbols rise above simple associational relationships because they are understood to possess significant contexts or messages.

It is important to recognize that signs and symbols, which include the written language, highly influence visual weight in all of its forms. A large rectangular shape in the design (Fig. 10.7 **a**), center right-hand side, functions rather well as part of the overall composition. It holds its place and does not attract undue attention.

We can assess the visual weight of symbols and words by inserting each, in turn, into that rectangle. Figure 10.7 **b** shows a cross imposed on the rectangle. Because of their psychological visual weight, symbols override all other components in the design by immediately drawing our attention and holding it there. In the next example (Fig. 10.7 **c**), the words *Hong Kong* have been placed in the rectangle. These words carry such a heavy visual weight that we can hardly avert our eyes. It utterly destroys the design's composition, which now seems to exist only to support the words. Would the reaction be the same for an illiterate person or for a foreign national who could not read English?

Ordinarily, we must not place a recognizable symbol or word in any work of art unless its communication significance overrides all other considerations; or, unless its impact is balanced by a profusion of similar symbols/words in a hierarchy of weights throughout the composition. It may be necessary, when painting a cityscape or an abstraction that includes letters or words, to weaken such signs by garbling or diffusing the letters, by cutting them off or overlapping them with other elements, by greatly reducing their contrast with their background, or by using not one or two, but many such signs in the composition.

Figure 10.7 c might be suitable as a title of an article in a magazine or a TV show or motion picture, but little else.

Symbols are a kind of visual shorthand. They enable an artist to communicate complex ideas efficiently, with minimal space, and with minimum detail (complexity), yet with maximum understanding and impact. Of course, symbols often become clichés. Yet a symbol would not be a viable symbol if it did not originally possess considerable energy. Such energies can be redirected. Turning a symbol inside out, giving it a new setting or context, or combining it creatively with another may make it fresh and compelling again.

An artist should be especially knowledgeable about symbols since they often permit more direct and economical solutions to visual problems. They are some of the best tools at an artist's disposal.

Summary

It is possible to create dominance with size alone although that is usually not a very effective choice in the long run. When principles of visual weight are correctly understood and applied, an object of any size can be made dominant.

Just as we do with an actual seesaw, we can add weights on the lighter side until balance is achieved or remove weight from the heavy side.

Basic patterns can be reinforced, enriched, and elaborated on through the use of counterpoint (psychological contrast and physical contrast). Counterpoint is combining in a single visual two or more conceptual ideas that have harmonic relationships although each retains its individuality. Rich and poor persons can be contrasted. Human figures are harmonically and rhythmically the same because they are similar in size and shape, but their *status* can be differentiated by their clothing or appearance or even by the way that they stand or sit. This is a leveling and a sharpening process.

Leveling and sharpening can produce extreme simplification on one side and extreme complexity on the other. What is right or what is wrong in each instance is determined by the conceptual objectives of

10.8 Francisco Goya. *And They Still Will Not Go, Los Caprichos*, No. 59. 1793. Etching and aquatint, second state; $8^{11}/_{16} \times 5^{1}/_{4}''$ (24 × 13 cm). The Metropolitan Museum of Art, New York. Gift of M. Knoedler and Co., 1918. Observe the orientation of the enigmatic monolith. What is the emotional effect?

each individual work. The idea is to trap the viewer for as long as possible, that is, to *hold the viewer's attention.*

Consider the emotional reaction to Goya's *And They Still Will Not Go* (Fig. 10.8). Goya uses a supported diagonal as a compositional device to convey visually the idea of repression. The support is a skele-tal figure, weak from deprivation. We know this is a person who struggles to maintain balance and that he will ultimately fail against superior strength (weight). That is the genius of Goya. The emotional effect is no mystery. Goya has simply applied intuitively the perceptual principles of organization, visual weight, and meaning.

Review of key terms

association A mental connection, joining, or linking of thoughts, feelings, ideas, or sensations. A recognition of the functional relationships existing between things that habitually accompany, or are operational components of, one another.

consumer behavior A marketing term that refers to the study of factors that motivate human behavior. It concerns the general public's response to products, services, subjects, or sets of circumstances as determined by statistical research.

meaning In this text, the term is used in its most generic sense: to refer to perceptual recognition, naming, or identification of a figure-object. The term, as used here, does not necessarily imply *message. See* **message**.

message A correlation of "meanings" in a specific context or structure for the express purpose of communication—transmitting a purposeful thought, concept, or idea.

recognition A simple act of identification that gives a "name" to a familiar figure-object—the most fundamental level of deriving "meaning" from sensory data.

symbol A figure or a sign that "stands in" for something else; something that represents an entire idea of concept. A kind of "shorthand" used to indicate an operation, quality, relationship, and so on.

The anatomy of meaning

CHAPTER ELEVEN

Communicating visually

Visual cues in the arts and advertising

We can generate emotions of fear, anger, disgust, and sadness within ourselves simply by making a face. Studies suggest that the emotional change is very strong. Although, for some unknown reason, this does not seem to work with faces of happiness and joy, we will spontaneously join in another person's laughter even when we do not know what the other person may be laughing about. Is it easy to see how the entire entertainment industry (theater arts, film and television) utilizes human characteristics, cues, to arouse emotions? Meaning from theatrical performances is communicated more forcibly with appearance, body language, and sound of voice (delivery) than it is with the words. Even a dog or cat may respond more to the tone of the voice rather than to specific words.

Of course, the public relations, marketing, and advertising fields use visual cues to sell ideas, services, and products. Appropriate visual cues induce consumer reactions favorable to the point of view being expressed by the advertiser. Persuasion is a more effective means than coercion to get anyone to do anything.

Our survival instinct has taught us to be ever ready for fight or flight. Sensory data related to basic needs, like love (reproduction), food (sustenance), and self-preservation may produce virtually instantaneous hormonal changes in the lower brain, and our response is, at the primitive level, highly emotional.

Basic meanings about our condition are derived from environmental, representational, and symbolic cues. These are the same sorts of cues already discussed—cues or codes that can be imbedded in works of visual art and decoded by the viewer or audience. Initial responses to all sensory data are emotional. Though many of these emotional responses are universal, that response is relatively weak.

In order to build a powerful image, all related visual components must be coordinated in precisely the correct mixture just as would be required to produce a valuable chemical formula, a functional mathematical equation, a symphony, or even a prizewinning recipe. The elemental visual components of visual processing (and also of design), along with their associated affective responses, are the raw materials—the building blocks. Creatively used, they can underscore, reinforce, and strengthen the inherent emotional drama in any pictorial field. With like responses overlaid, so that a particular emotion or mood is reinforced by every single element in the picture, affective responses (emotional influences) may be converted into effective results.

We are all irresistibly driven to deduce meaning from any visual field (a perceptual imperative). When a field possesses no clear meaning, it fails to satisfy our (the viewer's) basic emotional need to find it.

11.1 Karl Schmidt-Rottluff. *Three Nudes*. 1913. Oil on canvas, 41⅞ × 38⅝" (106.5 × 98 cm). National Gallery, Berlin. The artist is not really interested in the nude women but in the shapes and forms and his feelings about them. This example of German (or figurative) expressionism shows influences of cubism, but it has no refined structure. Is there any area of similarity with Pearlsteins's painting, Figure 5.2 — a similarity of dissimilars?

Two emotional modes in works of art

The subjective

When artists express their own feelings in the art for their own sake, that is a subjective approach. The artist is primarily concerned with what is taking place in his or her own mind unaffected by the external world — a kind of baring of the soul, filled with personal metaphors and symbols, and expressed in gestural form.

Most often we place this kind of work into one of two stylistic categories: *figurative (German) expressionism* (Fig. 11.1) and *abstract expressionism* (Fig. 11.2), a nonobjective form.

Although such works may be appreciated on an intellectual level, they often hold little interest for the untutored viewer who lacks professional guidance.

The objective

In the objective mode, artists reach out to touch the viewer, to stimulate a viewer's reaction. The feelings aroused by the work may not necessarily represent those of the artist at all. Most works of art fall into the objective mode predominantly, although there are but few works that are not combinations of the subjective and objective.

Even when the artist is calculating a response, if he or she does not also feel the emotion, the work may not be convincing and, as a consequence, is often diminished. The subjective work is an emotional outflow, governed by mood and chance and wholly "intuitive." For the trained artist, however, *intuition* is a consequence of years of trial and error experience, academic study, and judgments acquired (almost by osmosis) through associations with professional colleagues and acquaintances. Therefore, the subjective work may possess objective qualities introduced on the subconscious or intuitive level. Evaluate Figures 11.2 and 11.3.

In the objective mode, self-expression is allied with purposeful communication. That includes all art for advertising: sales of products, services, or ideas for public relations; for corporate identity; for any sort of promotion; and for information or instruction, that is, for the dissemination of information. Obviously, it also includes most of fine art and design.

Communication has been the primary purpose of art from the beginning of time.

Creating moods

Our emotions dwell in the deep primitive recesses of our brain. Although we can sometimes control them intellectually, primitive emotions often vigorously express themselves before higher brain functions can intercede. Often we do not wish to control them. There is catharsis in the release of emotions. Given an acceptable social framework, we want to laugh, to cry, to scream out loud!

The objective of an illustration is to produce an emotional setting, a mood, appropriate to the story line. The image should raise adrenaline levels to thrill and excite; lower them for calm and tranquillity; bring about sexual arousal for moods of love and romance. Examine Figure 11.4.

left: **11.2** Robert Motherwell. *Elegy to the Spanish Republic No. 34.* 1953–1954. Oil on canvas, 80 × 100″ (2.03 × 2.54m). Albright-Knox Gallery, Buffalo. Gift of Seymour H. Knox 1957. Do the huge black calligraphic "marks" move a person emotionally? Motherwell uses them virtually to blot out color and "image," to externalize his internal emotions. Has he coupled to universal concepts, or are his ideas too personal to elicit a response from the viewer?

below: **11.4** Keith Henderson. Frontispiece design from *Green Mansions* by W. H. Hudson. Note how the strong lighting and heavy shadows help the artistic design as well as help establish the "mood." No words are needed to tell the viewer what is happening.

below: **11.3** Franz Masereel. *Despair.* Woodcut. Note the body language: The head is thrown back, facing God (both questioning fate and supplication or resignation); one hand covers the face (hopelessness, agony); another is raised in defiance (a struggle to the very end). The stark luminance contrast, the overall darkness (amount of black versus white), the declining movement—all are *visual cues* (graphic symbols) that do not require explanation for viewers to understand. We respond emotionally.

Communicating visually **163**

11.5 Michelangelo da Caravaggio. *David with the Head of Goliath.* ca. 1605. Oil on canvas, 49¼ × 39¾" (125 × 101 cm). Borghese Gallery, Rome. What is the emotional reaction to this painting? There are ambiguous implications. On the one hand, does the harsh, spotlight effect and the contemplative appearance of David imply a classic tragedy? Or, on the other hand, does David merely look sickened and disgusted by the bloody sight? Does it stretch imagination to see this David as the one who slew Goliath?

In advertising and marketing, we want to motivate the viewer to do something related to the product, service, or idea being promoted. Any emotions may be appropriate to this purpose. Creating a sense of self-worth coupled with sharpened stereotypes that sexually differentiate men and women may sell a deodorant expressly aimed at one or the other. Perceptions of integrity, stability, and friendliness may sell a viewer on the virtues of a bank or a political candidate.

Evaluate the differing emotional qualities in two paintings of the same subject, *David with the Head of Goliath,* painted by Caravaggio less than a year apart (see Figs. 11.5 and 11.6). The earlier version is calm, introspective; the later one bristles with vigor and movement.

For producing the strongest stimuli and, consequently, the strongest response, all affective emotional responses must be coherent; that is, they must all be similar, so that they reinforce each other.

I am me and you are you

We must always be cognizant of the fact that our own responses to specific situations may not be generic—that is, the same as those of the majority of viewers. Without realizing it, we may be out of touch with general opinion. For example, our ethnic heritage may determine color preferences common only to our group. We may have irrational personal color prejudices, which are shared by no one else. If I have a strong dislike for any color, I should ask myself, "Why?"

The following story illustrates how different individual perceptions can be, although I have been unable to discover its origin, or to verify its authenticity at this time. Even if apocryphal, it serves a purpose.

As an art project for Halloween, an elementary school teacher asked students to draw pictures of the most frightening monsters they could imagine— ghosts, goblins, witches, and so on. When the works were submitted for grading, all but one lived up to expectations. The exception was a drawing of a rabbit. Later, the teacher discovered that the child had once been bitten by a rabbit infected with rabies. There had been a series of painful shots and many weeks spent

11.6 Michelangelo da Caravaggio. *David with the Head of Goliath.* ca. 1606. Oil on canvas, 35½" × 45¼" (90.17 × 114.93 cm). Kunsthistorisches Museum, Vienna. Is this a much more forceful work than Figure 11.5? How has the mood changed? Note the tension that runs through the body of David: The face is alert, the sword arm is upraised, and the arm that supports the head of Goliath does not appear to droop as it does in the earlier painting. The body is in action rather than repose. We should feel the energy and movement.

in a hospital. To that child, a rabbit was a dreadful monster.

Personal symbols, in jokes, favorite colors, favorite expressions, or personal experiences mean absolutely nothing to persons whom we have never met.

Communication begins with shared experiences.

The keys to visual communication

Inherent in the character of the visual components of design are symbolic, associative, and emotional (affective) responses that are derived directly from the way in which our brain processes sensory data. Therefore, these coincide with most viewers' expectations. It is essential for the artist to be in touch with them as they are the means to create powerful and compelling works of art. When an individual stimulus (from a shape, for example) is combined with additional affective responses of the same character (originating from an edge, a color, or a movement), intensity levels are raised.

In previous chapters as the opportunity arose, we defined the emotional and the conceptual implications of a topic. Affective constituents are part of all elemental visual components: change and motion (in all their forms); edges; lines; shapes (both open and closed

forms); space; and, of course, color. As not all these topics have been thoroughly covered, nor been tied together properly, we shall do so in the following.

Change and motion

Remember that we are primarily aware of change in our environment. Because of this, any form of change possesses enormous attraction. The differing forms of change that we have already discussed were displacement (physical evidence of movement too fast or too slow to be observed); metamorphosis (the transformation of one shape or form into another); direct motion; inferred motion; interval (movement through time); and the effects of time on figure-objects and the environment. Let us say that, in general, our emotional reactions to these are consistent with our general understanding of such events in a visual field of any sort.

A displacement that occurs because of movement too fast for us to see is usually frightening. A bullet moves faster than we can see. Its sound and the evidence of its impact are guaranteed to shake us. Slow movements are allied with growth, aging, evolution, weathering, erosion, decay, and oxidation. Metamorphoses (caterpillar-chrysalis-butterfly) is a wonder for

11.7 Robert Longo. *Untitled* lithograph from *Men in the Cities* series. 1982. Courtesy Metro Pictures, New York. How does a person respond emotionally to this image of a twisting and turning figure?

us to behold whether child or adult. The process is at once puzzling, disturbing, incredible, beautiful, fascinating, and almost incomprehensible. Attach some of these ideas to the metamorphosis of a human figure, for example. Then what do we have?

Each of these concepts has vast possibilities. Movement can occur only through time. Movement is also a component of both two-dimensional and three-dimensional space. We recognize various kinds of motion events in a visual field as indicative of our past experience (assimilation), and we respond with associated feelings.

Meanings of movements

The following chart categorizes 11 differing movements and the affective emotional responses associated with them:[17]

Types of movement — affective responses

1. *Revolving:* mechanical energy, disorientation, vertigo (dizziness) (Fig. 11.7).

2. *Pendulum:* monotony, time passing (like a metronome or a clock).

11.8 Max Ernst. *Les Obscures*. 1957. Oil on canvas, 46 × 35″ (116.84 × 88.9 cm). Museum Folkwang, Essen. Cold, dark blues, nightmare images, and the engulfing radiating lines, like a spider's web, combine to make a viewer distinctly uncomfortable. This is exactly what Ernst had in mind.

11.9 Jan Lenica. Poster for a performance of Alban Berg's opera *Wozzeck*. 1966. Lithograph, 37⅝ × 26⅜″ (95.5 × 67 cm). Muzeum Plakatu, Wilanow, Poland. How can we say "opera" visually? Lenica's solution to this visual problem was a series of concentric shapes around an orifice, the mouth. The associative response of one of our senses to another sense is called *synesthesia*. Does this visual design evoke the sensation of sound?

3. *Cascading:* lightness, sprightliness, effervescence (like a fountain, a waterfall, bubbles in champagne or a soft drink, fireworks, or a group of children rolling down a hill).

4. *Spreading or radiating (centrifugal forces):* warmth, reaching out, all-encompassing like radiating lines, expansion, suffocating, snaring, or capturing (as with a net). See Figures 11.8 and 11.9.

5. *Converging (centripetal forces):* drawing inward, consolidation, concentration, restriction compression (like squeezing in a vise, cramming clothes in a suitcase, a whirlpool, or a tornado).

6. *Inward spiral:* tension, conflict, violent movements, draining (emotional or physical exhaustion), out of control.

7. *Interrupted progression:* varieties called a "jump cut" or a "freeze frame" in film and TV; syncopation in music. It is stopping action in midstep, so to speak, or dropping out chunks of time. Remember that movement is progression through time. It can also be a reordering of natural progressive intervals (syncopation). Such effects are startling and

11.10 Arnold Newman. *Andy Warhol.* Photograph. The "interrupted motion" suggested by this combination of two different portraits taken some time apart creates affective responses consistent with surprise, fear, the unworldly. A similar effect called a "jump cut" as used in motion pictures simply drops out chunks of otherwise continuous action. It is guaranteed to startle a viewer. Is such an emotional framework appropriate for an image of Warhol?

attract attention because they are unexpected. They not only appear to make the music skip a beat, but they also make the heart skip a beat. They suggest hesitancy or stumbling; intoxication; otherworldly interference; frightening speed or sudden, inexplicable, and frightening cessation of all activity (like a heart attack), both beyond human control. Though most effective in film, the concept can be applied as well to nonkinetic pictures (see Fig. 11.10). It increases the varieties of expression.

8. *Horizontal:* travel; momentum. Left-to-right movement is easy, correct, natural, fast (the customary visual flow for persons from Western countries). It is both positive and progressive. Right-to-left action is slow, difficult, unnatural; the associations are negative and recessive. Keep in mind that these characteristics are mostly cultural characteristics.

9. *Ascending vertical:* freedom, escape, exaltation. Movement up a vertical axis is associated with magnitude and increasing growth; movement up and right suggests growth through time.

10. *Descending vertical:* crushing weight or power, heaviness, danger, loss, doom, death, destruction, declines of all types. Observe the way this characteristic has been employed by Käthe Kollwitz (Fig. 11.11); also review Figure 10.8.

11. *Diagonal:* movement, fear, danger, stress, conflict if counterpointed with opposing angles. A hand moves diagonally to strike us, torrential rains come diagonally, and all things that depart from their verticality (a stable position) fall. Falling things are threatening.

Even though our preference for left-to-right, top-to-bottom movements is largely a cultural manifestation, it resists change or redirection. Producing move-

11.11 Käthe Kollwitz. *Memorial to Karl Liebknecht.* 1919. Woodcut. Compare this print to Figure 11.3. What components are similar? Which ones are different? Note the descending movement and the distribution of "darkness."

ments in static pictorial fields counter to these is not easy; it may be impossible if we do not know the right thing to do. On the other hand, there is no reason not to take advantage of this inherent tendency; no one has, as yet, exhausted the possibilities.

In a communication, the expected order may be essential to permit information to be grasped readily. Differing orientations are likely to prove irritating and distracting. Coupling to biases, cultural or otherwise, anticipates the viewer's expectations, and uses them to advantage: to support a message, to establish an appropriate mood, or to supply a context for any form of presentation. Sequences in natural order or in unnatural order possess affective (emotional) characteristics consistent with such understandings as we have already learned.

The distinctive qualities of edges

All artists should learn to sensitize themselves to

the qualities of edges. Too often figure-objects in works of beginning artists look like cardboard cutouts. Such hard-edged, closed shapes are compatible with decorative design, stylization, and formal types of nonobjective work, but not with naturalism or realism. Nor are hard edges necessarily appropriate to abstraction or to expressionistic works. Failing to give adequate consideration to an edge is like throwing away half of one's art supplies; it is not a rational thing to do without a lot of very careful thought.

The meanings of soft edges (a symbol of things that yield easily to weight or pressure, of luxurious velvet, clouds, a baby's skin, or of roundness and movement) together with their opposite, the hard unyielding edge (the razor-sharp cutting edge, the architectural stud, and the geometric form) give to any artist a range of emotion and mood on which to play, as with a musical instrument: sweetness or bitter stridency, passion or cold detachment, merriment or deep

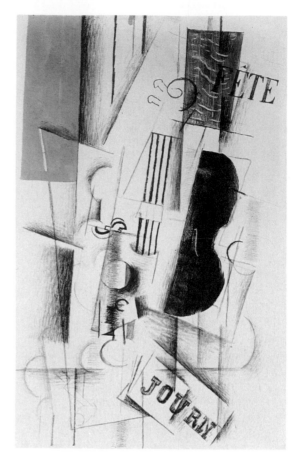

11.12 Georges Braque. *Musical Forms.* 1913. Oil, pencil and charcoal on canvas; 36¼ × 23½″ (92 × 60 cm). Philadelphia Museum of Art. Louise and Walter Arensberg Collection. Hard-edged shapes dominate this work. Braque has softened the severity with coarse textures and forced edges that suggest surface modeling. Mostly positive connotations are evoked; but what kind of emotional response is produced? Is it warm or cold, involving or detached, lifelike or mechanical?

gloom—whatever is in mind; whatever a concept demands.

Hard edges

Hard edges advance. They have these associational meanings:

1. Flat design, decoration.

2. Spatial distinction: clear separation of figure and ground.

3. Explicit, lucid, or clear images.

4. Industry, machines.

5. Sharp edge like a knife or a shirt collar.

6. Sharp corner like a box.

The emotional, conceptual, or intellectual implications of hard edges are pragmatism (practicality), realist attitude (especially a hard or bitter one), businesslike efficiency, mechanical action; and all the positive and negative associations with the words *sharp* and *hard*.

The painting (Fig. 11.12) is one example of a work with hard edges.

Soft edges

Soft edges are at the opposite end of the scale. They normally recede. They have these associational meanings:

1. Softness in feel or texture, luxury; soft focus, fuzziness.

2. Distance: atmospheric contaminants like snow, rain, fog, smoke: translucency.

3. Roundness.

4. Inferred motion.

5. Life: living creatures or beings.

The emotional, conceptual, and intellectual implications of soft edges are romanticism, allusiveness, indication, expressiveness, emotionalism, fantasy, dreamlike states, improvidence (wastefulness, negligence), shiftlessness, and unreliability. Soft edges may

induce emotions of suspense and fear because they reduce the clarity of vision, a quality we prize very highly.

The photograph (Fig. 11.13) is one example of a work with soft edges.

Intermediary edges

When edges are intermediary between the two extremes, they drift toward neutrality. However, the viewer response would be relative, determined by the contrast with other edges in the same visual field and by the context in which they appear. A gradation of intermediary edges, from very hard to very soft, could help to establish spatial relationships, and it could also be used to create a transformation from a lack of clarity to sharp focus.

Lost and found edges

Lost and found edges are characteristic of figure-ground melds, of open shapes, not closed ones. They have these associational meanings:

1. Unity and unification.

2. Variety.

3. Puzzle.

The emotional, conceptual, and intellectual implications are naturalism (like nature), intrigue, mystery, danger, hesitancy, indecisiveness, and camouflage (cloaked, covered, hidden). Take another look at Figure 4.42.

Line meanings

Never forget that contours are lines and that the path of a moving object or a moving eye creates lines of movement. Depending on how lines are used and in what form, meanings may reinforce the affective responses of other visual components to produce an effective result. Please refer to Figure 11.14 as we go through the following list.

1. **Verticals** express a mood of dignity, austerity, and stability. Weighted lines suggest grandeur and strength. Heavy lines are inherently masculine

11.14 Line meanings. Always keep in mind that *contours are lines* and that there are *lines of movement*. Thus, these characteristics of lines are not only applicable to linear works, like pen and ink drawings, but to **every** type of painting, illustration, or design.

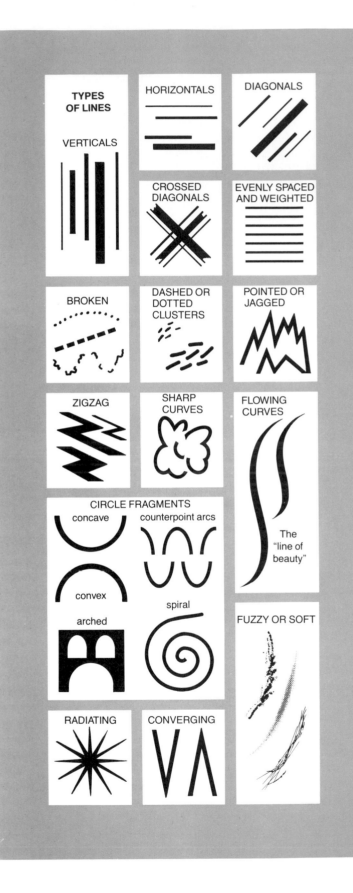

11.15 Pablo Picasso. *Woman Weeping.* 1937. Oil on canvas, 24 × 19" (60 × 49 cm.). Tate Gallery, London. Reproduced courtesy of the Trustees. Though this is a painting (a tonal work), its linear quality is very strong. Note how the nervous, jagged lines contribute to the emotional effect. How do the perspective distortions and image fractionalization contribute to communication in this case?

(stereotype). They express our commonly understood resistance to gravity.

2. **Horizontals** suggest rest, peaceful moods, reclining or leveling positions such as a sleeping figure or a landscape. They imply vast space: open fields, expanses of water. Given an appropriate visual image, horizontals may also suggest speed and momentum.

3. **Diagonal or oblique lines** are inherently unstable. A powerful sensation of movement is created in whatever direction a line inclines. We "know" anything tipped at a diagonal cannot long stand. Attributes are energy, violence, instability, fear, oppression.

4. **Crossed diagonals** suggest conflict, opposition, a battle or contention, especially if heavy or weighted. A diagonal network may suggest support (reinforcement) or impenetrability, denial of access (like a fence), hence prohibition or confinement.

5. **Equally spaced and weighted lines,** or repetitive patterns of the same shape and spacing, in any orientation, suggest boredom and monotony. They are perceptually irritating because no meaning can be derived from such visual fields. *See* Figures 1.1, 2.19 **a**, and 4.3.

6. **Broken lines** suggest a mood of nervousness or insecurity; hesitancy and indecisiveness. Dashing, dotting, or otherwise breaking a line of any orientation levels or weakens its response.

7. **Random dots or dashes in clusters** create staccato rhythms against simple grounds, pulsing beats, moods of excitement like twinkling lights or fireworks; draw our attention to their "busy-ness." Tiny and light in visual weight, they establish atmosphere, create "air."

8. **Pointed or jagged lines** like a mountain range or jagged rock formations imply difficult passage. They remind us of the rough edges of something broken or cracked—splintered wood or broken glass. Emotional attributes are harshness, hardness, and brutality.

9. **Zigzag lines** or movements express excitement.

Communicating visually 173

11.16 Aubrey Beardsley. *The Peacock Skirt,* an Illustration from *Salomé* by Oscar Wilde. Note the long "S" curve, single-weight line, organic forms throughout. A much different emotional quality from that seen in Figures 11.3 and 11.4.

11.17 Kurt Wiese. Illustration for *The White Panther* by Theodore J. Waldeck (New York: Viking). Does the soft, fuzzy quality of this dry brush ink drawing add to the poetic quality of the scene?

Dissension, irritation, anger, or electricity are suggested, especially when quite irregular or erratic in character. (See Fig. 11.15.) Sometimes schizophrenia is implied. When horizontal, zigzag lines suggest stealth or evasion.

10. **Sharp curves in short lengths** indicate violent or sudden action, merriment, liveliness, vivacity, or confusion. Seen in the context of rapidly expanding smoke, gas, or clouds, they suggest menace.

11. **Flowing "S" curves** are the so-called lines of beauty. Lazy "S" or vertical "S" shapes suggest sensuality, romance, softness, beauty, grace, continuous flowing action or movement. See Figure 11.16. Inherently feminine (stereotype), the vertical "S" also suggests verdancy, fertility, and growth. Especially long, drawn-out vertical "S" shapes suggest tranquillity, sadness, gloom, or melancholia.

12. **Circle fragments:** *Concavity* suggests containment. It is inviting, protecting, sheltering. Less confining than concentricity, it nevertheless shares similar attributes. *Convexity* opposes concavity and concentricity; it expands, repels, and releases. *Counterpoint convex and concave arcs* imply alternating motion, waves, dancing figures, muscular action — life. It is tension — advancing or progressing, followed by relaxation, receding (or recession). *Arches*, especially when rhythmically repeated, suggest strength, support, harmony, buoyancy, spiritual contemplation. *Spirals* are one of the fundamental rhythms of nature, seen in whirlpools, currents — in all types of atmospheric movements, as well as in patterns of growth — seashells and flowers. Wound tight, like a coiled spring, spirals suggest tension and stored energy; falling loosely wide open, spent energy or dissolution.

13. **Radiating lines** are symbolized by rays from the sun — radiant energy that bathes us in light and warmth. Such lines have the quality of spirituality, but the form also suggests divergence, branching, dispersion, repulsion, and explosive disintegration, and — like a net swung over us — entrapment and confinement.

14. **Converging lines,** the arrowhead shape, generally take their affective emotional responses from the apex or point where the lines join because the visual weight is somewhat stronger there. We will call this tendency "inherent." However, that can be easily reversed (inverted) by careful distributions of visual weight.

Lines that appear to converge (like vanishing point perspective, capital *A*'s) imply space and distance. Inherently pointing up and out, they suggest motion away from the viewer (like convex forms), rejection, and repulsion. If the tip is clearly vertical and weighted, the affects of upward movements are recalled.

Lines that appear to diverge like a *V* open up, expand, and lift, give rise to attributes of freedom, lightness, and growth as long as movement appears to be up and out. When movement is seen to be inward and down, with weight on the point, this form may take on all the negative attributes of downward movements.

Lines that sharply change character or direction suggest energy and dynamism, assuming that the line is long enough to have clearly established strength of movement in one direction before the change occurs. A line that deviates from absolute frontality suggests volume and space. Michelangelo has been credited with the discovery that living creatures have a serpentine rhythmic motion to their limbs. To give the quality of life to his figures, Michelangelo emphasized this rhythm by first accenting one side of the limbs and then the other (counterpoint arcs). Try this technique.

The qualities of lines may be leveled by making them soft and fuzzy, which tends to reduce their contrast; or sharpened by making them harder, sharper, crisper with increased luminance contrast. They may be leveled by making them thinner and of uniform width; or sharpened by giving them variation: weighting the line. Soft, fuzzy lines are often considered more expressive; they may confer a poetic quality on images (Fig. 11.17), intensify feminine characteristics (stereotype), or make masculine characteristics impotent. Vertically oriented, soft lines accent solemnity; horizontal ones accent tranquillity.

Lines are artistic conventions

Most lines we have been discussing are artistic conventions and do not actually exist. A contour is the edge of a volume as seen against a ground. Though there are some linear elements in the natural environment, such as tree branches, plant stems, and manufactured objects like railroad tracks, girders, and wire, most real figure-objects are masses, with length, width, and girth.

11.18 Lester Beall. *Untitled,* ca. 1952. Ink. The *weighted line* is a line that varies in thickness or in grayness throughout its length. Beall's drawing is very gestural, almost abstract. It is calligraphic, like writing, and simplified almost to the point of a pictogram. Does it suggest not only a vigorous artist but also a vigorous woman?

The line as "sign" goes back to the first mark humans placed on a surface. **It has inherent two-dimensionality as a connection between two points on a 2-D surface.** It takes creative intelligence and a lot of knowledge to give it substance and form and ultimately to confer on it the qualities of expression and communication.

Because lines are perceptual contours, they possess the quality of containment. Configurations bounded by lines are perceived to be parts of a whole. Like lead channels in a stained-glass window, even the most disparate colors or shapes will be seen to be "tied together" when bounded by a line that is perceived to be edge of figure and edge of ground simultaneously. Caution: Be wary of using this device to solve visual problems. When we feel impelled to surround something with a circle or box, it is often an indication of a fundamental failure in the design itself. A design should be so well integrated that it holds together as a unit and needs no outside crutch to support it. A circle or a box is not an easy alternative to other unifying procedures, nor will it ever rescue a

poor design — the problem is only compounded. A border demands at least several very good, sound reasons for its use.

Weighted lines and heavy lines

A *weighted line* is one that varies throughout its length; in other words, it changes from light (thin, gray) to heavy (thick, black). A sequence of weighted lines, from light to heavy, when used in natural order may establish strong spatial relationships (see Fig. 11.18; also Figs. 8.33 and 8.34). When superimposed on any type of line it adds variety and life — organic qualities of living things, of growth, of variegation, and of change. Weighting a line may be used as a sharpening procedure to suggest expressiveness, boldness, forcefulness, tension, roughness, immaturity, crudity, a lack of culture and refinement (when coarse), or, conversely, an indication of culture and refinement (when transitions are smooth and precise). Evaluate these qualities in Roman style (thick and thin stroke) of type styles (see Fig. 11.19). Note how the affective

Soft

love

PASSION

Elegance

OLD

Responsible

BRIGHT

reliable

abnormal

Graciousness

silver

Mechanics

COLORFUL

Nostalgia

fantastic

IMAGE

DiMiNiSH

PRESTIGE

WINTER

character in the line qualities of type styles may be used effectively to convey meaning.

A *heavy line* is one that is very thick and bold, many times the thickness of a single pen stroke but one always understood to be close to, or exactly of, a single width throughout. Superimposed on any type of line, a heaviness sharpens them, makes them hard, mechanical, unyielding, and unfeeling, indicating insensitivity and repulsion. Such lines are also strong, masculine (stereotype), bolstering, and suggestive of durability. Heavy lines, like channels in stained-glass works, isolate one figure from another and tend to flatten space. Evaluate these qualities in Gothic (single stroke, nonserif) type styles.

Thinning a line sharpens its delicacy and refinement, but it may also simply indicate weakness and instability. Applied artists must use caution when employing relatively thin lines in a design as they often drop out (disappear) or break up when reproduced.

Use the knowledge just acquired to evaluate all the line illustrations in this chapter.

11.19 Choice of type has almost as much effect on communication as choice of words. Here are some type choices made by art directors for their advertising headlines. Note how the affective responses associated with the linear qualities of each type style conform to or match the subjective emotional responses appropriate to that particular word or idea.

11.20 *One must learn to get by the obvious.* Dealing literally with a square, a circle, and so on, is only a small concern. The larger picture emerges when we consider these shapes as a means of composition. Whether literally closed or perceptually "closed," basic geometric forms exhibit affective characteristics that can be profitably employed as a basis for the overall shape of the basic mass in any design or composition.

Stereotypes

We possess stereotypical impressions of almost everything we have ever seen, not just ones related to sex. Making stereotypes (generic models or paradigms), remember, appears to be a fundamental characteristic of the manner in which our brain processes and stores sensory data. It is counterproductive to try to change this process. We should sensitize ourselves so that we will not be caught unaware of our own storehouse of stereotypes (generic models), which establish prejudicial points of view. It is said that lawyers do not trust men who wear bow ties. Obviously, there is something going on in this case. The question is how did the stereotype come about, and what are its implications? What reasons could be proposed?

Stereotypes eliminate sensitivity in observation and variety in graphic expression. In other words, they are deadly to artistic vision. Stereotypes should be clearly recognized for what they are. If we clearly understand and evaluate their positive and negative attributes, then stereotypes may be profitably employed as elements of communication and expression. Making stereotypes is a leveling procedure (a simplification), and departing from a stereotype is a sharpening procedure (increasing contrast in either or both concept and detail). Can one depart from a stereotype and still simplify? Of course. One simplifies conceptually by selectively eliminating nonessential details—details not relevant to the expression or communication—not by randomly dropping out ordinary descriptive details of a shape as in Figure 2.15.

Eliminating descriptive details of shape or form

(stereotyping) may not be simplification, only simple-minded. The creative artist always knows which is which.

Meanings of closed geometric shapes

Closed geometric shapes (Fig. 11.20) have the following alternative meanings:

1. **The square:** symbolizes the "four corners" of the earth; the "four elements"—earth, air, fire, and water; the number four; construction; solidity; solidarity; firmness; or correctness or conformity.

2. **The triangle with one face horizontal:** the most stable of all shapes, symbolizes strength, permanency, longevity, communication between heaven and earth, *or sight or insight.*

3. **The triangle sitting on one point:** the most unstable shape; symbolizes dynamism, implied movement, or scintillation (a spark or flash) therefore light. *Note:* triangles take on qualities of converging or diverging lines and possess other qualities not necessarily related to specific orientation such as the Trinity; the number three and all of its mystical associations; or a situation in which two persons are in love with a third.

4. **The circle:** symbolizes perfection; completeness; unity; and well-being; but also confinement. It is the ultimate equilibrium.

5 & 6. **The "star" shape, regular or irregular:** symbolizes excitement; attention or significance; general qualities similar to radiating lines.

A geometric construction represents that shape's

ultimate sharpened form. It may be strengthened or reinforced by manipulating characteristics of visual weight. Leveling is possible by breaking up the form, either the contour or the internal coherency; by altering (reducing) contrast; by rounding pointed corners, by squaring round corners; or by destroying the rigid geometry of the line, that is, giving free expression to the line: wavering, dotting, or weighting.

When line configurations or basic geometric forms are used as basic structures for composition, some of their attributes are inevitably transferred to the work's meaning or message. If meanings compete, ambiguous results are obtained, and the total effect of the work is diminished. If meanings reinforce one another, effectiveness is enhanced.

Combinations of line and shape affect the meanings of all sorts of figures or objects, including letterforms. Type or lettering used in conjunction with layout or design should leave a subliminal impression consistent with the subject matter. **Good type supports the message; it does not get in the way.**

Spatial meanings

The emotional characteristics of any visual field are related to the perceived perimeters. Outside, in a broad, open space, we may feel free and liberated or lonely and lost, depending on our state of mind and other visual cues that may be present. A visual field that reveals to us that we are in a confined space, like a small room, for example, may impress us as stifling, imprisoning, confining sometimes to the point of panic; or it may seem safe, secure, and comforting. These attributes, associated with natural visual fields, are transferred virtually intact to pictorial fields. A large figure-object in a small frame may appear confined and cramped or may be perceived as an economical use of space, of concentration, or of focusing attention. It may imply conservatism and restraint. A small figure in a large picture frame will produce exactly the opposite reactions. It may appear open and free, luxurious (in the "wasting" of space), or simply wasteful, libertine, diffuse, and uninteresting. Obviously, other factors will help to move our reactions to the stimulus toward a more specific response, one that should be specifically controlled by the artist. (Refer to Figs. 2.21, 2.22, 3.9, and 3.28.)

One advertiser of merchandise may find a layout with a great deal of white space incredibly extravagant and wasteful because every square inch is expensive to reproduce whether something is printed on it everywhere or not; however, one promoting an expensive luxury item may view the same amount of white space as reflective of the product's worth and status. These differing responses reflect a difference in worth placed on the utility of space. Such concerns are appropriate to fine art as well as to advertising layout.

In a portrait, more "air," that is, space, must be placed on the side that the subject faces; otherwise, feelings of anxiety are planted in the viewer's mind. Why? If the edge of the picture frame is closer to a person's face than the edge of the frame behind, it is claustrophobic and associated with having something thrust into our face; it is irritating at best, frightening at worst. The confining closeness provides no air for breathing, and personal space has been invaded.

When illustrating a speeding vehicle or object, more space must be placed behind the figure rather than in front. Why? If there were more space in front, would that suggest that the vehicle was not traveling very fast? Remember, we make judgments of speed based on how fast the object transverses our visual field. If, when we first see it, it is already about to escape our visual field, it must be traveling very fast indeed. The illusion of speed may sometimes be enhanced by permitting the object actually to leave the confines of the picture frame or to be observed in that process (Fig. 11.21).

Review the entire discussion of balance and orientation found in Chapter 6. Our emotional reactions (a viewer's reactions) to spatial positions, both position and attitude, reflect the same emotional responses as experienced in actual situations transposed to the pictorial field. Examine Figure 11.22.

The affective responses associated with color will be reviewed in Chapter 18.

Summary

Inherently opportunistic, natural selection has provided us with a variety of sensory cues with which we evaluate our environment. Our survival instinct has taught us to be ever ready for fight or flight. Our response to this type of sensory stimulus produces hormonal changes designed to cause us to spring into action. Initial responses to all sensory data are intuitive and emotional.

Intuition must be educated and refined to enable the desired results to be produced. Anyone can improve their intuitive powers. Intuition is a deep-rooted, subconscious response to any specific stimuli that is produced by the sum total of each person's life experiences up to that point. Scientists do not fully understand how it works; like perception, there are some elements of genetic memory, but it is not magic. It is the brain's shortcut to action—fight or flight—even though all the data have not yet been intellectually analyzed in full. It is our capacity to make *inferences* from incomplete data. It is a kind of sixth sense that helps prevent us from waiting too long to respond to life-threatening situations. If we are willing to educate our intuition, it can also become a

11.21 Jayme Odgers and April Greiman. Poster for the Los Angeles summer Olympic Games, 1984. In this two-dimensional outdoor poster, how fast is the runner traveling that enables him to *escape the bounds of the picture frame*?

180   The anatomy of meaning

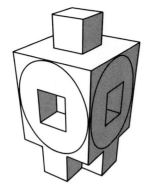 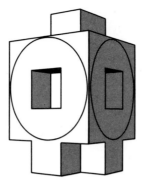 

11.22 **a** *High eye level.* Bird's-eye or omniscient point of view: airborne or "floating," noncommittal or "standoffish," detached, uninvolved, of superior attitude, God-like, spying, or surveilling. *Viewer:* important, large, or high. *Subject:* insignificant, small, or faraway.

b *Eye level.* Normal point of view: correct, easy, natural, right, ordinary, on-the-level, conventional, intimate. *Viewer* and *subject* are on equal terms.

c *Low eye level.* Worm's-eye point of view: danger, fear, in hiding, concealment, sinking, decline, depressed, low esteem, subordinate, and subservient. *Viewer:* insignificant, small, or underneath. *Subject:* important, large, or overhead; also, rising, therefore light in weight or very powerful. Review ascending and descending movement in text.

remarkable creative tool.

Visual cues in pictures stimulate audiences to respond emotionally in the arts (painting, printmaking, theater, film, television), education, entertainment, public relations, marketing, and advertising. Affective responses establish the emotional context (mood) appropriate to any given message.

Knowledgeable prior planning and programming of a composition, design, or advertising layout can move a viewer or an audience through a prescribed visual pattern toward predictable emotional responses.

Remember that the visual language was the first language.

How can we say it visually?

Just a few things to think about:

How can we say "small" visually? (Reference, Fig. 3.28)

How can we say "relative worth" visually? (Fig. 3.30)

How can we say "stress" visually? (Fig. 4.38)

How can we say "pain" visually? (Fig. 6.2)

How can we say "rescue is doubtful" visually? (Fig. 6.30)

How can we say "robotics" visually? (Fig. 9.24)

How can we say "blind" visually? (Fig. 10.5)

How can we say "oppression" visually? (Fig. 10.8)

How can we say "sound" visually? (Fig. 11.9)

Study lists

Types of movements	Types of lines
ascending vertical	broken lines
cascading	circle fragments
converging (centripetal)	arches
descending vertical	concave arcs
diagonal	convex arcs
horizontal	counterpoint arcs
interrupted progression	spirals
inward spiral	converging lines
pendulum	crossed diagonals
revolving	diagonal or oblique
spreading (centrifugal)	equally spaced and weighted
spreading/radiating	flowing *S* curves
	horizontals
	pointed or jagged
	radiating lines
	random dots/dashes in clusters
	sharp curves in short lengths
	verticals
	zigzag

Review of key terms

affect To influence or bring about a change in. To touch or to move the emotions. Also, a strong feeling that has active consequences.

emotion Any strong, generalized feeling; subjective responses such as love, hate, or fear that involve physiological changes as a preparation for action.

expressionism A type of artwork in which the artist permits his or her emotions to dominate the character of the color, structure, and imagery (if any). As this is a highly personal, subjective experience, the communication aspects of the art may be sacrificed totally or subordinated to such "expression." There are two types: *figurative expressionism,* sometimes called "German expressionism," in which representational forms are subordinated to the artist's aesthetical motives; and *abstract expressionism,* a development of the 1950s, which is nonobjective in character.

feminine (stereotype). Qualities commonly associated with the feminine gender — beauty, softness, sensuality, romance, weakness, hesitancy, indecisiveness, and so on; also those qualities when attributed to other figure-objects: flowers, for instance, or type styles. *See* **masculine; stereotype.** *Note:* Mixing perceptions of gender characteristics (masculine/feminine) can produce a girl/woman who is a tomboy, a feminist, or a business-woman, for example; or a boy/man who is sensitive, aesthetic, an artist, or a Don Juan. Pushed to extremes, mixtures transmit meanings of homosexuality to the viewer.

intuition A deep-rooted, subconscious response to any specific stimulus that is produced by the sum total of each person's life experiences up to that point, including instinctive responses like emotions (genetic components). Also, a capacity to make inferences from incomplete or missing data. Contrary to popular belief, our intuitive faculties draw on all assimilated knowledge and, therefore, can be developed and enhanced.

line Theoretically, a closely spaced series of points; a continuous mark made by a pen, pencil, brush, or other writing or drawing instrument. Also, any conceptual, intellectual, or theoretical correspondence to this figure. There are lines of vision, lines of motion or movement, contour lines, and so on.

masculine (stereotype). Qualities usually attributed to the male gender — strong, forceful, muscular, bold, hard, mechanical, cold, insensitive. Also, similar qualities as applied to figure-objects like machines or type styles. *See* **feminine.**

objective Based on knowledge; factually presented without influence of, or regard to, emotions, supposition, or personal prejudice. Also, things viewed dispassionately; the opposite of *subjective.*

perceptual imperative An autonomic psychophysical drive to find meaning in every visual field, or, more broadly, to derive meaning from all sensory data.

stereotype A vastly oversimplified model, concept, opinion, or belief in which things typify or conform in an unvarying manner and without individuality.

subjective Existing only in the mind of the person having the experience; therefore, not possible to confirm scientifically. Also, an individual personal experience or response not necessarily like, or even similar to, those of any other person; the expression in the arts of any such experience, response, or attitude; the opposite of *objective.*

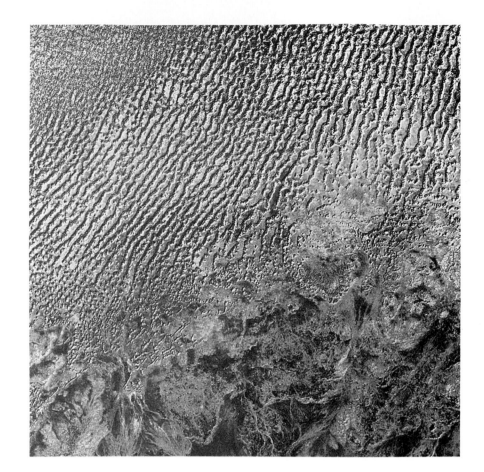

CHAPTER TWELVE

Expanding the mind

Connections of the broad kind

Connections of the broad kind associate one sense or mode with another, one profession with another, one society with another, the earth with the universe, the finite with the infinite. Broad connections sharpen our art by giving it transfusions of the blood of life from sources outside ourselves, outside our social circle, our country, and outside of the arts.

If I am a man, a connection is knowing and feeling how a woman feels; if I am a white Caucasian, it is knowing and feeling like a black person; if I am a Republican, it is knowing and feeling like a Democrat; if I am a citizen of the United States, it is knowing and feeling like an Iranian.

It is knowing and feeling *the likenesses* as well as the differences among things: apples and oranges, pine trees and cypress trees, leaf cells and body cells, the animate and inanimate.

The raw materials of the arts are these *cross-modalities.*

One thing, one concept, one mode fertilizes another; gives birth to a new hybrid; sharpens; produces unified or cohesive structures from apparently incompatible elements; synthesizes disparities; creates similarities from dissimilar figures, objects, and ideas.

The more narrowly we perceive our field, the greater the difficulty of finding success within it.

Nothing in the arts stands in isolation from anything else. We are always interconnected in every

12.1 *Geopic*™ Courtesy Earth Satellite Corporation. An abstract painting? No, a "maxiworld"; a snapshot of our planet from a satellite. Computers re-create and color the images broadcast back to earth in the form of electrical signals. This is a view of our universe that few persons will ever be privileged to see except through photographic means.

183

12.2 A marijuana monster. Tiny spider mites are frequent visitors on the leaves of marijuana plants. This mite is unable to leave. It has become stuck to one of the leaf's resin nodules, which contain the plant's hallucinogenic chemicals. Magnification: × 600. This is a "microworld," one revealed to us only by using instruments that extend our limited vision. Around us, all of the time — every moment of our lives — are images of things we fail to see either because the mind is blind (we do not critically observe) or because the biological construction of our eyes makes them physically blind to such events! Keep this in mind: Our eyes are our primary information-gathering system.

phase of expression or activity. To the question "What else do I need to know?" the artist must reply, "Everything!"

Getting in touch

If we wish to advance beyond the most elementary accomplishments, we must have an awareness of, and couple with, as many connections as is humanly possible to do, connections both narrow and broad.

Figures 12.1 and 12.2 contrast two broad connections, the living earth with a living creature, a contrast of the very large with the very small: sights ordinarily beyond the limits of the naked eye — but not beyond technology imagined by the human mind, a synectic mind.

We have to know what is going on in the political arena; we have to know what is going on in psychology, what is going on in science, whether that is physics, chemistry, genetics, or social science; we have to know what is going on in absolutely every existing field. That is because something in one of these fields may be exactly the one thing we need to solve the visual problem we are dealing with — right now. It may be that thing that will separate us from the pack. That is the name of the game — synectic thinking.

Developing fresh and unusual solutions to visual problems that command attention is the name of the game.

We have to become voracious readers; we have to see everything; we have to read everything. We do not have to become a physicist in order to know what is generally going on in that field. We can scan the reports. We don't have to become a fashion designer to know what colors and characteristics of style are appropriate this year. We can scan reports. We do not have to compromise our own personal aesthetics to be aware of and to appreciate works of art that differ in all respects from our own, whether these are created by our culture, foreign cultures, or cultures long vanished from the face of the earth. Perhaps it should be soberly realized that crossing the bar into history is the inevitable fate of all cultures, past and present and future. It will be true of our own. Immortality is a mark on a surface.

Whether a manager of a corporation (president, for example), the manager of genetic research program, or the manager of line, color, and shape on a two-dimensional surface; intelligent managers know that it is not possible for the brain to retain every bit of data required for superior performance. They may try even though memory is imperfect. That is a limiting concept.

12.3 Images, Julius Friedman (Designer) and Joe Boone (Photographer). © 1982 Julius Friedman. For the Art Center Association. How does a plate of worms appeal to a person? What are the symbolic and psychological implications? How have the artists combined dissimilar concepts — made connections — to produce a compelling, fresh image?

12.4 Piere Brauchli. *Babylon Today.* Poster. The artist combines the image of a modern nuclear energy plant's cooling tower with Peter Brueghel's 1563 painting, *The Tower of Babel.* Think about the inferences — connections between millennia past and the nuclear age!

Intelligent and creative managers remember fundamental concepts (an overview) and the context in which that information resides, so that they may quickly locate any specific detail or quantity of detail when they need it. That is a broad concept. Preplanning, research, and testing (experimentation) are not inhibitors to creative work. As in any other human endeavor, they represent a straight path toward viable solutions to problems. Achievement, though, usually depends on inserting an incubation period, during which the brain is allowed to associate freely, transpose, and reorganize the data — to "fool around."

Fooling around allows the brain to make inferences. For the artist, this often means fooling around visually, with thumbnail sketches, brainstorming, and the like. Though visual problems are best solved visually, it is not the hand that exercises control.

Creativity is a product of the mind. It depends on knowledge, skill, and motivation. Creativity's operating mechanism is "sweat."

Synectic thinking

Most creative work in this world is due to the perception of the similarity of dissimilars as Aristotle observed long ago — to innovation and synthesis, to synectic thinking. The term *synectic* implies the merg-

12.5 James E. Loyless. *Vertigo.* 1987. Computer graphic image created by fractal geometry. Dot matrix printer (24-pin) on white paper, 8 × 8″ (20.32 × 20.32 cm). Courtesy the artist. Fractal geometry, an element in the chaos theory — a new variety of mathematics, has been used to control a computer image derived from a Mendelbrot set. It is another example of design by process.

12.6 Michael Heizer. *Complex One City, Central Eastern Nevada.* 1972. Cement, steel, earth, 23½′ × 110′ × 140′ (7 × 34 × 43 m). Courtesy M. Knoedler & Co. Heizer said that *Complex One City* was the art of the Atomic Age; it was designed to survive a blast that would blow away everything else. Like Oriental gardens (Fig. 1.10), earthworks and environmental works are for contemplation. They involve connections of all sorts.

ing of different and incompatible things into cohesive and unified forms or structure.

Was the wheel invented by some Middle Eastern person who observed that a person slipped and slid around when walking on rounded stones? Native Americans, who are supposed to have come here by crossing the Bering Sea land bridge some 30,000 years ago, never invented the wheel although they used circles in their art, crafts, toys, and they used circularly shaped implements.

There is a story that James Watt observed that the pressure of steam from boiling water raised the lid of his mother's teakettle. He did not see a common household event as thousands of persons had seen before him, but a new source of abundant power — a source of power that brought about the industrial revolution.

Pablo Picasso saw in African art a powerful artistic expression that collided squarely with his own. A completely new vocabulary for the visual language

emerged from his fooling around with its superficial characteristics (Fig. 12.7). While those early cubist works have little intrinsic worth, they are significant visual evidence of an uncommon event. They permit us to be witnesses of an amazing process of transformation and synthesis (Figs. 12.8 and 12.9) — a creative mind at work — a synectic mind.

In each of these events, *chance* probably played a significant role. Louis Pasteur said that chance serves only the prepared mind.

One of the foremost designer-illustrators, Milton Glaser, advises young designers:

The best designers I know have a very broad cultural understanding, besides just outstanding techniques. You have to know the history of visual phenomena; you have to know something about psychology, semiology and so on, in order to be really first class in this profession. And by that I don't mean making a lot of money doing something well — like working for a record company and

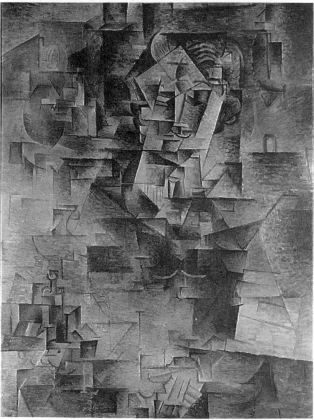

above left: **12.7** Pablo Picasso. *Mother and Child.* 1907. Oil on canvas, 31⅞ × 23⅝″ (81 × 60 cm). Musée Picasso, Paris. Picasso's fascination with the superficial characteristics of African art led him to "fool around" with its forms. So long as he tied himself to these, the works seldom seemed to be going anywhere.

above: **12.8** Pablo Picasso. *Fan, Saltbox, Melon.* 1909. Oil on canvas, 32 × 25″ (81 × 63.5 cm). The Cleveland Museum of Art. Leonard C. Hanna, Jr., Fund. Once Picasso understood that the emphasis in African art was on form, not imitation of nature, he began to apply such concepts to his paintings rather than copy the external shapes of African Art. This flash of insight produced works like *Fan, Saltbox, Melon.* It was a new visual language for Western culture!

left: **12.9** Pablo Picasso. *Portrait of David-Henri Kahnweiler.* 1910. Oil on canvas, 39⅝ × 25⅝″ (100 × 73 cm). The Art Institute of Chicago. Gift of Mrs. Gilbert W. Chapman in memory of Charles B. Goodspeed. Within a year, cubism emerged full-blown—one of the most influential art forms of the 20th century.

doing a lot of record covers. To be really good you have to be very smart and you have to be very purposeful.

You have to know a tremendous amount, not just whether something should be set ten point or twelve point type. The more education and the more background you have in the world in general, the better off you'll be.[18]

Sources for information acquisition

If we know what to look for, the daily newspaper is a treasure chest. One example is the cover of a section on weddings in which the designer has used Art Deco motifs — not design of the 1920s or 1930s, but contemporary design. More styles are revived in variations than are created new. High style furniture has Art Deco influences at the moment these words are written. Tomorrow?

On the fashion page of another paper is an article "Spice Up Spring with Colors and Patterns," which describes current trends in women's and men's clothing. If a male illustrator is going to do a layout with women in the composition, he has to know what is going on. It is not an option but a vital necessity. Persons in an illustration must be clothed in fashions that look like what people are currently wearing, not stereotypes derived from what we think they are wearing. It is no different from tackling a historical project, whether illustration or fine art mural, where we have

to research the nature of costumes worn at that time in that place. Current fashions are contemporary history.

If we wish to do contemporary advertising, communication, or applied design, we must stay current with contemporary trends. Sometimes we must even project them into the future.

A reader writes a columnist, "Why are the interlocking rings on the Olympic flag black, blue, red, white, and yellow?" The reply states that at least one of these colors appears on every national flag. A small article says different gasses are used to produce colors in neon signs. Argon makes blue, neon is red, helium is yellow, and carbon dioxide makes white. This is important information to know if we wish to create a neon sculpture. Another article reports on a book describing how to select colors for clothing and makeup appropriate to skin, hair, and eye colors. Another, "Hey Big Boy! Marketers Make Heroic Effort to Lasso the Macho Consumer," suggests that advertisers sell products by appealing to traditional working class male stereotypes: symbols like cars, trucks, weapons, physical prowess, sports (especially football), outdoors, and freedom. "Birthday Beatings" reports on a psychological study showing that teenagers unknowingly select humorous birthday cards that offend grandparents who resent fun being made of wrinkles, infirmities, and age. These were just a few articles

clipped over a four-month period, over a dozen in all.

The *Journal of Chemical Education* published a series of articles on the chemistry of art, including light and color and the preparation and properties of artists' colors. *Scientific American* devoted an entire issue to light and vision. *Chemical and Engineering News* prepared a special report on the chemistry of vision. In unlikely places, articles appear almost continually that bear on aspects of the arts. The point being made here is that we will never get the whole story from reading just art magazines or art columns.

There is the library. There is the *morgue,* an artists' picture or clipping file. There is interviewing professional persons. There are trips to museums of every description. To scratch the surface, we have to learn to see, to observe. We have to make an effort!

We must reach out, extend our experiences, extend our mind — make connections.

How do we manage all this? One way is to learn good scanning techniques. Read headlines; read subheads, if those suggest that the material may be beneficial; then read the first sentence or the first couple of lines in each paragraph. The first sentence should tell us the general content of the paragraph. If it is a book or a very long article, first sentences from a half dozen or so paragraphs after each chapter head or subhead should provide a good estimation of its worth. If the work looks promising, read it thoroughly, or set it aside for future reading, or copy it for later reference. We may miss a few nuggets this way, but little of long-term significance will be overlooked, and we can cover ten times more material.

Being prepared

The star of stage or films always is observing how different personalities behave. What does this person or that one do with eyes, with hands, with feet, under any particular circumstance? How does the mouth go, the jaw set, the head toss? This is the material for acting — becoming someone else. It is also the material for illustration and portraiture — depicting someone else. The illustrator and the painter must be actors of vision, setting visual design components to work on a conceptual stage. Guiding figures through their pictorial roles is one of the processes of design.

A good photographer always carries a camera. The shot of a lifetime may appear at any moment as it did for Ansel Adams (Fig. 12.10). As illustrators, designers, or painters, are we ready to take similar advantage of fortuitous circumstances? (Serendipity!) Opportunity does not wait on our convenience, nor does it hang around until we are ready to catch up.

To paraphrase Pasteur, *opportunity* serves only the prepared mind.

If we were asked to draw the outline shape of a flag, right now, what would it look like? What shape

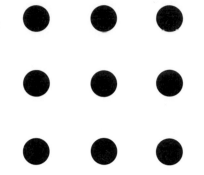

12.11 Problem: without lifting the pencil from the paper, connect all nine dots using no more than four straight lines. No cheating.

would we have drawn? When asked, most everyone draws a simple horizontal rectangle, approximately in a ratio of 3:5.

If that is what we drew, our brain has locked onto a stereotype. Though most national flags today are a plain rectangle, a rich variety of flag shapes have been devised during their long historical development. When we draw a rectangular flag shape, does it show narrow thinking and a lack of creativity—a lack of information? Think about that before looking at the end of this chapter at Figure 12.31 for a diagram of 16 differing flag shapes. True, some of these shapes are used for specific purposes, but we were not asked to draw a specific flag, just a flag shape. Could it have been any shape?

Mental blocks

Take a look at Figure 12.11, an array of nine dots. Solve this puzzle by crossing through all nine dots using no more than four (4) absolutely straight lines. Do not lift the pencil from the paper. Take some time to think seriously about this, and try to solve it before checking the possibilities, which will be found in the notes to this chapter at the back of the book.[19]

The purpose of this example is to demonstrate how most persons have mental blocks. Often these are due to the manner in which our perceptual mechanisms operate. Our perceptions are designed to produce leveled states—to give our world stability and equilibrium. A failure to recognize stereotypes and other forms of perceptual blocking, like constancies, seriously limits creativity. These things limit our capacity to acquire knowledge. They limit flexibility and

understanding. They limit our ability to see scientifically and creatively and to associate dissimilar elements freely.

Understanding perception not only enables us to apply its characteristics profitably but also to avoid being caught in its drawn net, trapped and unable to escape.

Every person who aspires to creative work in any field must be cognizant of how common perceptions restrict thinking and reasoning—the ability to distinguish facts (knowledge) from superstition; to distinguish individuality from symbols and stereotypes; otherwise, the solutions to problems, the answers which we all desperately need, may be staring us in the face, *but we will never see them!*

How pictures began

Pictorial form goes back at least to the early humans who placed marks on the walls of their caves (Fig. 12.12). Such a mark was a *sign*. That sign (mark) on a surface was the first link in an emerging process of communication. It says, "I am here. Recognize my presence." It was purposeful. Depending on where and how the mark was made, it endowed its creator with a certain kind of immortality since its existence sometimes extended beyond the human life span.

Marking or signing appears to be a characteristic of many types of living creatures. Only human beings have taken the mark and built an elaborate structure for its exhibition. This structure not only permitted ritual communications with the gods but also communication with other persons of their own time and place, as well as, unknowingly at first, with future

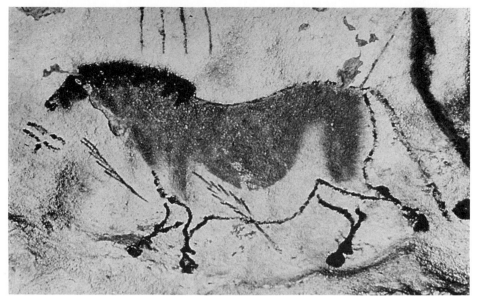

12.12 *Horse Pierced with Arrows*, Paleolithic cave painting. ca. 15,000–10,000 B.C. Approximately life size. Lascaux (Dordogne), France. Immortality is a mark on a surface.

generations. One aspect of the structure developed into an increasingly abstract and symbolic image, a pictograph, which came to represent an idea or a sound and ultimately lead to the written language. Another aspect continued to remain visual — wholly graphic and pictorial.

Art began as a mark of visual communication. Persons were motivated to make pictures from some deep-seated urge not fully understood. The process is repeated every time a writer or an artist touches paper or canvas. The first mark is the sign of the creator's presence.

The written language depended almost wholly on shape and its repetition in prescribed sequences that were eventually called words and sentences (pattern/structure). Picturemaking, like written language, evolved a more elaborate system of visual components necessary for sensory data reception and perception as well as individual expression. Most often these components are listed as follows: line, shape (or form), color, texture, and balance. Sometimes any or all of the following replace balance in the list or are added to expand the concept: contrast, emphasis, interval, orientation, proportion, repetition, rhythm, scale, and so on. When we discuss three-dimensional design, space and material become requisite elements. In the performing arts (theater, ballet, film, and television) and in some contemporary and conceptual art, motion and interval (distance, proportion, and time) are essential.

All these elemental abstract visual components are always organized into a pattern whose purpose, like that of the written language, is to convey a meaning.

Over the centuries, evaluations of the organization of pictorial elements has evolved certain "aesthetic" qualities such as harmony, contrast, rhythm, and unity. Such evaluations inevitably involve the concept of "taste".

Aesthetics is a branch of philosophy that deals chiefly with the nature of beauty (a work's appeal), theoretical standards by which its essential character may be evaluated (a work's form), and its relation to the human intellect (a work's worth). Aesthetics is also the branch of psychology treating the sensations and emotions evoked by all the visual arts.

Taste is the power of discernment and appreciation of fitness, beauty, order, and whatever constitutes excellence especially in fine arts and literature. As taste is culturally determined, the social guidelines by which it is measured are continually redefined.

The nature of pictorial form

The nature of pictorial form is sign together with aesthetic qualities, perceived by the artist, which are recognized and responded to by viewers both intellectually and emotionally. Its dominant characteristic is pattern (structure), and that pattern characteristically employs the principle of domination as a means of organizational integrity.

Like literature, picture making assumes many forms, which slide easily from classification to classification and from style to style. Today artists mix approaches, forms, styles, and techniques as easily as they mix colors. Sometimes it is a matter of form substituting for substance. All too often when anything

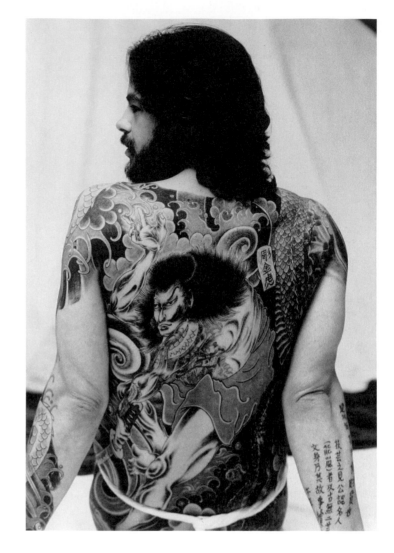

12.13 Tatooed person. Photograph. Here is body decoration of an extreme sort, a direct descendent, however, of a tradition that began long before recorded history. The purposes included beautification (to attract the opposite sex) or to make one more fierce (to frighten enemies). Modern applications include everyday cosmetics as well as theatrical makeup.

appears to be nailed down, it shifts or changes. More likely it is our point of view that changes and evolves. Each era reworks earlier ones in the context of its own.

A glimpse of the richness of diversity

We have no idea when surface decoration began, but studies of the more primitive societies still existing today suggest that it may have started with body decoration designed to enhance the attractiveness of the male for the female, and vice versa. (See Fig. 12.13.) Decoration enhanced the worth of any object to which it was applied. There is ample circumstantial evidence for us to suppose that this was an activity in which all persons in an entire community engaged. The specialization of crafts was a much later social development. This interest in decoration and picture

making appears to be an intrinsic part of the psyche of every single human being. Its expression takes many forms, but few individuals are so intimidated by sophisticated or academic art forms that they are discouraged from participating in picture making of their own.

Virtually every child draws pictures. Perhaps no single home is without its prized "objects of art." What we evaluate as art, however, is often determined by the place where it is viewed. A work intended to be framed and hung in an art museum, in an art gallery, or in a home as an art object is viewed differently from other pictures that lack that *intention*. If there is a gulf between this public and official art circles, perhaps it is because the communication link has been bent. Modern art does not always speak in a language the layperson is able to understand.

above: 12.14 Folk art advertising. The creators of this artwork did not *intend* to create "art." Their work was not intended to be framed and hung on a wall as decoration or in an art gallery. Commonly art philosophers, art historians, artists themselves, and often the general public evaluate artworks by their intended purpose and the *environment in which they are displayed.* In other words, the significance we give to any individual work of art is often related to "place."

above right: 12.15 John Kane. *Self Portrait.* 1929. Oil on canvas over composition board, 36⅛ × 27⅛″ (91.8 × 68.9 cm). Collection, The Museum of Modern Art, New York. Abby Aldrich Rockefeller Fund. Usually considered one of America's best folk (naïve or "primitive") artists, Kane's works exhibit strong formal characteristics. Whether considered unsophisticated or not, *this work is intended to be exhibited for its aesthetic value, and hung on a wall to be perceived as "art."*

Folk art

Picture making by untrained artists we categorize as *folk art,* sometimes, as *naive art.* It was the first art, the art of the common folk, and it is still vigorously expressed today. It ranges from the personal decoration of our homes, from what is sometimes derisively called arts and crafts, to folk art advertising (Fig. 12.14); from Indian art (Fig. 8.8) to kindergarten art; from weather vanes to duck decoys; from discount store wallpaper patterns to framed easel paintings intended to take their place among other paintings in galleries and museums.

John Kane's *Self Portrait* (Fig. 12.15), a stiffly posed, basically symmetrical composition, includes decorative arches above the head, which combine with the inverse arch formed by the arms and clenched fists below to form an architectural parenthesis. It is individual dignity and strength that is portrayed—a personal symbol with internal resemblance as well as the external. It is formal art in the strictest sense.

Using things around us

The directness, simplicity, and innocence of folk art, children's art, and the art of peoples thought to be "primitive" have long attracted sophisticated artists who have tried to capture these characteristics in their work.

In 1912, Pablo Picasso took a commercially printed material with a chair caning pattern and incorporated it into a work (Fig. 12.16). It was the first *collage,* a coined word derived from the French *coller* meaning "to glue" or "paste." This action emphasized the flatness of the work and helped to point out pic-

12.16 Pablo Picasso. *Still Life with Chair Caning.* 1912. Collage, 10½ × 13¾″ (26.67 × 34.92 cm) Musée Picasso, Paris. Picasso changed the language of painting forever with this work in two ways: (1) He emphasized the flat surface and (2) he invented the technique we call *collage* by incorporating a "real" object, a commercially printed imitation chair caning.

opposite: 12.17 Robert Miles Runyan (Designer) and Stan Caplan (Photographer). *17th International Design Conference in Aspen.* Offset Lithograph, 36⅞ × 24⅜″ (93.65 × 61.9 cm). Collection, The Museum of Modern Art, New York. Gift of the designer. The brain erupts in plumes of fire! What a metaphor. Other symbols that enhance communication are the heart (emotion) and the newspaper (language and communication). Are there more?

ture making's essential difference from nature. Picasso also included lettering and eliminated the picture's traditional square corners. These things reinforced his idea and drew the first clear line of demarcation between the picture as an object and the picture as a window. The contemporary technique of combining ordinary items into works of art or presenting them as works of art, melded and transformed physically or conceptually, began there — at that moment.

Making differences

It is the differences in the products of "the arts" art that account for their long existence and their significance to civilization. Artists usually point up differences; they make comparisons between dissimilars, which enhance communication and understanding.

Analogies

An analogy, whether literary or visual, points out that there is a logical correspondence between certain aspects of dissimilar things. The visual comparison between the trunk and branches of a tree, the main channel of a river and its tributaries, and the network of veins and arteries in the human body would be an analogy. As a sensitizing exercise, we could use geometric forms as a basis for exploration of analogy. What forms are inherently circular, for example, or triangular? Which ones radiate from a center point or possess a spiral shape or overlap like fish scales (imbrication) or have a vertebral structure (like a backbone)?

Metaphors

The metaphor is a common technique that has been employed by all types of writers, actors, and visual artists over the centuries. The headline on one pharmaceutical advertisement reads, "Hemorrhoids are a pain in the neck."

Simply stated, a metaphor is a case where qualities of one thing are transferred to, or presented as,

17th
International
Design
Conference
in Aspen
Order
and Disorder
June 18-23

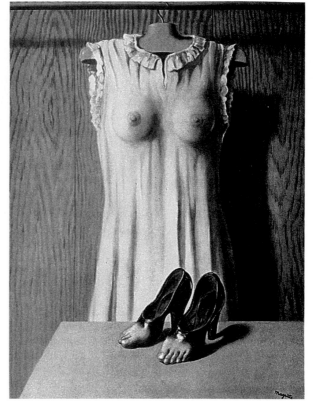

12.18 René Magritte. *Philosophy in the Boudoir.* 1947. Oil on canvas, 31⅞ × 24″ (81 × 61 cm). In this painting, has Magritte violated our perceptual expectations?

characteristic of some other thing; it may not only involve concepts or ideas but figure-objects or physical or physiological systems. The purpose is to explain or to make clearer some point of view or characteristic of dissimilar elements *(leveling)* or, conversely, to point up or emphasize differences between similar elements *(sharpening)*. *The mouth of a river* is a metaphor because rivers do not have mouths, but the term is an easily understood way to indicate the opening or vent through which a river empties into a larger body of water. *Dead end* is also one. *Dead* emphasizes the fact that this *end* limits further progress, whether along a street or along some other type of progress in life. Ends, that is, conclusions, are generally satisfying, logical terminations of events—the end of a sentence, the end of adolescence, the end of the journey. Ends usually provide unlimited possibilities for new beginnings. A dead end emphasizes the negative aspects of termination, the prevention of an exit, an indication of a lack of opportunity, or an impediment to progress.

A visual metaphor expresses these ideas in visual form. Take a look at Figure 12.17.

Paradoxes

A paradox is a contradictory statement, situation, or image that defies logic. Impossible images (Figs. 3.15 and 3.16) are paradoxes. The surrealist artist René Magritte, in particular, has used visual paradox to create stunning images. Shoes do not possess human toes, nor gowns possess human breasts (Fig. 12.18). Such arousing images with their enormous psychological potential have made Magritte perhaps the most imitated artist in modern history. Legions of communication artists have used his ideas as springboards for developing compelling advertising art. Also become aware of how Magritte's ideas have entered the mainstream of contemporary fine art.

Puns

A pun is a humorous or anecdotal metaphor.

Expanding the mind 195

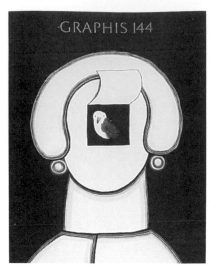

top: **12.19** Josse Goffin. Cover for *Graphis* 144. Reproduced with permission. A "bird brain," a visual pun.

above: **12.20** Milton Glaser. Two clichés combined into one new symbol for the School of Visual Arts, New York.

WILLIAM HOGARTH. *'Gin Lane'*, engraving

62

196 The anatomy of meaning

These are usually based on words that sound alike or
figures of speech that have double meanings. A *visual
pun* is a similar idea presented in graphic form. Consider the humorous possibilities of these presented in
visual form: monkey wrench, boat shoe, jailbird, photo
bug, or bird brain (Fig. 12.19). Try extending this list.

Synthesizing

Milton Glaser combined two clichés, a palette and
a rainbow, into a new symbol (Fig. 12.20). This is a
form of synthesizing, the creation of a new image out
of the combination of two or more existing symbols.
Much of what we do in art is a kind of synthesis,
creating patterns out of chaos. Synthesis involves the
melding or total integration of any two or more representative figures, objects, or concepts.

Satire, ridicule, and humor

Humor in art is very old. Written evidence goes
back at least to the ancient Egyptians although we can
logically assume that it has been a part of our character almost from the beginning of the species. In the
19th century, Honoré Daumier, a great caricaturist,
attacked the French legislature (Fig. 12.21) as well as

French society; and William Hogarth, the evils of
liquor (Fig. 12.22). Today political cartoons grace virtually every newspaper, their importance significant
enough to win Pulitzer prizes.

Anecdotal references in the cubist works of
Picasso and Braque (Figs. 11.12, 12.9, 12.16) found
relationships in the later works created by artists in
the Dada and surrealist movements, who used humor
with telling effect on every conceivable target, as ridicule, as satire, even as pinpricks to deflate the pom-
posity of "art" itself.

One of the best-known comic books, Marvel
Comics, interests many young people in art careers
through adventure strips such as *Kilraven* (Fig. 12.23).
and underground comics like Clay Wilson's *Portfolio*
(Fig. 12.24) rebel against bucolic concepts of beauty
by featuring the ugly and the disgusting. (Remember
the concept of contrast; without ugliness is there any
beauty?) A leader in the pop art movement, Roy Lichtenstein adopted the superficial forms of comic art
(Fig. 12.25) and turned them into monumental paintings.

Amusement and education

If humor can amuse, it can also inform. Messages

12.24 Clay Wilson. *Portfolio*. Art intended to shock, but that will amuse some persons and disgust others.

in the guise of humor are more acceptable to a target audience than the same information clothed in statistical, preachy, academic, or dogmatic forms. People will pay attention to, and better remember, entertaining presentations than those that are in a dry, lecture form. Humorists and cartoonists often turn our eye inward on our soul where we can see ourselves bathed in a revealing light. Humor can teach. It can place important truths in a form that an audience will remember. The cartoons that appear on the frontispieces for each section of this book have something important to say about us as creative persons as well as about humankind in general.

Ridicule is often a stronger weapon than the sword. Satire dares take on those who sit in the seats of power. Humor can bite without hurt; disarm without alienating. Emerson wrote that if we want to rule the world quietly, we must keep it amused.

Sometimes humor pries open minds that are otherwise vacuum-sealed against ideas: the new, the unfamiliar, and the psychologically threatening and unacceptable. It casts the warm sunshine of hope on our day-to-day problems and lifts our spirits when nothing else will serve as balm. Laughter makes the unbearable bearable. For this, the work of humorous writers and artists is often dismissed as lightweight and frivolous. A clown is somehow less than a doctor of medicine.

A Shakespearean tragedy would be seriously diminished without its contrast of humor. Humor is one of our most telling elements of contrast: the light against the dark. The qualities of each are immeasurably sharpened.

Humor is the most serious of all our art forms — it dares to challenge us when we least expect it, when we are least prepared. It does not fear to challenge the powerful leaders of governments, nor is it embarrassed to make a child laugh.

Whether a medium is regarded as a recorder of facts or an art form depends not on the media but on the intention of the artist. The word, the pen, the brush, the computer, and the camera function very well as recorders. In the hands of a creative person, they function equally well as a means of giving expression to ideas. The medium is not the message, except for those persons whose vision runs no deeper than surface gloss.

It is the challenge of imposing concept on form that is the substance of picture making; the medium is a kind of vehicle whose influence over the resulting form is coincidental, one choice—just one—of the enormous variety of choices artists must make in the process of giving birth and substance to an idea.

opposite: **12.25** Roy Lichtenstein. *Whaam!*. 1963. Acrylic on canvas, two panels, 5′6″ × 13′ (1.67 × 3.96 m). The Tate Gallery, London. Reproduced by courtesy of the Trustees. In a style based on cartoon strips, Lichtenstein employs scale (massive size), clichés (overused symbols), and exaggeration to create works filled with energy and dynamism. It is art intended for the art gallery, not the comic book page.

Summary

Some persons march to the beat of a different drummer. R. Buckminster Fuller created a unique map projection that offers an almost distortion-free view of the world's land masses (Fig. 12.26). It was Fuller who invented the geodesic dome, whose architectural possibilities seem to expand continually.

Surrealist Salvador Dali was moved to transform the rigid, metallic substances of which watches are constructed into flowing soft material as a metaphor for *The Persistence of Memory* and the passage of time (Fig. 12.27). Limp watches!

Photographer Jerry Uelsmann synthesizes fragments of the natural world into disarming wholes with skill and with wit (Fig. 12.28).

Illustrator David Wilcox takes off from René

below: **12.26** R. Buckminster Fuller. *Dymaxion Airocean World Map.*™ © 1981 Buckminster Fuller Institute, Los Angeles. All rights reserved. Fuller devised a revolutionary new map projection that provides the most distortion-free view of the earth's land masses yet devised. **Creative vision is not limited to artists.**

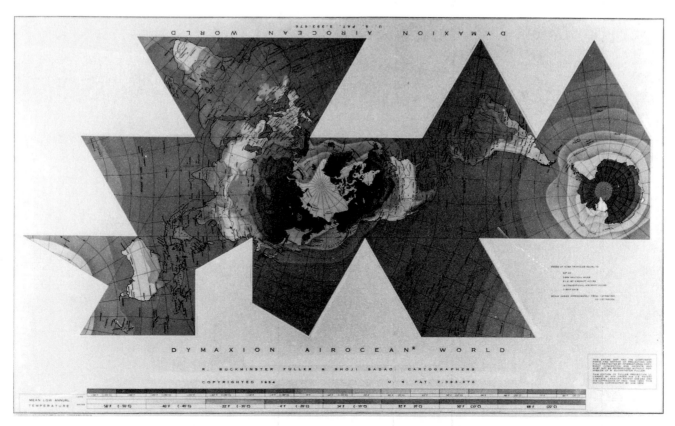

above: **12.27** Salvador Dali. *The Persistence of Memory.* 1931. Oil on canvas, 9'6" × 13' (2.9 × 23.96 m). Collection, The Museum of Modern Art, New York. Anonymous gift. Dali transmuted the hard, metallic substance of watches into a substance that flows and drapes itself over surfaces. Artists were now free to transpose the inherent substances of all things for whatever aesthetic purposes they had in mind. **Creative vision is seeing potentialities.**

below: **12.28** Jerry Uelsmann. *Floating Tree.* 1969. Photograph. Uelsmann assembles his photographs from bits of images he shoots everywhere. Each is a unique vision, which obeys no natural laws except those of the artist. **Creative vision forges other worlds out of fragments of our own.**

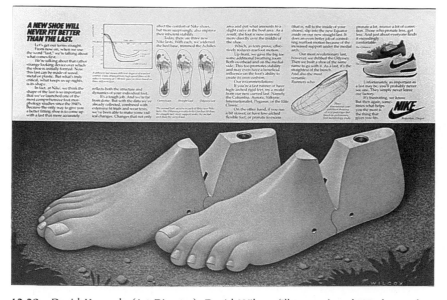

12.29 David Kennedy (Art Director), David Wilcox (Illustrator) and Wieden and Kennedy (Agency). Advertisement for Nike Corp. 1983. Acrylic on masonite, 27 × 15." (68.58 × 38.1 cm). Illustrator David Wilcox turns to René Magritte (Fig. 12.18) for an inspiration appropriate to the theme of this advertisement: "A New Shoe Will Never Fit Better Than the Last." How can we say "foot comfort" visually? Sometimes creativity is knowing where to locate a good idea and making an original variation on that theme.

12.30 Brown Design Group of Brown University, Allen Wong (Art Director/ Designer). 1984. Poster advertising a performance on the topic of the role of emancipated women in today's society; 9¾ × 20¾" (24.76 × 52.70 cm). How can we say "Women in Transition" visually? There may be many ways, but the designer chose to synthesize two widely divergent type faces and type sizes into one. The result is fresh, challenging, and provocative. Creative vision sees possibilities in incompatible forms. It makes uncommon CONNECTIONS.

Magritte's idea (Fig. 12.18) to create an analogy between feet as a reshaper of shoes and the mechanical device designed to do the same thing, shoe stretchers, in an ad for running shoes (Fig. 12.29).

Designer Allen Wong uses halves of two radically different type styles for each letter in the headline of a poster to telegraph visually his subject: *Women in Transition* (Fig. 12.30).

The only thing these artists exhibit in common is the mental capacity to innovate—*synectic thinking.*

Throughout this book are innumerable examples: from the cave artists to the Greeks; from Leonardo to Michelangelo; from Picasso to Pollock; from Eadweard Muybridge to Ansel Adams; from Maxfield Parrish to Milton Glaser. All the examples of professional artworks used to illustrate this book have been chosen specifically with the concept of diversity in mind. Reexamine them all, especially works that have withstood the test of time. The history of art is a compendium of visual problems and successful solutions. Look for aesthetic content and worth that have triumphed over style, over time, and over contemporary criticisms.

It is not style that lasts but substance.

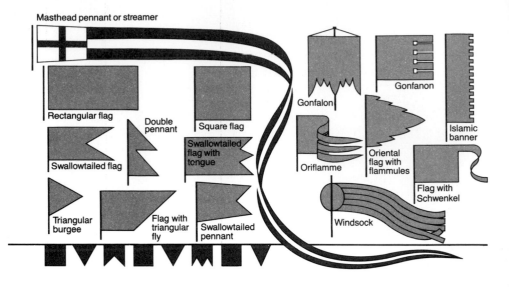

12.31 Flags of all shapes. There may be many reasons why nations elect to make their flags conform to one basic rectangular shape, but there is no reason why artists should so limit their vision to one boring shape. Variety, goes the old saying, is the spice of life. It is also the substance of good art. **Creative vision avoids stereotypes.**

Masthead pennant or streamer
Rectangular flag
Double pennant
Square flag
Swallowtailed flag
Swallowtailed flag with tongue
Gonfalon
Gonfanon
Islamic banner
Oriflamme
Oriental flag with flammules
Flag with Schwenkel
Triangular burgee
Flag with triangular fly
Swallowtailed pennant
Windsock

Review of key terms

aesthetic Of or pertaining to the sense of the beautiful and the accepted notions of what constitutes good taste artistically. (From the Greek *aisthetikos,* of sensory perception.)

analogy An actual or an implied correspondence between things that are different in all other respects. Relationships may be based on any sorts of conceptual, formal (shape and structure), or perceptual characteristics.

connection Something that connects. To *connect* means to join, fasten, link, unite, or consider as related. *Connections* may provide a logical ordering of ideas, establish common interests, conjunction, or coincidence. **Connections of the narrow kind** establish visual relationships between internal pictorial elements within a composition, or establish associational pattern similarities between works in a series. **Connections of the broad kind** are specific references that join a work of art together with elements in the world at large: typically, the environment, society, culture, politics, or the sciences. These stimulate more creative solutions to visual problems and also enhance communication.

delimit To establish limits or boundaries.

folk art Art by the common folk, that is, by persons who lack any formal art training or experience; sometimes called *naive art,* such works are characterized by a lack of sophistication in drawing and painting, and they often depict nostalgic subjects in a simplistic manner. Images, however, may be powerfully evocative and display an innate sense of beauty in patternmaking. Graffiti could be considered a form of folk art.

humor The quality of being amusing or comical; therefore, visual art that displays these qualities. There is a wide variety of types: *humorous illustration* depends mostly on situation with little unnatural exaggeration or stylization of figures; *satire* employs irony, derision, or caustic wit to expose human folly, stupidity, or vice (political cartoons are a satirical form); *ridicule* is mean — it derides, mocks, or contemptuously makes fun of an individual person in order to belittle and embarrass; the *comics,* or "cartoons" are generally all fun, though today they vary from thrilling adventure stories to thinly veiled political and social commentary, from the gentle art of *Peanuts* to the campy ugliness of underground comics.

metaphor A figure of speech in which one object is given attributes characteristic of another object, from which it clearly differs, in order to suggest or to point out likenesses between them not ordinarily observed; a visual equivalent to this literary form. A humorous or anecdotal metaphor is called a *pun.*

paradox A true, but apparently contradictory, statement, circumstance, or image. Also, what is illogical, inexplicable, or contrary to accepted opinion or expectations.

synectic Relating to the merging of different and incompatible things into a new cohesive and unified whole; that is, to synthesize.

taste The power to determine what constitutes beauty or excellence and the expression of that power.

The anatomy of color

Cartoon by Robert Weber

"It comes in five important colors."

CHAPTER THIRTEEN

Light

The nature of light and color

Discard all previous assumptions about the nature of light and color. Most persons have a fairly mixed-up view of what these are all about. We will attempt to put this material in order. Eventually we will learn to use light and color as tools that we can manipulate with confidence and ease. Start with an open mind.

The details will be presented as clearly as possible, and we will look at only those things that are essential to our needs. Follow along carefully; eventually it should all make logical sense. How we apply all this information specifically to design projects is the subject of Chapters 15, 16, and 17.

Light is an interpretation by the brain of the collision of energy waves with photoreceptors in our eyes. Light waves may originate in two ways: (1) directly from an original light source, which are called *incident* light waves; or (2) from secondary sources, "redirected" waves that have been reflected from surfaces, transmitted through substances, or scattered by collisions with particles in the air, water, or other substances.

13.1 Claude Monet. *Rouen Cathedral, West Facade.* 1894. Oil on canvas, 39½ × 26" (100.4 × 66 cm). National Gallery of Art, Washington, D.C. Chester Dale Collection. Impressed by the effects of light that he had observed in some of the works of J.M.W. Turner, Monet set about trying to capture light on canvas. It became an obsession with him.

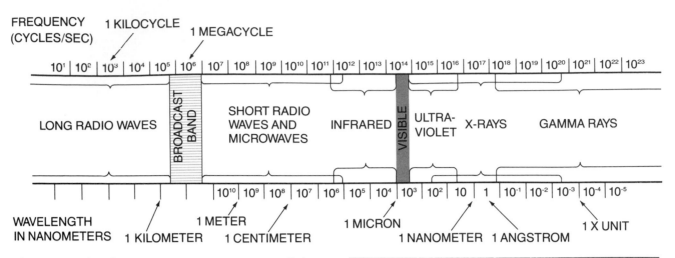

FREQUENCY (CYCLES/SEC)   1 KILOCYCLE   1 MEGACYCLE

10^1 | 10^2 | 10^3 | 10^4 | 10^5 | 10^6 | 10^7 | 10^8 | 10^9 | 10^{10} | 10^{11} | 10^{12} | 10^{13} | 10^{14} | 10^{15} | 10^{16} | 10^{17} | 10^{18} | 10^{19} | 10^{20} | 10^{21} | 10^{22} | 10^{23}

LONG RADIO WAVES   BROADCAST BAND   SHORT RADIO WAVES AND MICROWAVES   INFRARED   VISIBLE   ULTRA-VIOLET   X-RAYS   GAMMA RAYS

10^{10} | 10^9 | 10^8 | 10^7 | 10^6 | 10^5 | 10^4 | 10^3 | 10^2 | 10 | 1 | 10^{-1} | 10^{-2} | 10^{-3} | 10^{-4} | 10^{-5}

WAVELENGTH IN NANOMETERS   1 KILOMETER   1 METER   1 CENTIMETER   1 MICRON   1 NANOMETER   1 ANGSTROM   1 X UNIT

above: **13.2** The *Electromagnetic spectrum* categorizes all the varied forms of electromagnetic radiation in terms of their frequencies and wavelengths. Note that what we call "visible light" is just one small, narrow band, roughly 400 to 700 nm (nanometers), in a continuous spectrum.

right: **13.3** The behavior of visible light is like particles that travel in waves similar to those produced by dropping pebbles into a pond.

Light: A form of electromagnetic energy

What we call "light" is a form of electromagnetic energy. Electromagnetic energy waves are a basic force in the entire universe. They range from gamma rays to electrical power waves, Xrays, TV, and radio waves. All these together, including light, are referred to as the electromagnetic spectrum. The very tiny section of that same electromagnetic spectrum to which our eyes respond is called the *visible light band.* Examine Figure 13.2.

The band of visible light

Visible light travels in waves very much like waves produced on the quiet surface of a pond when a pebble is thrown into it (Fig. 13.3). An ever-expanding circle of waves radiates outward from the point where the pebble entered, small rings close in expand as they move further and further away.

A *wavelength* is the distance from the crest of one wave to the crest of the next as shown in Figure 13.4. The relative energy level, the *intensity* of the light, is indicated by the difference in height between the crests and troughs of the wave. In the case of light coming from a source, such as the sun, the relative energy level would indicate the amount of incident light present and would be measurable with a photographic light meter, an instrument that is designed to measure light's *intensity* (relative energy level).

We need to examine white light; that is, just the band of "visible" electromagnetic energy. The reason it is visible is because the photoreceptors in the eyes of human beings are biologically attuned to those particular wavelengths. It is something like tuning radio or television to receive a favorite broadcasting station. Other creatures are not tuned to exactly these same wavelengths.

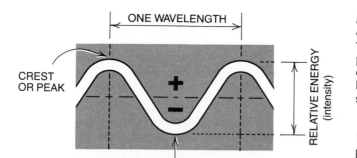

ONE WAVELENGTH

CREST OR PEAK

TROUGH

RELATIVE ENERGY (intensity)

left: **13.4** A *wavelength* is the distance from one point on the crest of one wave to a similar point on the crest of the next. The *frequency* is the number of such single wavelengths that pass any given point in space in one second. Although colors are overwhelmingly determined by wavelength, they have a small frequency component that is not well understood.

13.5 A diagram of "white" light being dispersed by a prism.

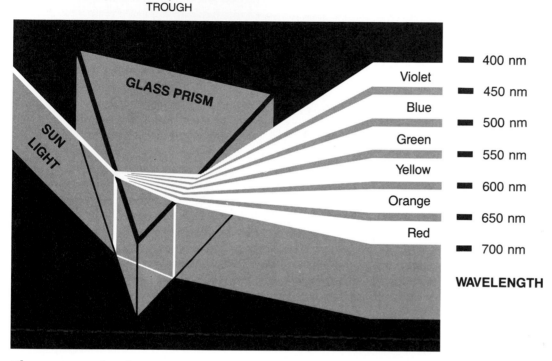

GLASS PRISM

SUN LIGHT

Violet — 400 nm
Blue — 450 nm
Green — 500 nm
Yellow — 550 nm
Orange — 600 nm
Red — 650 nm
— 700 nm

WAVELENGTH

The nature of color

In order to see how white light is composed of a variety of colors, pass a light ray through a prism, which spreads out the band of light and reveals individual hues (Fig. 13.5). All the colors of the rainbow are visible as represented by their individual wavelengths: violet, blue, green, yellow, orange, and red. This is the *color spectrum.*

The photoreceptors in our eyes have the ability to distinguish individual wavelengths ranging from 400 to 700 nm. The "nm" stands for *nanometer,* which is a measure of wavelength, each of which is one billionth of a meter. If our eye detects mostly wavelengths around 700 nm reflected from an object, our brain tells us that it is "red" because we have become accustomed over the centuries to identify that wavelength with the term *red.* The same thing would be true of blue or of green wavelengths. We should call

these *generic hues* in order to distinguish them from pigments like Cadmium Orange. A *pigment* is a substance capable of reflecting or transmitting a particular group of wavelengths (hues) and absorbing others; it is not a "color" in and of itself!

At the beginning, it is important to make clear that the light reflected to our eye does not consist of a single wavelength, but of all wavelengths no matter what color it is that we perceive. This fact is one that creates problems for everyone when mixing pigments for painting and design because it makes it difficult to obtain pure, vivid colors. The more that we mix, the grayer or muddier a color becomes. If we know why that happens, we can do a better job of mixing hues (colors), any one for any purpose.

Color is a property of light

Color is not a property of things, but a response of our brain to a certain group of reflected or transmitted light waves. Color is not out there—around us—it's up there in our heads.

To describe a color accurately, we need three terms.

The first term, *hue* is the generic color name such as "red." Each of these names is a traditional one long identified with a specific wavelength of light that strikes photoreceptors in our eyes.

A list of the wavelengths for generic hues follows:

Wavelengths of generic hues in the color spectrum

	Scale mark	Actual range
violet	400 nm	380–424 nm
blue	450 nm	424–491 nm
green	550 nm	491–575 nm
yellow	600 nm	575–585 nm
orange	650 nm	585–647 nm
red	700 nm	647–760 nm

Observe that there are no magenta or red-violet hues. These are not "spectral" hues, but are created in our brain perceptually from light that contains both blue and red wavelengths.

Luminance, the second term, is the ratio between the amount of light reflected from, and the amount absorbed by, a surface, that is, the relative light energy that our eyes receive. Luminance pertains to the lightness or darkness of a hue but *not* to its vividness or grayness. When we refer to pigments, the comparison is usually made to a gray scale of nine equal steps plus white and black.

Luminance is a dimension of color commonly called "value," a term whose popularity is attributed to Albert H. Munsell. In the Munsell system, white is rated 10.0, the presence of all light—an "additive" measure pertaining to the mixing of light sources. Yet, in character, most two-dimensional design is *subtractive*, a term that pertains to light (or color) reflected from a surface like paint. Some respected color authorities like Joseph Albers refused to use the term *value* because they reasoned that careless use of the term and false examples in books have destroyed it as means of measure. This text prefers the term *luminance* as a less ambiguous, more precise and workable alternative to *value*. In addition, the term *luminance* is able to accommodate a gray scale based on density, a subtractive measure, which is of more practical benefit to designers. The density gray scale is discussed in Chapter 16.

The third term, *purity*, is a dimension dependent on the monochromatic quality of the light reflected or transmitted by a substance. *Monochromatic* means one-hued. Purity, then, is a measure of how close a ray of light comes to a single wavelength.

Purity establishes a scale ranging from the most vivid hue physically possible to neutral gray but *does not* involve the lightness/darkness of a color. There is no universally accepted descriptive term for this dimension. Though some persons use *purity*, others prefer *intensity*, and still others prefer *saturation*. Some say intensity and saturation mean different things, and both terms are required. Some persons prefer the term *brightness*, but that is a term most frequently used to describe a combination of dimensions rather than a single one. In the Munsell system, this dimension of color is called *chroma*. No single term is accepted by a majority of persons. The term *purity* can be clearly defined as monochromatic light of a single wavelength giving it a precise meaning, and, for that reason, it is preferred in this text.

Hue, luminance, and purity are referred to as the "three dimensions" of color because all can only be expressed together visually in the form of a three-dimensional solid as shown in Figure 13.6.

Selective Absorption. All reflecting and transmitting surfaces selectively absorb particular wavelengths of light. The body color (or what artists often call the "local" color) of an object is determined by the dominant wavelength of light waves that are received by the eye and detected by the brain.

Types of original light sources

In order to understand how we perceive light and color, we need to understand a little bit about the physical characteristics of light and the chemical and physical characteristics of pigments, plus something about how the eye receives and interprets light waves

opposite: **13.6** As color has three dimensions, all three can be displayed together only in a solid form. Any point within the solid will identify a color of a specific wavelength (hue), a specific degree of purity (relative vividness–grayness), and a specific luminance (lightness–darkness). Luminance variations range up and down vertically, the purity range extends from the outside (or surface) edge to the center, and the hue range follows around a circumference horizontally from top (white) through the equator to bottom (black). Because pigments naturally vary in their degree of purity, when we substitute actual pigments for generically pure hues, the solid will become an irregular shape rather than a sphere. The purer the hue, the more steps there will be between it and neutral gray.

THE COLOR SOLID
A means to classify color dimensions

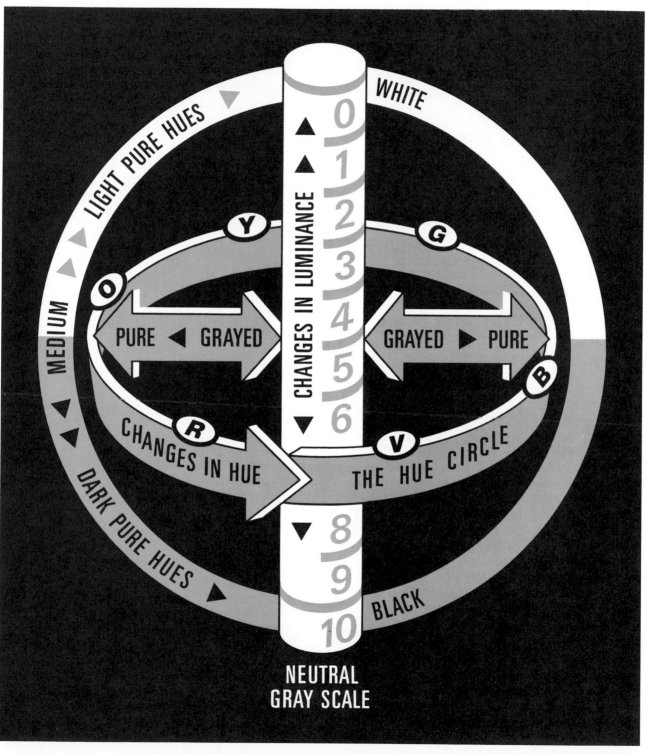

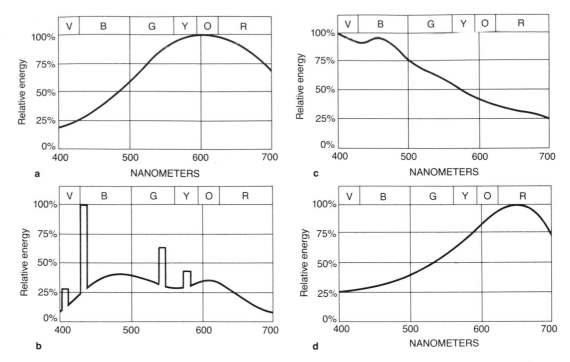

13.7 The *emission curve* for any single light (incident, reflected, or transmitted) is a graph that shows the relative energy level (intensity) of each hue (wavelength in the color spectrum) present in the composition of that light. Shown are emission curves for **a**, the yellowish light of a tungsten filament (incandescent) light bulb; **b**, daylight fluorescent tubes; **c**, natural summer daylight at noon; and **d**, natural daylight at sunset.

reflected from, or transmitted through, those pigments.

We have many different types of light sources. Of course, the sun is the predominant one. It is overhead most of the time except for early morning and late evening.

Incandescent light is produced by a burning body such as the sun. A common household lamp bulb is also an example of an incandescent light source because light is created by a glowing or burning tungsten filament. Also, there are arc lamps that create light by passing electric current across a gap between two carbon rods. All burning bodies create incandescent light. It should be easy to think of at least two other common sources of incandescent light.

All light that is not produced by burning is classified as *luminescent light*. Light can be produced by biological, chemical, or electrical/electronic means. This is a very broad category, which includes fluorescent lamps, neon tubes, and the picture tube in a television receiver as well as light from fireflies and glowworms.

Physical color temperature

Physical color temperature designations were orig-

inally based on burning bodies (incandescence). The higher the temperature, the bluer the hue; the lower the temperature, the redder the hue. The same measures, now applied to all light sources including luminescent ones, do not necessarily indicate relative heat intensity. Differences in physical color temperature are expressed in degrees *Kelvin* (K). Following is a chart for some common light sources:

Physical color temperature chart

Prime light source	Approximate degrees Kelvin	Hue
Candle	1800–1930° K	yellow-red
Sunrise/sunset	about 2000° K	·
40-watt tungsten bulb	2650° K	·
100-watt tungsten bulb	2900° K	·
600-watt quartz photoflood bulb . . .	3200° K	yellow
GE Deluxe Cool White Fluorescent . . .	4150° K	"white"
Average noon sunlight	about 5000° K	"white"
Electronic flash tube	6000° K	·
Average daylight (sun and sky)	6740° K	·
Overcast daylight	7500° K	blue-white
Blue sky (north light)	10,000–18,000° K	blue

The light from a candle flame is very orange-red. Light from a 40-watt household bulb is redder than a 100-watt bulb. A quartz photoflood bulb for taking indoor pictures with tungsten color slide film is cooler, but yellowish. A camera's electronic flash tube is about 6000° K and requires daylight color film for correct color balance.

Efects on the perception of colors

Figure 13.7 **a–d** shows the relative energy levels of individual wavelengths in particular light sources. These are called "emission curves." Read the captions.

Figure 13.7 **a** shows the wavelengths produced by a 100-watt tungsten light bulb with a color temperature of 2854° K. Note the peak of energy is in the yellow-red wavelengths. Figure 13.7 **b** is the curve for a daylight fluorescent bulb, which is high in blue and green but very weak in the red wavelengths. Figure 13.7 **c** shows the response of average daylight, a color temperature of about 6740° K. Figure 13.7 **d** shows what happens to the hue of sunlight at sunset. Average daylight has the peak in the blue area, but at sunset the peak shifts to yellow-red. Notice that the curve of outdoor light at sunset is much closer to the tungsten light bulb than to average daylight.

We should observe three important facts from these diagrams. (1) Though there is a peak in one or more wavelengths, each light source includes all, or most all, of the visible spectrum. (2) Natural daylight is neither constant in hue nor relative energy (intensity) even though we perceive it to be. It is the extreme adaptability of our eye-brain mechanisms together with perceptual constancies that suggests to us that daylight is unvarying. (3) Each of these light sources differs considerably in both hue and relative energy from one another. This is true of all light sources of any type and is also true of all transmitting or reflecting surfaces, including all artists' paints, dyes, and pigments regardless of generic hue.

How to evaluate the accuracy of colors

The effects of the differing emission (spectral) curves of daylight and tungsten light sources on perceived colors may be observed by examining Color Plate 5 (p. 259).

Both of these light sources appear normal to our vision, and we interpret them both as white light. We are not usually aware of the color temperature differences unless they are drawn to our attention through direct comparisons. The color films we use to make prints or slides see hues in their natural colors, as they cannot adapt to the varying hues and luminances as our eye-brain mechanism does.

Yet the hues of these prime light sources significantly alter the way that we perceive and mix colors. When we paint in tungsten light, we compensate for the excessive yellow-red by increasing the purity of blues because they seem duller and grayer. We do exactly the opposite in the cool north daylight because the blues appear to be too intense. In this instance, we increase the purity of the yellows, oranges, and reds.

In Color Plate 5 **a** (p. 259), the "true" hue, center, is a very pale purple-blue. The color would normally appear more like the color below when observed in daylight and more like that above when seen under tungsten light, both obviously different.

The same effects may be observed on a range of hues in Color Plate 5 **b** (p. 259): Daylight 6000° K bottom, center is normal perception, and top is tungsten 3200° K.

Color Plate 5 **c** (p. 259), center, shows a white handkerchief as we perceive it to be. The picture below shows the effect produced by bluish noon daylight 6000° K, and above, that of tungsten light, 3200° K. Under normal circumstances our brain compensates for white light differences, and the handkerchief appears white under *both* lights, not blue- or yellow-hued. This is a form of perceptual constancy.

Balancing light sources for painting

Eastman Kodak Company evaluates color prints under 4000° K, a compromise between ordinary incandescent light bulbs and noon daylight. Artists are well advised to work under lighting conditions similar to viewing conditions. Paintings and illustrations should probably be done in light of around 3500° K to 4000° K unless we know the work will be viewed primarily under daylight or daylight fluorescent lights.

Museum conservators have determined that paintings, prints, drawings, even the paper itself, are damaged by light. Daylight and some types of fluorescent light are harmful because they contain high percentages of ultraviolet wavelengths. Even diffused natural light is best avoided. Many museums use only low levels of ordinary incandescent light, whose only harmful component, heat, is easily counteracted with air conditioning. In homes, incandescent light is the most common artificial light source that is used for viewing.

A good formula for painters to use consists of one 100-watt incandescent bulb for every two 40-watt

13.8 Strips of polarizing film, each with differing orientation, laid on a sheet of the same material. Note the passage of light progressively declines as the alignment of the film's crystalline structure becomes more and more transverse (crossways).

cool white fluorescent tubes. If there is a large amount of daylight, banks of incandescent lamps should be used to adjust temperature based on color meter readings. Overall illumination levels should be about 50 foot-candles at working surfaces as measured with a light meter.

In a naturalistic work, a recognition of the differing color temperatures of light sources can contribute to the mood desired. Of course, photographers must always balance such factors with filters in order to provide accurate color rendition of any subject.

Chromatic light

When the hue of the light becomes strong enough that our brain can no longer compensate for the deviation, we then see "colored light" rather than white light. Again, the total effect is not always observable because the brain continually attempts to compensate. Only direct comparisons provide the clearest view. We will use the term *chromatic light* for light that we perceive to have a definite hue.

In Color Plate 6 (p. 259), the vegetable or flower appears normal only when the hue of chromatic light most nearly matches the hue of the object. As can be seen in the photograph, the hue of the light substantially affects perceived hues of objects. The reason for

the dramatic changes in colors under chromatic light is that chromatic light eliminates substantial portions of the visible spectrum (white light), greatly limiting the wavelengths that can be reflected.

No matter what sorts of wavelengths are being transmitted or reflected into the eye, our brain will try to make things appear correct. Remember our brain always interprets the visual field being received. If we see a tomato under green-tinted light, our brain will probably reject the idea that tomatos are yellow, and it is likely we will still perceive a *red* tomato. It takes a very strongly hued light to make differences unmistakably observable.

Polarized light

Light waves vibrate in every direction perpendicular to the direction of travel. When such vibrations are confined to one direction, the light is said to be polarized. This occurs naturally for a portion of sunlight due to the reflection and scattering of light waves. It is not necessary for us to know too much about the physics in order to use this phenomenon to our advantage (see Figs. 13.8 and 13.9).

The polarizing of light can be accomplished through the use of a polarizing filter or sheets of polarizing film. We can think of the work of the filter

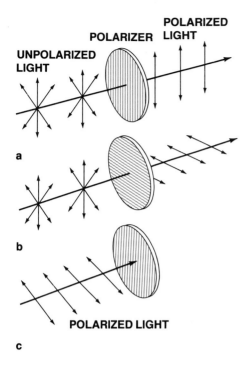

UNPOLARIZED LIGHT

POLARIZER

POLARIZED LIGHT

POLARIZED LIGHT

a

b

c

13.9 **a Polarizers make order out of chaos of scattered light:** Lined-up crystals in polarizer allow unpolarized light rays vibrating in one plane to pass through the filter. Most natural light is not polarized.
b Turning the polarizer: The alignment direction of the filter crystals always determines the plane of the light ray vibration allowed through. Here we have turned the filter 90° so that only the horizontal vibrations pass through.
c Getting the polarization effect: If light is already polarized by being reflected from the correct area of sunlit sky or is a reflection from the correct angle and type of shiny surface, it is already vibrating in only one plane to begin with (here horizontal). Therefore its intensity can be reduced or eliminated by turning the polarizer so that its crystals are perpendicular to the light ray vibrations. The polarized sky becomes underexposed and appears dark; or reflections are eliminated from surfaces such as water or glass.

as if it were a venetian blind, opened just enough to allow narrow slits of light to pass through, thus creating rays of light all aligned in one direction. For a moment, however, let us consider the light as if it were thin pieces of cardboard. If the cardboard were lined up with horizontal slots in the venetian blind, it would pass through. If the sheet of cardboard were turned vertically, it would not pass through the blind. Essentially this is what the polarizing filter does to the light. As light is not cardboard, we can partially polarize light if desired. Obviously polarization reduces the amount of light energy present.

Using polarized light in art

A polarizing filter enables a photographer to control reflections in all sorts of shiny surfaces. Polarizers can darken the blue of the sky and add drama and contrast to subjects. They accomplish this feat by filtering out much of the scattered light, which substantially reduces the amount of *atmospheric blue* (a factor in aerial perspective). This means that polarizers tend to increase color purity (and dye saturation) both indoors and outdoors.

When polarizing filters are used for photography, the exposure must be increased about two and one-half times, that is, two and a half "stops."

The stop: A luminance interval for all arts

A *stop* is either one-half the amount of light (50 percent less) or double the amount (a 200 percent increase). Stops may be varied by changing a camera's aperture (F5.6 to F8, a 50 percent decrease in light); or, by changing exposure time (1/30 second to 1/60 second, also a 50 percent decrease in light). If only one stop difference is needed, do not do both of these. Changing F8 to F5.6 would double the amount of light, as would changing 1/60 second to 1/30 second.

Whenever we operate a camera of any kind (photostat, view, or copy camera), adjustments in exposure should employ full stops if any appreciable difference is to be obtained. Half stops are the smallest adjustment one would ordinarily make.

Keep this principle in mind because it is also the way that we perceive even steps of change in luminance on a gray scale, for example, any density change. It is a concept, therefore, that applies to all forms of artwork. (See Figs. 13.10 and 13.11.)

Photographing animation and painting

Polarizers give us the ability to control reflections from windows, from glass-covered paintings, or from varnished or other glossy paint surfaces. All animation

LEFT: Perceptually, handkerchiefs remain white, and illumination may appear relatively constant.

RIGHT: What actually happens:

FULL ILLUMINATION

½ ILLUMINATION (50% of light), ONE STOP LESS

¼ ILLUMINATION (25% of light), TWO STOPS LESS

left: 13.10 Whiteness constancy. Our brain will tell us a white handkerchief is white (like the photographs on the left) even though the intensity of the light varies greatly (like photographs on the right). This quality of perception is illusionary and cannot ordinarily be photographed. The declining illumination on the handkerchiefs, right, merely makes them look dirty or gray in still photographs.

ARITHMETICAL GRAY SCALE

GEOMETRIC GRAY SCALE

13.11 Wilhelm Ostwald (creator of the Ostwald Color Notation System) demonstrated that simply adding the density of a gray to itself, 1, 2, 3, or 4 times (upper chart) displays less and less difference across a scale. In order to perceive an even progression of steps between white and black, the density of each step must be twice the preceding one, 1, 4, 8, 16, and so on (bottom chart). This concept is the same as "stops" in photography, and conforms to the *inverse square law* of physics.

work on acetate cells is photographed using polarizers. When photographing artwork, a polarizer is placed on the light source as well as on the camera. The camera polarizer is rotated, and the light source (for example, a photoflood lamp) is moved about and adjusted until the reflections are minimized or completely eliminated.

Colorful effects using light as a medium

For creative artworks using light, for experimental light shows using light as a medium, for multimedia presentations, or any kind of slide show, colorful effects may be generated by placing various transparent materials between sheets of polarizing material. For example, in a slide mount, cellophane may be sandwiched between one polarizer at the rear and a piece of clear acetate at the front. Figure 13.12 shows how a slide made from small slivers of cellophane appears—completely colorless. When a second polarizer is placed over the projector lens, the colors magi-

cally appear (Color Plate 7 **a**). If the front polarizer is rotated, the colors change continuously throughout the rotation.

Surfaces modify light waves

Light wave behavior is governed by the characteristics of the surface that they strike. There are two basic types: (1) opaque reflecting surfaces through which light does not pass; and (2) transmitting surfaces through which light passes, although both the light's intensity and our perception of it may be altered by such things as the hue, particle density, and refraction index of the transmitting material. Because light waves are modified by such materials, the quality of the color (but not necessarily the perceived hue) is also modified.

Reflecting surfaces

Most of the light waves that we perceive in our

13.12 This is a photograph of a slide sandwich consisting of tiny slivers of clear cellophane between one sheet of polarizing material and one sheet of clear acetate, fastened in a 35 mm slide mount. The black and white image faithfully reproduces the colorless result. Only when another polarizing sheet is laid on top or placed over the lens of a projector, will we see the brilliant colors created by light wave interference. See Color Plate 7 **a**.

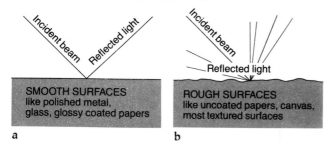

a   **b**

visual field are reflected from relatively opaque surfaces. Opaque surfaces are a general characteristic of most natural things although a few exhibit varying degrees of translucency.

There is a contrast range of reflecting surfaces from matte to extreme gloss. As a rule, luster adds depth and brilliance to colors. Some artists wonder why a pigment that looks bright, pure, and dark when applied shiny wet on a surface looks so much duller and grayer after it has dried. If we varnish the surface filling in tiny spaces between the particles of pigment (Fig. 13.13), the luster returns, and the color's brilliance is restored. This effect is due to the fact that very smooth surfaces do not scatter as much light. Like a mirror, glossy surfaces reflect light directionally (Fig. 13.14 **a**).

Matte surfaces diffuse, or scatter, the light in all directions (Fig. 13.14 **b**). When light is scattered, it contains more of the entire color spectrum. Individual colors will appear less vivid and pure (grayer).

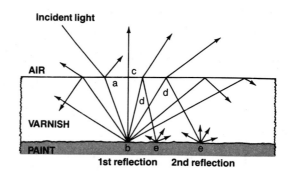

13.13 Internal reflection of light within a varnish layer increases contrast of hue and luminance in the paint layer. In **a**, incident white light strikes the varnish layer—part of this light penetrates the layer; **b** shows the first reflection of the light from the paint surface; in **c**, a beam of reflected light escapes through the varnish; in **d**, a beam of reflected light is reflected through the varnish layer again; **e** shows a second reflection of a light beam at the paint surface. Contemporary painters and designers should not be ignorant of how varnishes and glazes can enhance certain qualities in their works like color purity and depth.

left: **13.14** Differing surfaces reflect light differently, but all surfaces reflect some light, including clear transparent surfaces like glass. A smooth, or polished, flat surface, **a**, reflects most light at an angle of 90° to the incoming beam. In this case, a bright light reflection may be sent to the eye from one particular direction, and almost none from another. Such a surface condition is usually called *lustrous*. The rougher the surface, **b**, the more the light is scattered in all directions, meaning that less light is reflected back to the eye from any single direction. The surface appears more evenly lighted but not very bright.

Transparency and translucency

Transmitting surfaces or substances range from clear, completely transparent materials through varying degrees of translucency to opaque. Transparent living things are so unusual that we think them otherworldly, like ghosts, or curiosities like jellyfish and insect wings. The natural transmitting substances we encounter are air and water. Glass and plastics are manufactured products.

The difference between the terms *transparency* and *translucency* should be clearly understood, for each possesses particular qualities not shared by the other. A *transparent* material does not hinder, in any way, the passage of light and vision. The overlap of layered transparent materials is always *darker* than either member.

A *translucent* material is semiopaque. It always contains, to a greater or to a lesser degree, particles that obstruct the passage of light and vision. Such

Light   215

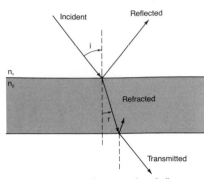

above: **13.15** *Refraction:* the deflection of a wave (light or sound) at the boundary between two differing mediums or in the passage through such mediums. Here the diagram shows the behavior of light rays encountering a transparent medium (such as a glass plate) at an angle **i**. An image viewed through such a medium is likely to appear offset from its actual location. The thicker the medium, the more the image is dislocated.

right: **13.16** Paul Browning (Artist) and Robert Burns (Art Director). Screenprint, with fishing fly attached, 24 × 26″ (61 × 91.4 cm). The artist uses "light refraction" as a design concept in this self-promotion piece for a Canadian Design Studio.

below: **13.17** *Constructive interference* reinforces (a beat or increase in energy), and *destructive interference* cancels out (a null or decrease in energy) both waves of light and sound rather similar to the effects seen in Figure 4.4.

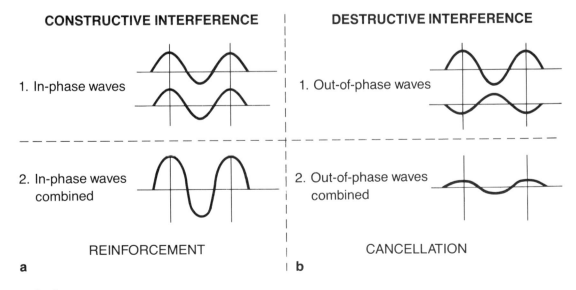

CONSTRUCTIVE INTERFERENCE	DESTRUCTIVE INTERFERENCE
1. In-phase waves	1. Out-of-phase waves
2. In-phase waves combined	2. Out-of-phase waves combined
REINFORCEMENT	CANCELLATION
a	b

materials always appear cloudy or foggy to the viewer because particles of light are scattered and reflected back to the viewer. Overlaps of layered translucent materials will appear lighter than any single layer. The effect will always be proportional to the number and size of the opaque particles trapped in the substance, a lesser amount giving more transparency and a greater amount giving more opacity. The hue of the upper layer overwhelms the hues of any underlying layers. Mixtures are never equal: the more opaque, the greater the upper layer influence.

Scattering, refraction, and interference

Scattering is the random deflection of rays of light by very small particles like molecules of dust, water, or any other substance. In the atmosphere, water molecules create fog; haze is a combination of fog, dust, and perhaps smoke. Short waves (blue and violet wavelengths) are more easily scattered than long waves (red wavelengths). This explains why scattered light is often bluish and why the sky appears blue during the daytime. We do not see the violet rays because our eyes have little response to these wavelengths. The white of snow crystals results from the fact that these much larger particles scatter all wavelengths more evenly.

Refraction is the bending of light waves when they cross a boundary line between two different types of transparent materials (Fig. 13.15). Perhaps, most commonly, we recall the way that a pole in water appears to be bent the moment it penetrates the surface. It is a characteristic that realistic painters must be careful to incorporate into their work. Refraction is the characteristic of glass that makes lenses possible. The light entering one of its surfaces can be designed to emerge in a new direction by altering the shape, thickness, or composition of the glass itself. This effect, like all the others, can inspire a creative solution to a visual problem if we are always sensitive to the possibilities. (See Fig. 13.16.)

Light wave *interference* occurs when two light waves from the same source are superimposed. When the waves match, that is, when they are in-phase, the interference is "constructive," and the relative energy increases because that of one is added to the other. When the waves are out-of-phase, energy is decreased because one is subtracted from the other: Wavelengths are transformed or mutually destruct. See Figure 13.17. The beautiful colors in soap bubbles are due to wavelength interference. They are produced by partially out-of-phase light waves that are reflected from the rear surface of the bubble film colliding with light waves reflected from the front surface of that same bubble film. Interference occurs because the thickness of the bubble film is less than the width of one wave of visible light. Colors seen in films of oil on water, mother-of-pearl, peacock feathers, and many butterfly wings are similar phenomena. These substances (like Fig. 13.12) may have no pigmentation of their own. We commonly call these effects "iridescence."

Body colors

Every color we see is not composed of one wavelength, but of many wavelengths. In fact, each contains the entire spectrum of hues though each hue may be at differing energy levels. In other words, no common incident, transmitted or reflected, light produces *monochromatic light*, that is, light of a single wavelength. Neither will any dyes or pigments. In fact, outside of the laboratory, there is virtually no such thing as monochromatic light.

To avoid perceptual confusion, the brain has learned to disregard all parts of the spectrum except the dominant wavelength in order to determine the body color of the figure-object. This is a characteristic of color constancy.

The emission (spectral) curve for transmitted green light, like a green spotlight, is shown in Figure 13.18 **a.** In Figure 13.18 **b** is the curve for a red body, that is, an object painted red such as a red ball. In

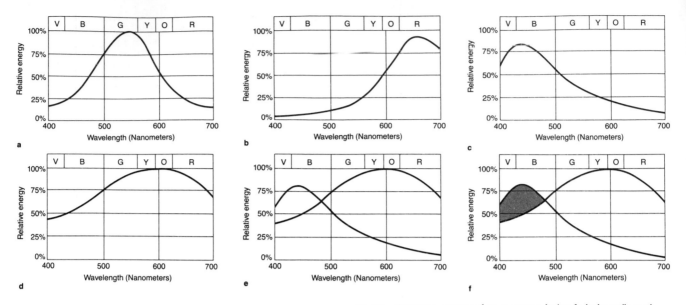

13.18 Emission curves for: **a** green light; **b** light reflected from a red body; **c** light reflected from a violet body; **d** light reflected from a violet body viewed in yellow chromatic light. Under the condition **d**, only part of the reflection **e** can be perceived; part **f** cannot. (Rough simplification.)

this case, the light is reflected from the object. Figure 13.18 **c** is light reflected from a violet body, like a purple sweater. And Figure 13.18 **d** is that same purple sweater in yellow chromatic light. Be sure to observe that these colors, transmitted or reflected, do not only have peaks in the expected wavelengths, but also have wavelengths of most all other hues.

Note in Figure 13.18 **a** that though there is a strong peak in the green wavelength, around 550 nm, the green light also contains red, yellow, blue-green, blue, and ultraviolet wavelengths. When a reflection containing a peak of 550 nm enters our eye, the brain rejects all the other information it receives and says, "That is green." It ignores all other wavelengths present except as *influences* on the green. If strong blue wavelengths are present, the green will appear "cool"; if there are strong red wavelengths, the green will appear "warm." We should be able to see exactly the same thing occurring in Figure 13.18 **b** and **c** for the red body and the violet body.

The wavelengths present in the reflection, but not perceived, always influence the perceived hue. If we observe a red, and there are considerable blue wavelengths present, the red will appear "cool" like magenta; if there are more green than blue wavelengths present in the reflection, the red will appear yellowish or "warm," like Cadmium Red Light. Is it possible to determine what color we will perceive in Figure 13.18 **d** from the data presented?

Why all of this is critically important

When we take our paints out to mix a purple using blue and red pigment, for example, we have to understand that the red we have chosen also reflects wavelengths of all other hues, to a greater or lesser degree, depending on which particular red pigment we have chosen. The blue is also reflecting all other wavelengths. So whenever we mix two or more colors together, we are also mixing together all other hues (wavelengths of light), not just the pigments chosen.

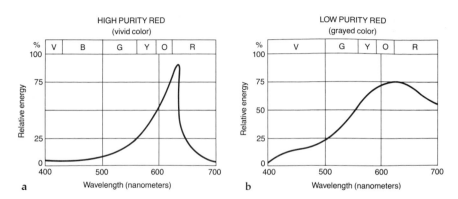

HIGH PURITY RED
(vivid color)

LOW PURITY RED
(grayed color)

13.19 A pigment with a high purity, **a** will have a reflection with a strong, narrow peak in relative energy at the wavelength of the generic hue with sharply tapering reflections in all the other wavelengths. A low purity pigment, **b** will have a comparatively lower and broader peak in the generic hue's wavelength and gradually declining reflections in all the other wavelengths.

This means that if the red is yellowish (like Cadmium Red Light) and the blue (like greenish Phthalocyanine — Thalo or Monastral — Blue) includes a yellow component, the sum of the energy levels of both yellows are added to the mixture. When both pigments include wavelengths of a hue (yellow) complementary to the hue we wish to mix, in this case violet, the resulting mixture will be a color greatly reduced in purity — a grayed, muddy color.

Hue contaminants

In the reflections of every dye and pigment, wavelengths of all hues present, except the dominate hue, are color-mixing contaminants. These must be taken into account whenever we mix colors. At the beginning, we must consider them consciously and deliberately; after time and practice, their consideration should become intuitive. This is one of the methods through which we gain absolute control over color pigments.

A high purity hue (Fig. 13.19 **a**) is one that has a very high, narrow peak close to one single wavelength (the generic hue), but only low reflections in all other wavelengths. That would be what some persons would call a vivid or intense or saturated hue. A low purity hue, that is, a grayed color (Fig. 13.19 **b**), has strong reflections all across the spectrum and a much lower and broader peak in the generic hue. Remember Figure 13.18 **d** the violet body in yellow chromatic light? It will appear grayish to us, with the high yellow-red curve turning it a brownish gray. For the technically minded, the curves in Figure 13.18 **e** and **f** show why.

Obviously, which pigments we choose to mix together becomes very important. If we want the purest colors, one rule is not to mix them at all, but buy a tube of paint that exactly matches the color we want. In many instances, that may be impractical or impossible. The point to remember is that to get the color we need, we should do as little mixing as possible. Yet there are virtually no hues found in nature exactly matching those of artists' pigments.

How to put this information to work in painting and illustration is the subject of Chapter 16.

Concepts of white and black

Approximately equal reflections of all wavelengths at high energy levels will produce white light, which is the presence of all wavelengths of electromagnetic energy. Black is the absence of all waves of visible electromagnetic energy — no light at all, in other words. We seldom experience such a situation naturally because the atmosphere scatters light; there is some light even on the darkest night. Real blackness can be experienced only if we go to the bottom of a mile-deep mine and turn off all the lights.

Light exists in every visual field

Keep in mind that black is the absence of all light. Look at any black object, book cover, piece of clothing, whatever. We can always make it blacker by shading it with our hand or some other object. There is no black material found in our environment that does not reflect some light, including all black pigments regardless of media. Unless we are electing to use flat colors applied decoratively, shadows cast by

13.20 As there is no actual "black" (except in a totally enclosed, sealed space without light), even the darkest shadows should be defined and contain detail, including those cast on dark surfaces like black textiles, for example. Otherwise artwork will not appear realistic or naturalistic.

figures should be defined even when they fall on black surfaces. See Figure 13.20. Generally, even the deepest shadows should exhibit some detail. A good rule: Avoid black shadows unless deliberately creating decorative effects.

Perceptually, gray light does not exist, as our eye-brain mechanisms fully adjust for most differences in illumination. Theoretically it could be observed only when white light is also present in the same visual field for comparison.

Achromatic and chromatic colors

We usually divide colors into two types: chromatic or achromatic. It is common practice to refer to white, black, and grays as achromatic colors — hueless colors. Though that may be a convenient way to describe them, it is literally not true. Achromatic colors actually reflect all wavelengths about equally. Chromatic colors are those that include a clear recognition of their dominant wavelength, such as 700 nm, red. *Chromatic sequence* refers to the hues of the spectrum arranged in natural order; that is, they follow one another around the hue circle like a rainbow.

The drama of light

We should take advantage of differing qualities of light in painting, design, and illustration.

Chromatic light for example, is a means of unifying any work of art. It is also a means of controlling the affective (emotional) responses appropriate to the subject matter. Color Plate 8 (p. 260) shows four different views of the Grand Canyon photographed at different times of the day all from the same camera position. Upper left is early morning, right is noon, below left is midafternoon, and right is sunset. Not only do we see significant hue changes, but we have all sorts of changes in the shadows due to changes in the direction of light striking the landscape. Each is a completely different picture and evokes a completely different mood. These ideas, whether applied abstractly or realistically to a work, offer virtually unlimited alternatives to explore, each with its own special qualities. Exploring alternatives is a direct path toward fresher and more original work.

Become aware of how light has been used to create drama when watching stage plays, TV shows, and motion pictures. Obviously, realistic painters and illustrators should take special note. However, nonobjective and abstract artists should also realize that the use of light in a dramatic sense is conceptual and must be a consideration in their work just as with any other form of art. When at an art exhibition or going through books on contemporary painting or art history, become sensitized to the qualities of the light that other artists have incorporated into their works.

Cues to light's relative energy level

Our brain recognizes cues to differing light intensities (relative energy levels). The more intense the light source, the sharper detail in an image seems, up to the point where the light becomes so intense that it blinds us. At that point images become pale (washed out), purer in hue, with unstable edges that seem to shimmer and dissolve before us.

When the intensity of light declines to very low levels, darkness beyond where our eyes fully adapt to them, images become colorless, more diffused, and meld together. Spatial planes are poorly separated.

The intensity of reflected light, that is, light that strikes some surface and is reflected back to our eye, is very much less intense than the intensity of a light source itself. The overall luminance range of surface characteristics, such as the lightness-to-darkness of the coloring matter or paint on that surface, is independent of the light source. In other words, everything drawn, painted, or printed on a surface has a certain luminance range that it is capable of reflecting. This range, overall, may be darker or lighter, depending on how much light (the intensity) is falling on that surface. Thus, the pages of this book will appear much brighter outside in sunlight than indoors under a 60-watt lamp; but the range of tones, luminances from white to black, which appear printed on the pages *will not have changed at all*.

The words and pictures may be easier to define or appear sharper or more detailed, but the *range* is unaffected. This concept is a very important one for artists to understand.

An important point

The average person can clearly distinguish about 25 steps of luminance from white to black on a surface such as ordinary paper, photographic paper, painted canvas, or illustration board, for example. A trained eye might double or triple distinctions within that range, but that does not make the range greater.

The luminance range from any reflective surface is very small when compared to a natural outdoor visual field, where light intensity ranges from the sun to the darkness of a cave. Indoors, where a room may be lighted from a 100-watt bulb, for example, light intensity ranges from the bulb itself to deep shadows under the furniture at the opposite end of the room to the gloom in an unlighted room beyond, the point furthest from the source.

No reflective surface like a painting on canvas — or the printing on the surface of the pages in this book — can match such ranges of illumination in any respect whatsoever. The white of the paper or canvas may reflect up to 80 percent of the light. The blackest ink or paint on that surface will reflect as much as 10 percent of the light. The luminance difference between the white and the black is a mere 15 to one.

We can easily prove this to ourselves by placing a very shiny metal object or piece of aluminum foil right on the surface of this page. Notice how the room lights reflected in the metal are ever so much brighter than the paper itself. In fact, the white paper really looks quite dark by comparison.

Outdoors on a sunny day, the differences in intensity (the relative light energy) may exceed eight hundred thousand to one. For any viewer, a painting will never become a window.

The significant fact to be understood is that the surfaces on which most artists work have an extremely narrow range of luminances available to manage. To achieve a sense of light pervading a work of art requires very precise ordering or control of these limited luminances.

Summary

Making two-dimensional art is learning to manage images composed of light waves that are reflected from a surface or transmitted through a surface.

Light is important to artists in five basic ways. These provide a wide variety of alternative possibilities.

1. Light is a means to help establish volumes (chiaroscuro) and planes (cast shadows), as described in Chapter 8.

2. It is a means of establishing emotional drama and evoking moods.

3. Light itself can be used as a medium both in applied art and in fine art.

4. When we compare the range of light intensity in a natural visual field to that of a reflecting surface, like a picture, we appreciate some of the luminance problems every artist faces, particularly those who wish to work naturalistically.

5. The physical properties of light exert a crucial influence on our perception of colors and also on the manner in which pigments mix. In principle, we do not mix pigments; we mix reflected or transmitted light.

Exactly how this information can be put to practical use by an artist is explained in Chapters 15–17. But first we must look at how human physiological mechanisms receive images composed of light rays and transmit collected sensory data to the brain.

Understanding light is the cue to understanding how color and how pigments work, and how to mix pigments as well as light to achieve whatever ends are desired.

Review of key terms

achromatic Pertaining to colors without any distinctive hue, for example, black, white, and gray. Achromatic colors are often called "neutral colors."

body color The "colored" appearance of any matter or substance (like a paint film), caused by differences in the molecular structure of such substances. Molecular differences determine which wavelengths of light are absorbed and which are reflected. Such colors are affected by the spectral composition of the incident light.

chromatic Exhibiting a definite color or hue.

chromatic sequence *See* **spectrum.**

color A property of light, not of bodies or pigments. As sensed by photoreceptors in the eye, our perception of color results from a certain bundle of wavelengths of electromagnetic energy bombarding the retina. Color has three "dimensions" or characteristics. *See* **hue; luminance; purity.**

color temperature The sensation of "warmth" or "coolness" associated with colors. There are two types: *physical* color temperature, which is measurable in degrees Kelvin; and *relative* color temperature, which requires the presence of two or more colors (hues) for direct comparison. Though reds, oranges, and yellows are said to be "warm," and blues and greens "cool," there are cool and warm reds, cool and warm blues.

electromagnetic spectrum The entire range of electromagnetic waves from very short, high-frequency vibrations, such as cosmic rays, through (in the order of decreasing frequency) gamma rays, X rays, ultraviolet radiation, *visible light*, infared radiation, microwaves, and radio waves to very long, low-frequency vibrations, which include heat waves and electric currents.

hue The traditional color "name," such as "red," which is attached to a specific wavelength of visible light (electromagnetic energy). Red, for example, is 700 nanometers (nm). If 700 nm is the dominant wavelength in the reflection of light from an apple, our brain interprets the hue of the apple to be "red."

hue circle A circle composed of primary, secondary, and intermediate hues in any color-mixing system. This text prefers the term *hue circle* to *color wheel* because these ordinarily deal only with hue, just one of the color dimensions.

incandescence A type of original (prime) light source created by a burning body. The sun is an incandescent light source as are common items such as light bulbs, candles, campfires, kerosene lamps, projector bulbs, and carbon arc spotlights. One of two broad categories. *See* **luminescence.**

interference An interaction of waveforms whereby the overlap of two sets of waves weakens some waves but reinforces others. If one peak coincides with another, the wave is reinforced; if a peak coincides with a trough, the waves cancel out one another. Light wave interference is responsible for the iridescent colors we see in soap bubbles, record grooves, some butterfly wings, and birds' feathers.

light A small portion of the electromagnetic spectrum capable of stimulating the photoreceptor cells (cones and rods) in the retinas of our eyes. The *band of visible light* extends from about 400 nm to 700 nm. *See* **electromagnetic spectrum.**

luminance An index of the amount of light reflected from a surface viewed from a particular direction. It relates to the lightness or the darkness of reflected colors and is compared to a gray scale.

luminescence (loo mi NES' enz) Any prime light source not attributable to incandescence, that is, all nonthermal lights such as those produced by chemical, biochemical, or electrical processes, including fluorescence and phosphorescence. Do not confuse this term with luminance (LOO' mi nans).

monochromatic Possessing only one hue, though possibly varying in luminance and purity; consisting of only one wavelength of light. In addition to a single hue, *monochromatic color schemes* commonly include white, grays, and black.

nanometer One-billionth of a meter (10^{-9}); approximately .000000039 inch. Formerly called a "millimicron," this unit of measure is applicable to wavelengths in the visible light band.

purity One of the dimensions of color that identifies the monochromatic quality of any hue, that is, its relationship to light of a single wavelength. This relationship establishes a scale ranging from the most vivid hue physically possible to neutral gray.

reflection Light waves bounced back to the eyes from any surface.

refraction The bending of light waves as they pass through one transparent medium into another, for example, a lens or a glass of water.

scattering Random dispersion or deflection of light from any surface, substance, or airborne particle.

spectrum More precisely, the *color spectrum*: the distribution of hues in natural order according to their wavelengths. Also, the colored image formed when light is spread out after passing through a prism. Spectral sequence or chromatic sequence describes hues in prismatic order.

wavelength The distance between any two similar points on a given wave; usually specified as the center of one wave crest to another.

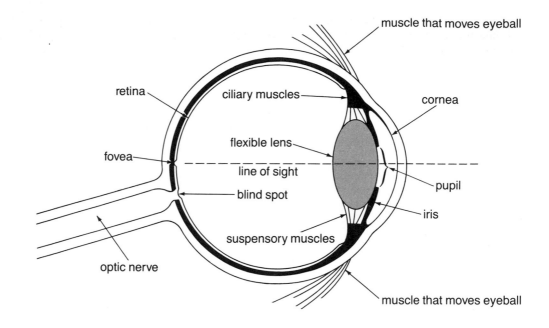

Labels in figure: muscle that moves eyeball, retina, ciliary muscles, cornea, fovea, flexible lens, line of sight, pupil, blind spot, iris, optic nerve, suspensory muscles, muscle that moves eyeball

CHAPTER FOURTEEN

Vision

We do not see as a camera does

The eye is not an objective, impartial mechanism that observes or records images like a surveillance camera or a videocassette recorder. They eye does not record discrete images at all. It simply responds to the stimulus provided by waves of light with nerve impulses (electrical signals), which it transmits along the optic nerve often to different parts of the brain. These transitory bits of sensory data are sorted, restructured, and then modified by memories of past experiences (assimilation).

It is a common practice to compare the eye to a camera. There is the lens through which light passes; a diaphragm (the pupil), which adjusts to permit greater or lesser amounts of light to pass through; and a surface (the retina) on which the images are brought into focus. Although it is true that the eye shares these superficial characteristics with the camera, except for the pupil, the functions of neither of the others is simulated by any camera. Such a comparison is

thought to be a convenient way to explain the workings of the eye to young people. However, this does a good deal more harm than good because most persons tend to accept that concept as truth, and that colors all future concepts about vision. The facts suggest that it is not a worthy comparison.

Seven ways the eye differs from a camera

Please place a marker by Figure 14.1, and continue to refer to that diagram even though we will also look at other illustrations.

The light enters the eye through a hole in the iris, called the pupil, which is a kind of diaphragm. The

14.1 The site of the optical image is the retina, which contains the terminations of the optic nerve. In the tiny retinal depression known as the *fovea*, the cone nerve endings are clustered. Their organization and dense packing make possible a high degree of *visual acuity*, the ability to resolve very fine detail.

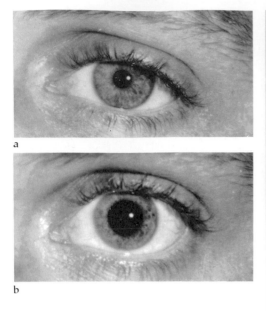

a

b

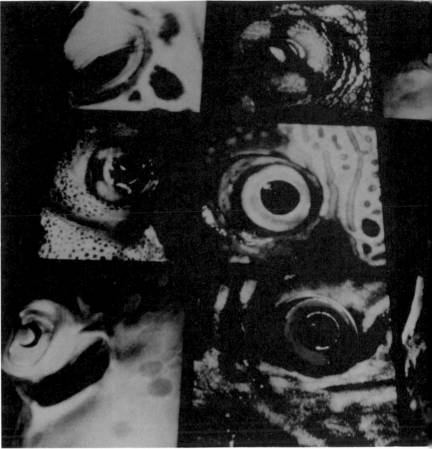

pupil responds to the intensity of the incident, transmitted, or reflected light entering the eye by automatically opening or closing (Fig. 14.2). Within a considerable range, adjustment occurs virtually instantaneously and without awareness. This factor prohibits us from judging the relative amount of light present unless the change is extreme (bright sunlight to dark cave). The pupil is able to change in area by a factor of 10 giving it a working range in light intensity of 100 million to one.

There are many different kinds of pupils. Ours is round, but if we examine other types of animals, we find that nature has been rather luxurious in the creation of pupil design (Fig. 14.3). Some are slits, like those of cats, which prove much more adaptable to extremes of light and dark than our own. Many other creatures have shapes particularly adapted to the living environments and requirements of the individual creatures. Knowing about varieties of pupil design could solve a visual problem for an illustrator. How could we say, "Alien being," visually?

1. Our flexible lens

Behind the pupil is a very different lens from the ones used in cameras. First, our lens is flexible. It's rather like a bubble of transparent jelly that will deform when we press or squeeze on it. Focusing from figure to figure occurs not by moving in or out, but by changing shape. Muscles attached to the pupil pull to flatten or relax to make it rounder. Second, the amount of effort required by the muscles is sensed by the brain as an important cue to the location of the figure-object in space (its spatial station). This is the quality of the lens called *accommodation*.

The lens is a simple one. It cannot bring all colors to focus sharply together; blue hues actually focus ahead of red ones.

2. The retina: A data "bit" receiver

Light that first strikes the *cornea*, the eye's outer transparent protective shell, and passes through the pupil is focused by the lens on the *retina*, a thin sheet

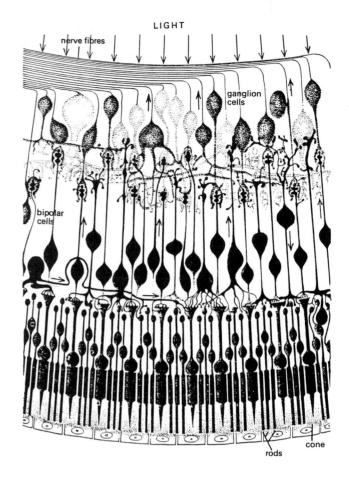

LIGHT

nerve fibres

ganglion cells

bipolar cells

rods · cone

opposite, far left: **14.2** Within a rather wide range of illumination, we may be hardly aware of changes in light intensity. The pupils in our eyes open and close to "smooth out" fluctuating light energy (intensity). Illustrators and portrait painters should note that in low light levels, **a**, as the pupil widens to its fullest extent, so does the eyelid! In strong light, **b**, not only does the pupil close, but the eyelid also closes somewhat partially shading the iris.

opposite: **14.3** Cambridge Seven Associates and Stephen Althouse (Photographer). National Aquarium, Baltimore, mural wall, detail, 9 × 90' (2.74 × 27.4 m), with 63 backlit transparencies, each 3' (0.91 m) square. The richness of nature's diversity is glimpsed here in the variety of pupils and eye shapes and in the configuration and textures of the surrounding tissues (skin). If there were no models to look at, could a person be so inventive?

right: **14.4** The retina. From R. L. Gregory. *Eye and Brain,* McGraw-Hill Book Company, 1966. Reproduced by permission. Light travels through layers of blood vessels, nerve fibers, and supporting cells to the sensitive photoreceptors (the rods and cones). These lie at the back of the retina, which makes it functionally inside out. In vertebrate eyes, the optic nerve is not joined directly to the receptors, but is connected via three layers of cells, which form part of the brain externalized in the eyeball.

of light-sensitive tissue at the rear of the eyeball (Fig. 14.4).

The retina contains around 125 million rod cells and 7 million cone cells, which are the eye's light receivers (photoreceptors). They are called rods and cones because of their general shape.

When struck by light, a rod or a cone undergoes a chemical transformation triggering a response that is passed along through two other cells, bipolar and ganglion cells, before the signal reaches the optic nerve. Each ganglion cell gives a minute electrical charge, "fires," only in response to the cone or rod with which it is associated even though it is not directly attached. The optic nerve takes the bits of "on and off" (binary) data and passes them along the optic nerve, which feeds the information directly to the brain through an exit in the back of the eye.

The hole in our visual field

The passage of the optic nerve out of the eye creates a hole in our field of vision. We are not aware of this missing chunk because the brain takes information from the surrounding parts of the image and combines it with data from the other eye, then synthesizes and fills in the empty space continually and automatically. The presence of the hole provides clear evidence of how the brain is able to fabricate a sharp visual field from incomplete, fuzzy, and confusing data. Of course, the process enables us to function more comfortably in the natural world as do many other perceptual characteristics.

If we make a spot about one inch in diameter (use a bright color like red) on a piece of paper about five inches to the right of a check, or cross, mark, we will be able to find our own blind spot. Hold the paper at arm's length. Close the left eye tightly, and focus on the check mark with the right eye while moving the paper slowly closer. At one point the red spot will vanish.

Rods: Luminance responses in dim light. The 125 million rods are mostly color-blind, responding to a

14.5 David Hockney. *The Desk, July 1st, 1984.* 1984. Photocollage. David Hockney's criticism that ordinary photographs "stare you down" led him to the photocollage, which, he says, represents "how we actually see."

broad band of wavelengths. They are responsible for our vision in dim light. A number are gathered together in a "bundle" so that they are more likely to respond when light levels are low. Rods are so sensitive that they may become overloaded and incapable of signaling in bright daylight.

Cones: Our color detectors. Seven million cones of three different types provide our color vision. As most of these are associated with their own ganglion cell, light must strike each individual cone directly in order for it to fire. Cones hardly respond at all in very low light levels. This is the reason that as light diminishes, everything seems to become much less colorful. In very dim light, there may be no color response at all because an important part of our visual mechanism is not working. Bright light activates a color response. This is one reason why color advances (*pulls*) perceptually but gray tones recede (*push*).

The chemical trigger. The substance in the rod and cone cells that actually absorbs light is called *opsin,* of which there are four types. When exposed to light, the opsin produces a chemical action that the ganglion cells convert to electrical signal. Rhodopsin is the visual pigment in rods, which have a peak absorption in the 500 nm range (bluish green).

An individual cone contains only one of three

different opsins, which distinguishes three different types. When struck by a colored light, cone cells do not "see the color"; each simply responds to the very narrow wavelengths of light to which it is sensitive with an "on" or "off" signal. A nearly monochromatic (single wavelength) appears to stimulate each respective cone the most. Peak absorption for each of the three cells is 477 nm purple-blue, 540 nm yellowish green, and 577 nm yellowish red. The interaction of these three cone types enables us to perceive a full color visual field. One or more of the cone types is missing or inactive in color-blind persons.

To the cones and rods, it makes no difference at all whether the source of the light waves coming through the lens of the eye are direct from a light source, transmitted, or reflected from a surface although, in each of these cases, there is a substantial change in the light intensity. This difference in relative energy level (luminance) is the primary means by which the brain discriminates between the qualities of light waves whatever their hue or source. Review the illustration and caption for Figure 1.12.

How we see sharply

Take another look at Figure 14.1. Directly in line with the lens is a tiny depression in the retina, not much larger than the period at the end of this sen-

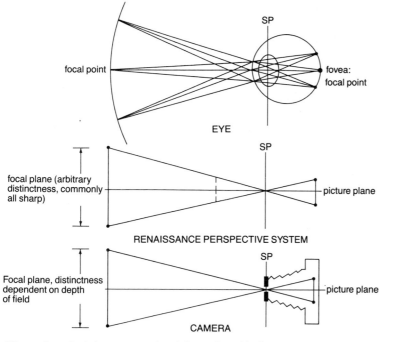

14.6 A comparison of visual systems: the eye, Renaissance (vanishing point) perspective, and the camera. To be perfectly accurate, we should have pictured the eye twice. Note: the eye focuses on a point; the other systems have a focal plane.

SP = station point (where one stands relative to the subject)

tence. Called the *fovea*, it is densely packed with 4,000 cones, each one associated with a single ganglion cell attached to an optic nerve fiber. It is the fovea that gives humans visual acuity, an ability to resolve fine detail. Distinct vision occurs *only* for that bit of an image falling on the fovea.

Our apparently very sharp, full color visual field is synthesized by the brain. It is a kind of mosaic field consisting of an array of tiny bits of the total image, each bit having been brought, in turn, to rest on the fovea. See Figure 14.5. Dense around the fovea, the number of cones declines rapidly moving outward, peripherally, around the retina. None remain at the furthest distance.

Those professions requiring good night vision suggest that, after the eye has adapted to darkness, persons look a little to the right or left of the subject in order to see it because, in the darkness of a moonless night, the exact center of our vision, the fovea, is completely blind.

3. The eye sees points, not planes

A fixed, unmoving camera lens focuses an image on a plane (the film, which is usually held rigidly flat or in a gentle curve). Our eyes focus on points, not planes. Examine the differences shown in Figure 14.6. If we select some very small detail of any object about

a yard away and fix our gaze upon it for some moments, gradually we will become aware that immediately outside of that point everything is fuzzy and unclear. To create the complete image we perceive, the eyes must jump constantly from one fixed point to another, gathering bits of visual data. The brain knits these bits together to help synthesize a sharp and clear visual field. The movements, called saccades, provide a new retinal image every few hundred milliseconds, that is, about every one-fourth second.

4. The eye is never still

Like the heart (pumping blood) and the lungs (breathing), the visual organs, the eyes, are engaged in continual activity of which we are hardly aware. Stabilizing our visual field both physically and mentally is one of the vital functions of the brain.

The eyeball is equipped with three sets of muscles, one each for movement—up, down, and from side to side. Not only do the eyes move in their sockets, but we will find our head moving as well. We are normally unaware of these constant movements: To become aware for a time, we simply need will to do so. To become sensitized, look all about, at every part of the room. Let the head follow eye movements only when they reach the limits of their sockets; do not move the head arbitrarily. Sense how everything *opposite:* 14.7 **a** What we think we see. Assume these circles are an array of 15 tennis balls viewed straight on. Our brain tells us that they are all perfectly round; edges are sharp. As tennis balls are all alike, the size differences seen here indicate that some balls are further away than others. **b** Approximately what each individual lens projects on the retina. The image is sharp only on the center ball; every other ball is increasingly fuzzy toward the outer edges of the visual field. *Note* the increasing distortion of the circle's roundness as the distance from the center focal point increases.

c The approximate appearance of the combined images of both eyes. Call it "image doubling." This is the type of visual sensory data that the brain receives every waking, but not dreaming, moment. As in **b**, only the center ball is critically sharp. Outer images grow fuzzy.

looked at is being brought to the center of our field of vision, the fovea.

In addition to head movements and eye movements (*saccades*), each eye vibrates at between 30 and 150 cycles per second. These minute tremors shift an image bit from one set of photoreceptors to another in order to place components of an image continually on fresh cells. Each ganglion cell, once fired, takes a moment to recover before it can fire again and is momentarily blind (a characteristic often called "fatigue"). We blink to close off visual stimuli and rest the receptors, the rate rising under tension.

These physical mechanisms are largely responsible for various fatigue illusions, usually called *optical dazzle*, which we have already discussed in Chapter 9 (see Figs. 9.27 and 9.28), and psychophysical color qualities called *afterimage* and *simultaneous contrast*. Color vibration as seen in Color Plate 12 **e** (p. 263) is also an example.

5. Peripheral vision

The retina is roughly spherical, not flat or a curved flat plane. The field of vision extends around the walls of the eye in excess of 180 degrees, giving us significant peripheral vision. The extreme boundaries are filled with visual noise from the central nervous system with little ability to resolve detail.

Our peripheral vision is the brain's surveillance equipment, ever alert to any change in the visual field that might signal danger. Recent studies suggest the primary purpose, perhaps the only purpose, is to detect movement. Any element attracting attention is

instantly brought to the fovea for detailed examination.

6. Binocular vision for close distances

We have two eyes, whose overlapping images are combined in the brain to give us a three-dimensional view of our world. We should recall from Chapter 8 that it is most effective within 25 feet of us and disappears altogether at about 1,200 feet. Beyond this, the images received by each eye separately are indistinguishable. What is important to remember is that the brain senses muscle movement as well as image differences in order to estimate distances.

7. Image doubling

We have learned both that our eyes focus on a point, not a plane, and that acute vision is limited to a tiny part of each eye. These factors combine with binocular vision to create even greater visual confusion, *image doubling*. Some idea of how this works may be obtained by examining Figure 14.7 **a**–**c**. What we perceive is shown at the top, Figure 14.7 **a**. Research studies indicate that the actual image from one eye looks something like Figure 14.7 **b**, which shows that outer edges of shapes grow increasingly fuzzy and distorted. In Figure 14.7 **c** the effect of both individual eyes is combined.

Conclusions

It should be obvious that our eyes are no straightforward optical mechanism. It is the brain that

IMAGE DOUBLING AND DISTORTION

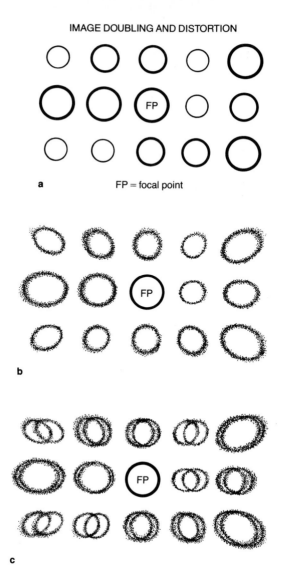

a

FP = focal point

b

c

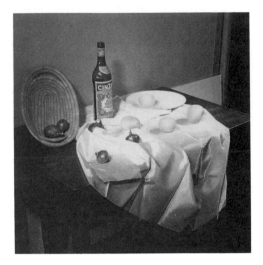

14.8   Paul Cézanne. *The Basket of Apples.* ca. 1895. Oil on canvas, 25⅝ × 31½″ (65 × 80 cm). The Art Institute of Chicago. Helen Birch Bartlett Memorial Collection.

above: 14.9   Photograph of a still life with the camera directed at the center of the table.

totally controls our perception of distinctness, or image sharpness, not our visual detection mechanisms. We see very differently from the way we think we do.

Our brain synthesizes the entire perceived visual field. Taking tiny bits of images, it unites them together to form a wide, sharp, dimensional color visual field—a kind of mosaic. This characteristic of the brain provided the means by which our species has learned to negotiate and eventually exercise control over the world in which we live.

Getting in touch with the way we see

In his book *The Visual Dialogue,* Nathan Knobler reconstructed an example of what he called "contemporary spatial representation" using Cézanne's *The Basket of Apples* (Fig. 14.8) as an example.[20] Figures 14.9, 14.10, and 14.11 are the photographs that he used. Compare these photographs with David Hock-

ney's photograph, shown in Figure 14.5.

Of course, Cézanne did not plan to exemplify a perceptual concept in his work. He was simply in touch with the way that he perceived subjects—sensitized would be an appropriate term. Though this is an essential characteristic for all artists, such sensitivity must be continually and aggressively pursued and nourished.

This work of Cézanne may still look a little odd to some persons because we are accustomed to Renaissance perspective. The table appears to be tipped up on end and seems distorted; the bottle looks as if it is tipped back. When the public first saw these and similar paintings in the last decade of the 19th century, they said that such art distorted nature and vision.

Yet, the way Cézanne painted was much closer to the way our vision works, as we have just learned.

a   b   c   d

above: **14.10** Four views **a–d** of the same still life, Figure 14.9, with the camera lens directed at differing portions of the table rather than at the center.

left: **14.11** A photomontage of the same still life, Figure 14.9, made up of individual sections only of the views seen in Figure 14.10 **a–d**. Compare this effect to Cézanne's painting, Figure 14.8.

Renaissance perspective: How cameras, not persons, see

Since the 15th century, we have become accustomed to one type of visual field, Renaissance (vanishing point) perspective. Its invention, acclaimed by both artists and scientists as a scientific discovery of major importance, is usually attributed to the architect Filippo Brunelleschi. At about the same time, the portable camera obscura was developed. This device, similar in construction to today's cameras, could project a one-eyed view on a pane of glass, which an artist could use to draw from or trace. These things supported one another—after all, visual perspective was right there, projected on the glass for all to see. Painters as diverse as Canaletto, Dürer, and Vermeer are known to have used such devices. Leonardo da Vinci wrote about them.

Since the middle of the 19th century we have had the photographic camera, a one-eyed cyclops that sees a plane and not a point. Pictorial fields featuring this point of view are with us everywhere today.

Figure 14.9 shows the way the scene looks to a camera. It is more distant, less intimate and immediate. Take another look at Cézanne's painting (Fig. 14.8). Knobler asks the question, "Which picture gives a more accurate representation of the table?"

The point: We have not only been told that we see as a camera does, but we are assaulted with such images virtually from birth to death. We have grown accustomed to flat planar images—the movies, the photographs, TV, the entire historical record of Western paintings and drawings up to the 20th century. Our visual mechanisms work very differently from the way we think they do. Is it any wonder?

The psychophysical qualities of color vision

The combination of the physical properties of light and the physiological eye–brain processing is called a "psychophysical" response because each factor contributes something to our perception. Most perceptions are the results of such a combination.

The afterimage

When light causes selected cones to react, our vision is, for an instant, blinded to the positive image. Momentarily present is a negative image of the full color visual field. This negative image, represented by cones that did not fire, is called the *afterimage* (or sometimes "successive contrast"). The hues we see are the light complements of the original colors. Normally the afterimage is so weak that we are unable to detect it although it is always present in our visual field. If we were able to detect it, a neutralizing effect on vision would occur, and we would be unable to function.

If we stare intently at an image for a time, about 20 seconds, then shift our gaze to a blank sheet of white paper, the afterimage will become visible. We can test this out with Color Plate 9 (p. 261).

The afterimage can be employed as a creative concept. In one of a series of flag paintings, Color Plate 10 (p. 261), the painter Jasper Johns uses that very same idea. At the top, a complementary color image of the flag and at the bottom, a flag with no color. Is it possible to analyze the psychological significance of this? We are confronted with a negative image of the flag, followed by a flag drained of all color! Obviously a kind of political statement, it is a very strong one.

Even though the afterimage is visually weak, it influences almost every color that we see.

Simultaneous contrast

In early 19th-century France a problem with woven textiles first raised scientific questions concerning the mixing of colors. Michael Eugène Chevreul, a chemist appointed superintendent of the dye laboratory at the Gobelin tapestry factory, was asked to solve a riddle: Why did certain thread colors combine to produce unpleasant grays instead of the bright colors expected? Everyone blamed the quality of the dyes. Chevreul discovered that the problem was "simultaneous contrast," as he called the phenomenon, the optical fusion of colors. His observations recorded in a book, *The Principles of Harmony and the Contrast of Colors* (1839), marked the starting point of all modern color theory. We are just beginning to understand some of the psychophysical aspects of Chevreul's discoveries.

Managing color through simultaneous contrast

Understanding how simultaneous contrast affects our perception of images and colors enables us to increase the richness and interdependency of the color relationships. These can help us to draw together and to unify designs. Different colors can be made to appear to be the same, or the same colors appear different, a useful problem solver. The apparent hue, luminance, and purity of some colors may be made to appear different even though colors applied in a work of art are not actually varied. This ability is particularly useful where color is limited, as in some printmaking (saves plates and runs) and illustration where a production cost or time saving will result.

We can also use simultaneous contrast to help *push-pull* edges, causing them to advance or recede at will. Simultaneous contrast is particularly strong at edges or junctures between contrasting pure hues and opposing luminances.

Therefore, the effects of simultaneous contrast represent one of our most important means of solving visual problems.

It is now time to bring together a number of important pieces of knowledge that we have studied separately in different contexts. Our perceptual mechanisms do not work alone, but each one in concert with all the others. In Chapters 1 and 2, we discussed *irradiation*, which accentuates the differences in contrast between masses, making dark edges darker and light edges lighter. So, too, are the elements of relative visual attraction surveyed in Chapter 7, where, for example, an orange on a blue ground (near complements) advanced over a purple red (an analogous hue). In Chapter 8 we learned about the three principles of *aerial perspective*: distinctness; "atmospheric blueness," which also defines a basic principle that pure colors advance; and luminance contrast. All these are manifestations of *simultaneous contrast*. Let us take a closer look at some of these illusions, which anyone can encode into their work. Please place a marker by Color Plate 11 so that it will be easy to flip back and forth.

Color Plate 11 a (p. 262): The effect of area on lumi-

nance and purity. As an area becomes smaller, apparent luminance and purity *decrease.* The large magenta block and the small magenta circle pictured here differ only in their physical area. We should be very sensitive to the difference. Notice that the small circle appears darker and less colorful. Yes, it is subtle, but effective nevertheless.

Color Plate 11 b (p. 262): The effect of sharpness (distinctness) of contour on purity and luminance. Observe that these two circles differ only in the sharpness with which their edges are delineated. The effect, subtle but clearly seen, is the result of irradiation (remember Fig. 1.4)? The white space along the sharp edge of the right circle causes the color edge to darken perceptibly. (Is this what happened to the small circle in Color Plate 11 **a**?) The phenomenon does not occur or has less emphasis when the edge is softly blended.

Color Plate 11 c (p. 262): The effect of the contrast of grounds or backgrounds on purity. The two green rings are exactly alike. The differences in purity are created by the relationships with the background. A cyan (green-blue) afterimage created by the red wavelengths in the red background, left, reinforce those already present in the green ring and increase its apparent purity. The gray ground, right, contains a relatively even mixture of all wavelengths. The afterimage affect upon the green ring is negligible, and it is perceived as printed.

Color Plate 11 d (p. 262): The effect of simultaneous contrast on hue. Two identical magenta rings appear to be different hues because each one has a differing relationship to its ground. The presence of a very strong cyan afterimage created by the red ground dulls and cools its magenta ring. The cyan afterimage contains green wavelengths that are complementary to the magenta (dulling it) and also blue wavelengths that shift the hue toward violet. This effect does not occur when the ground is neutral gray, allowing the magenta to be seen in its natural hue.

Figure 14.12 a: The effect of simultaneous contrast on luminance. The gray centers of both the black and the white circles are exactly alike. The apparent change in luminance is due to the contrast (irradiation) effect. Such effects are proportionally uniform throughout the luminance range.

Figure 14.12 b: Example of a size change. The white

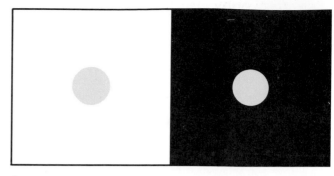

a

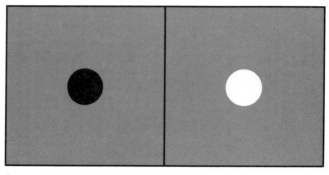

b

14.12   The effects of simultaneous contrast. Center dots in **a** are identical gray patches. Cover the left portion of **a** with a hand. Note that the center circle, right, appears to be as white as the white paper in the margins of this book. In **b**, the white circle appears larger than the black one, yet both are identical in size.

14.13 Examples of the illusionary effects of *contour contrast,* a special case of what is called simultaneous contrast or *irradiation.* If a small figure is surrounded by a forced edge (a dark band) that figure will appear to be lighter than the surrounding white ground, or the opposite effect may be produced on a dark ground. The *larger* the figure's area, the *less* effective is the phenomenon. For maximum effect, figures should be quite small and the edge should be very hard and sharp inside and blend away outside. This is one means by which an artist can extend the luminance scale of two-dimensional works beyond what is physically possible.

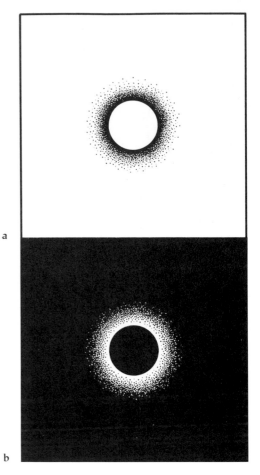

a

b

and the black circles on the middle-gray ground appear to be a different size although they are actually identical. The irradiation effect causes the white circle to appear to advance and it seems larger than the black circle, which recedes, because its edge contrast is comparatively weaker. Note that the white circle takes on the quality of a figure, although the black circle appears to be a hole. The gray ground occupies a spatial plane somewhere in between.

Naturally, we should expect that all the qualities of simultaneous contrast just discussed also produce effects on our perception of space and depth as they cause things to advance or to recede.

Border and contour contrast

"Border contrast" and "contour contrast" are qualities of simultaneous contrast given specific names. They deal with edge effects and are a characteristic of distinctness (aerial perspective). *Border contrast* is considered as a fundamental working tool in painting and design. As an art technique, it is more commonly called "the forced edge." We have dis-

cussed this before in Chapter 7 as a means to vary spatial relationships.

One aspect of border contrast, *contour contrast,* uses the forced edge to create a luminance change. It differs from border contrast in that contour contrast deals with perimeter (see Fig. 14.13 **a–b**). This is not a new artistic concept even if just recently understood. Take a look at Figure 14.14, an 18th-century Korean vase, for example. It is important that the area enclosed be relatively small for the effect to appear astonishingly believable. Is there a connection with Color Plate 11 **a**?

The effects of contrast on visibility

Refer to Color Plate 12 (p. 263). The visibility of any figure-object in a visual field may be enhanced (*pulled*) by increasing both luminance and color contrast with the ground. The tools used for this purpose are complementary, or nearly complementary, hues and strong light-dark contrast. Conversely, the visibility of any figure-object may be reduced, camouflaged, or

14.14 Korean vase. Yi dynasty, ca. mid-18th century. The Asia Society, New York. Mr. and Mrs. John D. Rockefeller 3rd Collection. The vase provides an excellent example of a dark band, a forced edge, between areas. The moon appears to be brighter than the sky directly below it, but the actual luminance is just the reverse.

hidden (*pushed*) by leveling the contrast. In this approach, the object and ground differ hardly at all: consisting of analogous hues and little or no luminance contrast. Also, we should recall from aerial perspective that hue purity affects visibility, that is, pure hues advance (*pull*), and grayed hues recede (*push*).

Managing edges and adjacent color relationships

As we have discussed, there is a perceptual tendency for any two adjacent hues to move toward their own complements at the edge where they meet. Effects along the edge grow more pronounced as the hues approach their complements. If we create more edges by breaking up colors, as with Pointillism (Divisionism), optical fusion is increased. The phenomenon can be put to very practical use in any work of art or design by employing this principle to level or to sharpen the contrast of edges, as well as to increase the variety and aesthetic quality of color work.

In a simplified form, the process works as follows. Please place a marker by Color Plate 13 (p. 263).

Edges may be forced to recede (*push*) or advance (*pull*) by respectively forcing edges of two different hues to become more analogous or by forcing those same edges to become more complementary. In Color Plate 13 **a** (p. 263), for comparison purposes, are plain red and blue panels of approximately equal luminances. In all examples, luminances have been kept very close so that hues will be emphasized. This is not ordinarily necessary. According to the additive and subtractive systems (hue circles Figs. 15.1 and 15.7), yellow and blue, magenta and (yellowish) green, and cyan and (yellowish) red are pairs of complementary hues. Refer to the circles as necessary.

In Color Plate 13 **b** (p. 263), a reddish violet has been laid in along the edge of the blue and blended into the red. Note how the edge drops back (melds). The same thing has been done in Color Plate 13 **e** (p. 263), except, in this case, the blue has been modified by placing a violet along its edge and blending it away. By combining the techniques used in both Color Plate 13 **b** and **e** (p. 263), the edge will virtually disappear, with an increased melding of figure and ground (Color Plate 13 **f**, p. 263).

In Color Plate 13 **c**, yellow-orange has been painted along the blue edge and blended back into the red. The edge now comes forward, with considerable visual activity along the edge. In principle, the same thing was done with Color Plate 13 **d** (p. 263), except, in this case, the blue was modified by blending in green along the edge. In both instances, the edge has been sharpened.

Pay particular attention to the fact that all these effects (Color Plate 13 **b** through **f**, p. 263) generally appear more "colorful" and aesthetically pleasing than the original patches of blue and red. We have not only made the edges dance to the tune we wanted, but we increased the variety and excitement as well.

Every edge in every kind of work, abstract, realistic, nonobjective, applied, may be similarly worked. These techniques are not related to concepts of style but are universal visual tools that can solve problems regardless of style, technique, or subject.

Out of the discussions in this chapter, we should be able to distill three fundamental principles applicable to all cases. It is a good idea to commit these to memory, so that this knowledge will eventually become intuitive.

1. When complementary colors of equal, or nearly equal, luminances are placed next to one another, the wavelengths of each complementary color are reinforced, creating an unstable or vibrating edge — optical dazzle. When luminances are not equal, edge visibility and brilliance of both hues are increased.

2. When colors that are not complementary are placed next to one another, each shifts toward the complement of the other, not only in hue but also in purity and luminance. The activity along the edge increases as colors approach complementary status.

3. All visual mixing effects are fundamentally additive in nature.

Summary

We do not see as a camera does.

Vision does not concern itself with just the immediate visual field because that field is a mental construction influenced by previous experience and attitudes (assimilation). In other words, vision, including our perception of color, is complex and subjective. Visual individuality extends from psychological processes to physical anatomy. Every eye is so individual that recently developed security systems are based on the unique vascular pattern of the retina — just like fingerprints.

Yet the way in which we process visual data is the same for all normal human beings. The characteristics of these biological mechanisms together with the physical characteristics of light — the psychophysical characteristics of perception — provide us with an array of tools to help us achieve artistic goals, that is, solve visual problems. Of these, simultaneous contrast is especially useful.

Techniques employing principles of simultaneous contrast provide a reliable means to extend significantly the limited luminance range of colors and tones on reflective surfaces, increasing the apparent purity and variety of pigments on those surfaces. The advancing and receding characteristics of figures and grounds may be determined not only by edge quality (hard-soft) or by subject matter but may also be managed by creative understanding and use of the principles of simultaneous contrast.

Review of key terms

accommodation The ability of our eye's flexible lens to change shape in order to adjust focus between far and near figures. The muscle movements required are detected by the brain as an indicator of a spatial station.

acuity Sharpness or clarity. The ability to resolve very fine detail in the visual field.

afterimage A psychophysical characteristic of vision in which an image persists after the original stimulus has been removed. The hues of the image are ordinarily the additive complements to those originally observed. *See* **simultaneous contrast.**

blind spot The point where the optic nerve leaves the retina of the eye. As this area possesses no rods or cones, it does not respond to light or images.

cones Photoreceptors in the eye that provide visual detail and detect color. There are three types, each capable of discriminating between very narrow wavelengths of light: one for red, one for green, and one for blue. Concentrated in and around the fovea, numbers decline rapidly moving outward, peripherally, around the retina. Cones respond primarily to bright light levels.

fovea A tiny depression in the center of the retina densely packed with cones. The fovea is responsible for visual acuity, that is, sharp, vivid, detailed images.

irradiation A perceptual illusion in which our brain makes a dark edge darker and a light edge lighter in order to clarify and strengthen the formation of the edge. It is observed as ghostly gray dots at the intersections of white bars on a black field.

lens In reference to the eye: a flexible, oval-shaped, transparent body behind the iris, which changes shape to bring objects into focus on the retina.

photoreceptors Light-sensitive cells in the retina of the eye: the "rods" and the "cones."

psychophysical A term used by psychologists to indicate a response that is dependent on combined physical, biological, and mental processes.

retina A multilayer, light-sensitive membrane lining the inner surface of the eyeball that is connected by the optic nerve to the brain. The retina contains the eye's photoreceptor cells.

retinal fatigue Overloading of the retinal system commonly experienced when viewing contrasty linear patterns. It may be partly a result of eye tremors causing receptors to signal on/off, thus sending a heavy load of confusing signals to the brain. The effects may also be due to the fact that once a photoreceptor cell has "fired," it is momentarily blind, and a sensation of the additive complementary color appears. *See* **afterimage.**

rods The most numerous light receptors in the retina of the eye; important to vision at low levels of illumination. Rods are essentially color-blind.

simultaneous contrast The psychophysical effect of our visual mechanism where the stimulus of any color on our retina generates a subtle sensation of its opposite, additive complementary hue. The presence of red will make blue appear greener, especially along edges; the blue will cause the red to appear to contain more yellow—to look orangy.

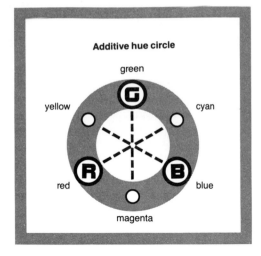

Additive hue circle

green

yellow   cyan

red   blue

magenta

CHAPTER FIFTEEN

Color mixing systems

Additive principles of color mixing

The additive system applies to all forms and applications of colored light. More than most of us realize, *this affects virtually everything we do when painting or designing with color.*

The beginning point for additive mixtures is black—the absence of all light. The additive primaries are red, green, and blue (which correspond to the peak absorption of the eye's cone cells). The addition or mixture of these three hues will produce white light. See Color Plate 14 **a**, p. 264; please place a marker there. Light energy is *added* as each primary is introduced, thus increasing the number of cone cells stimulated. An increase in luminance is experienced. The mixed color is *always lighter* than its component parts.

Mixtures of any two of the additive primaries will produce an additive secondary; see the additive hue circle (Figure 15.1.) Superimposed, red and green light produce yellow light; green and blue light produce cyan light; and blue and red light produce light. (See Color Plate 14 **b**, **c**, and **d**, p. 264.)

Complementaries on the additive hue circle will mix to produce white light. Blue and yellow are complements, and their combination results in white light (Color Plate 14 **e**, p. 264). This is an especially important fact when an artist is combining light sources for effect. In stage lighting, never light a set with alternate blue and yellow spotlights if green light is expected. This combination produces white, not green, light.

How additive color is used

IN APPLIED ARTS: Color television broadcasting and reception; computer graphics; laser light shows; interior and exterior decorative lighting; decorative color spotlighting of architecture, parks, gardens, fountains, landscape details; neon and other illuminated signs; slide presentations; multimedia shows; color separation of full color photographs or artwork for reproduction (color printing) in magazines and books; plus all fine art applications below.

IN FINE AND CONCEPTUAL ARTS: Light sculpture; all light media; color separation for printmaking; Pointillism; op (optical) art; optical dazzle and fatigue illusions; fluctuating spatial effects; aerial perspective and all such atmospheric effects; all qualitative effects of subtractive (pigment and dye) mixing; effects of all reflections from colored surfaces on all

15.1 Primary hues are indicated with large circles; secondary hues with small circles; complementary hues appear at opposite ends of the dashed lines. Complementary hues, like yellow and blue, for example, mix to produce white light. See Color Plate 14, **a–e**.

238

15.2 Georges Seurat. *Sunday Afternoon on the Island of La Grande Jatte.* 1884–1886. Oil on canvas, 81¾ × 121¼" (207.6 × 308 cm). The Art Institute of Chicago. Helen Birch Bartlett Memorial Collection. *Divisionism* (Pointillism) was an attempt to produce additive optical fusion and thus increase the brilliance and luminance of colors.

figure-objects or grounds; **all effects of the after-image and of simultaneous contrast** on hue, luminance, and purity of colors and their interaction.

IN PHOTOGRAPHY AND PERFORMING ARTS: All floodlighting and spotlighting for photography; all lighting for the theater sets: stage, ballet, opera, motion pictures, television plays, and advertising; color television broadcasting and reception; computer image processing; slide presentations; multimedia shows; additive color transparency films such as Polachrome; filtration for all printing from color negatives; color separation for additive color printing and dye transfer prints; all effects of color filters on both black and white and color film.

IN GENERAL: Research on all physical phenomena: color perception laws and vision; all light phenomena; all color phenomena; international color standards for industry, color reproduction, technical control, and specification of color tolerances.

Additive color mixing applications

Additive color formation will occur in any situation where small dots, dabs, particles, splotches, or geometric arrays of various colors are present. The particles must be small enough or distant enough that they cannot be clearly and individually resolved by the eye. The edges of adjacent colors (especially complementary colors) will provide additive color generation

(simultaneous contrast). Movement enhances fusion.

In painting, examples of additive color mixing are to be found in the works of the late 19th-century artists Georges Seurat and Paul Signac, who developed a technique they called *Divisionism.* More commonly referred to as *Pointillism* today, it is perhaps the most misunderstood technique in the history of art. Seurat was aware of new discoveries in physics relative to the nature of color. He had studied Chevreul and also O. N. Rood, an American physicist, who had discovered that color mixed by the eye was more intense than premixed color. Seurat attempted to combine science and art by reducing color to a scientific theory that any artist could use. He wanted to make use of the concept of optical color mixing, *optical fusion,* in order to increase the atmospheric brilliance of his hues. The method he devised was to apply pure, vivid colors in small dots on the canvas. Seurat expected that the dots would be fused by the eye of the viewer into the color desired. For the proper effect, the viewer would stand at a distance so that the individual dabs or spots of color could not easily be distinguished. In other words, the dots were not intended to be seen. This effect cannot be printed in a book unless the reproduction approaches actual size. *Sunday Afternoon on La Grande Jatte* is almost seven by ten feet (Fig. 15.2).

Optical fusion

If the concept of optical color fusion was to work successfully, it was necessary for Seurat to understand that little dabs of blue paint next to little dots of yellow pigment *did not* fuse to green optically, but to gray (or olive-gray). The viewer needs to understand that the dots or dabs were incidental to the technique, a means to an end, not an end in themselves. Seurat's Divisionism was *not* analogous to pen and ink stipple, but to color television and additive color transparency films.

In order for the concept to work effectively, differing hues are best adjusted, raised or lowered, to approximately equal luminances for application to a subject of that luminance. Dots of alternating light and dark pigments do not provide very satisfactory optical fusion, especially when hue and purity are concerned. View Color Plate 15 **a**, p. 264, from at least seven feet away. The large color patches of orange and blue in the left block can clearly be distinguished from one another. At the same time, the block composed of very small patches of exactly the same colors, right, appears to be a uniform pink. Its luminance is lighter than the blue but darker than the orange. This effect occurs because the luminance factors are added together. A similar block of colors (Color Plate 15 **b**, p. 264) has orange and blue hues of equal luminance. Fusion is easier, in this instance, and the overall luminance does not change. Is it possible to explain why we see "pink"?

In cases where optical fusion is the primary goal, as in Pointillism/Divisionism or in some of the op art works of Victor Vasarely and Richard Anuskiewicz, the optical effects that we observe are dependent on how the coloring matter is deposited on the surface and on the optimum distance the viewer must stand away from the work.

In one example, Color Plate 16 (p. 265) simulates a segment of Richard Anuskiewicz' *Glory Red*. The original acrylic painting is 60 x 60 inches (1.5 x 1.5 cm) composed on a one-inch grid. Although the work includes a chromatic sequence of cool hues (blue, green-blue, green, and yellow-green), the red is painted in exactly the same pigment throughout. The red *appears* to change hue because reflected light waves from the cool colors and the red mix in our eye additively.

Most effects of this type can be photographed because a camera lens also mixes light waves and color film will respond accordingly. However, the photograph will depict the work *as modified by the camera lens*, rather than show the appearance of the

painting as it actually exists. Make careful comparisons between Color Plate 16 and the photograph on the cover of this book. It should be obvious that such works can best be understood only when the original is seen.

Additional examples of optical fusion are shown in Color Plates 17 and 18 (p. 266). In Color Plate 17 **b**, the range of colors varies from yellow through gray to blue, not shades of green as is commonly expected.

Light as a medium

Fine artists will find that light sculpture and light paintings, techniques employing light as a medium, will benefit from a clear understanding of additive color mixing principles. Those who paint naturalistically need to understand that the colors of reflections mix additively, not subtractively.

Every artist who works with pigment and light must be aware of the effect that the physical color temperature of light sources has on their work. Interior decorators may think that a pale purplish-blue wall will look stunning in daylight; but, under incandescent light, rich in red-yellow transmissions, that wall is likely to turn dull gray and ruin an entire decor (Color Plate 5 **a**, p. 259). The same thing will happen to a stage set or to a patch of color in a design or painting. Colors must be critically examined under all types of light likely to be present during expected viewing.

When lighting a theater stage, one could place red spots on one side and green spots on the other. Any subjects that interrupt the beams, such as an actor or a dancer, will cast multicolored shadows, each bearing the hue from the unblocked spot. Where green would cast a shadow, red will appear; where red would cast a shadow, green will appear; and wherever the beams overlap, on the body or on the floor, that area would be defined in brilliant yellow. The result would be interesting, exciting, and theatrical. Almost infinite variations of this concept are possible in all application of all the arts, wherever colored light is used. The same idea can be applied to display lighting and to show window lighting.

In slide shows, colors mix additively

Artists who develop slides shows using dissolve units will find that slides combine additively when projected on a screen. For example, if a red field is projected and held, then green lettering against a black ground dissolved onto it, the lettering will be displayed yellow against a red field. If the red field is allowed to fade to black, the lettering (depending on the rate of dissolve) will gradually change from yellow to green as the red field dims to maroon, reddish brown, and then fades to black. Such a colorful effect may be produced with a piece of red acetate placed in a slide mount and a Kodalith black and white slide dyed green with ordinary food colors — using no color film at all.[21] The possibilities are too numerous to discuss here. Experiment.

Additive color photographic films

The first practical color films, such as Autochrome, Agfachrome, Dufaycolor, and Finlaycolor, were additive in principle. These films were made by covering the surface of a conventional black and white emulsion with one transparent layer of colored dye particles consisting of an equal distribution of the three additive primary colors — red, green, and blue — randomly dispersed, in ruled parallel lines, or in a checkerboard grid structure similar to the surface of a television screen (Color Plate 20, p. 267). These dye particles acted like filters when light passed through them, causing a variation in the exposure of the black and white film underneath. When the black and white emulsion was processed to a positive transparency and viewed together with the same dye pattern, a full-color image resulted. The process's main faults were that the dyes absorbed much of the light, producing a dim picture, and on close observation, the grain or grid of dye particles was visible. See Figure 15.3.

a

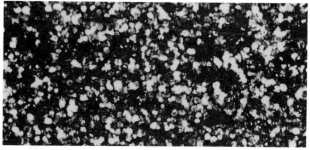

b

15.3   a Alfred Stieglitz. *Mrs. Selma Schubart in a Yellow Dress.* ca. 1907. Lumiére Autochrome, 5 × 7″ (12.7 × 17.8 cm). Metropolitan Museum of Art, New York. The Alfred Stieglitz Collection, 1955. Autochrome, the world's first commercially successful color process, debuted in 1907. The resolution (sharpness) and film speed of early additive films were very limited.
b Autochrome's grain pattern as seen in this black and white × 30 photomicrograph is a mosaic consisting of a random dispersion of "potato starch grains" dyed red, green, and blue. Other early additive films employed regular grid patterns of various sizes.

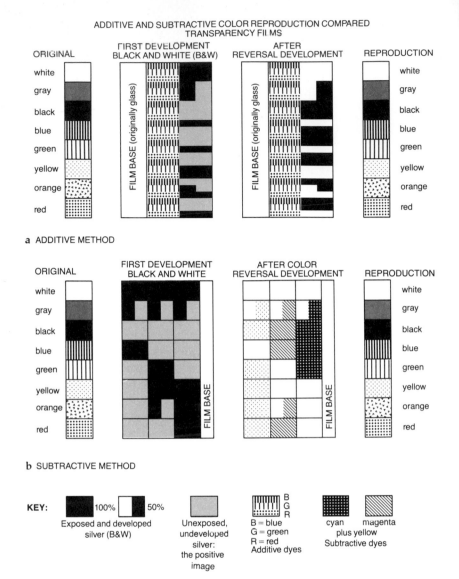

ADDITIVE AND SUBTRACTIVE COLOR REPRODUCTION COMPARED
TRANSPARENCY FILMS

a ADDITIVE METHOD

b SUBTRACTIVE METHOD

KEY: 100% 50% Exposed and developed silver (B&W)

Unexposed, undeveloped silver: the positive image

B = blue
G = green
R = red
Additive dyes

cyan

magenta

plus yellow
Subtractive dyes

15.4 In the *additive* method, top, the three color separation images are recorded side by side as they are in modern television picture tubes. Color reproduction depends on interaction of the silver black and white image (which remains as part of the film) and these color "filters." In the *subtractive* method, bottom, superimposed dye images control hue, luminance, and purity of color although these layers are initially formed by three black and white emulsions, each sensitive to only one additive primary hue. All silver is removed in the processing.

With the invention of Kodachrome in 1935 by the Eastman Kodak Company, additive-based films rapidly disappeared from the marketplace. Kodachrome was the first film producing a subtractive transparency. A comparison of additive and subtractive color films is shown in Figure 15.4. Today the only film employing additive principles is the instant color slide film Polachrome, marketed by the Polaroid Corporation.

Double exposures: Filters mix additively

The artist-photographer should understand that the principles of additive color mixing apply to multiple exposures through color filters, to the effects of colored multiple flood or flash exposure, and to filter selection when color correcting during the printing of color negatives.

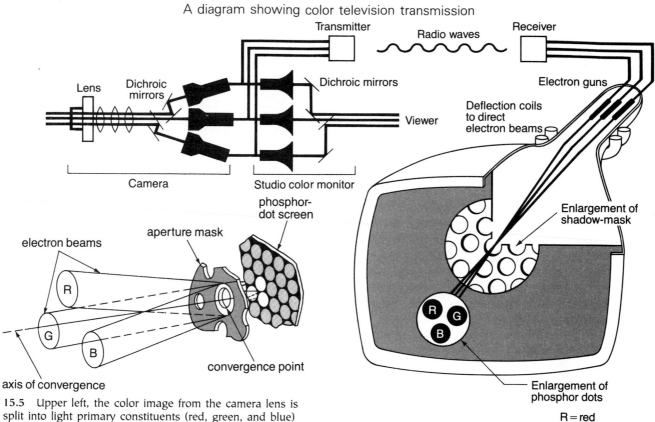

A diagram showing color television transmission

15.5 Upper left, the color image from the camera lens is split into light primary constituents (red, green, and blue) using "dichroic" filter. These are converted to electron beams (not colored themselves) differentiated only by data pertaining to their hue and purity. The luminance signal, which determines lightness or darkness, is separated out so that the signal is compatible with black and white receivers, which are sensitive only to luminance variations.
The electronic components in the receiver reconvert the luminance and color data bearing signals to feed three separate electron guns in the picture tube that simultaneously scan a viewing screen, composed of a triplet pattern of red, green, and blue dots or bars. See Color Plate 20.

This is analogous to what happens in human visual systems.

above left: 15.6 The three electron beams carrying information for each of the additive primary colors converge on the phosphor array on the inside of the picture tube. Each beam is prevented from hitting a phosphor of the wrong hue by the *shadow mask*, a perforated metal plate. The shadow mask in a 21-inch tube has 357,000 holes so there are well over 1,000,000 phosphor triplets on the screen. Only when a beam actually strikes a color phosphor is color visibly recreated for us to view. The angle of convergence is exaggerated in this diagram.

One of many possible effects, for example, would be to photograph a white object, say, a swan, placed against a dark ground. Expose first through a green filter (No. 61). Relocate the swan in the frame so that it only partially covers the first position, and double-expose using a red filter (No. 25). In the developed slide, wherever the subjects overlap, the image will be yellow. Red will appear only on those portions of the image where no green exposure occurred, and vice versa. Theoretically white could not be produced, but the film could be overexposed sufficiently to wipe out the yellow and give white instead. When this is done, blacks often take on the hue of the filter. There

are enormous creative potentials in this idea although results are usually unpredictable.

Television and computer graphics: Additive systems

Computer graphics and color television transmission and reception function, in principle, exactly like the additive color transparency films. See Figures 15.5 and 15.6. On a television screen, observe the mosaic of red, green, and blue phosphors (dots or dashes) against a black background (Color Plate 20, p. 267). These can easily be seen with any ordinary magnifying glass. The phosphors do not overlap, nor

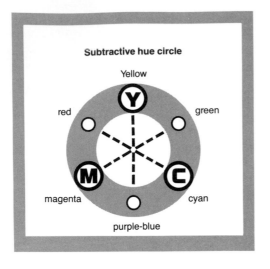

Subtractive hue circle

Yellow

red · green

magenta · cyan

purple-blue

15.7 Primary hues are indicated with large circles; secondary hues, with small circles; and complementary hues are at opposite ends of dashed lines. Complementary hues theoretically mix to appear "black," the absorption of all visible light energy (electromagnetic wavelengths from 400 to 700 nm). See Color Plate 21. In actuality, paint or ink mixtures do not absorb all light.

can white be added. Luminance levels are altered by applying greater or lesser amounts of energy to excite the phosphors. Maximum excitation of all three hues (the additive primaries) simultaneously produces, through optical fusion, a sensation of white light. If the subject is red, the blue and green phosphors will be wholly or mostly dark. We then see red. If only the blue phosphors are dark, the lighted red and green phosphors fuse in our eyes, and we see yellow additively. The yellow will appear greenish or orangy depending on whether the dots are stimulated equally or whether the red or the green is less stimulated than the other. All this is controlled by a black and white (luminance) image, which contains the coded color information in exactly the same way additive color films do.

Subtractive principles of color mixing

The starting point for the *subtractive mixing system* is white light, the presence of all visible electromagnetic vibrations. There are two types of grounds: a pure white reflecting surface such as the paper on which this book is printed or a crystal clear transparent surface through which white light can be transmitted. A translucent surface is a combination of both of these. The terms *pure white* and *crystal clear* are intended to indicate that the surface reflects or transmits a relatively equal distribution of all wavelengths. Although these surfaces may alter the relative energy level of the light, theoretically they do not modify wavelengths. As we have already discovered, that is not necessarily true. All white light has a hue called a *color temperature*. The sensation of white is largely a subjective evaluation made by our brain.

The subtractive system is more easily understood if we think of it as composed of only transparent pigments (rather than opaque or semiopaque ones). The primary hues are yellow, magenta (purplish red), and cyan (greenish blue). See the hue circle (Fig.

15.7). The sum of the luminant levels of individual hues—the mixed color—is always *darker* than any of the component hues. Overlapping all three primaries theoretically prevents passage of all visible light, producing a sensation of black. See Color Plate 21 (p. 267).

Each pigment layer acts like a selectively absorbent "filter," restraining some light waves while reflecting (or transmitting) others. The hue we see is entirely dependent on the dominant wavelength in the reflected light. The effect of the mixed color is partially influenced by the hue of the pigment in the uppermost layer.

Each of the subtractive primaries is a complement to one of the additive primaries and is formed by taking away, that is, absorbing, one of those from white light. Cyan is white light minus red, magenta is white light minus green, and yellow is white light minus blue.

Hue contaminants and subtractive mixing

As we discovered in our study of light, every surface reflects every wavelength of light though each is at a different energy level. In the light reflected from a red tomato are green wavelengths and blue wavelengths as well as red wavelengths. Our brain says that the tomato is red only because the red end of the spectrum dominates. What tells us the tomato is pinkish or orangy depends respectively on whether there are more blue or more green wavelengths present. These blue and green wavelengths represent hue contaminants when mixing pigments. A failure to understand this fact will frustrate all attempts to mix pure hues. Methods by which each artist can manage these and other factors likely to cause problems when mixing pigments are discussed in the next chapter.

Subtractive color mixing occurs whenever light passes through, or is reflected from, one or more selectively absorbent surfaces or coatings (layers of transparent or opaque pigment). The dominant wavelength establishes the hue, and the amount or quantity of electromagnetic energy determines the luminance—the relative lightness or darkness of the color we perceive.

How subtractive color is used

IN APPLIED ARTS: Color printing for magazines, books, posters, and so on; all work with transparent dyes (such as Dr. Martin's or Luma); work with transparent inks; all illustration, design, or craft work with opaque or transparent media, such as acrylics, designers colors, markers, textile paints.

IN FINE AND CONCEPTUAL ARTS: All painting with transparent or opaque colors, such as acrylics, oils, gouache, egg tempera; glazing; pure aquarelle (transparent) watercolor; all craft work with fired enameling materials and glazing frits; stained-glass work and glass collages; transparent dyes or pigments for textiles, batiks, etc.; relief, intaglio, lithography, and screen (silkscreen) printmaking.

IN PHOTOGRAPHY AND PERFORMING ARTS: Most color photographs, prints, and transparencies (slides); photographic color correction for direct positive color print materials such as Cibachrome or Kodak Ektaflex; color correction filtration for matching color temperatures of films and light sources; set decoration; color makeup.

IN GENERAL: All forms of photographic reproduction; standardization for pigments hues (all sorts of paints and finishes for products, such as textiles, cosmetics, and automobiles): in the United States, ISCC-NBS system (Munsell); all wood stains and varnishes; lacquers or enamels for wood, metal, or glass; pigmentation of flora and fauna, geological formations, and other science applications.

How to identify a subtractive system

The mixing system attributed to the viewing of any color surface or field is the predominant one. The section of this book printed in color, for example, is printed subtractively and dominantly viewed that way. Therefore, color printing is referred to as a subtractive process even though there may be additive viewing (optical fusion) effects and even though additive color filters were used to prepare the color separations (Color Plate 22, p. 267).

Subtractive color photographic films

Subtractive color transparency films, such as Kodachrome, Ektachrome, Agfachrome, and Fujichrome contain at least three black and white (silver) emulsion layers stacked one on top of the other, each sensitive to only one of the additive primary hues: red, green, or blue. Take another look at Figure 15.4. In the first developer, all of the exposed silver is processed to a negative just as with ordinary black and white film. The unexposed and undeveloped silver represents the positive image. In the color developer, this unexposed silver is developed and simultaneously encapsulated or coupled with color dyes: the blue sensitive layer with yellow dye, the green sensitive layer with magenta dye, and the red sensitive layer with cyan dye. When the film is fixed, both positive and negative silver images are removed, leaving only the dye particles. This developing procedure is called the reversal process. Superimposed on one another, these positive dye images, one layer for each of the subtractive primaries, produce a full color image of high purity and a wide range of luminant levels. Films with small silver grains (slow-speed films) are capable of resolving very fine detail.

How additive and subtractive systems work together
Color negative films

Color negative films used for color prints record the additive complements of the original colors of the scene (Color Plate 23 **a**, p. 268). When a print is made from this complementary-hued negative, the original hues are restored (Color Plate 23 **b**, p. 268). We view the result subtractively.

Compare Figure 15.4 with Color Plate 22. Are the similarities becoming clear? "Color separation" by additive filtration is characteristic of all forms of reproduction of any full color visual field: color slides, color prints, color printing in magazines and books, color television, and computer graphics. It is also essentially a characteristic of the way that our eyes receive and process light waves.

It is not possible to photograph or to reproduce color directly. We must separate out from the color visual field each of the subtractive primaries as encoded black and white data. We then use these three black and white images, appropriately dyed or printed in colored inks, layer on layer, to recreate the original hues.

The act of color separation for commercial printing purposes is usually done by photography or, in recent years, by the laser scanner, but illustrators for greeting cards and commercial designers are frequently required to "hand color separate" their work for reproduction (printing) purposes. The same is true for the fine art printmaker. A knowledge of subtractive mixing of transparent inks is especially valuable to them. A full and complete understanding of all color mixing, both additive and subtractive mixing systems, will add significantly to the options at the disposal of any artist.

15.8 Jan van Eyck. *The Marriage of Giovanni Arnolfini (?) and Giovanna Cenami (?)* 1434. Oil mixed with tempera on panel, 32¼ × 23½" (81.8 × 59.7 cm). Reproduced by courtesy of the Trustees, The National Gallery, London. An example of what used to be called "mixed technique," now a term with much broader meaning. Such paintings set a standard for the Renaissance and for the centuries that followed.

Color separation with additive color filters

Additive color filters[22] are used to make color separations: A blue filter permits us to record the yellow information; a red filter provides the cyan; and a green filter, the magenta data. It is analogous to the three layers of silver in the color film where the blue sensitive layer is ultimately dyed yellow. Because the density of dyes used in the film is proportional to the amount of processed silver, the dyes can be very dark and pure, yet yield both a light and a dark yellow. When overlapped, they produce a good "black." However, printing inks must be applied in a single layer of only one density. Though lighter hues (luminance differences) are created by the dot pattern imposed by the halftone screen, the base density of the ink is not affected. A transparent yellow ink, light enough to appear pure and brightly hued when reflected from the surface of the paper, does not have sufficient density when combined with similarly formulated magenta and cyan inks to produce black. The resulting overprint is a kind of muddy brown (Color Plate 24, p. 268), and the contrast of the original work is lost or substantially compromised. To restore contrast, a fourth plate—a black plate—is added, giving color printing its name, *four-color process.*

Glazes and varnishes

Although scholars no longer agree, the invention of oil painting has often been attributed to a Flemish painter, Jan van Eyck, who worked around the beginning of the 15th century (Fig. 15.8). He used a combination of a tempera underpainting and oil glazes—a "mixed technique." The brilliance and richness of his colors set a standard for the entire Renaissance and established the basic operational methods practiced by most painters. These masters separated the acts of drawing and painting in the following manner. The composition was drawn on a gesso-coated canvas or wooden panel tinted a neutral brownish hue. A careful drawing in monochrome was done on this surface. Color was added to the monochrome drawing through the use of thin glazes that allowed the underlying drawing to show through.

In more recent times, Maxfield Parrish employed an approach similar to that of the Renaissance painters. A rare unfinished work reveals his technique (Color Plate 25, p. 269). He completed the entire painting as a tonal (monochromatic) study in blue. Color was added entirely with glazes. This method resulted in superior quality reproduction, a factor that made him an outstanding figure in the world of illustration during the 1920s and 1930s.

One of the most neglected tools available to the contemporary painter is the "glaze." A *glaze* consists of a transparent medium, such as oil, to which a transparent pigment has been added. The glaze is usually applied over a dry underdrawing, or underpainting, either of which may be monochromatic or in color. Like layering of colored glass or cellophane, glazes can intensify colors, creating jewellike qualities. In creative hands, marvelous qualities of transparency and translucency are possible. If anyone has ever wondered about the subtle, almost tactile qualities of flesh in 16th–early 19th-century portrait paintings as seen in art museums, it is more likely than not that these effects were created with glazes. It is a quality virtually impossible to capture in a slide or printed reproduction although it always influences the reproduction. The original must be seen to be appreciated.

Glazes act like filters, selectively absorbing certain wavelengths of light. A color glaze over a color paint film increases or decreases the purity of a hue depending on whether the glaze matches or complements the underlying color. If, for example, a red

glaze is placed over red pigment, purity is considerably enhanced because hue-contaminating green and blue reflections from the red pigment layer will be reduced—that is, filtered out. Light passes through the glaze, which narrows or restricts the wavelengths of light reaching the pigment layer underneath, which, in turn, selectively absorbs green and blue wavelengths before reflecting the light back through the red glaze to the viewer's eye (see Fig. 13.13). Thus filtered three times, the red light reaching the viewer's eye is more nearly monochromatic, producing a purer and more vivid color. The price the painter pays for these more intense colors is a reduced luminance (a darker color). One simply compensates by making the underpainting color lighter (a higher luminance) than desired, so that the glaze will make it correct, not darker. Any accomplished painter must learn to trade off such negatives.

Not only can glazes be used to enrich colors, but they can also modify all three of its dimensions: hue, luminance, and purity. If a green glaze is placed over a red pigment layer, the result will be a brown hue because the red light energy available to be reflected back to the eye is reduced. Thus, a red, too bright for its position in a painting, may be modified to cut its purity slightly with a weak bluish-green glaze or virtually turned black with a heavy bluish-green glaze. A light hue may be darkened with a glaze of a darker pigment of the same generic hue. This type of luminance adjustment can be made without totally repainting any part of a work.

Surface finish: A few pros and cons

Variations in the surface characteristics of a painting are creative tools for the fine artist—impasto textures here; smoothness there; a shiny, reflective quality here; a dull matte surface there. Such an interplay enriches the tactile quality of the surface. Though these usually do not reproduce well, a fine art painting is intended to be appreciated as it exists — as an entity or object in its own right — not as a reproduction.

Conversely, applied artists must understand that their works must be uniformly matte or uniformly glossy for best reproduction, containing no mixtures of matte and glossy surfaces. The reproduction camera will pick up differences in surface finish as differences in color density (luminance).

Differing densities produced by light reflections from matte or glossy surfaces may totally destroy a work judged only by the quality of the reproduction. For this reason, a final varnish is always worth considering. It adds depth to dark colors and to the blacks. The same problem occurs with heavy impastos. In this case, a varnish only compounds the problem. Though wonderful in fine artworks, it is a technique that should be carefully considered or totally avoided in works intended primarily for reproduction.

Using transparent colors in printing

In printmaking, the concept of subtractive mixing with transparent inks can extend hue, luminance, and purity control just as one can do with glazes. It becomes an especially valuable approach when it is necessary to get the most out of a limited number of colors. When transparent inks are used rather than opaque ones, blue and yellow can be overprinted to produce a green — two runs, but three colors. The luminance level of the green will be approximately the sum of the yellow and the blue added together, so three luminances are also produced simultaneously with just two runs. If, for example, we now add one run of a pale reddish orange, we can increase both hues and luminances by four: pale reddish orange;

golden orange-yellow, olive green, and gray-blue. Thus a few colors may suggest many hues, luminances, and degrees of purity.

A red and green of the correct luminances will overprint to produce black. If screens or textures are used, we may be able to have brown, olivey-green, neutralish grays, pinks, and sky blue also. Two colors will look like many (see Color Plate 26, p. 269). The hue of the paper can also be used as an additional creative color tool.

The applied artist can employ exactly the same idea to create color-separated art for reproduction. Such concepts enhance color options available when the designer is faced with a limited budget. Fewer colors reduce printing costs for the client. Economy does not necessarily need to limit creativity.

Partitive color formation

Partitive color mixing is not a separate system. It results from viewing colors in which the wavelengths reflected to our eye are modified partially in an additive fashion and partially in a subtractive fashion.

Our brain will average the hue (wavelength), purity, and luminance of the combined colors in any specific area of the visual field, with the lightest luminance and the most active hue (purest) influencing the result. Opportunities for partitive color formation are, of course, numerous. Virtually all pictorial fields exhibit this characteristic to some degree, including the color printing in this book.

Though Seurat had hoped through Divisionism to achieve an additive mixing of the colors, an imperfect application of the theories resulted in a partitive response when viewing his work. Remember that the dots were not meant to be seen.

A contrasting idea was *Orphism*, in which much

15.9 Robert Delaunay. *Window on the City No. 3.* 1911–
1912. Oil on canvas, 44¾ × 51½″ (113.7 × 130.8 cm). The
Solomon R. Guggenheim Museum, New York. The patches of
color seen in this work were not intended to produce optical
fusion, but to create a poetical quality in surface texture,
space, and color. Although they vary considerably in size,
the patches average about 1/2 × 11/16″ (1.1 × 1.9 cm).

larger patches of color were a deliberate artistic concept rather then an attempt to create optical fusion. In this case, the broken color was meant to be observed as part of the character of the work (Fig. 15.9).

Summary

The additive and subtractive color systems account for all the varieties of color we perceive throughout our lifetime. They are the basis for all color used in the arts, and each has a wide variety of specific applications. What is not common knowledge is how the additive system, light, affects our mixing of color pigments, which are viewed in the subtractive system.

For example, the physical properties of light govern our ability to match in paint any form of natural light effect such as transparent or translucent objects and reflections of one color on another. These combine additively, not subtractively.

A significant point that any painter or illustrator must remember is that all effects of simultaneous contrast are additive in principle. The colors in after-image we see are the additive (light) complements of original hues, not subtractive complements.

At the present time, there is no system for reproducing natural color without additive color separation of primary hues for additive or subtractive reproduction. Nor is there any viable proposed theory to accomplish this feat. Actually, they are both characteristics of light, one the obverse of the other—two sides of the same coin. Artists then, as well as scientists and engineers, are wise to learn about and to understand the mechanisms of light in order to be able to apply this knowledge to the solution of visual problems.

Understanding how the additive and the subtractive systems work together jointly provides artists with many additional creative alternatives they would not otherwise possess.

Review of key terms

additive color The color mixing system of light. When the primary hues, red, green, and blue are added together, the result is white light. Yellow is seen when red and green lights are mixed; cyan is a combination of green and blue light; magenta, of red and blue.

Divisionism A technique developed and named by Georges Seurat and Paul Signac that attempted to apply the scientific concept of *optical fusion* to painting. The works were characterized by an overall pattern of tiny dots of pure colors. The term *Pointillism* is more commonly applied to these works, but in a manner that tends to distort the painters' objectives.

glaze A thin, medium-rich application of transparent color over an underlying drawing or painting in order to add, alter, blend, enrich, or unify colors. It is a means of creating transparency and luminosity in works of art. Glazes may be used to alter any of the three dimensions of color: hue, luminance, and purity. Glazes may be worked over dry grounds or applied with a wet-in-wet technique.

optical fusion The blending in the eye of two or more discrete elements in any visual field so that each loses its separate identity. For example, if we spin a disk half white and half black at high speed, we will see a shade of middle gray, not black or white. The variety of colors on a TV set are created by the optical fusion of many tiny triplet patterns of red, green, and blue phosphors.

Orphism One of several similar styles that were characterized by surface patterns composed of dashes, dabs, or dots of paint, used as a means of endowing the works with a poetic quality. Objectives were very different from those of Divisionism.

Pointillism *See* **Divisionism.**

primary colors The irreducible number of hues in any color system from which theoretically all other colors may be mixed.

secondary colors Hues mixed by combining any pair of primary colors.

subtractive color The basic form of color mixing and viewing we experience with paint, ink, and most color photography. Pigments absorb (subtract) certain wavelengths of white light. The color we perceive consists only of reflected or transmitted wavelengths. The primary hues are yellow (white light minus blue); magenta (white minus green); and cyan (white minus red).

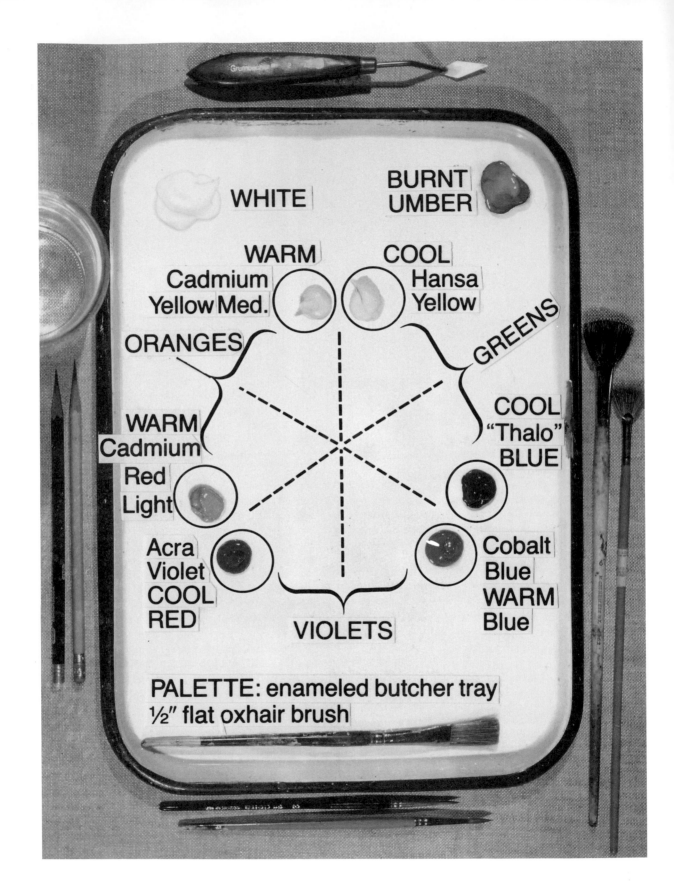

WHITE

BURNT UMBER

WARM
Cadmium Yellow Med.

COOL
Hansa Yellow

ORANGES

GREENS

WARM
Cadmium Red Light

COOL
"Thalo" BLUE

Acra Violet COOL RED

Cobalt Blue WARM Blue

VIOLETS

PALETTE: enameled butcher tray
½" flat oxhair brush

CHAPTER SIXTEEN

A practical basic palette

For those persons beginning to study art seriously or those persons with little practical experience, the *double primary palette* (Fig. 16.1) offers some distinct advantages.

The double primary palette takes into account the fact that *no satisfactory true artists' primary pigments exist.* In other words, there are no specific hues in permanent artists' paints (dyes or pigments) meeting theoretical requirements. To fulfill such requirements, the pigments should not degrade the purity of the mixed hue. This would permit the mixing of a full range of generic hues at high purity levels. These pigments should also meet artists' requirements for stability and permanency. The double primary palette most nearly satisfies all three of these requirements.

For design studies, acrylic paints are recommended. They dry fast and can be worked over without disturbing the paint layer underneath. Paint is essentially made up of pigments combined with a vehicle, *the binder* that fastens pigments to the surface. Acrylic polymer emulsion is the vehicle for acrylic paints, for example, as linseed oil is for oil paints and gum arabic is for watercolor. Before we can proceed, there are some things we need to know about *pigments.*

A few words about pigment characteristics

Fugitive and permanent pigments

Permanency has long been a problem for artists concerned with the longevity of their work. In years past, many colors were fugitive; that is, they faded or changed hue within a relatively short time. Alizarin Crimson, long thought relatively permanent, has recently been given a lower rating. The culprits include not only the ultraviolet radiation in sunlight and daylight but also atmospheric gases, for example, and adverse chemical reactions from mixing incompatible substances together. Some pigments made out of lead compounds reacted with those made from organic dyes. Pigments are chemicals, and certain ones, like true Vermilion, a bright orange-red made from a sulfide of mercury, behaved unpredictably (it sometimes turned black). In the past many of these pigments were used because no adequate substitute hues were available. Today chemical technology has made it possible to replace most fugitive colors with more permanent ones in a range of bright colors of high purity. There is rarely any need to use pigments whose permanence is unreliable.

Transparent, translucent, and opaque pigments

Some artists' pigments are transparent; others, opaque; and some, intermediary between the two, semiopaque or translucent.

Transparent pigments, when applied thinly, allow the light to pass right through, striking the ground before it is reflected back to the eye. This may increase their apparent purity. Transparent pigments, even when applied in a thick layer, do not always cover well; be prepared for some underlying color or ground to show through.

Opaque paints reflect light from the surface of the paint film. They cover most grounds well except when too diluted with media or when combined with transparent pigments. Because glazing and scumbling techniques depend on such knowledge, artists should know which pigment is which. A list will be found in the Appendix.

opposite: **16.1** Double primary palette. This photograph of a palette is arranged as a diagram. For painting, it is best if the paints are placed around the outside edge in natural order, leaving the center free for mixing.

Relative color temperature

In the chapter about light, we found out about physical color temperature, which is expressed in degrees Kelvin. Artists understand that there is also subjective color temperature. It is important to make clear that subjective color temperature is relative. However, broadly speaking, yellows, oranges, and reds are considered warm; and greens and blues, cool; violets are often seen as neutral.

Relative color temperature is determined by direct comparison of two or more patches of color. There are warm and cool aspects to every hue. For example, a warm green has significant red wavelengths (600–700 nm) in the reflection, causing it to lean toward the yellows (remember, in light, red and green mix additively to produce yellow); a cool green has strong blue wavelengths (400–500 nm) present, causing it to lean toward cyan (greenish blue). Similarly, a warm red contains significant green wavelengths, causing it to lean toward orange; and a cool red leans toward violet because it has significant blue wavelengths in its reflection.

The physical wavelength composition of the reflection from color pigments and the physical color temperature of the light always affects our perception of relative color temperature. That is a point worth remembering.

The physical effects of hue contaminants

Never forget that reflected wavelengths differing from the perceived generic hue (the dominant wavelength) of a surface represent *hue contaminants* that may adversely affect purity. These additional wavelengths often mix additively to produce the complement of the hue desired. Examine Figure 16.2, for example.

A warm yellow, like Cadmium Yellow, has very high red (700 nm) reflections. An attempt to mix a green by combining Cadmium Yellow with Ultramarine Blue will result in a very muddy color with an olive tone. Ultramarine Blue has strong wavelengths in indigo (400 nm, near ultraviolet), as well as some red. The blue causes the combined red wavelengths present to shift toward magenta, the additive complement to green. The mixture of these hues in a reflection results in a loss of light energy and a neutralization of the distinctive hue, a gray with a greenish tint. These two warm pigments cannot be mixed to provide a pure, vivid green. Correct use of the double primary palette eliminates this type of problem.

Familiarity with warm and cool qualities of each pigment we use is essential for mixing vivid, pure colors. A list of warm and cool pigments will be found in the Appendix.

The double primary hue circle and palette

A list of pigments needed for the double primary palette follows.

A Basic Palette
Employing the "double primary" principle

Advantage: Ability to maintain highest possible purity of hue throughout the color spectrum with a limited number of paints.

Lumi-nance*	Hue/Pigment Identification	Opacity**	Temper-ature***
D 1.0	Hansa Yellow Light (or Lemon)	T	cool
D 2.0	Cadmium Yellow Medium	O	warm
D 5.0	Cadmium Red Light (not medium)	O	warm
D 6.0	Acra Violet (preferred)	T	cool
	or Permanent Magenta****	T	cool
D 7.0	Cobalt Blue (good grade!)	O	warm
D 9.0	Phthalocyanine ("Thalo") Blue	T	cool

Add neutrals to TOTAL 9 COLORS:

D 0.0	Titanium White	O	—
D 9.0	Burnt Umber (preferred)	SO	warm
	or Raw Umber	SO	warm
D10.0	Ivory (or Lamp) Black	SO	—

Optional: **To expand palette to** *12 colors,* **add:**

D 3.0	Cadmium Orange	O	warm
D 9.0	Phthalocyanine (Thalo) Green	T	cool
D 9.0	Dioxazine Purple	T	—

Optional: **To expand palette to** *14 colors,* **also add these:**

D 6.0	Raw Sienna	SO	warm
D 4.0	Yellow Ochre (or Yellow Oxide)	O	warm

*Approximate luminance given as a *density factor,* D.

**Transparency/opacity abbreviations used are as follows: T = completely transparent pigment; O = opaque pigment; translucent, or semiopaque, pigments are marked SO.

***These color temperatures are not just subjective but indicate the physical presence in their reflection of wavelengths other than that of the generic hue. These are "hue contaminants," which often adversely affect mixing pure, vivid colors.

****A product manufactured by Windsor and Newton.

Note: Not all pigments listed are available by name in some manufacturers' lines of artists' paints. This is particularly true when adapting the palette to other media, such as oils and watercolors. Check the labels or product literature for pigment identification of trade names like Windsor Violet (W&N) that is primarily dioxazine.

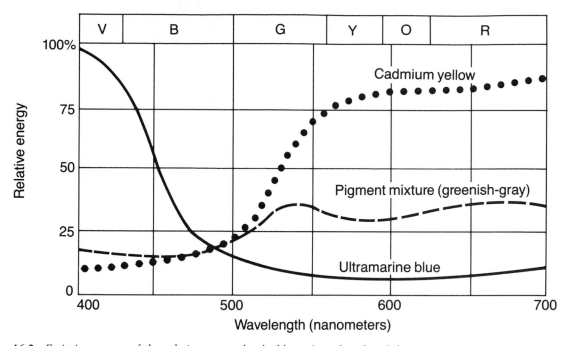

16.2 Emission curves of the relative energy level of hues (wavelengths of the color spectrum) in the light reflected from Cadmium Yellow and Ultramarine Blue paints, together with the reflection of their mixture, a greenish gray. Note the high reflectance of red wavelengths (700 nm) in yellow and violet as well as red in the blue. Because the expected hue of the mixture, green, is the subtractive complement to red, these two pigments are incapable of mixing a "pure" green. A combination of Cadmium Yellow and Cobalt Blue will produce similar results.

The special characteristics

How warm and cool pigments are managed

Observe that the double primary palette consists of a cool and a warm yellow; a cool and a warm red; and a cool and a warm blue. Figure 16.2 shows that Cadmium Yellow (warm) and Ultramarine Blue (warm) will not produce a vivid, pure green when mixed. What is needed to obtain purer greens is a cool yellow and a cool blue. Hansa Yellow Light, when mixed with Thalo Blue, will enable us to produce a wide range of very pure, vivid greens. Purer greens can be obtained only by purchasing a pure green pigment such as Thalo Green. The diagram in Figure 16.1 shows how the warm and the cool pigments are combined to mix any hue desired. When Thalo Blue is mixed with Cadmium Red (light, medium, or dark), the result is a dirty, unsatisfactory hue rather than a pure violet. What is needed is a cool red and warm blue. Acra Violet (actually a kind of magenta) and Cobalt Blue will provide a range of very good violets. Of course, a warm yellow and a warm red would be needed to provide the brightest oranges. This pattern of mixing avoids virtually all adverse effects of hue contaminants.

The density factor, D

The *density factor*, D, is the obverse of the Munsell color system's *value*. Conversion from one to the other is accomplished simply by subtracting the original number from 10. The D factor possesses certain desirable characteristics: (1) It is compatible with printing densities expressed as a percentage of color (density factor 1.0 is equivalent to 10 percent black, for example, a very light gray); (2) when mixing paints, it aids in determining luminances, that is, the relationship of individual colors to the gray scale; and (3) it is similar to photographic density scales, for example. The density factor is subtractive in principle, the Munsell value notation is additive. In the applied arts, luminant levels are more often specified as a percentage of darkness

16.3 Most art materials use density markings, that is, an indication of the darkness or density of a color in which, as the percent of density increases, numbers become larger up to 100 percent, for example. When a light, medium, or dark "value" is mentioned, the reference usually means density, not a reference to Munsell "value," in which numbers grow smaller as the color becomes darker rather than as it becomes lighter. One brand of artists' paints, however, marks tubes with Munsell "values." Conversion is easy. See text.

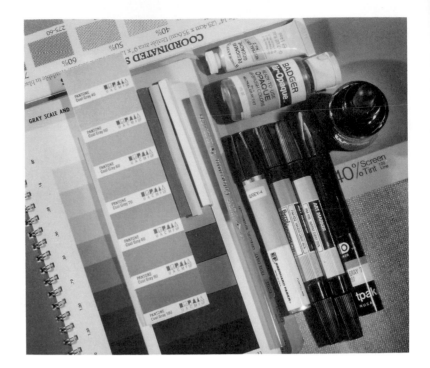

(density). For instance, "values" shown on markers and "values" shown on retouch grays are all actually density notations (Fig. 16.3).

Body colors

Remember that the body color is the colored appearance of a substance based on the dominant wavelength of light reflected to the eye. Differences in hue, luminance, and purity are based on the molecular structure of the substance. When we mix different pigments together, we alter the composition and proportions of such substances.

Even the physical alteration of the same substance may produce a change in hue. All cadmium colors are made of exactly the same pigment. Yellow is produced by grinding the cadmium crystals very fine. Reds are composed of large crystals of exactly the same substance, and orange is a mixture of both large and small crystals. When we mix Cadmium Yellow Medium with Cadmium Red Light, we get virtually the same paint film packaged in a tube of Cadmium Orange.

How pigment choice changes purity

Some pigments that are complementary to others have widely different luminances. One may be light, the other may be dark. For example, mixing Cadmium Yellow with Dioxazine Purple (or Cobalt Violet Deep) not only changes the yellow's purity but also significantly alters luminance because both violets are very dark.

An important principle: To alter purity but not luminance, the complement must be adjusted (raised or lowered) to the *same luminant level* as the original hue (the yellow), then mixed.

Whenever the greatest purity of hue is required, select a pigment as close to the desired color as possible so that very little or no mixing is required. This is one reason why many professional artists use an extended palette. This statement is especially true for watercolor because colors appear somewhat duller on the surface than acrylics and oils — the result of light-scattering reflections from the rough paper ordinarily used.

The double primary palette provides artists with the best opportunity to create a full range of pure hues at maximum purity, using a limited number of pigments.

Artists' colors are composed of dyes or pigments formulated to produce maximum hue purity from source materials. These paints are meant to provide artists with as much flexibility as possible in the selection of intense, vivid, pure hues for whatever purpose they have in mind. None are specifically manufactured

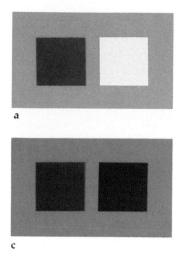

a

b

c

d

CP.1 **Color attraction.** In **a**, color advances; gray (an achromatic color) recedes. In **b**, hues complementary to grounds advance; hues analogous to the ground recede. In **c**, colors whose luminance contrasts with the ground usually advance; but those whose luminance is similar to, or the same as, the ground tend to recede. **d** Pure hues advance; grayed, or impure, hues recede.

CP.2 **Prism with a black pattern.** A student project employing *process* as a design principle. Rendered in pen and ink, the black pattern shown in Figure 4.28, was photostated on a transparent sheet of acetate and placed over a coordinated color pattern consisting of one chromatic (prismatic) sequence and one tonal sequence, each consisting of a minimum of eight steps. (Courtesy of Amy Taylor.)

CP.3 Foreground rock formations are within the boundaries of Bryce Canyon National Park. Note bright oranges, reds, and yellows of various rock layers. Though rock formations on the far distant cliffs (horizon line, upper left) are not so interesting in shape, exactly the same brightly hued rock layers exist. The difference in the colors observed is due to the presence of the atmosphere, which moves distant hues toward purple-blue.

EVERY CHILD

EVERY CHILD HAS THE RIGHT TO BE BORN FREE OF SYPHILIS. PROTECT YOUR FUTURE CHILD. GO TO YOUR DOCTOR OR A CLINIC FOR A CHECKUP INCLUDING A BLOOD TEST.

CP.4 Ben Shahn. Poster design for an antisyphilis campaign proposed by Columbia University for the U.S. Public Health Service. ca. 1951. This graphic image was rejected on the ground that it was ''too strong'' and might frighten away contributors.

258

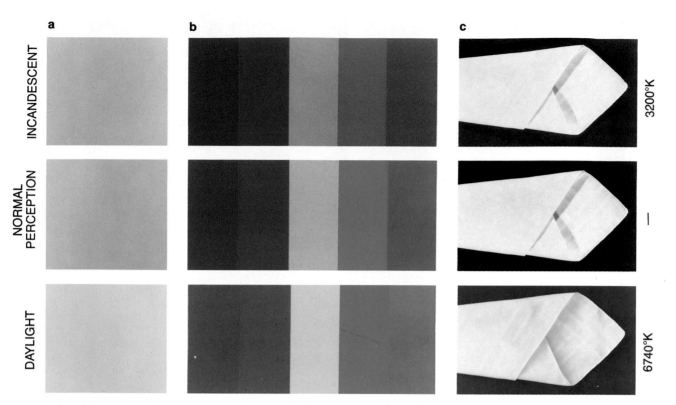

CP.5 In all three parts of this composite photograph, the center strip shows hues as we should perceive them "normally." The top strip shows those same hues as modified by incandescent light (yellowish). In the bottom row colors are modified by the hue of noon daylight (bluish). Even though we are not ordinarily aware of these differences in the hue of light sources, **they alter the way in which we perceive and mix pigment colors**! The effect is always additive.

CP.6 Photographs of an orangy red tomato, a green sweet pepper, and a violet-hued hydrangea blossom under three different strong chromatic lights, each lacking one of the additive primaries. Photo **a** was taken in greenish blue light (cyan) light; **b** in yellowish green (yellow) light; and **c** in bluish red (magenta) light. The objects reflect significantly different color mixtures back to the eye because the object cannot reflect a hue whose wavelength is not present in the light source.

259

a

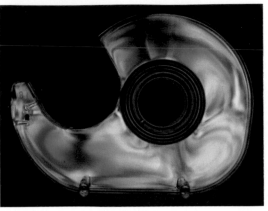

b

above: **CP.7** Variations in the angles of reflection and refraction of light waves as revealed by polarizing the light produces the colors seen in these clear, transparent materials. In **a**, slivers of cellophane in a 35 mm slide sandwich. In **b**, an ordinary clear plastic dispenser, which comes with small rolls of transparent tape. The colors seen are the result of light wave interference.

below: **CP.8** Hopi Point, Grand Canyon. The camera was pointed in the same direction, unchanged for all four photographs. The differences in the apparent shape and texture of the landscape and in the moods are due to the orientation and hue changes of the prime light source (the sun) at different times during one day: **a** sunrise, **b** noon, **c** afternoon, and **d** sunset.

a

b

c

d

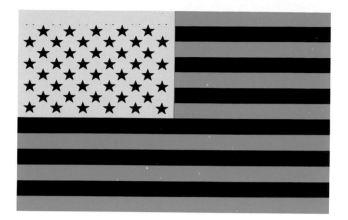

CP.9 Experiment with the afterimage. Stare intently at the center of this flag for approximately 20 seconds; then shift attention to the small black dot in the white space next to it. What is observed?

below: CP.10 Jasper Johns. *Flags.* 1965. Oil on canvas, 72″ × 48″ (183 × 122 cm). Courtesy Leo Castelli Gallery, New York.

a

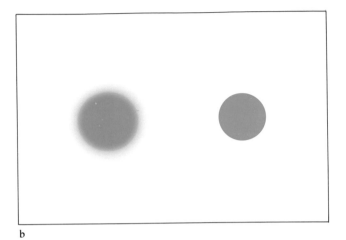

b

c

d

CP.11   EFFECTS OF SIMULTANEOUS CONTRAST ON HUE, LUMINANCE, AND PURITY. In a, size changes apparent purity and luminance. The small round spot (right) seems darker and less pure in hue than large rectangular mass (left) of *exactly the same color*. **In b, sharpness (distinction) of contour changes perceived purity and luminance.** A spot (right) with hard edges seems darker and less pure in hue than a soft-edged spot (left) although both are identical colors. **In c, color of ground changes perceived purity.** A green ring with a neutral gray ground looks different from exactly the same green with a complementary ground (red) because the cyan afterimage (from red) reinforces its purity making it seem to be more vivid (intense) and lighter. **In d, color of ground changes perceived hue.** Though both magenta rings are exactly the same color, the ring with a red ground looks distinctly "cooler" because the afterimage hue (cyan) from the analogous red ground shifts the hue toward violet.

262

a

b

c

d

e

f

CP.12   VISIBILITY A wide luminance range and complementary hues *increase* visibility. A narrow luminance range and analogous hues *reduce* visibility. Note how words stand out in **a**, **b**, and **c**, but are much more difficult to read in **d**, **e**, and **f**. Could these concepts be used to emphasize an object in a painting or in a room, or, conversely, to camouflage an object or mass?

below: CP.13   USING SIMULTANEOUS CONTRAST TO MANAGE ADVANCING AND RECEDING EDGES.   In all the examples shown, there has been a deliberate attempt to maintain very close luminances so that attention can be strictly focused on hue. This is not ordinarily necessary. Part **a** shows patches of red and blue with a hard edge between them. In **b**, moving the red patch edge toward violet, an analogous hue, causes the edge to recede. In **c**, moving the red patch edge toward orange (yellow), a complementary hue, causes the edge to advance. In **d**, moving the blue patch edge toward green (cyan), a complementary hue, causes the edge to advance. In **e**, moving the blue edge toward violet, an analogous hue, causes the edge to recede. In **f**, moving both edges toward their shared analogous hue, violet, results in a hue sequence in natural order, which virtually causes the edge to disappear.

a

b

c

d

e

f

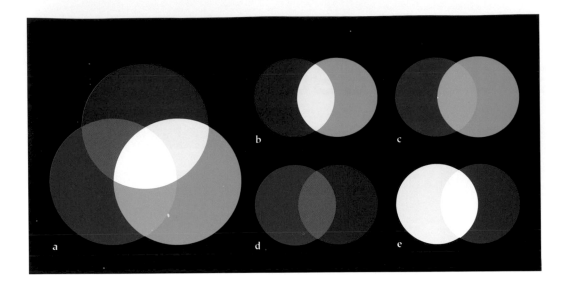

CP.14 THE ADDITIVE COLOR MIXING SYSTEM. The illustration simulates three different spotlights focused on a white screen in a dark room—one for each of the three additive primaries, red, green, and blue. These mix to produce white light, **a.** Mixtures of any two additive primaries produce additive secondaries: red and green mix to yellow, **b;** blue and green mix to cyan, **c;** and blue and red mix to magenta, **d.** Complementary hues mix to *white light.* For example, yellow and blue mix to white light, **e.**

below: CP.15 OPTICAL FUSION. In **a,** although the larger patches, left and center, remain clearly distinguishable, additive optical mixing of the small patches of color (far right) produce a pinkish hue when viewed from a distance of about seven feet. Differing luminances inhibit the effect. In **b,** when the smallest blue patches are matched to the same luminance level as the orange ones, optical fusion is easier, and the result is stronger and more predictable. Even the very large patches are less distinguishable from one another.

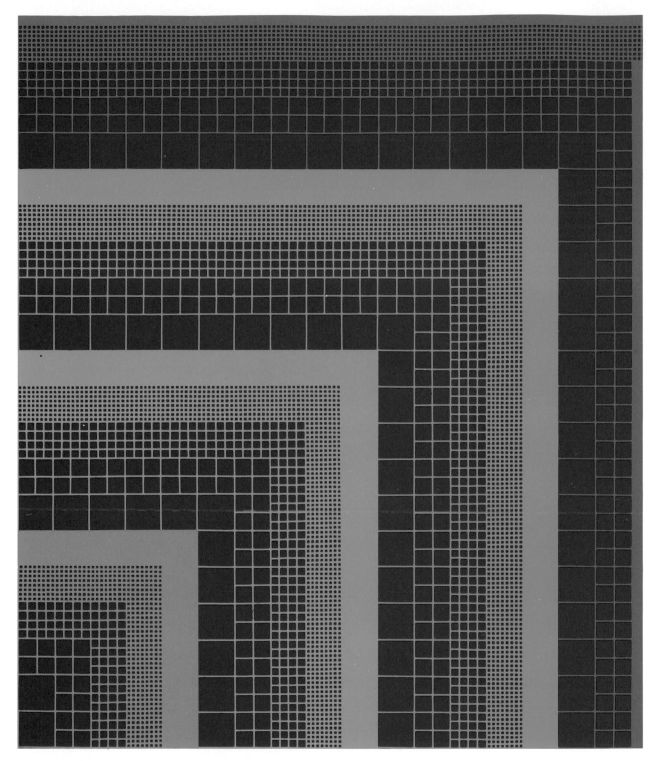

CP.16 Using special graphic art techniques to eliminate optical fusion of colors in a camera lens, this approximately one-third size reconstruction of Richard Anuskiewicz' *Glory Red* (see cover of this book) provides a more accurate indication of the true appearance of the painting. Optical fusion is intended to occur in the eye not in the camera. Effects are most pronounced when this example is viewed under very bright light at some distance away (10–12 feet). Note how the red seems to change hue and how the fine green lines (lower left corner) turn yellow.

265

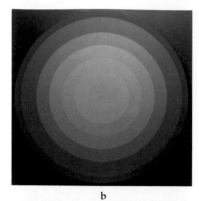

a

b

CP.17 The fluting, or Mach effect, occurs when areas of uniform luminances, one light and one dark, placed side by side, are separated by a hard edge. It is a result of perceptual *irradiation*. When the disk **a**, left, is spun, the result is not a smooth progression of steps from light to dark as we would expect to see, but a series of fluted bands **b**.

a

b

CP.18 Differences between mixing pigments and mixing light: If the orange-red, green, and blue pigments used to paint the disc, **a**, were mixed together on a palette, they would absorb much of the light producing a muddy gray, but when this disc is spun, **b**, the light reflected by each hue is mixed optically in the eye. The luminance of each hue is *added to the other*, producing secondary mixtures that are lighter than either component.

a

b

CP.19 In **a**, the green light reflected from the green wall has little observable effect on the blue jeans, merely moving their hue toward cyan, an analogous hue. In **b**, the red light reflected from the red wall is almost the additive complement of the blue jeans. Their hue is moved towards gray-violet. Is that what we should expect from the additive hue circle (Fig. 15.1)?

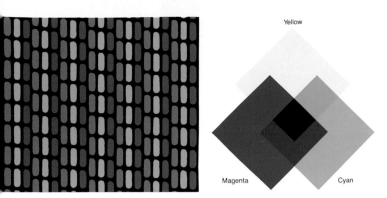

Yellow

Magenta   Cyan

far left: **CP.20** The phosphors in many modern TV color picture tubes are arranged in triplets of vertical dashes rather than dots. This is particularly true of high resolution *RGB* computer monitors. RGB stands for red-green-blue, the additive color primaries. Note that a dense black pigment fills spaces between the phosphors — there is no "white" at all.

left: **CP.21** **THE SUBTRACTIVE MIXING SYSTEM.** In the subtractive mixing system, the primary hues, yellow, magenta, and cyan, theoretically combine to block all transmission or reflection of visible light, producing the appearance of "black."

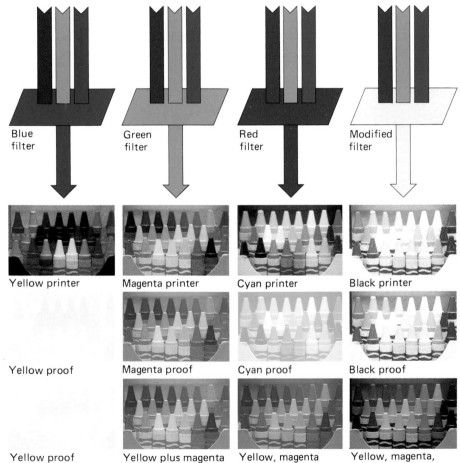

Blue filter	Green filter	Red filter	Modified filter
Yellow printer	Magenta printer	Cyan printer	Black printer
Yellow proof	Magenta proof	Cyan proof	Black proof
Yellow proof	Yellow plus magenta	Yellow, magenta plus cyan	Yellow, magenta, cyan plus black

CP.22 A diagram of *four-color process* reproduction. All full color reproductions in this book, as well as those in every other type of printing — book, magazine, or brochure — are made using this process. It is not currently possible to print color directly. Color reproduction is possible only by separating primary hue data out of the original and recombining them as shown. Note the similarities (**connections**) with color transparency films (both additive and subtractive), television, and our own visual mechanism. Color separation is a black and white process. Actual color does not return until the printing plates are on the press. Each color of ink must be laid down one at a time just as is required for a linoleum block or a silk screen print.

267

a

b

c

above and left: **CP.23 COLOR NEGATIVE FILM:** Additive in the negative—subtractive in the print. In **a**, a "masked" color negative just like those returned with the prints from the processors who develop the film. The orange *mask* improves color brilliance and fidelity. Colors seen are the additive complements of the natural colors (all three dimensions). In **b**, a print from the color negative (left). Note that the yellow bottle, center, is blue on the negative; and vice versa, the blue bottle is yellow on the negative. In **c**, a color negative with the orange mask removed, the additive complements are easier to detect. *Note* that the collie dog's red tongue is cyan blue, and the tan and brown fur is purple-blue. Are these the complementary hues we should expect to see?

left bottom: **CP.24** A greatly enlarged detail of a four-color process halftone like that seen lower right in Color Plate 22. The halftone dot pattern is clearly visible as are the dots of the subtractive primaries, yellow, cyan, and magenta. Observe the characteristic muddy brown hue of the overlap of these primary hues. *Note* the few black dots. An ordinary magnifying glass will reveal this pattern in most books and many magazines, however, some dot patterns are so small that a microscope may be required.

opposite: **CP.27** The Hue/Luminance Chart with hues at maximum purity. Refer to Figure 16.5 and the gray scale, (Fig. 16.6). The luminances are approximately correct when bars appear to run horizontally rather than vertically. Check luminances by laying color chips next to the appropriate gray tone. If the edge can be seen clearly, the luminance is not the same. When the luminances are the same, the edge will disappear.

a

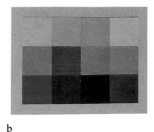

b

above: **CP.25** Maxfield Parrish. *October (Dreaming).* 1928. Oil on a panel, 32 × 50″ (81 × 127 cm). Private collection. Courtesy Alma Gilbert Gallery, San Mateo, Calif. This unfinished painting shows his technique, which included a monochromatic underpainting in blue. Colors were added with glazes. Parrish's uncommon technique resulted in unusually good color reproduction for his time.

above right: **CP.26** THE TWO-COLOR PALETTE. Part **a**, shows some of the hues possible to mix from only two colors: an orange-red (similar to Cadmium Scarlet or to Vermilion) and cyan-green (similar to Thalo Green) or equivalent hues in inks. The colors are shown on a white ground. Such a combination would be called a *limited palette* in painting and a *two-color printing job* in applied art. Part **b**, shows exactly the same colors seen in **a** but as they would appear rendered in transparent pigments (or inks) on a pink paper. Although both of these diagrams are simulated by four-color process, effects are relatively faithful to the original.

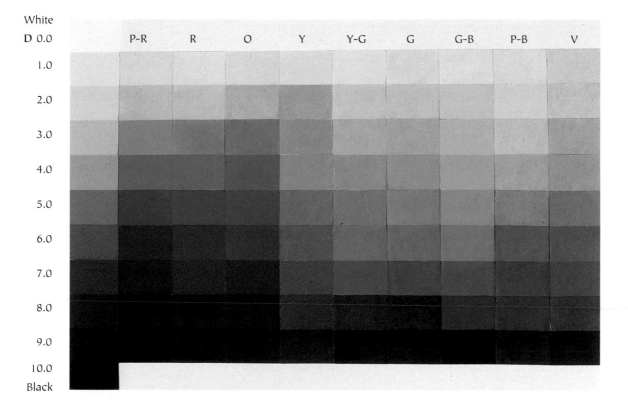

CP.28 HOW TO MIX NINE STEPS OF THE HUE YELLOW In **a**, a yellow scale from light to dark in nine steps using black pigment to darken the yellow. The hue shifts toward green. In **b**, a yellow scale from light to dark in nine steps is constructed according to directions in the text. It is a more convincing sequence for yellow because the yellow does not appear to change in hue.

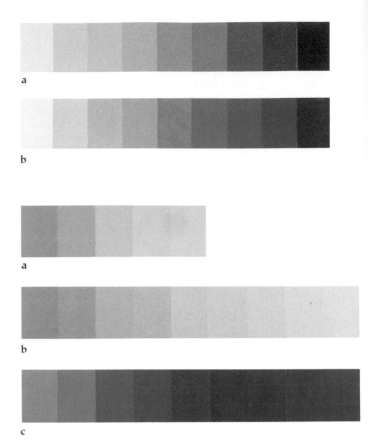

CP.29 PURITY CHART. Parts **a**, **b**, and **c** refer to Figure 16.7. The center chip in each strip is a neutral gray. Cadmium Orange (D 3.0) is at left and Cobalt Blue (normally D 7.0) is at far right. Read the text. In **b**, the Cobalt Blue has been "adjusted" to a D 3.0 luminance before mixing it with the Cadmium Orange.

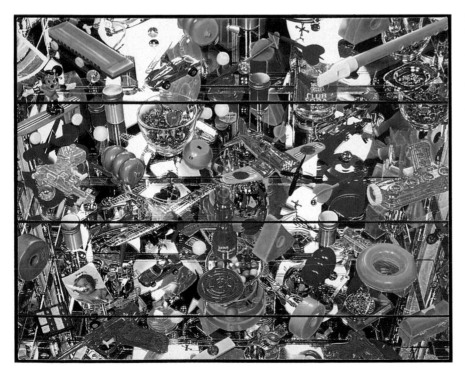

CP.30 Don Eddy. *C IV*. 1981. Acrylic on canvas (airbrush), 30″ × 38″ (76 × 96.5 cm). Courtesy Nancy Hoffman Gallery, New York. Note color balancing: each hue is repeated in differing parts of the composition so that there is, for example, a "red pattern," which runs throughout; also a "green pattern." In fact, there is a pattern for each basic hue.

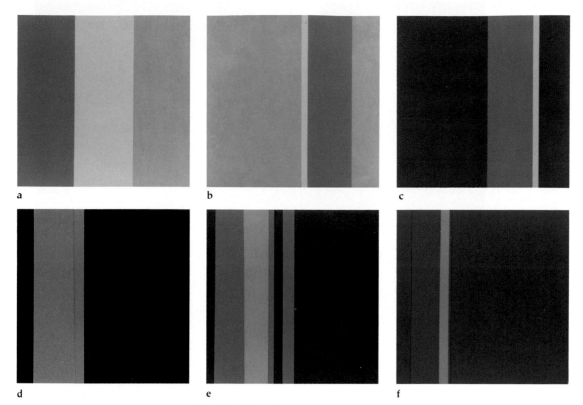

a   b   c

d   e   f

CP.31 COLOR SCHEMES. In **a**, a ''poor'' color scheme:
equal luminances, purities, and areas. In **b**, same hues and
luminances unchanged but differing areas. In **c**, same hues
but differing purities, luminances, and areas. In **d**, **e**, and **f**,
exercises for students are shown employing the concept in **c**.
Hues were literally drawn out of a hat.

below: CP.32 STUDIES IN HUE SATURATION: In **a**, an
original design by a student is shown. Hues were chosen at
random though with ordinary concern for overall effect. In **b**,
the same design is done over using the *dominant tint* technique. The dominant tint in this case is Cobalt Blue, a purplish blue. Colors appear to be more harmonious and uni-

fied. In **c**, the same design as **a** is done over again, this time
with hues as modified by purplish blue *chromatic light*. Colors
also appear to be more harmonious and unified, but the
common hue is less obvious and colors are brighter. (Courtesy of Christina Strnat.)

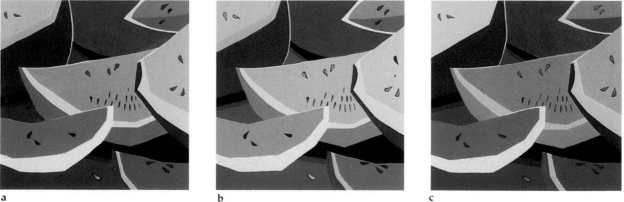

a   b   c

CP.33 Jack Beal. *Danaë II.*
1972. Oil on canvas, 68″ × 68″
(170.72 × 170.72 cm). Whitney
Museum of American Art, New
York. Purchased with funds
from Charles Simon and an
anonymous donor. *Note* overall
yellowish-red saturation; backlight is "cooler" yellow saturation.

CP.34 Kenneth Snelson. *Atoms.* 1988.
Computer image. This work is an
example of the rendering capability
afforded by one of the computer paint
programs currently on the market.
Snelson used a Silicon Graphics Iris
3130 system with software from
Wavefront Technologies. Note the
handling of transparent substances.
Color formation on computers, as with
television, is in the additive color-
mixing system.

-- Typical curve for black pigment/white pigment mixtures
— Typical curve for complementary-hued pigment mixtures

16.4 Two shades of gray may sometimes look alike to the human eye but their differences become readily evident when recorded by a spectrophotometer. Line **A** represents a shade of middle gray (luminance **D** 5.0) mixed from black and white pigments. Because it reflects all wavelengths about equally, it appears as a straight line. The gray of line **B** mixed from complementary hued pigments, however, reflects colors unevenly as indicated by the crests and troughs of its graph pattern. Under differing light sources, B exhibits considerable change in hue through A shows little or no change. This same thing happens with black pigments but the result is less obvious.

to duplicate hues found in nature—not even earth colors; nor rarely are any designed to meet theoretical requirements.

Altering luminances

The term *luminance* involves the lightness or darkness of a color. One common way to alter luminance has been to add black—easy, simple. When black is added, a color does get darker, but, in many cases, perhaps most cases, adding black is exactly the wrong thing to do. **When black (or white) is added to any pigment, it not only changes the luminance, but it changes hue and purity as well.**

White pigments and black pigments modify the molecular structure of the paint film. The reflected light from the resultant mixture contains a higher percentage of the additive complement to the original hue regardless of the total energy reflected. This means that the hue will shift both in average wavelength, and purity will be reduced.

Do not use black to change luminance

For example, when black is added to Cadmium Yellow, the result is a distinct shift to the green (Color Plate 28 **a**, p. 270). Cadmium Yellow has a strong red and green wavelength reflection with a dominant red, hence a warm yellow. (Remember that yellow *is produced* by a mixture of 700 nm, red, and 550 nm,

green, wavelengths.) When black pigment is added, it produces an increase in the percentage of both green and blue wavelengths in the reflected color. As blue is the complement of yellow, the color loses purity (muddies) as well as darkens. The hue is shifted toward the lemon yellows, and the result is an ugly grayish green yellow rather than a warm, bright yellow hue that is made darker.

We could compensate for the greenish shift of Cadmium Yellow by adding some orange to restore the characteristic hue. However, not only hue but also purity is affected. Even though orange is added to correct the hue, the loss of purity cannot be corrected, and the resulting color will be grayed. A little later on, we will learn of a better way to darken colors without altering purity and without altering hue significantly.

Illustrators and designers whose work is intended primarily for reproduction should be especially wary of using black in color mixtures. Purity and hue shifts are accentuated by the four-color reproduction process. The reproduction is likely to look significantly duller and less brilliant than the original work appears to the naked eye. Black is safely used for areas or lines that are to be solid black in the reproduction.

Some artists mix a neutral gray from black and white pigments of the desired luminance and add this to alter a hue's purity. However, this neutral can alter both hue and purity unpredictably (Fig. 16.4).

An idea worth considering: Take black out of the

A practical basic palette 273

Hue/luminance chart
at maximum purity

	D	purple-red	red	orange	yellow	yellow-green	green	green-blue	purple-blue	
WHITE	0.0									
	1.0				Hansa Yellow Light					
	2.0				Cadmium Yellow Medium					
	3.0			Cadmium Orange						
	4.0				Yellow Ochre					
MID-GRAY	5.0		Cadmium Red Light							
	6.0	Acra Violet			Raw Sienna					
	7.0								Cobalt Blue	
	8.0									
	9.0			Burnt Umber			Thalo Green	Thalo Blue		Dioxazine Purple
BLACK	10.0									

16.5 The Hue/Luminance Chart represents an entire circumference (the outside surface) of the color solid (Fig. 13.6). See Color Plate 27. Every dye or pigment has a "natural luminance" — for Acra Violet, it is **D** 6.0. Horizontally, each row is a complete hue circle at a single luminance level, one line of "latitude" on our color sphere.

regular palette, and put it aside to use sparingly for specific purposes, as in abstract design or in monochromatic color schemes.

Sometimes, however, this can be turned into an advantage. When a color mixed with black is placed next to a pure hue, that hue glows; it takes on a radiance and brilliance it would not normally possess. Of course, a pure hue will do that against any grayed color, such as *chromatic grays* mixed by combining two complementary colors. *Chromatic grays* are far richer and more aesthetically satisfying than ones made with black. If they lean toward the complement of the pure hue, they will be even more effective.

Creating better blacks

There is even a better black. Black pigments usually have a dull and lifeless quality compared to blacks mixed from dark pigments. For example, a mixture of Burnt Umber and Phthalocyanine Blue will produce a black that will actually appear darker than black pigment. In addition, the artist can allow one or the other of these pigments to dominate, giving a brown-black or a blue-black color with a velvety quality. To create the illusion of dark black materials or deep shadows requires creativity, skill, and an understanding of light. Remember that there is no absolute black on the surface of the earth; our atmosphere normally prevents that. Any black figure-object can always be made darker by covering it or enclosing it. In bright sunlight, the blackest material is, comparatively, a middle gray. Cast shadows must be seen even on black materials unless the composition is being deliberately simplified for design or decorative goals.

An important point to remember: To make something look really dark and black, surround the darkness with light—*never paint it flatly black.* **It is "contrast" that makes it work, not "blackness."**

Other combinations of pigments will also produce good blacks. Experiment: Try Cadmium Red Deep and Phthalocyanine Green. If they are not in the palette, try any dark red or violet, such as Acra Violet, with the Thalo Green. Any black can be made to appear much darker and richer with varnish or a glaze, both to the viewer's eye and to the lens of a reproduction camera.

Adding white changes the hue

Most warm colors are made noticeably cooler by the addition of white. When white, which reflects all wavelengths about equally, is added to a color, the relative percentages of wavelengths present are changed. The hue shift of the warm colors, yellows,

oranges, and reds, is most obvious; it is less noticeable in blues and greens. Be prepared to make adjustments by adding a bit of a warmer (or, occasionally, a cooler) pigment to any color mixed with white if a constant hue is to be maintained. A common fault in airbrush work is to highlight with pure white pigment. This results in a chalky effect that looks fake even in a reproduction. Highlights should be built up with pure light hues, using white for just a final sparkle.

Changing luminance without changing hue

Understanding what we are trying to do will help us understand what to do.

An important principle to remember: When a darker color is needed, use a dark pigment of the same generic hue rather than adding black to a lighter color. Adjust hue, when necessary, by adding tiny bits of the next sequential cooler or warmer spectral hue, preferably of about the same luminance D factor.

See the Relative Color Temperature Chart in the Appendix for a list of the generic hues for a number of common dark pigments.

How to mix for purity achievement

Refer to the Hue/Luminance Chart (Fig. 16.5) and Color Plate 27 (p. 269); please place a marker by them so that it is easy to flip back and forth.

These examples show an 11-step gray scale from white to black along with 9 hues in 9 steps from near white to near black, a total of 92 chips. These all have been mixed at maximum purity from the 14 pigments of the double primary palette in accordance with the instructions in this chapter although it could be very closely matched by using only the first 9 pigments on the list. Duplication of this chart is a very good exercise in learning to mix colors.

Luminances are approximately correct when rows appear to run horizontally rather than vertically. View the chart upside down and from a distance for an easier evaluation. Squint; if vertical columns are observed, luminances are out of position. Intermediate hues should not appear to be closer to the hue on one side than to the hue on the other side. Each horizontal row forms a complete chromatic sequence of hues (the spectrum). Just think of **D** 1.0 across as a hue circle struck by bright light, for instance, and **D** 9.0 across as hues in very deep shadow.

Each vertical hue column represents a vertical line from pole to pole down one side of the color solid (Fig. 13.6).

The way to begin

To create the gray scale for the left side of the chart, refer to the luminance density scale (Fig. 16.6) as a guide. A more accurate reproduction of the scale will be found on the back cover.

First, prepare a white chip, a black chip, and a middle-gray chip. Then create four steps from mid-gray to white, and four steps from mid-gray to black. Apply white paint right out of the tube to a medium-weight drawing paper (or one-ply bristol board, cold pressed). It is necessary to thin the paint in order to produce a very smooth flat coat. Use a flat, soft, reddish amber natural "oxhair" brush, 1/2" to 3/4" (1.1 to 1.9 cm) wide. The black chip should be created in the following manner: Add a few drops of waterproof india ink and a little water to Ivory Black. Be sure the paper is completely coated. If necessary, paint it again. When the chip is dry, give it two very light coats of fixative.

Use the D 5.0 block as a guide for mixing middle gray. If more accuracy is desired, compare the chip to a rapidly spinning disc that is one-half pure white board and one-half black velour pastel paper. Keep in mind that the hue of the room light will affect the neutrality of the gray. A light source of about 4000° Kelvin would be best for viewing the neutral gray as well as evaluating all other hues being mixed.

How to mix nine steps of the hue yellow

Question: How can a sequence of Cadmium Yellow Medium hue (orangy yellow) be maintained in a luminance scale of nine steps from light to dark? The first sequence discussed is based on a palette of nine colors. Follow it closely.

Always keep comparing the yellow chips to the sequence on the gray scale. Lay them side by side; squint. If the luminance is correct, the edge will disappear. If the color looks darker, lighten it. If the color appears lighter, darken it.

1. Cadmium Yellow Medium is approximately D 2.0; use it straight from the tube to create step D 2.0; just thin it a bit.

2. To create D 1.0, add white. The white will cool the mixture slightly; to maintain hue accurately, add a touch of orange. As there is no orange in the nine-color palette, first mix an orange by combining Cadmium Yellow Medium with a bit of Cadmium Red Light.

3. To darken Cadmium Yellow Medium for D 3.0, the best choice from the double primary palette is Burnt Umber. However, Burnt Umber has a peak in the orange wavelengths, making its hue orange—a warmer hue than desired. To adjust for steps D 3.0 and 4.0, use Hansa Yellow Light, a cool yellow, with Burnt Umber.

4. Return to Cadmium Yellow Medium with Burnt Umber for steps D 5.0 through 8.0, adding the yellow to the umber to lighten it. To be accurate, it may be necessary to cool the hue slightly with the tiniest bit of green. If green is not in the palette, mix a little by combining Hansa Yellow Light with a bit of Thalo Blue. Though the green will degrade the purity of the yellow, the amount required is very small, and the darkness should hide it. If it does not, too much green has been added.

5. Burnt Umber as it comes from the tube is D 9.0; just add a touch of green. If this is done correctly, the scale should look like the bottom half of Color Plate 28 **b** (p. 270) as well as the vertical sequence under Y in Color Plate 27 (p. 269). Compare it to the scale in which Cadmium Yellow Medium was mixed with black (Color Plate 28 **a**).

An alternative method

While the results of using only pigments in the basic 9-hue palette will be very good, a professional is likely to create these steps a little differently. With the 14-hue palette, we can do it virtually the same way.

1. The first two steps, D 1.0 and 2.0 would be completed the same as described earlier.

2. D 4.0 would be Yellow Oxide (or Yellow Ochre) right out of the tube.

3. D 3.0 would be a mixture of Yellow Oxide and Cadmium Yellow Medium.

4. D 6.0 would be Raw Sienna right out of the tube with a slight touch of green added to cool it slightly.

5. D 5.0 combines Yellow Oxide with the Raw Sienna mixture.

6. D 7.0 and 8.0 could be created by adding the Raw Sienna mixture to Burnt Umber. When Burnt Umber (an orange) is used, a touch of green is required to adjust the hue (cool it). Actually, the professional is more likely to use Raw Umber (a yellow) as D 9.0 because no adjustment is necessary, but we have

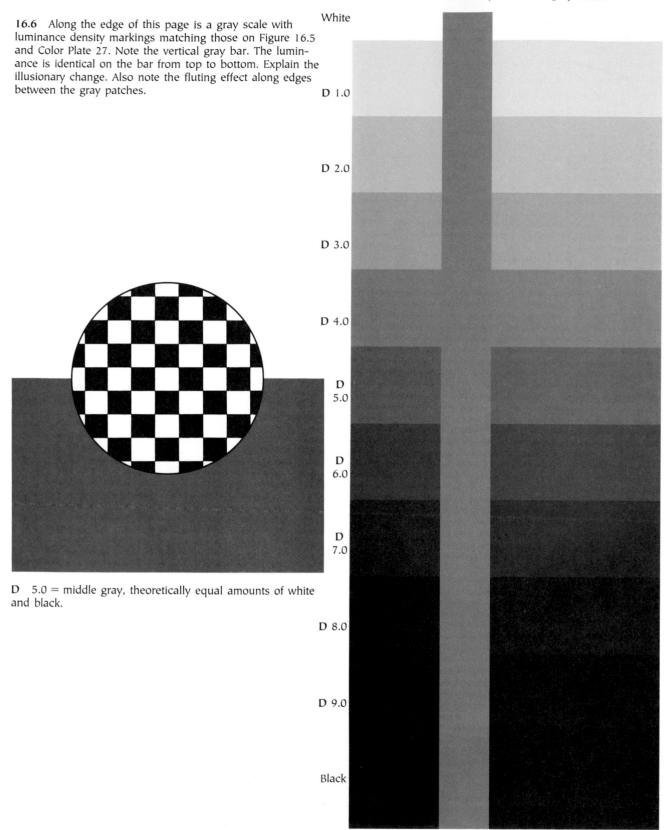

Luminance density scale (the gray scale)

White

D 1.0

D 2.0

D 3.0

D 4.0

D 5.0

D 6.0

D 7.0

D 8.0

D 9.0

Black

16.6 Along the edge of this page is a gray scale with luminance density markings matching those on Figure 16.5 and Color Plate 27. Note the vertical gray bar. The luminance is identical on the bar from top to bottom. Explain the illusionary change. Also note the fluting effect along edges between the gray patches.

D 5.0 = middle gray, theoretically equal amounts of white and black.

not included it in the suggested palette. Differences are perceptually slight.

If care was taken when mixing colors from the basic nine-hue palette, the observed results will vary little, but obviously the professional approach is easier, and hues will be slightly purer or more intense.

Expanding the luminance scale

Sometimes we may want a larger number of luminances than this basic scale provides. When required, the procedure is very easy. Be sure to keep in mind that though the number of steps will be increased, the range from light to dark will not have changed.

Imagine that each density step has been subdivided by 2. A D factor of 4.5, then, would be a luminance halfway between 4.0 and 5.0. This would produce a gray scale of 21 steps, 19 grays plus white and black. If ever necessary, we could subdivide by 10.

Following purple-blue through nine steps

Let us look at another hue, purple-blue, vertical strip P-B on Color Plate 27 and the chart in Figure 16.5. The procedure is a bit simpler than with yellow.

1. Cobalt Blue is approximately D 7.0. Use it right out of the tube; just thin it a bit.

2. To darken Cobalt Blue for Steps D 8.0 and 9.0, add Phthalocyanine Blue (a greenish blue), which will cool the color. To correct the hue, add just a bit of Dioxazine Violet.

3. Next add enough white to Cobalt Blue to match the middle gray, D 5.0.

4. Using the 5.0 mixture and Cobalt Blue from the tube, mix 6.0.

5. Add enough white to Cobalt Blue to match the gray luminance D 1.0. The white will noticeably cool the hue. Though a bit of Dioxazine Violet will warm it properly, it will also change the luminance. *Tip:* Add enough white to the violet to make it a D 1.0 before adding a bit to the Cobalt Blue. Lay the purple-blue mixture D 1.0 next to the gray scale D 1.0. Squint; if the edge can be seen, the luminances are different. When luminances match, the edge will vanish; we will simply be aware of a hue change.

6. Using proportions of the D 1.0 and 5.0 mixtures, create three steps: D 2.0, 3.0, and 4.0.

opposite: 16.7 This is a diagram of the purity chart shown in Color Plate 29 a, b, and c. Bar b represents *one luminance level from the outside edge of the color solid to the center and across to the other side* (Fig. 13.6). Bar C represents a diagonal through the color solid. Under a single light source, differences between color chips in a and those in the left half of b may not be obvious, but under differing light sources, b will exhibit greater changes (see Fig. 16.4). This color mixture, then, is said to be more "dynamic." A principle to remember: Grays are more visually interesting when mixed from complementary pigments rather than mixed from white and black pigments.

If the palette is limited to nine hues, a substitute "Dioxazine Violet" may be mixed by combining Phthalocyanine Blue with a little Acra Violet. Add a tiny bit of black if absolutely necessary but only for creating D 9.0 in the violet column.

A third example, greenish blue

Let us look at one more hue, Phthalocyanine (Thalo) Blue, a greenish, or cool, blue. It may have a D factor of 8.0 to 9.0, depending on variants that we have discussed before. Compare the luminance of the pigment directly out of the tube with D 9.0 on the gray scale. If it needs to be darkened a bit for the D 9.0 chip only, it is probably best to add a tiny bit of black—other pigments may have a stronger effect on the hue although a little Raw Umber may be used with little observable difference.

To lighten for steps 8.0 through 1.0, one needs only to add white and adjust hue as necessary.

How to make white whiter

To make white paint look "whiter," white pigment should be applied very smoothly so that the surface will reflect the maximum amount of incident light. When white is applied with an impasto (rough) technique or with visible brush strokes, it will always appear grayer because these things produce tiny gray shadows.

The obverse of managing black or darkness, make white appear "whiter" by surrounding it with darkness (*border contrast*).

Naturalistically, never paint a white object flatly with white because all the effect of illumination (light) will be lost. White (light) highlights cannot be added to paint that is already white. An exception, of course, is when deliberately simplifying shapes to conform to abstract, graphic design, or decorative concepts. Here, white highlights would not be required.

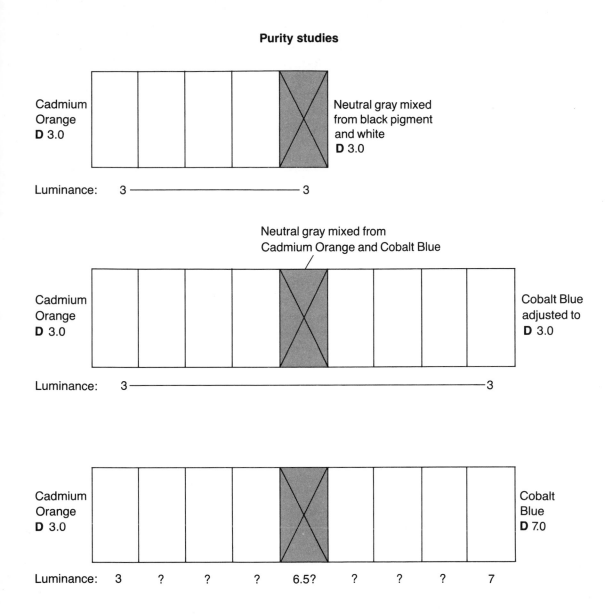

Purity studies

Cadmium Orange **D** 3.0

Neutral gray mixed from black pigment and white **D** 3.0

Luminance: 3 ———————— 3

Neutral gray mixed from Cadmium Orange and Cobalt Blue

Cadmium Orange **D** 3.0

Cobalt Blue adjusted to **D** 3.0

Luminance: 3 ———————————————— 3

Cadmium Orange **D** 3.0

Cobalt Blue **D** 7.0

Luminance: 3   ?   ?   ?   6.5?   ?   ?   ?   7

Working on colored surfaces or grounds

Mostly, painting is done on a white surface, but many artists prefer a colored ground. Once paint is applied to the working surface (support), all grounds become "colored." A few points: (1) Thin washes of color will be contaminated by any hue underneath. If the ground is analogous to the hue applied, the result may be beneficial; if complementary, the result may be disagreeable. (2) Additive color mixing (simultaneous and successive contrast) may come into play and visually alter perceived hues. (3) Hues and luminances mixed on palettes, particularly white palettes, may appear radically altered when applied to the work.

Similar problems occur when applying colors to any white surface although that may not be realized until the surface is covered. For this reason, some painters prefer to "mess up" that intimidating white surface before they begin to paint, usually with a wash of a near neutral hue analogous or complementary to the general tone anticipated in the final work.

How to adjust purity

Adjustments in purity are best made by employing complementary hues rather than black. A good exercise is outlined in Figure 16.7 and the results found in Color Plate 29 **a–c** (p. 270). Please place a marker there so that it is easy to flip back and forth.

1. Start by making three chips of Cadmium Orange (D 3.0), using the paint right out of the tube with a little water. These go on the extreme left of bars **a**, **b**, and **c**.

2. Next, from black and white pigment, mix a neutral gray, D 3.0, to create the chip center right, bar **a**.

3. Create three steps in between these to complete bar **a**. Squint to be sure you make even steps.

4. For the chip far right on bar **b**, add white to Cobalt Blue to create a D 3.0. This chip should match the P-B 3.0 on the Hue/Luminance Chart (Color Plate 27, p. 269).

5. Combine the 3.0 Cobalt Blue mixture with Cadmium Orange to create the center chip in bar **b**. Caution: Orange is the stronger pigment; use a lot less of it than blue. Take care that the center chip is truly a neutral gray. Compare it to the D 3.0 on the gray scale under differing light sources.

6. Create three steps between 3.0 blue, right, and 3.0 neutral gray, center on bar **b**.

7. Create three steps between 3.0 neutral gray, center, and orange 3.0, left, to complete bar **b**.

8. To complete bar **c**, make a chip of Cobalt Blue D 7.0, right out of the tube; place it far right.

9. Then mix a neutral gray for the center chip using Cobalt Blue and Cadmium Orange, both right out of the tube. Do not be misled by the luminance changes: in this procedure, equal luminance steps will not be produced. What we want are equal steps in *purity change*. Compare the center chip to the neutral gray of your luminance density scale. It should fall between D 6.0 and 7.0.

10. Mix three steps from the neutral gray mixture to the Cobalt Blue.

11. Mix three steps from the neutral gray mixture to Cadmium Orange.

Note: Bar **b** represents a horizontal line drawn through the color solid (Fig. 13.6). Bar **c** would be a diagonal line drawn through the same color solid.

If you are able to complete both the Hue/Luminance Chart and this Purity Chart accurately, you are well on your way to understanding how to mix pigments and how to achieve whatever degree of hue, purity, or luminance you desire.

Six traditional color systems

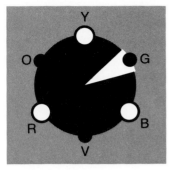

a MONOCHROMATIC

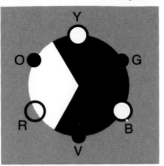

b ANALOGOUS

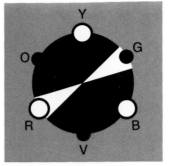

c COMPLEMENTARY

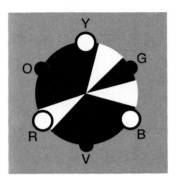

d SPLIT-COMPLEMENTARY

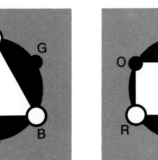

e TRIAD (3 hues)

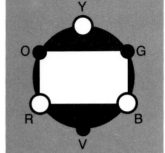

f TETRAD (4 hues)

We have explored all three dimensions of color, and we have produced two charts that can serve as a direct reference helpful for all sorts of future projects.

A word about harmony

One writer on art states flatly that "harmony is in the eye of the beholder." This is not exactly true. Yet many 20th-century artists and critics have used that idea as a pretext for dismissing every concept or theory of harmony.

Contemporary artists should throw these all out, Josef Albers advises. He writes "Our conclusion: we may forget for a while those rules of thumb of complementaries, whether complete or 'split,' and of triads and tetrads as well. They are worn out."[23]

Sometimes it is easy to forget that 20th-century color theorists all had a classical art training, which included a thorough study of such things. They arrived at their viewpoint from a base of knowledge that most of today's beginning artists do not share.

Every artist should be familiar with the terminology and meaning of the six traditional basic systematic variations on color relationships. Often called *color schemes*, these systems were, in the past, thought to be required to enable an artist to create "good" color

design and harmony. These "rules of thumb," as Albers called them, are diagrammed in Figure 16.8 and descriptions follow:

1. *Monochromatic.* A one-hue color scheme employing one hue plus black and white. Variations are all based on differing degrees of luminance or of purity or both.

2. *Analogous.* These hues are next to one another on the hue circle. Yellow, orange, and red would be an example.

3. *Complementary.* Color schemes based on hues directly opposite one another on the hue circle.

4. *Split-complementary.* Colors chosen include one hue plus the hues that lie on either side of its complement, making a total of three.

5. *Triad.* Three hues selected from a color circle so that they form an equilateral triangle. Generic red-yellow-blue form one, perhaps basic, triad.

6. *Tetrad.* Usually four hues equidistant from one another on the color wheel forming a square, but also any similar rectangle. A "double-split-complementary" would also fit this category.

A practical basic palette   281

Knowing and understanding these traditional color systems offer several important advantages to contemporary artists. (1) We will be able to understand the visual language of artists who worked in the past. (2) When we analyze historical works, we will be able to understand one of the artists' reasons for selecting the particular combinations of hues they did. (3) These systems provide us with a set of possible alternatives when we do not know what else to do.

The problem with these historical color systems is that they are based on hue. Studies in perception show that a person's concept of what constitutes harmony is not focused on hue at all, but on luminance and purity. Harmony is composed of things that are essentially alike.

What perception tells about harmony

Sometimes, according to art theories and styles, the term *harmony* means different things to different persons, to differing groups or art movements, or to differing times. Artists often argue about what constitutes harmony. Sometimes what happens is that concepts of harmony become distorted and confused by ideology.

Sometimes balance and similarity are confused with color harmony. When colors are properly distributed throughout a work, for example, a sense of harmony prevails, not because of any particular hues chosen (which may even be complementary), but because *every part of the composition is similar.* When one hue is dominant, all other hues are subordinated, placing things in equilibrium.

There really is no mystery about what constitutes harmony in any form. Our perceptual mechanisms and understandings define harmony in very specific terms.

They are the same characteristics originally proposed by the Gestalt psychologists as essential to visual patternmaking. We perceive things to be harmonious if they are coherent, similar in most ways or similar in all ways.

Things in any visual field that depict sequences in natural order, or that have similar shapes, similar colors, similar lines, or similar movements are viewed as harmonious.

Things are seen to be perceptually harmonious when the dominance principle is in evidence. Dominance creates harmony because everything is thus in its place, in order (a controlled environment).

Harmony is a leveled state. It is pleasing, comfortable, correct, stable, satisfying, mildly stimulating but not exciting. It is also enclosed and contained.

Attitudes about harmony are buried deep in the psyche of every normal individual. So, harmony *is not* "in the eye of the beholder." Every person comes equipped with very strong predispositions.

Color harmony

In a visual field, color is perceived to be harmonious if (1) hues are seen to be in a natural order, (2) if hues are of about the same luminance (lightness or darkness), (3) if hues are of about the same degree of muted purity, or (4) any combination of these three attributes. Strictly speaking, there are no other *harmonious* color relationships.

Natural order in color is a sequence of logical and progressive steps in hue, luminance, or purity. An analogous color scheme consists of such steps from one point on the hue circle to another point. A full spectrum in sequence — red, orange, yellow, green, blue, and indigo (violet-blue) — is in natural order. We

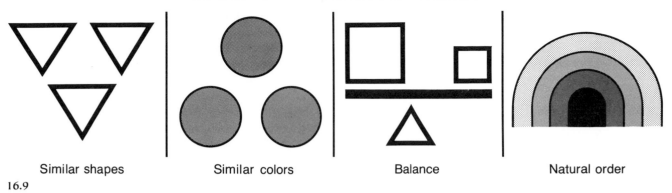

| Similar shapes | Similar colors | Balance | Natural order |

16.9

perceive that a preceding and succeeding hue have characteristics they share with the intermediary hue. For example, orange and green are perceived to have yellow in common. This is one of the reasons we think that a rainbow is beautiful.

Of the traditional color systems, only the monochromatic and the analogous have perceptual bases as harmonious.

When colors are all of about the same luminance (all of about the same degree of lightness, for example) they exhibit similarity, the Gestalt principle that causes figures to join together. The same thing is true when colors are the same degree of muted purity—"grayness" provides a common denominator. Gestalt similarity causes them to join together. Joining together is the primary quality of things that we interpret as harmonious. Harmony, then, is created by joining elements together.

However, there are other factors that we accept as broadly characteristic of harmony though they join things together in differing ways. One of these is balance. When forces are balanced, they are perceived to be in order or equilibrium. This includes the balancing of colors. When a little red is placed in a painting, it can be balanced by a little red placed somewhere else. Color Plate 30 (p. 270) is a painting by Don Eddy. Notice how every hue is repeated throughout the composition. Of course, this is only one form of color balance. (Balance and attraction were discussed in Chapters 6 and 7.)

Similar shapes, whatever their color, appear harmonious. In fact, for the vast majority of persons (except artists or creative people), *form (or shape) overrides color.*[24] Every elemental component of visual processing, such as line, shape, space, and texture

impacts on our attitude about color as an artistic or aesthetic concept.

Should harmony always be the objective?

In every case is harmony, in a perceptual sense, really what is wanted? In all forms of the arts, we want to engage the viewer emotionally. To do this, we do not want always to be obviously pleasing. Sometimes we want to arouse, disturb, excite, expand, extend. Sometimes we want to grate on a viewer's nerves, sour the stomach, upset the equilibrium. What would any visual or entertainment art be without tension?

Pure colors are not democratic. Used in a composition, each fights for attention. The artist must be a referee and assign each a place in the scheme of the composition by giving dominance to one hue by assigning that hue the largest area, some other hue a median area, another hue a smaller area, and so on. In other words, no hues should occupy the same amount of space or area in a composition unless that is a concept chosen deliberately, as in a perfectly symmetrical composition.

A never-fail means to make color work

There is a very simple method for creating a good color scheme that virtually always works regardless of whatever visual goal we have in mind. Though the principle involves only three easy steps, it takes practice and a good deal of wise discrimination to apply them successfully.

Here is the principle: **Do not give any hues in a composition (1) the same area (amount of overall** space), (2) the same luminance, or (3) the same degree of purity.

Color Plate 31 **a** (p. 271) shows a set of possibly the worst three colors we could pick for a color scheme. Color Plate 31 **b** (p. 271) shows that if only the surface ratio (area) of each is different, the result is quite acceptable. Color Plate 31 **c** (p. 271), which looks even better, has all three steps of the principle applied. It really does not matter at all what hues we start with. For example, pick any three hues out of a hat. That is exactly what was done to create the examples in Color Plate 31 **d–f** (p. 271).

We can select colors for their emotional content, in whatever arbitrary manner we like, rather than according to any set pattern, system, or scheme.

We can pick any hues that will best solve a particular visual problem. If we know what to do, any combination will work!

Of course, if we were creating a perfectly balanced symmetrical composition, we might not wish to follow this principle throughout. Also, at times, rather than make figures distinctive, we may want different ones to become homogeneous (join together) in order to create an overall mass (shape or form). In that case, different hues may be joined by giving them like luminances or like degrees of purity or both of these. Regardless of hue, figures seen to have the same luminance or purity of the ground tend to join with the ground and recede. Interior or exterior decorators may use this principle to hide unsightly architectural features. Fine and applied artists may use the principle to camouflage figures or to hold figures in prescribed spatial orientations.

Summary

The double primary basic palette and its hue/pigment circle provide artists with distinct advantages over other types of basic palettes. Using a relatively few pigments, the palette enables an artist to create a maximum range of differing hues throughout the color spectrum, and it does so in a wide range of luminances with very little degrading of purity in any hue. Using contemporary artists' colors, it comes as close to the theoretical subtractive mixing system as possible, without sacrificing permanency. The palette may be applied to any media.

Perceptual harmony describes things easily identified as being alike in some or all respects. Yet, for most persons, the concept of a harmonious visual field is usually governed primarily by the dominance principle, which establishes a hierarchy or sequential order for figure-objects.

A sense of harmony, then, may be created with things that are *different,* as well as with things that are *similar* (consonant), if a simple principle is followed: Give no colors the same area, the same luminance, or the same degree of purity. As an alternative, pure hues may be equally dispersed in all areas of the composition or design to provide balance.

Success in the application of any set of facts, of any formula or idea, concept, theory, or principle to any visual problem depends on an individual artist's capacity to *discriminate* between things. When we make sharp discriminations (or distinctions) that show insight or good judgment we call it *discernment.*

A discerning artist is likely to be an achieving artist.

Review of key terms

analogous colors Hues that are next to one another on any hue circle (color wheel).

body color The "colored" appearance of any matter or substance (like a paint film), caused by differences in the molecular structure of such substances. Molecular differences determine which wavelengths of light are absorbed and which are reflected. Such colors are affected by the spectral composition of the incident light.

density, density factor, *D* Density in design is related to the "darkness" of a color, that is, its relative light reflection, which is a subtractive measure. This can be directly related to the deposit of pigment or ink on a reflective surface in design and is often expressed in percent, as, for example, a 50 percent black (a middle-gray tone). A number 2 gray designers' color is a **D** 2.0. In the 11-step luminance scale, density is expressed in **D** factors like 5.0, which are directly convertible into percent by moving the decimal one place to the right. (D factors may be converted to Munsell "values," and vice versa, simply by subtracting the original number from 10. Thus, the two systems are compatible.)

harmony Agreement or consonance between forms, shapes, colors, concepts, or ideas, and so on; a perceptual understanding identified by the Gestalt psychologists as the principle of similarity.

luminance An index of the amount of light reflected from a surface viewed from a particular direction. It relates to the lightness or the darkness of reflected colors and is compared to a gray scale.

pigment A substance (mineral or dye) used as coloring matter in paint and other artists' materials. *Pigments are not hues* although each has its own distinctive hue. Cadmium Red Light is a pigment, whereas orange-red is a generic hue.

purity One of the dimensions of color that identifies the monochromatic quality of any hue, that is, its relationship to light of a single wavelength. This relationship establishes a scale ranging from the most vivid hue physically possible to neutral gray.

value A Munsell System term for lightness/darkness measures. It uses additive notation (white is 10.0; black, 0.0—the absence of all light); this term is the obverse of the subtractive luminance density scale. *See* **luminance; density.**

CHAPTER SEVENTEEN

Creating light effects

Light cues

This chapter is really about using concepts of light as tools in two-dimensional works of art such as Figure 17.1. It is about learning to recognize and to understand visual cues we need both to create imitations of naturalistic conditions for realistic works, as well as establishing, at the same time, the abstract concepts about light that result from our perceptual processing. Because light cues are perceptually abstract, most can be applied to any style or form of art, nonobjective as well as naturalistic, or to any stage of abstraction in between.

When working abstractly, an artist might choose to apply one or, at most, two or three cues. Even this severe limitation may produce a quite satisfactory result. However, for the most naturalistic effects in representational works, all cues that are appropriate to the specific situation being depicted in the picture should be applied—and applied intelligently. Remember that we bring our perceptions of the natural world to our viewing of pictures. To be convincing, we should know exactly what cues to encode in our work to produce a desired viewer response.

We already have learned a good deal about light and its effects although the points have been spread throughout the book. What we have learned has also been fairly circumscribed. Here we will examine how the bits and pieces fit together, and we will expand considerably on that knowledge.

A brief recap

We have learned how cast shadows help to define space, to establish the position and orientation of the ground planes, even to tell us whether there is any "ground" at all or just illusionary space (Chapter 8). (Review Figs. 2.6 and 8.35.)

In Chapter 13, we learned something about the physical properties of light. In these examinations, we found that changes in the direction and the chromatic content of the light made the Grand Canyon appear very different at differing times of the day. Artists control light hue and light direction simply by *exploring* alternatives; photographers control these by *observing* alternatives. Obviously, virtually any subject will yield to this kind of image management.

The relative light intensity and hue of various original light sources was also brought to our attention and contrasted with those of light reflected from a variety of surfaces. We distinguished between the terms *transparency* and *translucency*.

Many of the surfaces transmiting or reflecting light modify the qualities of light waves in ways that differentiate surfaces from one another. A piece of polished metal and a soap bubble appear quite different to us and also different from the surface of the paper on which this book is printed.

We understand that all light sources are colored; that is, they possess a hue regardless of what our eye-brain mechanisms tell us. We can use this information to advantage.

Chromatic light is light so strongly hued that our brain cannot wholly compensate, so we actually see colored light.

The luminance contrasts in a natural visual field are so great that it is impossible to simulate these in a picture. A picture is not a window, nor can it ever be. Yet it does have a "dual-reality"; it is conceived of as flat picture while at the same time it is seen to recall

or to stimulate our recognition of perceptual cues related to space and motion. A picture also can recall cues related to the qualities and intensities of light.

Because black, the absence of all light, is not a part of our perceptions about light, areas of pure black (like silhouettes) are best avoided in naturalistic works. This warning does not necessarily apply to decorative or abstract works.

In Chapter 14, we learned about simultaneous

17.1 Jack Fredrick Myers. *Fragments.* 1979. Whole egg emulsion tempera and oil on composition board, 30 × 48" (76.2 × 121.9 cm). Private collection, Cleveland, Ohio. The "frame" is not three dimensional but is, of course, like the broken "glass" part of the painting itself. Though the reflections in a glass surface are easily observed, most of us are not consciously aware that the entire surface reflects some light and that glass also absorbs some light. Whatever we see through the glass ordinarily is somewhat darker than it would otherwise appear. To depict a transparent or translucent object, paint what is behind it as modified by refraction and hue; then add reflected highlights.

17.2 a Jack Fredrick Myers. *Two from a Flea Market.* 1979. Whole egg emulsion tempera and oil on composition board, 32 × 48″ (81.3 × 121.4 cm). The Butler Institute of American Art, Youngstown, Ohio. Cast shadows, from a single light source, contribute to the overall pattern and organization of the composition, as well as help to unify the painting. The raking light angle brings out the textures in the objects depicted.

contrast and contour contrast, techniques that we can use to extend the very limited range of a reflective surface. Not only can we create the illusion that hues are purer than they really are or that they are lighter or darker, but we can make the same hue look like two or more different hues. We can create the illusion that white paper, canvas, or illustration board is whiter (has a higher luminance) in some places than in others. We have learned that through perceptual characteristics we can extend the limitations that reflective surfaces and pigments impose on creativity.

Every human being recognizes all these perceptual cues. Some are genetic, most are learned, but light cues tell us almost everything we know about our visual field, natural or pictorial.

Light-transmitting surfaces or substances

Transparent materials

An important thing to remember about transparent materials is that, through them, we can see what stands behind—the background. (See Color Plate 34, p. 272, and Fig. 8.42.) In fact, that is exactly the best way to approach painting a transparent object—**paint the background as modified by the transparent object;** then add the reflected highlights. The hue of the background is *always* influenced by the hue of the transparent figure-object. If we hold a piece of red glass against a blue wall, the glass will appear dark, almost black, not red at all. In this case, the red filter blocks cyan light (a combination of both blue and green) from passing through—no light, no color. Check the additive hue circle (Fig. 15.1). Red and cyan are complementary colors. A primary red filter theoretically would absorb fully two-thirds of the light!

Even with clear glass, some light energy is absorbed by the glass. The ground, as seen through the transparent surface, is subtly darker, if not slightly different in hue. See Figure 17.1. Most plate glass is slightly greenish. In addition, there may be significant distortions of anything seen through transparent materials, like a jar or vase. A flat piece of glass will distort (refract) images somewhat if observed from an angle.

If we see two transparent objects overlap, the area of coincidence, the overlap, is *always darker than either.* The combination is actually the sum of the indi-

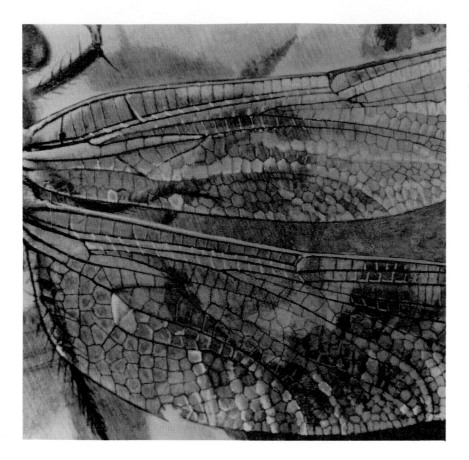

b Nearly actual size detail from Figure 17.2 **a**. The wings of the dragonfly are treated as a translucent surface. Observe that the wings cast shadows and that these shadows and other ground details can be seen through them.

vidual luminances. This can easily be approximated in any specific instance simply by adding together the apparent **D** factors of both. For example, a transparent yellow (**D** 2.0) combined with a purple-blue (**D** 7.0) will give an overlap of **D** 9.0. The hue will be olive-gray. Why? The totals of some **D** factors will exceed 10, theoretical black. In art, we create the *illusion* of reality, not reality itself. Therefore, it is best never to let the overlap become totally black, for black may be regarded by a viewer as a hole or as being opaque, and the illusion of transparency will be completely lost.

Our affective responses to transparency are similar to those of hard edges.

Translucent materials

Quite often the term *transparency* is mistakenly applied to surfaces or conditions that are translucent. There is an important qualitative and aesthetic difference. *Translucency* is a semiopaque quality. Unlike a transparent condition, particles opaque to the passage of light are involved. These particles reflect a quantity of white light that raises luminances (lightens) and

also degrades the purity of hues seen through the translucent material. Translucent materials dominate their backgrounds, which have substantially less influence in the visual mixture than transparent materials. The degree of such differences on elements seen through translucent atmospheres or materials will depend directly on the degree of opacity. Translucency is observed when viewing a visual field through rain, fog, or smoke or through surfaces such as dirty or dusty glass, sheer curtains, or fine netting. Observe the quality of translucency in the wings of the dragonfly in the detail of a painting (Fig. 17.2 **b**).

Our affective responses to translucency are similar to those of soft edges.

Working with colored light

Although we are not always aware of it, we experience chromatic light rather commonly in our lives.

At sunrise and sunset we see the hues yellow, orange, and red — chromatic light — as an influence on all the hues of figure-objects in the visual field. A red shirt seems to catch fire at sunset. Why? We are also

THE INFLUENCE OF THE DIRECTION OF LIGHT
ON A SUBJECT

a Flat front

d From behind

b Three-quarters front

e From the top

c Raking side light

f From underneath

generally aware of excessive blueness on heavily overcast days.

Indoors, during the day, when a tungsten lamp may be directly compared to window light, we usually will perceive one as white light and the other as chromatic. This perception may change, flip-flop, like the figure ground reversals. Whichever light source we look at will be white even though the differences in the hue of these light sources may be substantial (see Color Plate 5, p. 259). If both light sources are included in a work of art, we can take these facts into account. It is usually best to let the dominant light source be white and treat the lesser source as chromatic; or alternatively, allow only objects situated in the overlap of the light sources appear as if illuminated by white light. In these ways, the cool-warm dichotomy can be used creatively.

There are many other situations in which we experience chromatic light. Are we normally aware of the hue of street lights, for example? There are strong differences in hue between mercury vapor (bluish green) and sodium vapor (orange) lamps. What about the lighting at a disco, theatrical lighting for stage or films? There is no reason why the painter cannot employ these concepts of light in the same ways for the same purposes.

Hue saturation in works of art

The dominant tint technique (subtractive)

For comparison, Color Plate 32 **a** (p. 271) shows colors as they might be arbitrarily chosen for a simple design. Note the distinct change in mood when using the dominant tint technique (Color Plate 32 **b**, p. 271). In this technique, the artist adds a little of one color (blue, for example) to every color used in the painting. At least enough color must be added, even to white, so that the dominant tint (in this case, blue) can be seen in every color in the finished work. Observe that the technique gives the composition automatic color harmony and unity by relating all colors together.

Take a look at *Danaë II* (Color Plate 33, p. 271) by Jack Beal. Note how a warm orange color pervades the entire scene. Be especially observant of its effects on all the colors. Note how the relatively cool yellowish backlight alters these.

The chromatic light technique (additive)

Like the dominant tint, this is also a painting method that creates harmony and unity in a composition regardless of whatever arbitrary method may be used to select the hues (colors). It is a way of creating melds, that is, a merging of figure and ground. The application of the idea may be subtle or strong depending on the effect we wish to create.

In order to appreciate what happens when mixing light and pigment additively, experiment. Look at the Hue/Luminance Chart (Color Plate 27, p. 269) through a colored cellophane. A good exercise is to paint a small abstract design in any colors preferred. Then repaint the same work as it appears when viewed through blue cellophane. An example of such an exercise is shown in Color Plate 32 **a** and **c**.

The chromatic light technique is both physically and aesthetically different from the dominant tint. The dominant tint, however, is a faster and easier procedure. Learn to discriminate between subtle, but important, differences, which separate the two concepts.

Qualities of light direction or position

Light may originate from any point on a sphere surrounding the subject—visualize it. It may come from close-by or from far away. It may be very strong and intense or weak and feeble. It may be stark white or either subtly hued or strongly hued chromatic light. The possibilities are almost limitless.

Figure 17.3 shows a carved wooden mask lighted from six different directions. How many other possible positions are there?

Which angle is precisely the best one to solve a particular visual problem? It is not usually necessary to explore them all, but we should never be content with just one; we may be throwing away our best chance to create a much better work. That is a straight path to mediocrity.

The qualities of light direction should not be ignored, as novices sometimes do; nor should light direction be just a routine consideration. Compare the differing qualities of light coming from the back to that

opposite: 17.3 The qualities of various lighting orientations on a wooden sculpture. Each produces differing affective responses, as well as differing qualities of surface definition. That such variants profoundly affect the patternmaking (design/composition) elements in any work should be obvious.

from the side or front (Figs. 17.4 and 17.5, and Color Plates 33 and 34, p. 272). Notice what happens to the shadows in each case. Have the emotional qualities of the subject been enhanced by the artist's choice of light orientation? Direction or position is important because the choice can detract from, or considerably improve, both the drama (emotional quality) and the composition of the work. For example we perceive anything close to noonday sun as normal, and we tend to ignore such types of overhead lighting. If, however, a figure is surrounded by warm, analogous colors, all of a high luminance, and an image of barren earth, desert heat may be suggested.

According to constancy, when a light source is below eye level it MUST be late evening or early morning (with appropriate orangy hues). Otherwise,

above left: **17.4** The orientation of the prime light source (the direction from which it strikes the subject) significantly contributes to the affective responses evoked. The orientation of the light also is significant in patternmaking — the composition and the design qualities of any work. Back lighting, as shown here, unifies the figure, lifts and separates it from the background by a halo of scattered light. Clever artists will realize that such principles are applied equally well to abstract design and to realistic works.

left: **17.5** Side lighting defines volumes, brings out textures. Cast shadows define background planes and contribute to the overall design pattern. Edges of the figures merge with the ground (meld) creating naturally interesting lost and found contours. Take another look at Figure 4.40.

opposite: **17.6** Any low light orientation, a "raking" light that just skims across a surface, accentuates textures and makes them stand out. Conversely, to diminish texture, use light as diffuse as possible, and aim it straight on.

opposite, far right: **17.7** Never underestimate the importance of cast shadows as a compositional device. This photo is shown upside down in order to increase the ambiguity. Its pattern is composed almost entirely of shadows of interesting and varied shapes — shapes that all possess similarity — a characteristic that provides rhythmic repetition. Painters can easily employ the same technique; so can illustrators. Astute observers will note that the edges of shadows next to the human figures are sharper than the edges of these same shadows at the furthest distance from the figure.

something is terribly wrong. If those cues are absent, consider how the low light level would prompt a sense of the unexpected, of danger, even fear. Remember, our perception is that light, including artificial light, is always overhead. Long shadows cast by low or raking light sources (position) can be both an emotional device (drama) and an artistic device (pattern in composition). See Figures 17.5, 17.6, and 17.7.

Enhancing texture

When the light is low in the visual field, less light shines directly on the surface on which the figure sits, producing less light to illuminate the shadows. At low light angles, such as early morning or late evening, luminance contrast is increased. If the level is low enough that it just skims across the surface, textures are brought out, and the overall textural qualities enhanced (Fig. 17.6). Of course, this is also possible with artificial light as well by simply aligning the light about even with the surface (Fig. 17.3 c). At noon, with sun high in the sky, a light surface will reflect a great deal of light into the shadows, reducing luminance contrast. To paint realistic scenes convincingly, remember these important facts as they help to establish the time of day as well as the mood. They offer more alternatives to explore in our attempts to solve visual problems. Take another look at Color Plate 8 (p. 260). Note how differing hues, textures, and shadows contribute to the distinctiveness of each image. Be sure to observe that some parts of the landscape are not struck by direct light at all, but are illuminated from light scattered through the atmosphere or reflected from the sky. In what way would that modify the hues in the shadows?

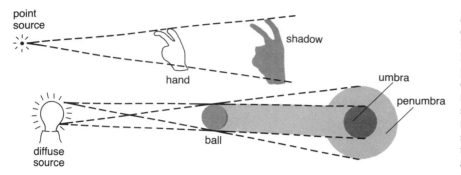

point
source

hand

shadow

umbra

penumbra

diffuse
source

ball

left: **17.8** The character of cast shadows is determined, to a large extent, by the character of the original (prime) light source. A pinpoint light source produces relatively sharp shadow edges (although they should rarely be made razor sharp). Diffuse light sources produce soft shadows; the more diffused the light source, the softer the shadows to the point where they disappear altogether. Perceptually, a moving light source produces soft shadows.

opposite: **17.9** Locate the desired light level from those identified across the top horizontally. Then follow vertical lines downward to align matching perceptual cues for that light level. These cues may be encoded into art works in order to evoke a mood, a time of day, a particular geographical location, or any other appropriate associations. Use guidelines with intelligence and sensitivity; do not slavishly or mechanically apply them.

Qualities of cast shadows

The quality and type of shadows cast by any original light source varies considerably. This is significant to the composition of any work, to spatial representation, and to a work's emotional qualities. See Figure 17.8. A pinpoint light source normally casts a hard-edged shadow; a diffused light source casts a diffused shadow. However, the distance between the figure-object and the ground also affects the sharpness of the shadow. Close to the figure, the shadow will be sharp; and further away, it will be softer and more diffused. This occurs under both conditions mentioned earlier and is effective in establishing spatial relationships.

Hard-edged shadows advance, and soft-edged shadows recede. We can examine these conditions by standing this book vertically on a table or desk between us and the light source. Observe that at the lower edge of the book, the shadow is quite sharp; moving out, it softens some. The further out the shadow extends, the softer it becomes. In strong sunlight, the shadow may appear to be sharper overall; in diffused light, overall softer; but the principle applies in every kind of light.

Cast shadow cues

The character of the shadows cast by the type of light source is important because it is also tied to constancy perceptions. The edges shadows cast by a candle flame or a roaring bonfire, for instance, are soft because flames flicker and move. The flame behaves like a diffused light source (Fig. 17.8). Sharply edged shadows would be *inconsistent* with this perception. Consistency is vital to creating a convincing effect.

The sun behaves like a pinpoint light source. It is the condition of the atmosphere that alters the character of shadows cast by the sun. If the atmosphere is very clear, the shadows are apparently sharp although it is best not to make them hard-edged. If the day is cloudy but bright, the shadows are lighter in luminance and have softer edges (more light is scattered, diffused). If the day is heavily overcast, shadows are still lighter and very soft if they can be seen at all. The character of the shadows can enhance the type of affective (emotional) response we strive to create in our work if we choose ones appropriate to the purpose. How does the emotional response to a bright sunny day contrast with the response to one that is dark and heavily overcast?

Placement of the light source

Is the light source inside or outside of the perimeters of the work (picture plane)? There are differing concerns in each case. If it is outside of the picture plane and is to be a source such as the sun, we perceive the light to be falling evenly over the entire

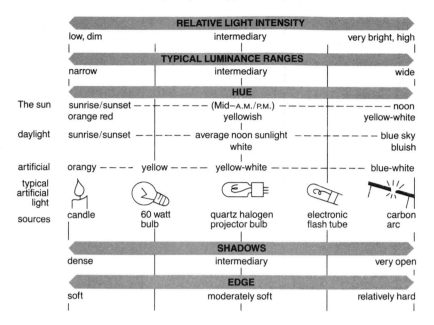

RELATIVE LIGHT ENERGY CUE CHART

Data provides starting points for experimentation

RELATIVE LIGHT INTENSITY		
low, dim	intermediary	very bright, high

TYPICAL LUMINANCE RANGES		
narrow	intermediary	wide

HUE		
The sun	sunrise/sunset — — — — — — (Mid–A.M./P.M.) — — — — — — — — — — noon	
	orange red	yellowish	yellow-white
daylight	sunrise/sunset — — — — — average noon sunlight — — — — — — — blue sky	
		white	bluish
artificial	orangy — — — yellow — — — yellow-white — — — — — — blue-white	

typical artificial light sources

| candle | 60 watt bulb | quartz halogen projector bulb | electronic flash tube | carbon arc |

SHADOWS		
dense	intermediary	very open

EDGE		
soft	moderately soft	relatively hard

visual plane. This is a common circumstance in any outdoor visual field and easy to understand in a work of art.

When the source of the illumination is placed within the frame, a very different set of conditions arises. This situation is not easy for the novice artist to handle. It is necessary to account for the brilliance or relative intensity of the light. If it were a sunset, for example, somehow we would have to make the sun appear bright. Yet we know a reflective surface such as canvas or illustration board permits only an extremely limited luminance range (a ratio of about 15:1) in no way equivalent to, or even suggestive of, the sun or any other light source. How, then, can the enormous natural luminance range of light even be inferred?

A few persons have great powers of observation and are able to sense just the right thing to do. For everyone else, there are guidelines to follow. What does the trick is contrast, both physical and psychological, always working light against dark, but in declining luminance ranges. Very close control of luminance ranges in every part of the work is required in order to capture the qualities of light. As a routine practice, we learn to work the light/dark pattern as a part of a work's basic design structure. We also learn to take advantage of the perceptual effects of simultaneous contrast.

Capturing the illusion of light

Inferring relative light intensity

The intensity of the light source may be suggested by certain cues implanted in the work. For instance, a candle flame, a very low light level source, is orangy red. Used for theatrical spotlights and searchlights, a carbon arc (a very bright, intense light source) appears bluish white. A cue to light intensity, then is (1) the hue (an aspect of physical color temperature). Other indicators or cues are (2) the purity of the hues of figure-objects, (3) the luminance ranges (within figure-objects as well as between figure-objects and the ground), and (4) the character of the shadows (density, luminance range, and edge quality).

In dim light, shadows are dark and dense with a limited or narrow luminance range. Figure-objects within these shadows are dull and relatively colorless (low purity). Conversely, in very bright light, details, even in the shadows, are fully illuminated, and colors tend to be vivid (high purity). Contrast range within shadows is comparatively much wider, but within it, the lightest objects should not average closer than two density steps below those in the light. The edges of light and shadow will be strong (these edges should be forced). Light intensity cues are charted in Figure 17.9.

Creating light effects 295

17.10 The inverse square law of the physics of light is a law that must be acknowledged when any light source is incorporated into the picture plane. The light of a candle that illuminates a one foot square surface at a one foot distance will cover four square feet at a two-foot distance, each point receiving just one-quarter of the light it received at one foot. And that same light will spread over nine square feet at a three-foot distance, producing just one-ninth the light intensity.

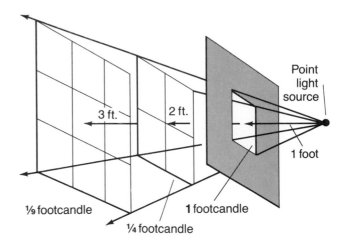

High key/low key

To create moods related to intense light (seashore, desert, "in the spotlight," inquisition, and torture), a work may be treated partly or entirely in "high key." *High key* refers to a type of composition in which the overall or prevailing luminances are above middle gray. For moods of dim light (night, gloom, fright, death, bizarre states), a "low key" may be appropriate. *Low key* refers to a type of composition in which the overall, or prevailing, luminances, are below middle gray. These differing moods are created by confining all colors to either the upper half (D 0.0 – 5.0) or the lower half (D 5.0 – 10.0) of the luminance scale. Just a very few delicate accents from the opposite end of the scale will add sparkle and interest and help establish dominances.

The inverse square law affects pictorial light

We have an innate understanding of how light behaves. One aspect of light behavior is stated in a law of physics: Light varies inversely according to the square of the distance. In a naturalistic pictorial field, this law cannot be totally circumvented; it is a component of light constancy.

What does the inverse square law tell artists? See Figure 17.10. At one foot from a candle, we have one footcandle of light. At a distance of two feet, there is one-quarter footcandle, *only 25 percent of the light*. At three feet distant, there is only one-ninth the light; and at four feet, just one-sixteenth. In other words, the

relative light energy (intensity) of the light declines dramatically as we move away from the light's source.

Actually, exactly the same thing happens with sunlight. The reason that it is not so obvious is that the sun is so many millions of miles away; distances from one point on the earth to another point are truly insignificant. Anyone good at mathematics should be able to prove this in short order. The law can be seen in effect, however, if we stand at a very high place at sunrise or sunset. It is then possible to see that where the sun is positioned, light is stronger on the earth and it is somewhat dimmer in the far opposite direction.

The effects of the inverse square law are important to the professional photographer who must light models, sets, or products with flash or flood lamps because the law has a critical effect on exposure. Unevenly lighted paintings or models may look all right to the naked eye (why?) but appear as a disaster in a photograph.

In naturalistic works of art, it is not necessary to reproduce the effects of the law with perfect accuracy; however, it must be *close enough that a viewer's innate understanding of the way light works will not be compromised.* If light effects are not accurately encoded, the illusion of reality will be lost.

Perhaps the painter most associated with this type of work is Georges de la Tour. His painting *Joseph the Carpenter* is shown in Figure 17.11. Today we under-

17.11 Georges de la Tour. *Joseph the Carpenter.* ca. 1645. Louvre, Paris. The light from the candle that is within the picture frame spreads throughout the space seen in the painting and is observed to pervade (influence) every figure and object. To be successful, an original light source (the candle flame) must be seen to conform approximately to the inverse square law, and the flame must appear to be the lightest object in the entire work!

17.12 **Matte painting**, from the film *Star Wars*. © 1977 Lucasfilm Ltd. All rights reserved. Courtesy Lucasfilm Ltd. About three-fifths of this scene (like many others) is a painting, not a photograph. The view of open space, top, is a miniature model. Almost in the exact center is a small spot "filled in" with live action as is the lower right-hand corner. Everything else consists of a painting on glass in which those spots were left unpainted. The artists who make matte paintings must thoroughly understand how light behaves; otherwise, results will not be believable.

stand that detail does not have to be totally eliminated from the shadow areas in order to be convincing.

A matte painting used in the motion picture *Star Wars* is shown in Figure 17.12. Small portions of the work were replaced with photography of real sets with live actors in the final combined print shown here. When viewing the completed film, how many persons would be aware that an artist *painted* most of the scene? The lights are convincingly real.

Figures 17.13 and 17.14 compare how illustrator Daniel Maffia and painter Vincent van Gogh dealt with similar problems. How successful were they? Is it possible to analyze how they instinctively applied correct principles?

Light sources are perceptually small

Perceptual constancy tells us that all prime light sources are extremely small in our visual field—the sun, electric light bulbs, even fluorescent tubes (though up to eight feet long, they are pencil thin). The sun is seen as a large source only when it is completely hidden by overcast clouds. We understand that diffused and reflected light may be many times

larger than prime sources, but we also understand that these are fundamentally much less intense.

We disregard reflected light altogether as an original source of light because we understand perceptually that the light actually comes from somewhere else.

Enhancing the luminance contrast range

One of the methods available to the artist to enhance the luminance range on board or canvas is to use *contour contrast*. As discovered in previous examples (Figs. 14.13 and 14.14), the effect is strong, but this perceptual illusion has limitations. It ceases to be effective over broad areas. In order to trigger the brain response that enhances the contrast of edges (irradiation), cues must provide dark contrast (or a forced edge) and consist of a small contained area. Ordinarily, this means a very small perimeter. The larger the shape, the less effective the result will be. Note that this is exactly compatible with our understanding of original light sources as being small. It is totally an edge phenomenon. To maximize the potential, clusters of small shapes with forced edges need to be placed

left: **17.13** Vincent van Gogh. *Café Terrace at Night, 'Place du Forum,' Arles.* 1888. Oil on canvas, 32 × 25¾″ (81 × 65.5 cm). State Museum Kröller-Muller, Otterlo. Van Gogh has intuitively captured the effect of artificial light at night. If we do not possess the same intuitive powers of an artistic genius like van Gogh or if our intuition does not get out of bed on the day we need it, how do we solve this visual problem? Knowledge is always more reliable than intuition and it enhances and expand intuitive powers. Farsighted persons fill their mental tool kits with as much knowledge as they can — everyday.

below: **17.14** Daniel Maffia. Cover for the Sunday magazine, *Plain Dealer.* In this illustration, Maffia had to make electricity "crackle." Is he successful? How has the mood of the work governed artistic choices?

against a dark ground.

Principles to remember

By understanding and following a few simple principles, it is possible to create a convincing illusion of light as long as works are not directly compared to reality.

To create the effect of a light coming from within a work of art, the light (1) must be small in size, (2) must be surrounded with darkness (at least, a forced edge, if not a relatively large area of darkness), and (3) no area in the work must exhibit a perceived luminance close to that of the light source. Note the term used above is *darkness* not *blackness.*

A prime light source always produces gradations in natural order. *Everything in a natural visual field is gradated.* There are no perceptually "flat" surfaces.

To be truly effective, painted lights must trigger the same cues that we expect of an original light source. Of these, two are the most important.

One is the inverse square law just discussed. Light declines in intensity very quickly as it extends out from its source.

17.15 Edward Hopper. *Sun in an Empty Room.* 1963. Oil on canvas, 28¾ × 39½″ (73 × 100.3 cm). Private collection, Washington, D.C. How has the mood of the work been affected by design choices that the artist made? Cast shadows define each of the various planes. Although this black and white reproduction does not show it, we perceive the walls to be of a uniform golden-yellow hue in spite of the variation in hue and luminances. Hopper has used a color sequence similar to that shown in Color Plate 28 **b**. Yellow mixed with black, as shown in Color Plate 28 **a**, would not have achieved the same convincing effect.

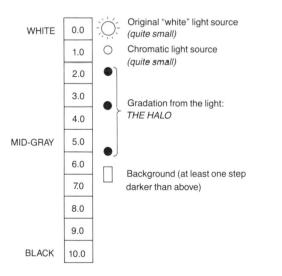

LUMINOSITY CHART

Scale: City Lights at Night

WHITE	0.0	Original "white" light source *(quite small)*
	1.0	Chromatic light source *(quite small)*
	2.0	
	3.0	Gradation from the light: *THE HALO*
	4.0	
MID-GRAY	5.0	
	6.0	
	7.0	Background (at least one step darker than above)
	8.0	
	9.0	
BLACK	10.0	

17.16 It is best to avoid total black masses anywhere in a naturalistic composition as it suggests outer space though, even in that case, a total black background is less successful than a modulated ground.

The second is the fact that a light is always seen to pervade a visual field, that is, to be present throughout or to flood over everything in its path. Take another look at all the Figures in this chapter. A point to remember: When a prime light source is included within a work of art, it must be seen to control everything seen in the composition—shading on figure-objects, cast shadows, whatever.

Important: A strong, single light source is, therefore, one excellent means of unifying a composition. It is a way of making the work appear all of one piece. Analyze the effect of such a light source in Figure 17.15, a painting by Edward Hopper, and in Figure 17.2 **a**.

Other light qualities

Creating effects of luster, luminosity, and iridescence are discussed by Faber Birren in several of his

17.17 Victor Vasarely. *Arcturus.* 1966. Oil on canvas, 63 × 63" (160 × 160 cm). Hirshhorn Museum and Sculpture Garden, Washington, D.C. Gift of Joseph H. Hirshhorn, 1972. Although this black and white reproduction does not precisely reflect the tonal qualities of this work painted in brown, violet, red, and blue squares, it is easy to see how these stepped hues conform to the luminance density (gray) scale (Fig. 16.6) with sequences in natural order. Note how Vasarely has managed them to provide a convincing effect of luminosity: light emerging from the surface of the painting.

books. Luster is seen in objects such as metals, satin material, or oiled wood. Luster, in the context used here, also implies a gradation from a soft sheen to full gloss. Why is luster among the other light effects? Simply because the light source that illuminates objects in a work of art is normally reflected in the lustrous or glossy surface.

Even though located outside the picture frame, *the light is moved within the frame* by virtue of being seen in a reflection. When the prime light source is reflected in a shiny object, it is within the pictorial field, and the composition should be treated accordingly.

A quality of light wave interference, iridescence is responsible for the delicate hues in mother-of-pearl, the colors seen in soap bubbles, and the glitter of a peacock's feathers.

Incandescence, light from burning bodies, includes a whole range from the soft glow of gently glowing embers of a dying fire, molten lava, to the mighty blinding-burning flash from an atom bomb. Luminescence includes the soft light of fireflies and luminous paint as well as fluorescent light bulbs.

The key to satisfactory representation of these effects is the very precise application of specific luminances according to the gray scale. Figure 17.16 shows a scale for controlling luminance intervals when placing lights within the pictorial field. When using the scale, peg each color used to the appropriate luminance as shown on the Hue/Luminance Chart (Color Plate 27). In *Arcturus* (Fig. 17.17), Victor Vasarely creates subtle glowing forms through careful application of stepped luminances.

To create the effects of light radiating from *within* the picture frame, luminance gradations should always follow natural order. *Do not* use any white in the composition except (1) to mix lighter hues and (2) to paint the small original light sources themselves.

Creating light effects **301**

General rules of thumb

For hues: Lights are the lightest (whitest) thing in the total work; gradation away from them shifts in natural order toward the hue of the ground or background.

For purities: Lights are pure; moving away from the light, purity declines in natural order toward gray. The brighter the light, the less or slower the decline.

For luminances: Light to dark gradation declines at differing intervals (fast or slow) for differing light effects. For example, a low level, like candlelight, produces a fast decline; though a very intense light produces a slow decline.

For backgrounds: *No highlights of any objects should ever be lighter than one step below the lightness of the original light source.* Total blacks in large areas (silhouettes) should be avoided, as they are not perceptual. General background hues should lean toward the complement of the hue of the prime light source. Virtually all background hues should be visibly less pure than the light source or than a light source reflected in an object. Do not use any large areas of unmodified white in naturalistic works.

Summary

For artists working naturalistically or for any artists who wish to employ light as a concept in their art, there is an array of perceptual light cues that will always prove beneficial. Such cues are important to add to our knowledge and to learn to apply with a degree of confidence and skill.

Light as a concept can offer an artist a means of adding special moods and other emotional qualities to works of art. Light can be a means of helping to unify works, of adding drama, or a means to bring out or to feature the texture of things. It is possible to create an acceptable illusion of light originating from within a work. For naturalistic or abstract artists, the techniques offer a considerable range of alternative possibilities. For the artist who, for the first time, creates a sense of light that appears to be emerging from within the painting itself, the accomplishment is very satisfying.

That needs only to be the beginning.

Review of key terms

chromatic light technique A melding technique in which colors are altered as if they were viewed only under one-hued chromatic light, an additive color mixing procedure.

dominant tint technique A melding technique in which a little of one hue (or pigment) is added to every color in a work of art, a subtractive color mixing procedure.

high key A composition in which the overall or prevailing luminances are all above middle gray.

low key A composition in which the overall or prevailing luminances are all below middle gray.

CHAPTER EIGHTEEN

Color psychology

Introduction

Although color has been significant to human beings in some ways from the dawn of time, scientifically based studies really began with René Descartes and Sir Isaac Newton in the 17th century and very early years of the 18th century. Psychological studies specifically related to color are a phenomenon of the 20th century. The application of color psychology in all sorts of ways — to art, to health and medicine, to communications and marketing, and to industry — is largely a development of just the latter half of this century. Widespread dissemination of the results of color studies has occurred even more recently. Interest

18.1 In this advertisement, color is used as a concept to sell clothing. The text refers to the architecture of Bermuda and reads in part, " . . . where cottages painted brilliant pink, green, blue, and beige are crowned with white roofs. Where stucco walls, painted layer upon layer, when chipped away, reveal a house's history and personality — much the same as color is used to lend character and depth to clothing." The words are more significant than the photograph which is in muted earth tones of browns and yellows.

303

is growing in this research because it reveals that color and light are major influences in our lives. *Color News* reports:

> Many scientists now believe that it is vital to our health and survival that we understand the importance of lighting and the colors emanating from those lights.
>
> In an article titled "The Guiding Light" from *Psychology Today,* science writer Hal Hellman states, "Researchers are becoming convinced that all aspects of our health, mental as well as physical, are affected by the density, duration, and even color of the light to which we are exposed.
>
> Dr. Richard Wurtman, a nutritionist at the Massachusetts Institute of Technology, stated in *The New York Times* that "it seems clear that light is the most important environmental input, after food, in controlling bodily function." Many studies have shown that various colors of light can affect brain activity, biorhythms, pulse and respiration rates.[25]

For the fine artist, for the communication artist, for anyone involved in the arts, a fundamental understanding of the psychophysical aspects of light and color appears to be an essential requirement for negotiating the last days of the 20th century and entry into the 21st century, only a hop, skip, and a jump away. Though traditional materials and methods may never completely be set aside, a substantial number, perhaps a majority, of artists caught up in the computer revolution, now in full swing, will find an electronic component fastened to their work. This is a technological age. The formation of new, original, and fresh, solutions to visual problems revolves around the exploration of alternatives, the bases of which are likely to flow from the broadest possible general and technological knowledge and understanding.

The state of contemporary research

Form dominant and color dominant persons

Children are often used for basic color studies because they do not possess the same inhibitions and prejudices that influence adult behavior. At a very early age, children are color dominant (stimulus responsive); that is, they respond to the color in a visual field before they respond to the shape or form. Later this reverses, with older children developing their powers of reasoning and exercising greater emotional control.

Ninety percent of the world's adult population is form dominant (stimulus selective), with tendencies to be more practical (pragmatic), thorough, conforming, stable, mature, and socially controlled.

Color dominant adults, around 10 percent of the world's population, are seen as highly sensitive, individualistic, and somewhat impractical. The terms

impulsive, immature, egocentric, and mentally unstable also have been applied to these people though research does not generally lend support to all these associations.

Deborah T. Sharpe writes in *The Psychology of Color and Design,* "One of the ingredients of creative ability seems to be naïveté (which some might call immaturity), the facility to be more or less free of the traditional modes of doing things and to see new possibilities, new relationships, unheard-of combinations."[26]

Is one good description of a creative person that of a nonconformist? A preponderance of evidence suggests that the creative adult is usually a color dominant personality. They tend to score very high in fluid intelligence, a creative, nonverbal kind of thinking involving visualization rather than step-by-step deduction.

The appeal of realism in pictures

Studies confirm that younger children prefer paintings based on subject matter and color without regard to the degree of realism present. As they grow older, they select paintings based on realism in increasing degrees. Any picture proved satisfying to older children in a direct ratio to its success in synthesizing the likeness of realism. Does that imply that adults are perceptually preprogammed to respond to a visual imitation of the real world in which we live?

Can we conclude from this that an appreciation of abstract and nonobjective art is an acquired taste?

Studies suggest that adults and college students who have had exposure to art studies tend to approve of paintings on the basis of artistic style. Such choices are attributed to a learned response (cognitive conformity) that authorities consider some styles and some artists superior to others.

How age affects selection of pure colors

Children prefer bright colors, but as they mature, they seem to develop a willingness to deal with a variety of purity and luminance differences. Early, the preference is for red—emotion and mass response—later, as the child moves toward a transitional stage, blue emerges.

Another commonly tested group in psychology, college students, aged 17 to 20, preferred blue, red, and green (the additive primaries) to orange, yellow, and violet. Overall, studies indicated that the preference for bright, primary colors continues from childhood into adulthood for uneducated or poorly educated persons. The more insecure individual tended to select bright colors that ranged from light to dark but the more self-confident, sophisticated personality favored colors of middle luminance that ranged from neutral to cool (gray, beige, green, blue).

18.3 Oskar Schlemmer. *Groupe Concentrique.* 1925. Oil on canvas, 38⅜ × 24⅜″ (97.5 × 62 cm). © 1989 The Oskar Schlemmer Family Estate, Badenweiler, West Germany. Photograph by Staatsgalerie, Stuttgart.

above right: **18.4** Statue of a cat. Egyptian. Late Dynastic Period. Bronze, height 11″ (28 cm). Metropolitan Museum of Art, New York. Harris Brisbane Dick Fund, 1956. Egyptians saw divine powers in black cats and dreaded red and brown ones.

Recent studies suggest that color choice may be influenced by personality. Neurotics and introverts generally favored dark, drab colors and irregular shapes, which, continued over long periods of time, could be a sign of emotional problems like depression. Extroverts preferred symmetry and bright hues. Some persons use bright colors as morale boosters or to attract attention.

As people grow older, into their sixties or seventies, there is a tendency for many of them to select somewhat brighter colors than they did in middle age. Researchers attribute this to the loss of some sensitivity in cone cells of the eyes consistent with a similar gradual decline in the sensitivity of other biological functions.

The effects of constancy on color choices

Most persons untrained in the visual arts respond to color constancies. These tell us that the sky is blue, grass is green, and apples are red. The child reaches in the crayon box for the "correct" crayon to color each of these. **Often the novice artist does the same thing. It is difficult to break the "crayon box mentality" because perceptual constancies are very difficult to overcome.** The sky is not blue, nor is grass green, nor is an apple red. Artists must sensitize themselves to the vast array of hues that every natural figure-object possesses. As we have already seen, there are enormous variations in virtually every respect.

A field of all bright colors tends to overload our

18.5 *Yellow Submarine,* film still from animated feature. Copyright © 1975 United Artists Corporation. All rights reserved. This black and white photograph does not show the many bright colors of high luminance and purity. Such colors were typical of the 1960s color revolution, "psychedelic color." In this case, the dark figure outlines help to harmonize the hues.

visual system, lose purity, and produce an overall gray response. The eye-brain mechanisms tend to discount extreme colors and see things more or less normal. Colors like red actually raise the blood pressure, and blue lowers it, but such effects are temporary. If physiological and psychological color relationships are to be actively maintained, constant change is required.

Culture influences color choices

Americans tend to think that their color preferences are just like everyone else's in the world. They are not. It takes very little study to become aware of the fact that there are widely differing national and racial responses to color. For instance, in the United States, black is the color of mourning. In Mexico, it is blue; and it is white in the Virgin Islands, Japan, and Africa. To Buddhists, yellow is the color of death.

There is now some evidence to indicate that racial groups may be perceived and reacted to by virtue of their colorcoding. It is possible that human response to lightness (sunshine, safety, growth, and warmth) and to darkness (night, fear, cold) may be buried very deep at the root of Caucasian prejudice against blacks and other dark-hued persons. When there is no light, only darkness, one cannot see. The loss of vision means a loss of control of personal security, placing a person *at risk*. This is one negative view of black that all peoples share, including black persons.

In Western societies, the majority of affective responses to black are negative, reinforcing the fear of

darkness. Conversely, African poets often attribute the same positive qualities (health, love, desire, passion) to black as Caucasians do to white.

Eras are color-coded

The colonial period made use of soft blues, pale (warmish) yellow, lilac, and delicate warm grays along with the tones of wood; Victorians preferred dark, rich colors of olive or emerald green, crimson red, midnight blue, and purple. The twenties were neutral — black, gray, and white with the metallics, gold and silver. The 1950s were pink. Obviously, color has major cultural significance.

In the 1960s, as a consequence of the social upheaval caused by the war in Vietnam and changing mores, a color revolution began. Artists, both trained and untrained, experimented with color as perceived by the drug culture, *psychedelic color.* Every possible combination of color was accepted; traditional concepts governing color schemes, such as complementary and discordant colors, became obsolete virtually overnight. Psychedelic color became a sort of trademark of the Beatle generation. The trend toward an increased variety of brighter colors is still with us.

A study of most times and cultures will show strong preferences for certain groups of colors. The association of purple with royalty goes back to the days of early Rome. Purple dye was so rare that only emperors could afford it. Purple was not chosen because its hue was preferred, but because it was unusual and expensive.

don't let it die

denver
denver
denver
denver
denver
denver
denver
denver
denver

18.6   Fred Colcer. Poster for The Colorado Open Space Council. ca. 1973. The black and white reproduction compromises the entire concept behind this poster because it places emphasis on the darker print at the bottom. In color, the emphasis is placed at the top instead, where "Denver" is printed in a very bright, pure green and blue. As "Denver" goes down the page, colors become dingier and darker, so that at the very bottom the word is almost black and white. **In this case, color is essential to meaning.**

Color language and symbolism

In the English language, color terminology plays a significant role. It is everyday vernacular. In order to grasp to some degree the extent that color terminology has entered common usage, turn to a dictionary of synonyms and antonyms.

In one thesaurus, there are more than 300 words associated with red alone. That does not include references like anger, revolutionary, radical, in the red, redbreast, red cent, red tape, red flag, red herring, red ribbon, and so on. Terms related to color pervade our everyday speech and our written language.

Check for every primary, secondary hue, and brown, blackness, darkness, colorlessness, gray, and purity; and while at it, also check variation and variegation. Keep in mind that such reference books do not always include slang, ethnic idiosyncrasies, and the wealth of temporary idioms that come and go every few years.

An old Southern mountain folk song goes,

Blue is true,
Yeller's jealous,
Green's forsaken'
Red is brazen
White is love, and
Black is death.[27]

There are many colorful songs. There are the Beatles' "Yellow Submarine," for instance, and Prince's "Purple Rain." What current songs use color in their titles?

We sing the blues when we are depressed. When we are healthy and feeling good, we are in the pink. Our lips turn white when we grow angry and we see red, although we turn purple with rage.

Affective responses to hues

Each of the hues possesses a set of affective responses, *cues*, that can be profitably used in works of art. Color *cues*, which are reinforced by a number of other visual cues, become an effective means of prompting a desired emotional response from the viewer. The affective responses of color hues, therefore, represent one of our best ways to help solve any visual problem.

A point: The emotional characteristics of colors are easily made invalid by specific applications where an attribute is not reinforced by other means. Reinforcement is an essential requirement. Do we respond in the same way to a green lawn as to green meat; a purple plum as purple skin; a red barn as a red room? As we have already pointed out, particular colors are subject to the fads of the times and to the fashions of merchandising products.

A few of the common affective responses for hues follow:

Red. The color of blood, passion, and aggression. A symbol of war and pestilence, red is also a warm hue associated with action, strength, zealousness, and religion. Women are attracted to red though men prefer blue. Together with yellow, it seems hypnotic. Red attracts attention and is used for this purpose in traffic signs, red-pencil corrections, and clothing accessories. Because it is so strong, it is not often used for broad, unrelieved expanses. Light pink is feminine, rosy, or healthy. Darker, vivid pink is tacky and cheap today, tomorrow?

Orange. A very warm color with energy and force as attributes. It is the color of a hot fire—glowing embers are red. Suggestive of good times and joy, it is also the color of knowledge and civilization. Peachy-hued oranges are fruity and juicy but yellow-oranges are golden and rich, a symbol of wealth.

Yellow. The color of sunshine, bright and cheerful; of radiant energy and light; also, of jaundice, cowardice, and caution. Unclear or impure mixtures, especially those containing black (greenish), suggest repulsion, ill health, and decay.

Green. The symbol of growth, renewal, and the rebirth of plant life (sometimes all life) on earth; an expression of fertility, freshness, youth as well as inexperience. It is the color of paper money. Some mixtures suggest envy, jealousy, guilt, disease, or terror. Green light is otherworldly because we experience almost no natural green light.

Violet. (Purple) The color of increasing distance and space (aerial perspective), it varies widely in hue, being perceived as warm or cool relative to the colors adjacent to it. Purple is associated with fantasy, mysticism, and homosexuality. Deep purple is a symbol of royalty. Other mixtures evoke nostalgia. When impure, pale and grayish, violets also suggest depression, loneliness, aging, disease, and death.

Blue. The symbol for peace. This is a hue that is in control, restful, serene; psychologically and physiologically calming. It is "transparent." The accepted symbol for fidelity, sobriety, and aloofness; in other contexts, blue indicates discomfort: cold, wet, and fear. Dark blue is conservative, sober, reliable, and dependable; sky blue is celestial.

Brown. The color of the soil, brown is earthy, cosy or comfortable, and fertile more often than dirty and dull. The hue suggests the stability and permanence of the earth. It possesses the familiarity and worth of wood. Like gray, brown is usually considered to be a neutral color but of a warmer sensibility. It seems to be a balm for depression. Except for Terre Verte, most other earth colors have similar connotations.

Black. The absence of visible light, it represents a void or a hole in the visual field, annihilation, as well as a sense of mystery, the powers of darkness, evil, and fear. But under other circumstances, it can be warm, engulfing, sheltering, comforting, and secure. Black is associated with depression, sorrow, gloom, and death in this country; yet it possesses a unique ability to lend force and great power to any figure. What is it that suggests a black panther is somehow more powerful and fearsome than the common variety of leopard?

White suggests death, fear, monotony, pallidness, and impenetrable cold as well as its more common

18.7 Brand New Limited uses the color of the aerosol can to symbolize *function* in a product line developed to fill a gap in the generic products market.

associations with light, purity, and truth. It is hospital cleanliness, the sign of a truce (white flag), a cover-up (whitewash) uselessness (white elephant), and deception (the white lie). We turn white with fright, are white-lipped with rage, or sear in white heat. White shapes are perceptually viewed as figures and advance but black shapes tend to be seen as holes and recede.

Gray is not perceived as being composed of colors, but as a noncolor. A kind of detachment or lack of commitment is reflected in this attitude. Gray is associated with cloudy days, the blahs; though it may be restful for short periods, long exposure is depressing because our senses are deprived of sufficient stimulation.

This list is only to start the process of thinking and of investigation. There are positive and negative attributes for each hue; environmental and biological attributes; national, social, ethnic, and symbolic attributes. We need to develop our own sensitivity to these through study and incorporate them into our intuitive responses. To avoid clichés, the cues should be used with imagination, in unusual relationships and combinations. More than simply augmenting object identification or brightening a drab environment, color greatly enhances and enriches the quality of our lives.

Contemporary artists emphasize individuality and tend to place trust in their own sensibilities. Yet it is clear that such determinations must be tempered by knowledge of the psychophysical nature of light and color. Our own responses to color may be too personal and subjective for clear communications.

Color symbols

Certain colors are associated with almost everything—with the seasons, with various festivals, with flags, with schools and colleges, with sports teams and events. A very long list would be required to include them all.

Colors mean different things to different audiences. Examine the chart by Gerald E. Jones (Fig. 18.8) from *Computer Graphics World*.[28]

Obviously, when a presentation or an advertisement is prepared for one of these groups, the choice of colors may be crucial to a full understanding.

Color applied

The structure of the arts is one that is designed to play up, or to take advantage of, the inherent psychophysical nature of human beings. Its purposes range from information (teaching); to motivation to buy a product, act a certain way, or support a certain cause; to entertainment; or to any combination of these. Elemental affective responses may be coupled to appropriate images (subjects), symbols, or suggestive shapes or forms to make them effective in application.

If we look at a drawing of just the outline of a drop shape and we are told that it is red, what is it? Blood! Are there any other possibilities? Then we are told the color has changed, and it is blue. What is it? Water? If the color is changed to white, what is it?

Color symbolism of various audiences

Hue	Movie audiences	Financial managers	Health-care Professionals	Control engineers
Cyan blue	Tender	Corporate	Dead	Cold, water
Yellowish green	Leisurely	Cool, subdued	Cyanotic	Steam
Green	Playful	Profitable	Infected, bilious	Nominal, safe
Yellow	Happy	Important	Jaundiced	Caution
Red	Exciting	Unprofitable	Healthy	Danger
Purple	Sad	Wealthy	Cause for concern	Hot, radioactive

18.8 This chart shows how the same hue may hold significantly different meanings for differing groups of persons.

It is at that point that we begin to get into serious difficulty. Blue and red colors for the droplet shape trigger very universal responses, but there is no equally strong symbol for a white liquid. In the United States, one answer is milk perhaps. However, many persons in the world never taste milk after their mother's breast.

These examples illustrate that, up to a point, responses to color are universal but only up to a point. Observe that it was a combination of shape and color suggested that produced the response, neither hue nor shape alone. Associations of color, shape, and emotion are inevitably linked and are symbolic in context. Such associative responses control the visual weight of any image. Properly executed, they are effective.

There are color symbols all about us.

We have safety codes, red for danger, stop signs, and stoplights, for example. Yellow is caution; green, safety and first aid. There are colors for signs of the zodiac, heraldry, and virtually every subject. Some color consultants say that the hue of our complexion together with the color of our hair should determine colors of facial makeup as well as the colors of garments worn.

What if all road maps were printed in black and white like the one shown in Figure 8.9? Sometimes, because things are so familiar, we do not appreciate how difficult it would be without colorcoding in all its forms. Here, various components of the map are easy separated when we look at a full color original.

Color expectations influence consumer choices

In one taste preference test, the rating of an inferior orange juice was raised when it was colored to match the hue of one of a higher quality.

In another experiment, when food colors, such as red, yellow, orange, and violet, were added to a colorless syrup, the flavor was attributed to a variety of fruits suggested by the colors of the drinks. Foods that are identified with specific colors are ordinarily accepted or rejected by consumers on the basis of that color although foods are seldom chosen for color alone. Not too long ago, an attempt utterly failed to introduce yellow-fleshed watermelons at the supermarket. Even preconceived notions about the texture of particular products alter the perception of flavors.

The dairy industry adds yellow color to butter when the natural carotene content is low. Carotene is a natural coloring matter found not only in butter but also in many plants. The natural color of orange juice is not strong enough to meet color expectations when it is used to make orange sherbet or ice cream. Mint-flavored ice cream would be white if it were not colored green. One manufacturer of ice cream has used that idea in a sales pitch: no artificial anything including color. Are they fighting a losing battle against consumer expectations? Cherry pies are colored red; even mother used a couple of drops of red food coloring when she made a pie from scratch. When cherries are cooked, they usually turn an unap-

18.9 Although some persons may be surprised to learn it, a majority of processed commercial food products contain coloring substances to increase their appeal *and perceived worth* to consumers. Read the labels.

petizing grayish red. Natural or artificial colors are added to a wide variety of the processed foods we purchase; check the labels.

Synesthesia

In a TV advertisement, one wine company claimed that its grapes were "orchestrated" to produce its fine wines, inviting the viewer to "taste the music." Many composers have associated specific hues with various tones or chords. Many persons see colors when listening to music.

Dark colors suggest strength though light colors are expected to be mild or weak. In general, the richness of color (pure and dark) affects perceptions of the effectiveness, flavor, and quality of products. How often are the terms *dark* and *rich* combined in TV commercials for coffee? Dark cough syrups are considered more potent.

The darkness or lightness of a color even affects perceptions of physical weight. Though weights were the same, tests showed that consumers estimated weights of dark-colored packages as heavier than light-colored ones.

Our senses do not operate independently. One sense seems to arouse correspondence with others. This quality of perception is called *synesthesia*, and it has enormous, though seldom acknowledged, effect on our choices of products, foods, and living environments, both as individuals and as a culture.

The uses of color

Color is used to solve visual problems in 12 basic ways:

1. **To attract attention by stimulating a viewer's emotional responses.** If a message is to be heard, it must first be seen.

2. **To symbolize abstract concepts or ideas.** Because responses to color are commonly emotional, color symbols combined with other images can often help express complex thoughts in visual terms.

3. **To produce an aesthetic response or endorsement through articulated order in visual relationships (patternmaking).** Our brain perceptually rewards us for perceiving "good" patterns. Responding to sensory patterns is a primary brain function. Patternmaking is creating orderly, coherent relationships; when we do that, we feel a sense of accomplishment. For the majority of artistic persons, color patterns are more significant than patterns of shapes, but the exact opposite is true of the general public.

4. **To create movement within the composition by directing and orchestrating visual weight (attraction).** Within a work of art, the application of the dominance principle not only establishes a focal point but also sets up the basic patterns of movement throughout the entire work. Managing color

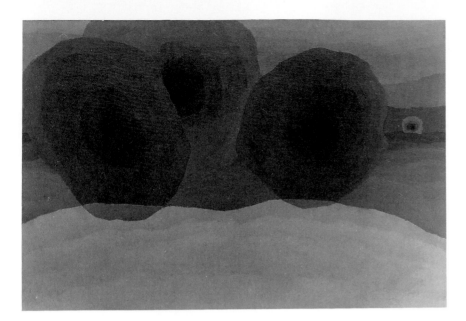

18.10 Arthur Dove. *Foghorns.* 1929. Oil on canvas, 18 × 26″ (45.72 × 66.04 cm). Colorado Springs Fine Arts Center. Anonymous gift. Here, using a visual field, Dove tries to evoke an audio response—synesthesia. Does the eye hear? The ear see? Compare this painting with Lenica's (Fig. 11.9).

is one means of creating a hierarchy of dominances and subdominances.

5. **To develop spatial relationships in the pictorial field.** No matter what the artist's style, concept, or application, color can be used to establish spatial relationships, to warp (*push-pull*) the two-dimensional surface through application of perceptual depth cues such as the principles of aerial perspective and relative visual attraction.

6. **To reinforce or modulate basic compositional structure.** Color may be developed as a motif, as a mood, tone, or emotional pyrotechnic; it can by itself (without considering shape) establish rhythms and patterns.

7. **To extend psychologically the perceived range of purities, luminances, and hues on a two-dimensional surface.** The reflective, two-dimensional surface has a very limited luminance range. Pigments are limited in vibrancy and intensity by the fact that they are not capable of producing monochromatic reflections. If we know how to apply the perceptual characteristics of simultaneous contrast, both the luminance range and the apparent purity of colors can be extended to create an illusion of light and of color brilliance that is physically impossible. The brilliance of colors can be improved through glazing, which increases the monochromatic quality of the reflection.

8. **To increase or decrease a figure-object's apparent size and weight.** Colors have qualities of dimension and weight, factors that can level or sharpen figures to create illusions of size and weight differences where none physically exist.

9. **To emphasize (point out) or de-emphasize (camouflage) figure-objects.** Color contrast permits an artist to cause figures to advance or to recede at will; it is a skill to learn and to use. It is not a mystery; it is knowledge.

10. **To provide a subjective, nonrational means to express personal feelings and emotions.** Emotions dwell in the most primitive parts of our brain. A large part of that primitive biological response is a reaction to colors in our environment. Color appears to be, by nature, more subjective (emotional) and less rational as a concept than shape (or form). Subordinating shape to color, therefore, provides artists with their best opportunity for personal and emotional expression.

11. **To describe objectively figure-objects by depicting their obvious surface characteristics.** Every natural figure-object possesses a kind of color model or a collection of color models (paradigms) by which they can be recognized by our brain. To equip a pictorial figure with colors that meet perceptual expectations is to create a satisfying connection for any viewer.

Color psychology   **313**

18.11 Andy Warhol. Advertisement for Levi Strauss and Co. 1984. It should be obvious even in this black and white reproduction that Warhol has used negative as well as positive images in the ad. What is not seen is that he has also used "negative color," hue complements of the natural colors.

12. **To enhance an object's utilitarian worth.** A stop sign is enhanced in its utilitarian worth by always being painted red; thus, color reinforces message. The colorcoding of traffic lights is a similar functional application of color, as is colorcoding on maps and other signage. A few drops of food color adds aesthetic appeal as well as perceived worth to such things as orange juice, mint ice cream, and cherry pie. Light, soft (somewhat grayed hues), or neutralized colors on the interior walls of a home have greater appeal to the majority of home purchasers than vivid wall colors like orange, lime green, or bright magenta. The monetary worth of a home, *its market value,* may be affected favorably or unfavorably by the colors of the wall paint or other decorative features.

Any individual piece of art may put to work some or all of these. A work of fine art will tend to be more expansive and subtle in the application; a work of applied art will tend to be bold, more obvious, and specific because the message must neither be ambiguous nor easily misunderstood.

Yet all these are fundamental to the creative use of color in any situation. When any artist is faced with a visual problem, they offer alternative choices virtually unlimited in scope and variation. Each should be given consideration in the conceptual planning of every work because failure to consider one is likely to diminish the work (as a whole) in some respect and make it less successful.

Summary

Psychological studies involving color and form are providing insights into the nature of creative persons. A profile is emerging. Studies suggest that a majority of creative persons respond first to color, then to form; that is, they are likely to be color dominant personalities and have an emotionally oriented personality structure. They tend to be more impulsive and sensitive, less imprisoned by logic and reason though commonly accomplished at both. They are often able to concentrate intently on one specific goal to the exclusion of everything else without regard to time, tedium, or travail.

Creative people seem able to hold onto a sense of childlike wonder and optimism about nature, about people, and about the essential goodness of things that the majority of children lose as they grow to adulthood. They are open to new ideas, able to shift gears easily, inclined to pursue untried or unpromising directions, and are not usually bothered by inconsistency or disarray. As a group, they are more intelligent than average. However, that intelligence may be expressed in the form of a creative nonverbal kind of thinking, easy neither to discover nor to evaluate by conventional testing methods. One characteristic is the ability to make inferences not obviously a result of logical reasoning (although the conclusion may be perfectly reasonable once understood); to see similarities in dissimilars; to make uncommon associations.

As children mature, studies indicate that they prefer pictures based on realistic representational subject matter and that approval of pictures is relative to the degree of perceived realism observed in the pictures. Our educational system appears to reinforce such associations. Therefore, the majority of adults are heavily predisposed toward realism in pictures.

Hue preference studies suggest that a majority of persons prefer hues that are components of our visual processing, blues, reds, and greens (the primary colors of light), before approving hues such as yellows, oranges, or violets. Bright primary hues are generally perceived to be less sophisticated than partly grayed or muted hues. Perhaps it is because a field of all bright colors perceptually grays and may possess no color dominance.

We have discovered that not all responses to color are subjective, but there are at least a number of physiological reactions such as the fact that the lens in our eyes cannot bring all colors to focus on the same point. A red-hued environment causes a temporary increase in blood pressure; conversely, a blue-hued environment lowers blood pressure for a time. Our initial responses to hues are part of the most primitive portions of our brain and are associated with basic emotions. These affective responses are tools that an intelligent image manager (the artist) can put to work.

Colors are ripe with symbolism; they possess all sorts of connections: biological, natural, cultural, professional, and political aspects, for example. They modify our responses to sounds and flavors and vice versa. To use them effectively requires a good deal of knowledge and sophistication. The key is to employ other symbolic forms, such as line, shape, space, and movement, to reinforce the affective (emotional) response a color can bring to an idea or to a concept. Coupled together, affective responses can become effective ones.

Color is one of an artist's most versatile tools. For exploration, it offers a range of almost unlimited alternatives.

Review of key terms

colorcoding A process through which figure-objects or their parts are distinguished from one another by color for a variety of useful purposes such as separating complex detail (as in a road map) or informing or warning (like yellow for caution or red for danger). Colorcoding is also applied prejudiciously to ethnic and racial groups.

color dominant personality A type of person who tends to respond first to color then to shape (or form). Comprising about 10 percent of the adult population, they are usually described as highly sensitive, individualistic, and somewhat impractical. They are said to have an emotionally oriented (stimulus responsive) personality structure.

crayon box mentality A state of mind in which colors are reduced to their simplest expression and things are viewed as having stereotypical hues (grass is green), a consequence of perceptual constancy.

form dominant personality A type of person who tends to respond to shape (or form) before color. Comprising about 90 percent of the adult population, they are usually described as practical, thorough, mature, and conforming. They are said to have a socially controlled (stimulus selective) personality structure.

psychedelic color A style of color usage introduced by the drug subculture of the 1960s and characterized by very bright pure hues applied as if viewed in a hallucinatory state. Psychedelic color has influenced almost every type of contemporary color application.

psychological Pertaining to the mind or to the emotions.

psychophysical A term used by psychologists to indicate a response that is dependent on combined physical, biological, and mental processes.

synesthesia A subjective event in which the responses of one sensory organ are linked to those of another, as seeing colors when listening to music.

Appendix

Relative color temperature chart (subjective)

A representative list of permanent artists' colors.
Luminance density, **D**, is approximate.

Luminance	Pigment	Generic hue**
Warm:		
D 6.5	*Bright Red Oxide	orange-red
D 7.0	*Burnt Sienna	orange
D 9.0	*Burnt Umber	orange
D 3.0	Cadmium Orange	orange
D 7.0	Cadmium Red Deep	red
D 5.0	Cadmium Red Light	orange-red
D 6.0	Cadmium Red Medium	red
D 1.0	Cadmium Yellow, Light or Lemon	yellow
D 2.0	Cadmium Yellow Medium	warmish yellow
D 3.0	Cadmium Yellow Deep	yellow-orange
D 6.5	Cerulean Blue	blue
D 6.0	Chrome Green	yellowish green
D 7.0	Cobalt Violet	reddish violet
D 6.5	*Green Earth (Terre Verte)	yellowish green
D 6.0	Grumbacher Red***	red
D 9.0	Hooker's Green	yellowish green
D 9.5	Ivory Black (carbon)	—
D 9.5	Lamp Black (carbon)	—
D 3.0	Naples Yellow	orangy yellow
D 5.0	*Ochre, Transparent Gold	orangy yellow
D 6.0	Permanent Green Light (mixture, includes yellow pigment)	yellowish green
D 7.0	*Raw Sienna	orangy yellow
D 9.0	*Raw Umber	yellow
D 0.0	Titanium White	—
D 9.0	Ultramarine Blue (violet overtones)	blue
D 7.0	*Venetian Red	orange-red
D 5.0	*Yellow Ochre	yellow
D 0.0	Zinc White (yellowish overtones)	—

Cool:		
D 8.0	Acra Red***	purplish red
D 9.0	Acra Violet***	violet-red
D 8.0	Cobalt Blue	purplish blue
D 9.0	Cobalt Violet Deep	reddish violet
D 9.0	Dioxazine Violet	bluish violet
D 1.0	Hansa Yellow, Light or Lemon	yellow
D 7.5	*Indian Red	purplish red
D 8.0	Naphthol Crimson	violet-red
D 8.0	Permanent Magenta***	violet-red
D 9.0	Phthalocyanine Blue ("Thalo")	greenish blue
D 9.0	Phthalocyanine Green ("Thalo")	bluish green
D 9.0	Viridian Green	bluish green
D 9.0	Windsor Blue (phthalocyanine)	greenish blue
D 9.0	Windsor Purple (dioxazine)	bluish violet

*Identifies "earth" colors.

**All descriptive words ending in *ish* or *y*, like *yellowish* or *orangy*, indicate that the generic hue (name that follows) is "influenced" by that color or leans toward it. For example, yellowish green is a green that leans toward the yellow. Hyphenated hue names describe intermediate hues, theoretically halfway between. Orange-red is a hue halfway between orange and red.

***Quinacridone reds.

Transparency/opacity of commonly used pigments

Caution: Qualities of pigments may vary considerably by grade and manufacturer. Good advice: Read the label.

Transparent: Clear hues of high purity, considered permanent by modern standards; especially suitable for glazing.

Acra Violet (quinacridone)

Cobalt Violet Deep

Dioxazine Violet

Hansa: yellows through reds, pure pigment only. (Caution: often used in mixtures with opaque pigments like white.)

Hooker's Green

Grumbacher Red (quinacridone)

Monastral: all colors, trade name for phthalocyanine

Quinacridone: reds, magentas, violets; usually sold under a trade name. Check label.

Phthalocyanine: all colors ("Thalo" for short)

Viridian Green

Windsor Blue (phthalocyanine)

Windsor Green (phthalocyanine)

Windsor Violet (dioxazine)

Translucent (semitransparent/opaque): These pigments may be used thinly as glazes. Caution: They may vary widely from relatively transparent to fairly opaque from manufacturer to manufacturer even in good grades.

Cobalt Blue (pure only; inexpensive grades may be mixtures of ultramarine and opaque white)

Cobalt Violet (pure only; not mixtures)

Ivory Black

Lamp Black

Ochre, Transparent Gold (very good transparency if original)

Paynes Gray

Red Oxides: Bright Red Oxide; English Red; Indian Red; Light Red; Venetian Red. Test them.

Sienna, Raw and Burnt (good grades are especially transparent and suitable for glazing)

Terre Verte (Green Earth)

Ultramarine Blue, also French Ultramarine

Umber, Raw and Burnt (good grades are especially transparent and suitable for glazing)

Zinc White

Opaque pigments: Usually unpleasant when used as glazes. Use for scumbling.

Cadmium: all colors

Cerulean Blue mixtures

Cobalt Blue or Violet, mixtures with white

Mars Black (iron)

Naples Yellow (lead)

Titanium White

Yellow Ochre (standard grades)

Notes: To learn more about pigments, see *The Artist's Handbook of Materials and Techniques* by Ralph Mayer (New York: Viking, 1982).

Any artist should also be aware of the toxicity of various pigments, mediums, solvents, and all other materials regularly used. The dangers are real; details can be found in *Artist Beware* by Michael McCann (New York: Watson-Guptill, 1969). Some manufacturers are now including warning labels on their artists' materials.

Common palettes

1. **Basic palette.** Such a palette usually consists of pigments whose hues conform to the primary and secondary hue names on the Prang hue circle (color wheel) plus white and black; sometimes a dark brown is added. There is *no* standard or generally accepted basic palette. The *double primary palette* is one form of basic palette.

2. **Basic palette plus Earth Colors.** Any basic palette with the addition of some, or all, of the earth pigments.

3. **Earth palette.** A palette that consists only of earth pigments. Because a strict earth palette has no blue hue, sometimes Cobalt, Manganese, or, more commonly, Ultramarine Blue is added.

4. **The extended palette.** Any number of pigments an artist might select for any reason, usually exceeding by far the number of pigments included in any form of palette called basic. This is an important type of personal palette.

5. **The limited palette.** A palette deliberately restricted to a very small number of pigments, possibly only two, but rarely more than three. Examples: Two-color, Cadmium Orange and Thalo Blue; three-color, Cadmium Yellow and Acra Crimson (Rembrandt sometimes used lead-tin yellow and Vermilion Red) plus black; or, try Yellow Ochre, Cadmium Red Medium, and Thalo Blue. This is a type of personal palette.

6. **Monochromatic palette.** One pigment (of any hue) plus black; also including white if opaque media (oil or acrylics) are used. Technique permits the use of grays, neutral ones mixed from white and black as well as chromatic ones mixed from black, white, and the chosen color.

There are also *warm* and *cool palettes,* based on the specific feeling of the pigments (hues) chosen. See *Relative color temperature chart.* Of course, most professional artists have their own personal palettes, chosen by preference after years of experience.

Notes

[1] Louis Prang of Boston published *The Theory of Color* in 1876. His ideas were subsequently adopted by the majority of American educational institutions for primary and secondary study.

[2] Morse Peckham, "Art and Disorder," in Richard Kostelanetz (ed.), *Esthetics Contemporary* (Buffalo, N.Y.: Prometheus Books, 1978), p. 115.

[3] Robert Rivlin and Karen Gravelle, *Deciphering the Senses: The Expanding World of Human Perception* (New York: Simon & Schuster, 1984), p. 165.

[4] Michael S. Gazzaniga, *The Social Brain: Discovering the Networks of the Mind* (New York: Basic Books, 1985).

[5] Maurice Pirenne, *Optics, Painting, and Photography* (Cambridge, England: Cambridge University Press, 1970), p. 165.

[6] Anna Berliner, *Lectures on Visual Psychology* (Chicago: Professional Press, 1948), pp. 1–2.

[7] Wucius Wong, *Principles of Two-Dimensional Design* (New York: Van Nostrand Reinhold, 1972), Chap. 2, pp. 9–13.

[8] Ralph Norman Haber, "Perceiving Space from Pictures: A Theoretical Analysis," in *The Perception of Pictures*, Volume 1, ed. Margaret Hagen (New York: Academic Press, 1980), p. 29.

[9] Ivar Peterson, "Computing Art" in *Science News*, 129:9 (March 4, 1986): 138–140.

[10] Donis A. Donis, *A Primer of Visual Literacy* (Cambridge, Mass.: M.I.T. Press, 1973).

[11] Herewood Lester Cooke, *Painting Techniques of the Masters* (New York: Watson Guptill, 1975), p. 43.

[12] The Troubador Press, 385 Fremont St., San Francisco, Calif. 94105, publishes *Stereo Views*, a collection of three-dimensional drawings and photographs using red and cyan glasses. Eclipse Comics, Guerneville, Calif., also continues to publish 3-D comic books.

[13] Holograms may be viewed at the Anhalt/Barnes Gallery, 750 N LaCienega Blvd., Los Angeles, Calif.; Gallery 1134, Fine Arts Research & Holographic Center, 1134 W. Washington Blvd., Chicago, Ill.; Holos Gallery, 1792 Haight St., San Francisco, Calif.; House of Holograms, 29291 Southfield Rd., Southfield, Mich.; and the Museum of Holography, 11 Mercer Street, in New York City.

[14] Herschel B. Chipp, *Theories of Modern Art* (Berkeley, Calif.: University of California Press, 1968), pp. 292–293.

[15] Werner Haftmann, *Painting in the Twentieth Century* (New York: Praeger, 1976) II, p. 113.

[16] Ideas about "pop-up" art may be found in *Ondori Pop-up Origami Architecture* by Masahiro Chatani (New York: Kondansha International/USA Ltd., 1984).

[17] The information presented was adapted from a book by Joseph V. Mascelli, *The Five C's of Cinematography* (Hollywood, Calif.: Cine/Grafic Pub., 1965).

[18] Nancy Aldrich-Ruenzel, "Interview: Milton Glaser," *Art Product News*, 5:6 (Nov.–Dec. 1983): 36.

[19] James L. Adams, *Conceptual Blockbusting*, 2d ed. (New York: W. W. Norton, 1980), pp. 24–25. Adams writes that just as it is sometimes difficult to isolate the problem properly, it is also difficult to avoid delimiting the problem too closely. (In other words, one should not impose too many constraints on it). The solution to the problem is below, example **a**. One of his correspondences solved the problem with only three lines, example **b**.

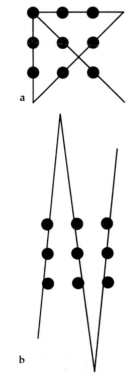

a

b

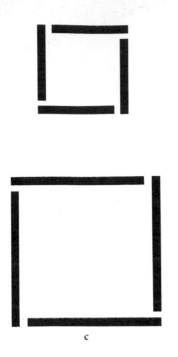

c

Example **c** is a totally different problem to try. Using the eight bars shown, make three equal squares. No part of any bar may extend beyond the edge of any square, nor can any bar overlap another.

[20] Nathan Knobler, *The Visual Dialogue* (New York: Holt, Rinehart and Winston, 1966), pp. 171–173.

[21] The formula for creating a dye immersion bath is as follows: to 8 ounces of water add a few drops of Kodak Photo-flo, 1 tablespoon of vinegar, and 6 to 8 drops of food color (transparent dye). Dr. Martin's Sychromatic Dyes also work very well. Test by immersing a scrap of film for two minutes. Adjust strength of color by adding a few drops more dye or thinning slightly with water. The correct color should appear in about two minutes as a stronger solution may cause streaks and uneven tinting. Rinse briefly and dry. Long rinsing may remove all color.

[22] The sharp cutoff filters, required for best color separation, are quite dense and need very long exposures. These are Kodak 98 Blue (for yellow separation), 99 Green (for magenta separation), 70 Red (for cyan separation). For experimentation, 25 Red, 61 Green, and 47 Blue filters may prove more useful.

[23] Josef Albers, *The Interaction of Color* (New Haven, Conn.: Yale University Press, 1963), p. 73.

[24] Debora T. Sharpe, *The Psychology of Color and Design* (Towata, N.J.: Littlefield Adams, 1975), Chap. 2, pp. 7–32.

[25] Article "Color and Light" in *Color News*, 1:1 (Spring 1986): 2.

[26] Deborah T. Sharpe, *The Psychology of Color and Design* (Towata, N.J.: Littlefield, Adams, 1975), p. 31.

[27] Samuel L. Forcucci, *A Folk Song History of America* (New York: Prentice-Hall, 1984), p. 79.

[28] Gerald E. Jones, "Color Use, Abuse in Presentations," in *Computer Graphics World*, 9:5 (May 1986): 119–20.

Glossary

abstract, abstraction Theoretical rather than applied or practical; something considered apart from physical existence. *In art:* An "abstraction" is a type of painting that uses representational shapes or forms as a point of departure but freely adapts or subjugates these to the aesthetical purposes of the artist. *See* **nonobjective.**

accommodation The ability of our eye's flexible lens to change shape in order to adjust focus between far and near figures. The muscle movements required are detected by the brain as an indicator of a spatial station.

achromatic Pertaining to colors without any distinctive hue, for example, black, white, and gray. Achromatic colors are often called "neutral colors."

acuity, visual *See* **distinctness.**

additive color The color mixing system of light. When the primary hues, red, green, and blue are added together, the result is white light. Yellow is seen when red and green lights are mixed; cyan is a combination of green and blue light; magenta, of red and blue.

aerial perspective Our understanding of the effects of the atmosphere on the distinctness, contrast range, hue, and purity of colors.

aesthetic Of or pertaining to the sense of the beautiful and the accepted notions of what constitutes good taste artistically. (From the Greek *aisthetikos*, of sensory perception.)

affect To influence or bring about a change in. To touch or to move the emotions. Also, a strong feeling that has active consequences. *See* **effect.**

afterimage A psychophysical characteristic of vision in which an image persists after the original stimulus has been removed. The hues of the image are the additive complements to those originally observed. *See* **simultaneous contrast.**

ambiguity Doubt or uncertainty in meaning. **Ambiguous:** capable of being understood in two or more possible senses; equivocal.

analogous colors Hues that are next to one another on any hue circle (color wheel).

analogy An actual or an implied correspondence between things that are different in all other respects. Relationships may be based on any sorts of conceptual, formal (shape and structure), or perceptual characteristics.

anamorphosis Optical magnification ordinarily in one direction or along only one axis. Anamorphic drawings or paintings are distorted images that may be viewed undistorted from a particular angle of view or with the use of a special instrument.

anomaly Deviation from the common rule or form; in particular, an irregular, abnormal, contrary, or missing element (or motif) in an otherwise regular field or sequence of identical figures.

assimilation A process by which a meaningful percept (a figure or an impression obtained by one or more of the senses) is compared to the vast body of personal knowledge and experience; placing things physically or psychologically in a familiar context.

asymmetry The principle of the seesaw transposed into pictorial form. Parts of a composition, unequal in area (size), are balanced in visual weight on either side of an imaginary fulcrum. The fulcrum is the center of visual balance, not the center of the picture.

autonomic Spontaneous or involuntary.

axial symmetry *See* **bilateral symmetry.**

balance Equilibrium of opposing visual weights, hues, or psychological and physical forces or a combination of these.

behavioral conditioning A term that encompasses anything learned by experience and practice: observation, imitation, formal education, and any behavior modification due to reward and punishment. This concept is often generalized as "nurture" as opposed to "nature," which consists of innate or genetic characteristics.

bilateral symmetry A form of design in which elements repeat themselves as perfect mirror images along a vertical (or horizontal) axis or bisector.

blind spot The point where the optic nerve leaves the retina of the eye. As this area possesses no rods or cones, it does not respond to light or images.

body color The "colored" appearance of any matter or substance (like a paint film), caused by differences in the molecular structure of such substances. Molecular differences determine which wavelengths of light are absorbed and which are reflected. Such colors are affected by the spectral composition of the incident light.

brightness An ambiguous term sometimes used to mean "purity," sometimes "luminance"; more often used to refer to a combination of these two dimensions of color.

change A transition from one state to another, altered state; a movement from one place to another place; a passage from one moment in time to another; any sort of transformation such as metamorphosis, growth, decay, and erosion.

chiaroscuro The arrangement of light and dark shading as defined by light rays flowing over a three-dimensional form. Chiaroscuro defines volumes in two-dimensional pictorial works. Also, a style of pictorial art employing only light and shade without the use of contour lines.

chroma *See* **purity**.

chromatic Exhibiting a definite color or hue.

chromatic sequence *See* **spectrum**.

chromatic grays Grays with a little color in them as opposed to neutral grays with no discernible hues.

cliché An excessively overused expression or image.

closure A Gestalt principle that describes an innate perceptual tendency for us to perceive multiple objects as a group or totality; to close "gaps" and to make "wholes" out of discontinuous lines, masses, or contours.

cognitive dissonance An internal conflict between one's beliefs and one's knowledge or behavior or both, for example, the opposition to the killing of animals and the eating of meat. It is a theory articulated by Leon Festinger, which states that when belief and behavior are in conflict, either one or the other must change.

collage Originating with the French word *coller*, to glue, a composition of materials and objects pasted on a surface, or portions thereof.

color A property of light, not of bodies or pigments. As sensed by photoreceptors in the eye, our perception of color results from a certain bundle of wavelengths of electromagnetic energy bombarding the retina. Color has three "dimensions" or characteristics. *See* **hue; luminance; purity**.

color temperature The sensation of "warmth" or "coolness" associated with colors. There are two types: *physical* color temperature, which is measurable in degrees Kelvin; and *relative* color temperature, which requires the presence of two or more colors (hues) for direct comparison. Though reds, oranges, and yellows are said to be "warm," and blues and greens are called "cool," there are cool and warm reds, cool and warm blues.

color wheel Used as an aid in painting, a color wheel is a circle with primary and secondary hues located at points equidistant from one another. The most prevalent version is based on one proposed in theories advanced by Louis Prang (1876). *See* **hue circle**.

complementary colors Hues that are diametrically opposite one another on any hue circle (color wheel).

composition The overall pictorial pattern or arrangement. *See* **design; form**.

cones Photoreceptors in the eye that provide visual detail and detect color. There are three types, each capable of discriminating between very narrow wavelengths of light: one for red, one for green, and one for blue. Concentrated in and around the fovea, numbers decline rapidly moving outward, peripherally, around the retina. Cones respond primarily to bright light levels.

connection Something that connects. To *connect* means to join, fasten, link, unite, or consider as related. *Connections* may provide a logical ordering of ideas, establish common interests, conjunction, or coincidence. **Connections of the narrow kind** establish visual relationships between internal pictorial elements within a composition, or establish associational pattern similarities between works in a series. **Connections of the broad kind** are specific references that join a work of art together with elements in the world at large: typically, the environment, society, culture, politics, or the sciences. These stimulate more creative solutions to visual problems and also enhance communication.

consonance Agreement, conformity, harmony. *See* **rhythm**.

constancy *See* **perceptual constancy**.

consumer behavior A marketing term that refers to the study of factors that motivate human behavior. It concerns the general public's response to products, services, subjects, or sets of circumstances as determined by statistical research.

continuity A Gestalt principle of organization that states that perception tends to move in one direction. Thus, we can easily follow the path of a single line, for example, even in a maze of many overlapping lines. This faculty is part of a survival characteristic required to distinguish contours and thereby separate figure from ground. Also, more broadly, continuity means to carry forward in natural order. In film, television, slide presentations, and storyboards or multipanel art, it is a natural flow of events in *chronological* sequence.

contour The outline of a figure-object or mass. The term commonly refers to the shape of a three-dimensional body as represented on a two-dimensional surface.

contour map A two-dimensional representation of topographical data derived from any kind of three-dimensional surface.

contrast Opposing qualities of things when compared or set side by side; the accentuation or sharpening of such differences.

cubism A style of art developed by Pablo Picasso and Georges Braque that is characterized by figure-ground ambiguity, flattened perspectives, and multiple points of view.

cue A sign or signal that prompts someone to do something. In psychology, it is a perceived signal for action that produces an operant response.

delimit To establish limits or boundaries.

density, density factor (D) Density in design is related to the "darkness" of a color, that is, its relative light reflection, which is a subtractive measure. This can be directly related to the deposit of pigment or ink upon a reflective surface in design and is often expressed in percent, as, for example, a 50 percent black (a middle-gray tone). A number 2 gray designers' color is a D 2.0. In the 11-step luminance scale, density is expressed in D factors like 2.0, which are directly convertible to percent by moving the decimal one place to the right. (D factors may be converted to Munsell "values" and vice versa, simply by subtracting the original number from 10. Thus, the two systems are compatible.)

density gradient A perceptual depth cue in which objects and the spaces between them become smaller and smaller as they recede into the distance.

design Creation of pattern. Human-made order, structure, and form. *See* **composition; form.**

discrimination The ability, act, or power to make fine distinctions, that is, to separate things by observing or distinguishing very small differences; differentiation; discernment.

distinctness The ability to resolve very fine detail in any visual field; visual acuity, sharpness, or clarity; also, a relationship or ratio between things such as hard and soft edges, wide and narrow luminance ranges.

Divisionism A technique developed and named by Georges Seurat and Paul Signac that attempted to apply the scientific concept of *optical fusion* to painting. The works were characterized by an overall pattern of tiny dots of pure colors. The term *Pointillism* is more commonly applied to these works, but in a manner that often distorts the painters' objectives.

dominance principle A perceptual characteristic that establishes psychophysical equilibrium in human beings. It is a rippling pattern of behavior in which first one thing, then another, is seen to dominate our field of view, mental state, or priority of action, preventing the sheer mass of sensory data from overwhelming us.

dominant Possessing the most influence or control; surpassing all others; paramount. When something is dominant, there must also be subordination.

effect Something brought about by a cause or agent; also, to produce a result. Do not confuse with *affect*, which means "influence."

electromagnetic spectrum The entire range of electromagnetic waves from very short, high-frequency vibrations, such as cosmic rays, through (in the order of decreasing frequency) gamma rays, Xrays, ultraviolet radiation, *visible light,* infrared radiation, microwaves, and radio waves to very long, low-frequency vibrations, which include heat waves and electric currents.

emotion Any strong, generalized feeling; subjective responses such as love, hate, or fear that involve physiological changes as a preparation for action.

equilibrium A Gestalt principle of organization that states that every psychological field tends toward "excellence" or precision, that is, the most regular organization possible. The concept reflects physical activity of natural forces that strive for balance. A water drop changes into a sphere as it falls; water seeks its own level; and so on.

equivocal Capable of being interpreted in more than one way; ambiguous.

expressionism A type of artwork in which the artist permits his or her emotions to dominate the character of the color, structure, and imagery (if any). As this is a highly personal, subjective experience, the communication aspects of the art may be sacrificed totally or subordinated to such "expression." There are two types: *figurative expressionism,* sometimes called "German expressionism," in which representational forms are subordinated to the artist's aesthetical motives; and *abstract expressionism,* which is nonobjective in character.

fatigue illusion *See* **optical dazzle.**

feminine (stereotype) Qualities commonly associated with the feminine gender—beauty, softness, sensuality, romance, weakness, hesitancy, indecisiveness, and so on; also those qualities when attributed to other figure-objects: flowers, for instance, or type styles. *See* **masculine, stereotype.** *Note:* Mixing perceptions of gender characteristics (masculine/feminine) can produce a girl/woman who is a tomboy, a feminist, or a businesswoman, for example; or a boy/man who is sensitive, aesthetic, an artist, or a Don Juan. Pushed to extremes, mixtures transmit meanings of homosexuality to the viewer.

Fibonacci numbers A geometric progression in which the Golden Section ratio 1:1.618 is a constant factor. Each subsequent number in the series is obtained by adding together the two that precede it, for example, 1, 1, 2, 3, 5, 8, 13, 21, 34, 55, 89, and so on.

field A space or ground on which something is drawn or projected or that which is perceived as such.

figure In this text, the term describes any shape or form perceptually enclosed by a boundary line (perimeter) or contour line that is seen as separate from the ground or background. Ground is neutral; figure is not. The term, as used in science, psychology, and in this text, does not necessarily imply a person as in the common expression *figure drawing.*

figure-ground A perceptual characteristic wherein whatever circumscribed area we look at is interpreted as figure and advances while everything else in the field of vision becomes background and recedes.

focal point The dominant point or area in any visual or pictorial field wherever the eye is directed or impelled to look.

folk art Art by the common folk, that is, by persons who lack any formal art training or experience; sometimes called *naive art,* such works are characterized by a lack of sophistication in drawing and painting, and they often depict nostalgic subjects in a simplistic manner. Images, however, may be powerfully evocative and display an innate sense of beauty in patternmaking. Graffiti could be considered a form of folk art.

form The shape or structure of a thing as opposed to its matter or substance. In the arts, the term is used broadly as a synonym for design or patternmaking; and it includes all aspects of composition, organization, and structure. For that reason, this text does not use the term *form* when only *shape* is meant. *See* **shape.**

formal balance *See* **symmetry.**

fovea A tiny depression in the center of the retina densely packed with cones. The fovea is responsible for visual acuity, that is, sharp, vivid, detailed images.

frequency The number of times that one wavelength of electromagnetic energy passes a fixed point in space in one second.

futurism An early 20th-century Italian art movement that focused on the violence, speed, force, and efficiency of modern society and on the mechanical energy exhibited by automobiles, trains, and industrial manufacturing.

genetic, genetic memory Pertaining to the biology of heredity; physiological body processes or characteristics, mental or physical predispositions, or actions due to genetic makeup of an organism. These are often called *innate.* Genetic memory in humans is generally allied to what we call "instinct" in lower animals and is often generalized as "nature" versus "nurture." (*See* **behavioral conditioning.**) *In this text, every reference is to genetic characteristics all human beings share, NOT to individual or family traits.*

gestalt An observation of a unified visual field perceived in its totality.

Gestalt psychology A branch of psychology originated by the German psychologist Max Werthheimer around 1912. Gestalt psychology emphasizes that behavior cannot be analyzed into independent units but must be studied as organized "wholes." Things are not a sum of their parts. Gestalt psychologists see relationships, patterns, and groupings as the primary elements of perception and have established a psychological basis for spatial organization and graphic communication.

glaze A thin, medium-rich application of transparent color over an underlying drawing or painting in order to add, alter, blend, enrich, or unify col-

ors. It is a means of creating transparency and luminosity in works of art. Glazes may be used to alter any of the three dimensions of color: hue, luminance, and purity. Glazes may be worked over dry grounds or applied with a wet-in-wet technique.

Golden Mean A term often used as a synonym for the Golden Section. In this text, the term *mean* is used to identify a method of dividing any rectangle into proportions that approximate the Golden Section.

Golden Rectangle A rectangle in which the ratio of length to width — and all subsequent divisions of interior space to infinity — will exactly conform to the ratio 1:1.618.

Golden Section A ratio of 1 to 1.618, and the geometric progression or proportions associated with this ratio. *See* **Fibonacci numbers.**

gradation A progression of change in natural order, with discrete or blended steps; a flowing transition in which adjoining parts are similar and harmonious; modulation.

gray scale A series of stepped gradations from white to black; a luminance scale (*see* **luminance**); a range of lightness to darkness in any color system. This text recommends conforming to the ISCC-NBS (Munsell) standard consisting of 11 steps, white, nine grays, and black. It also recommends converting the additive notation *value scale* to a subtractive *density scale,* which is consistent with the majority of applications in design, painting, and applied art. *See* **density.**

grid A pattern of lines commonly at 90° to one another like a checkerboard. Grids, however, may employ diagonal lines, circles and arcs, or arbitrary or freely chosen configurations. Grids are categorized as *regular* when they consist of geometric arrays of lines and as *arbitrary* if they consist of random or irregular lines. *See* Chapter 4.

ground The background against which figures are perceived. Grounds are fluctuating entities depending on whatever in the visual field is the focus of our attention. *Note:* The term is also commonly applied to any of several materials, like gesso, applied to a sup-

port in preparation for painting or drawing.

grouping An organizational principle of Gestalt psychology. Understanding how grouping takes place perceptually enables the artist to improve the unity of compositions and their structure.

harmony Agreement or consonance between forms, shapes, colors, concepts or ideas, and so on; a perceptual understanding identified by the Gestalt psychologists as the principle of similarity.

heavy line A line (or bar) that is very thick and bold, many times the thickness of a single stroke of pencil or regular brush. It is usually produced with a large, thick, or wide brush or a specially lettering pen (nib), or it is constructed with drafting instruments as an outline and filled in.

hierarchy A clearly defined relationship between things that establishes differing levels of dominance, emphasis, or influence, with each level subordinate to the one above it. Overall patterns with equally emphasized figures are sometimes called "nonhierarchical designs."

high key design A composition in which the overall or prevailing luminances are all above middle gray.

hue The traditional color "name," such as "red," which is attached to a specific wavelength of visible light (electromagnetic energy). Red, for example, is 700 nanometers (nm). If 700 nm is the dominant wavelength in the reflection of light from an apple, our brain interprets the hue of the apple to be "red."

hue circle A circle composed of primary, secondary, and intermediate hues in any color-mixing system. This text prefers the term *hue circle* to *color wheel* because these ordinarily deal only with hue, just one of the color dimensions. *See* **color wheel.**

illusion A perception that fails to give the true character of the object perceived; an unreal or misleading image presented to our vision; a deceptive appearance.

imbrication The overlapping of edges in a regular fashion like roofing shingles or fish scales.

incandescence A type of original (prime) light source created by a burning body. The sun is an incandescent light source as are common items such as light bulbs, candles, campfires, kerosene lamps, projector bulbs, and carbon arc spotlights. One of two broad categories. *See* **luminescence.**

incident light Light received directly from a prime light source (like the sun) rather than light reflected from a surface. Sometimes the term "ambient" light is used, meaning merely the light that is around us.

inference The act or process of drawing a conclusion from evidence or premises. Inferences are not necessarily the result of step-by-step logic but often are a consequence of deduction and supposition (a kind of sixth sense) that sees similarities or relationships between dissimilar things, activities, or mechanisms.

intensity *See* **purity.**

interference An interaction of waveforms whereby the overlap of two sets of waves weakens some waves but reinforces others. If one peak coincides with another, the wave is reinforced; if a peak coincides with a trough, the waves cancel out one another. Light wave interference is responsible for the iridescent colors we see in soap bubbles, record grooves, and some butterfly wings and birds' feathers. See **moiré.**

intermediate colors Hues that are mixed from one primary and one secondary hue to form a hue that is "in between"; also, more broadly, any color or hue perceived to lie between any two others.

interval The amount of spatial or chronological separation between things such as lines, figures, colors, areas, spaces, or points in time. Intervals are *regular* when spacing is all the same and *progressive* when the spaces change in natural order whether based on a simple numerical progression or on a geometric ratio.

intuition A deep-rooted, subconscious response to any specific stimulus that is produced by the sum total of each person's life experiences up to that point, including instinctive responses like emotions (genetic components). Also, a capacity to make inferences from incomplete or missing data. Contrary to popular belief, our intuitive faculties draw on all assimilated knowledge and, therefore, can be developed and enhanced.

iridescence An effect produced by the interference of light waves in which materials or surfaces, like soap bubbles, appear to reflect all the hues of the spectrum. *See* **interference.**

irradiation A perceptual illusion in which our brain makes a dark edge darker and a light edge lighter in order to clarify and strengthen the formation of the edge. Some psychologists call this "contrast"; this text prefers the term *irradiation* to avoid confusions with the broader meanings of the word *contrast.*

isometric perspective A form of parallel line perspective in which no construction lines are parallel to the picture plane. Three faces of an object are viewed simultaneously.

kinetic Moving; pertaining to motion; produced by motion.

lens In reference to the eye: a flexible, oval-shaped transparent body behind the iris, which changes shape to bring near or far objects into focus on the retina.

leveling Making things more alike; emphasizing similarities; commonly a stereotyping procedure.

light A small portion of the electromagnetic spectrum capable of stimulating the photoreceptive cells (cones and rods) in the retinas of our eyes. The *band of visible light* extends from about 400 nm to 700 nm. *See* **electromagnetic spectrum.**

line Theoretically a closely spaced series of points; a continuous mark made by a pen, pencil, brush, or other writing or drawing instrument. Also, any conceptual, intellectual, or theoretical correspondence to this figure. There are lines of vision, lines of motion or movement, contour lines, and so on.

linear perspective A method of encoding a two-dimensional surface to create an illusion of three-dimensional figure-objects. The term is usually meant to describe Renaissance perspective (vanishing point perspective) wherein parallel straight lines appear to converge on the distant horizon. However, there are other types of linear perspectives, including isometric, oblique, and orthographic, in which parallel lines remain parallel. The latter forms have been commonly employed by cultures other than our own and are especially important in 20th-century art.

local color The color of figure-objects seen independently of shadows, reflections, or atmospheric effects. *See* **body color.**

low key design A composition in which the overall or prevailing luminances are all below middle gray.

luminance An index of the amount of light reflected from a surface viewed from a particular direction. It relates to the lightness or the darkness of reflected colors and is compared to a gray scale. The term *luminance* is able to accommodate a gray scale based on density, a subtractive measure. *See* **value.**

luminescence (loo mi NES′ enz) Any prime light source not attributable to incandescence, that is, all nonthermal lights such as those produced by chemical, biochemical, or electrical processes, including fluorescence and phosphorescence. Do not confuse this term with luminance (LOO′ mi nans).

masculine (stereotype) Qualities usually attributed to the male gender—strong, forceful, muscular, bold, hard, mechanical, cold, insensitive. Also, similar qualities as applied to figure-objects like machines or type styles. *See* **feminine.**

mass Any body of matter perceived to be unified but without regard to specific shape; any cohesive group of objects so perceived.

meaning In this text, the term is used in its most generic sense: to refer to perceptual recognition, naming, or identification of a figure-object. The term, as used here, does not necessarily imply *message.* See **message; assimilation.**

melds A variety of artistic devices that merge figure with ground by exploiting Gestalt "continuity" — for example, extending figure contours, colors, or textures, into the negative space or ground (particularly at sharp changes in contour); softening or "blurring" edges; retention of normally invisible construction (compositional) lines; and so on. A leveling procedure, melds add homogeneity and unity to works.

message A correlation of "meanings" in a specific context or structure for the express purpose of communication — transmitting a purposeful thought, concept, or idea.

metamorphosis A transformation, or evolutionary change, from one form into another — appearance, character, structure, or function. *See* serial.

metaphor A figure of speech in which one object is given attributes characteristic of another object from which it clearly differs in order to suggest or to point out likenesses between them not ordinarily observed; a visual equivalent to this literary form.

model A preliminary pattern, prototype, or design, especially an example to be emulated. The term *paradigm* is preferred. *See* paradigm.

moiré The "beat" or visual reinforcement created by the overlapping (superimposition) of the same or similar wave patterns or periodic patterns. *See* interference. Moirés may be observed in overlapped window screens, curtains, and so on.

monochromatic Possessing only one hue, though possibly varying in luminance and purity; consisting of only one wavelength of light. In addition to a single hue, *monochromatic color schemes* commonly include white, grays, and black.

motif A design fragment, reduced to its most simplified form or configuration, that is used as a basic theme in a work of art. The motif may be repeated rhythmically, fractionalized, enlarged, and elaborated on; however, its presence always helps to provide coherency and unity in the work.

movement The visual act or appearance of change. The progression of events through time and space or across a two-dimensional surface. Visible displacement in space. When we observe movement it is called *direct* or simultaneous; when it is too fast or slow to be observed, it is called *inferred* or implied. *See* kinetic.

Munsell, Albert H. Inventor of the first practical color notation system. His system is now incorporated into the ISCC-NBS System adopted by the U.S. Bureau of Standards.

nanometer One-billionth of a meter (10^{-9}); approximately 0.000000039 inch. Formerly called a "millimicron," this unit of measure is applicable to wavelengths in the visible light band.

natural luminance Every pigment, when compared to a gray scale, has a luminance ordinarily associated with that specific pigment. For example, Cadmium Red Light is a middle gray, D 5.0.

natural order In regular or normal order or sequence: hues according to their spectral sequence (red, orange, yellow, green, blue, violet); even steps of gray from white to black or vice versa; and so on. Such sequences are psychologically comfortable, natural, easy, fast, and so on. *See* unnatural order.

negative space *See* ground.

nonobjective art "Pure" abstraction, that is, pictures that make no reference or bear no resemblance to the forms of nature or the natural world or to manufactured objects or structures; nonrepresentational.

normal value *See* natural luminance.

objective Based on knowledge; factually presented without influence of, or regard to, emotions, supposition, or personal prejudice. Also, things viewed dispassionately; the opposite of *subjective*.

op art A contraction of *optical art*, an art movement of the 1950s and 1960s that employed optical illusions, optical dazzle, simultaneous contrast, and other perceptual phenomena as a basis for their works.

optical dazzle A type of pulsating, shimmering, and dazzling optical effect attributed to the fatigue of photoreceptor cells (rods and cones) in the retina. Generally, strong contrasts of black/white or complementary hues are required.

optical fusion The blending in the eye of two or more discrete elements in any visual field so that each loses its separate identity. For example, if we spin a disk half white and half black at high speed, we will see a shade of middle gray, not black or white. The variety of colors on a TV set are created by the optical fusion of tiny triplet patterns of red, green, and blue phosphors.

organic Pertaining to living things or the attribution of the characteristics of living things to inorganic, nonobjective, or conceptual design forms.

orientation Alignment or positioning of anything with respect to a specific direction, reference system, or axis; also, familiarizing oneself or adjusting to any situation.

Orphism One of several similar styles that were characterized by surface patterns composed of dashes, dabs, or dots of paint, used as a means of endowing the works with a poetic quality. Objectives were very different from those of Divisionism.

orthographic Characterized by perpendicular lines and right angles. A form of linear perspective in which multiple views of a solid object are presented as if they were all in the same plane — the "plan" view used by engineers and architects.

paradigm A model or a blueprint, especially one perceived to be definitive.

paradox A true, but apparently contradictory, statement, circumstance, or image. Also, what is illogical, inexplicable, or contrary to accepted opinion or expectations.

percept A more or less single impression in the mind of something perceived by our senses.

perception An awareness of everything around us obtained through our sensual organs: sight, hearing, smell, touch, and taste.

perceptual accentuation That quality each individual brings to a figure, object, concept, and so on, that causes it to stand out or assume unusual importance; the result of past life experiences or perceptions; a factor in psychological weight.

perceptual constancy A human being's understanding that certain things remain the same regardless of the changing image sizes, shapes, and light qualities on our retina. It is part of the brain's mechanism to stabilize our environment. For example, we have no doubt that a person seen in the distance is of average height, five to six feet tall, even though the image on the retina appears smaller than that of a hand held up beside. This is size constancy; among others, we also have object, color, and shape constancy.

perceptual imperative An autonomic psychophysical drive to find meaning in every visual field or, more broadly, to derive meaning from all sensory data.

perceptual selectivity or set A process allied to assimilation. We see what we look for, that is, *what we expect to see,* while remaining unaware of things we do not expect to see.

periodic Recurring at regular intervals.

periodic patterns (or structures) Patterns of lines, dots, or other simple elements spaced at equal intervals or at geometrically progressive intervals. When a periodic pattern of vertical lines is overlaid on itself at right angles, the result is called a grid. *See* **grid**. Periodic patterns are inherently rhythmic.

photoreceptors Light-sensitive cells in the retina of the eye: the rods and the cones.

physics The science of matter and energy and of the interactions between the two.

physical Pertaining to the body as distinguished from the mind; pertaining to matter and energy.

physiological Pertaining to the biological science of life processes, activities, and functions.

pictorial space Illusionary three-dimensional space as observed from depth cues encoded on a two-dimensional surface.

picture plane The flat surface on which artists draw or paint as bounded by the edges of the material (the canvas, board, or frame) or by a line that circumscribes the area in which the artist composes a design or picture, length by width.

pigment A substance (mineral or dye) used as coloring matter in paint and other artists' materials. *Pigments are not hues* although each has its own distinctive hue. Cadmium Red Light is a pigment, orange-red is a generic hue.

Pointillism *See* **Divisionism**.

positive space *See* **figure**.

pragmatics That part of language that exhibits interrelationships with the reader, listener, or viewer — the existence of shared knowledge.

primary colors The irreducible number of hues in any color system from which theoretically all other colors may be mixed.

proportion Parts as related to a whole; wholes as related to one another with respect to length to length, width to width, girth to girth, and so on, or when compared in quantity, magnitude, or degree. Proportional relationships establish *geometric ratios* mathematically.

proximity In Gestalt psychology, the principle in which things spatially close together in a visual field join to make perceptual wholes or figures. *See* **tension**.

psychological Pertaining to the mind or the emotions.

psychophysical A term used by psychologists to indicate a response that is dependent on combined physical, biological, and mental processes.

purity One of the dimensions of color that identifies the monochromatic quality of any hue, that is, its relationship to light of a single wavelength. This relationship establishes a scale ranging from the most vivid hue physically possible to neutral gray. There is no universally accepted term or description for this dimension. Although some persons use the term *purity,* other persons prefer *intensity,* and still others prefer *saturation.* Some say intensity and saturation mean different things, and both terms are required; some persons prefer the term *brightness,* but it is a term most frequently used to describe a combination of dimensions rather than a single one. In the Munsell system, this dimension of color is called *chroma.* No term is accepted by a majority of persons. The term *purity,* as noted above, is easily tied to monochromatic light of a single wavelength giving it a precise meaning and, for that reason, is preferred in this text.

radial symmetry, or balance Mirror images on either side of both a vertical and a horizontal axes or along any even number of equally spaced radii.

rectilinear Formed or bounded by straight lines at 90° angles.

reflection Light waves bounced back to the eyes from any surface.

refraction The bending of light waves as they pass through one transparent medium into another, for example, a lens or a glass of water.

Renaissance A period of revived intellectual and artistic enthusiasm from roughly the 14th century to the 16th century; also, pertaining to the styles, characteristics, and attitudes of that period.

response A reaction or reply to a specific stimulus; all behavior that results when sense organs are stimulated. Motor responses occur when muscles are activated; glandular responses, when glands are activated; conscious responses are awarenesses that result when the brain is activated. *See* **subconscious**.

retina A multilayer, light-sensitive membrane lining the inner surface of the eyeball that is connected by the optic nerve to the brain. The retina contains the eye's photoreceptor cells.

retinal fatigue Overloading of the retinal system commonly experienced when viewing contrasty linear patterns or hues of high purity. It may be a result of eye tremors slightly shifting the image on the retina, causing photoreceptors to signal on/off, thus sending a heavy load of confusing signals to the brain. The effects may also be due to the fact that once a photoreceptor cell has "fired," it is momentarily blind, and a sensation of the additive complementary color appears. *See* **afterimage**.

rhythm Repetition of any visual component — interval, shape, color, or motif (figure) — in a regulated patternmaking process. Shapes or motifs may be repeated in their entirety, fractionalized, compressed or expanded, and so on, throughout a work.

rods The most numerous light receptors in the retina of the eye; important to vision at low levels of illumination. They are essentially color-blind.

saturation A term originally referring to the amount of pigment or dye a substance (textile or photo emulsion, for example) could absorb (soak up) as reflected in the vividness of colors that resulted. The term is now also applied to color purity factors (intensity) in TV picture tubes and computer monitors. *See* **purity.**

scale A visual relationship drawn between differing figures according to some easily recognized standard such as the human body.

scattering Random dispersion or deflection of light from any surface, substance, or airborne particle.

scumbling A technique in which paint is stippled, dabbed, or rubbed on with a very "dry" brush, dauber, rag, fingers, or anything else in a controlled application of opaque pigment over a darker color. In this way, a variety of textures may be developed with the underlying paint layer or ground showing through speckles of the scumbled color.

secondary colors Hues mixed by combining any pair of primary colors.

semantics In the grammar of any language, the recognition, tagging, or naming of a word or "figure" — its fundamental meaning.

serial Arranging in or forming a series or sequence in natural order. Serial development is the process of engaging in such an activity. Animation is serial development, and picture stories (like comic strips) are serial presentations.

shape The overall outline or contour of any perceived unit, figure or ground, particularly when related to a two-dimensional surface. *Shape* is a preferred term in this text as it is more specific. *See* **form.**

sharpening Making things less alike; emphasizing differences between things — contrast.

similarity The Gestalt psychology principle that states that like elements perceptually join to form wholes or figures.

simultaneous contrast The psychophysical effect of our visual mechanism where the stimulus of any color on our retina generates a subtle sensation of its opposite, additive complementary hue. The presence of red will make blue appear greener along common edges; blue will cause the red to appear to contain more yellow — to look orangy. The principle is this: The perception of a color moves toward the additive complement of the color that is next to it or surrounds it. The maximum color effect occurs when complementary hues of equal luminances are placed together causing "vibration." *See* **optical dazzle.**

space *See* **pictorial space.**

spatial attitude The position of any body relative to its normal or innate vertical axis, usually a position that takes the physical effects of gravity into account. Every figure-object possesses three axes about which it may rotate.

spectrum More specifically, the *color spectrum:* the distribution of hues in natural order according to their wavelengths. Also, the colored image formed when light is spread out after passing through a prism. Spectral sequence or chromatic sequence describes hues in prismatic order.

stereotype A vastly oversimplified model, concept, opinion, or belief in which things typify or conform in an unvarying manner and without individuality.

subconscious Below the level of conscious awareness. Subconscious responses are those usually associated with our autonomic nervous system, like breathing. *See* **autonomic.** Also, referring to deep-rooted psychological (perceptual) responses related to negotiating our world — instinct.

subjective Existing only in the mind of the person having the experience; therefore, not possible to confirm scientifically. Also, an individual personal experience or response not necessarily like, or even similar to, those of any other person; the expression in the arts of any such experience, response, or attitude; the opposite of *objective.*

subliminal Below the level of conscious awareness. It is a term commonly used to describe affective responses in an individual from stimuli (images or words) hidden or concealed in any sort of visual or audio materials — a secretive influence.

subtractive color The basic form of color mixing and viewing we experience with paint, ink, and most color photography. Pigments absorb (subtract) certain wavelengths of white light. The color we perceive consists of only the reflected or transmitted wavelengths. The primary hues are yellow (white light minus blue); magenta (white light minus green); and cyan (white light minus red).

successive contrast *See* **afterimage.**

symbiotic, symbiosis Relating to the "living together" or the living in close union of dissimilar organisms — usually where such association is necessary or advantageous to the survival of both. In the arts, *connections of the narrow kind,* that is, the consequences of a variety of means by which dissimilar elements are unified and brought into harmonious relationships in a composition.

symbol A figure or a sign that "stands in" for something else; something that represents an entire idea or concept. A kind of "shorthand" that may be used to indicate an operation, quality, relationship, and so on.

symmetry or symmetrical balance Exact repetition or correspondence of shapes on opposite sides of an axis or a point. When correspondence is not exact, but still similar, it is called "approximate" symmetry. *See* **bilateral symmetry; radial symmetry.**

synectic Relating to the merging of different and incompatible things into a new cohesive and unified whole; that is, to synthesize.

syntax Language structure, that is, the way in which words, sentences, or images are put together to form phrases or sentences—visual "strings"—in relative agreement and position sequentially according to rules of grammar.

synesthesia A subjective event in which the responses of one sensory organ are linked to those of another, as seeing colors when listening to music.

tangent A shape touching another or an edge, creating a point of emphasis—usually, an undesirable effect except in formal design.

taste The power to determine what constitutes beauty or excellence and the expression of that power.

tension The interaction of figures that tends to draw them together ("magnetic attraction") visually—a factor in Gestalt proximity. In general, the closer the figures, the greater the tension; the further the figures are apart, the less the tension up to the point where figures are perceived to have no relationship at all. Tension sets up stress points within a work of art that increase a sense of movement, direction, and dynamism.

texture gradient *See* **density gradient.**

unity The quality of any work of art that pulls it together and forms one whole as opposed to a random association of parts.

unnatural order Any arbitrary sequence like 7, 1, 5, 9, for example, or orange, blue, and red. Typical affective responses are "unnatural," slow, disturbing, jarring, and chaotic. *See* **natural order.**

value A Munsell System term for lightness/darkness using additive notation (white is 10.0; black 0.0—the absence of all light); the obverse of the luminance density scale. This text prefers the term *luminance*. See **density; luminance.**

veridical Pertaining to the properties of things considered objectively such as can be determined by measurement and without dependence on viewing conditions.

visual attraction The quality of "difference" in a visual field, observed uniqueness or novelty of any kind. Differences may be related to any form of change such as motion or metamorphosis.

visual field Essentially anything we see before us although, in specific instances, a visual field may be conceptually limited by perimeters such as a picture frame. In that case, it may be called a *pictorial field.*

visual literacy Comparable to literacy in language, it is the ability to understand and to use effectively all characteristics of the visual language.

visual weight The degree of attention or sustained interest that any single figure-object (or mass) commands related to all other elements in any visual field.

wavelength The distance between any two similar points on a given wave; usually specified as the center of one wave crest to another.

weighted line A line that varies in thickness (width) throughout its length—usually a gradation from thin to thick or a variation of luminance from light (gray) to dark (black).

Selected bibliography

Art aesthetics

"Cartoons as Art," in *Dialogue* (the arts journal). Special issue discussing the role of comics in fine art and popular culture. Four articles: "Is Comics Art?," "Comics and Popular Culture," "P. Craig Russell: Poet of the Panels," and "Don't Laugh That's Sick," 6:2 (November/December 1983): 7–11.

Chipp, Herschel B., editor. *Theories of Modern Art: A Source Book by Artists and Critics.* Berkeley, Calif.: University of California Press, 1968.

Kostelanetz, Richard, editor. *Esthetics Contemporary.* Buffalo, N.Y.: Prometheus Books, 1978.

Color

Albers, Josef. *Interaction of Color.* New Haven: Yale University Press, 1963.

Birren, Faber. *Color: A Survey in Words and Pictures from Ancient Mysticism to Modern Science.* New York: University Books, 1962.

————. *Color & Human Response.* New York: Van Nostrand Reinhold, 1978.

————. *Light, Color, Environment.* New York: Van Nostrand Reinhold, 1969.

————, editor. *Munsell: A Grammar of Color.* New York: Van Nostrand Reinhold, 1969.

————. *Principles of Color.* New York: Van Nostrand Reinhold, 1969.

Color News, a quarterly publication of the Pantone Color Institute, 6324 Variel, Suite 319, Woodland Hills, Calif. 91367.

De Grandis, Luigina, *Theory and Use of Color,* trans. by John Gilbert. New York: Harry N. Abrams, 1986.

Küppers, Harald. *Color: Origin, Systems, Uses.* New York: Van Nostrand Reinhold, 1973.

Marx, Ellen. *Optical Color & Simultaneity,* trans. by Geoffrey O'Brien. New York: Van Nostrand Reinhold, 1983.

Pavey, Donald, editor. *Color.* Los Angeles: Knapp Press, 1980.

Rossotti, Hazel. *Color: Why the World Isn't Gray.* Princeton, N.J.: Princeton University Press, 1983.

Sharpe, Deborah T. *The Psychology of Color and Design,* Totowa, N.J.: Littlefield Adams, 1975.

Verity, Enid. *Color Observed.* New York: Van Nostrand Reinhold, 1980.

Creativity and problemsolving

Adams, James. *Conceptual Blockbusting.* San Francisco: San Francisco Book Co., 1976.

Donis, Donis A. *A Primer of Visual Literacy.* Cambridge, Mass.: M.I.T. Press, 1973.

McKim, Robert. *Experience in Visual Thinking.* Monterey, Calif.: Brooks/Cole, 1972.

Roukes, Nicholas. *Art Synectics.* Worcester, Mass.: Davis Publications, 1982.

von Oech, Roger. *A Whack on the Side of the Head; How to Unlock Your Mind for Innovation.* New York: Warner Books, 1983.

Design, basic

Anderson, Donald M. *Elements of Design.*

New York: Holt, Rinehart and Winston, 1961.

Day, Lewis F. *Pattern Design: A Book for Students Treating in a Practical Way the Anatomy, Planning, and Evolution of Repeated Ornament.* New York: Taplinger, 1979.

Hofman, Armin. *Graphic Design Manual: Principles and Practice.* New York: Van Nostrand Reinhold, 1965.

Hornung, Clarence P. *Hornung's Handbook of Designs & Devices.* New York: Dover Publications, 1959.

Maier, Manfred. *Basic Principles of Design: The Foundation Program at the School of Design, Basel, Switzerland.* New York: Van Nostrand Reinhold, 1977.

Wong, Wucius. *Principles of Two-Dimensional Design.* New York: Van Nostrand Reinhold, 1972.

Geometry in art, periodic patterns, and grids

Baumgartner, Victor. *Graphic Games: From Pattern to Composition.* Englewood Cliffs, N.J.: Prentice-Hall, 1983.

Braun, Stephen R. "Crosscurrents: Botany with a Twist," concerning the Fibonacci numbers in nature, in *Science 86,* 7:4 (May 1986): 63–64.

Ghyka, Matila. *The Geometry of Art and Life.* New York: Dover Publications, 1977.

Hambridge, Jay. *The Elements of Dynamic Symmetry.* New York: Dover Publications, 1967.

Hurlburt, Allen. *The Grid: A Modular System for the Design and Production of*

Newspapers, Magazines, and Books. New York: Van Nostrand Reinhold, 1978.

Pedoe, Dan. *Geometry and the Visual Arts.* New York: Dover Publications, 1976.

Graphic design and applied art

Booth-Clibborn, Edward, and Daniel Baroni. *The Language of Graphics.* New York: Harry N. Abrams, 1979.

Brushwell, William, editor. *Painting and Decorating Encyclopedia.* South Holland, Ill.: Goodhart-Wilcox, 1982.

Cataldo, John. *Graphic Design.* Scranton, Pa.: International Textbook Company, 1966.

Favre, Jean-Paul. *Color Sells Your Package.* Zurich, Switzerland: ABC Verlag, 1969.

Ferriter, Roger. *Typerformance.* Palo Alto, Calif.: Communication Arts Books, 1983.

Hurlburt, Allen. *Layout: The Design of the Printed Page.* New York: Watson-Guptill, 1977.

Nelson, Roy Paul. *The Design of Advertising,* 5th edition. Dubuque, Iowa: Wm. C. Brown, 1985.

Light and color

Bedrick, Donna E. "Light: Your Best Friend or Worst Enemy" in *Airbrush Action* (November/December 1985): 6–9.

Hogarth, Burne. *Dynamic Light and Shade.* New York: Watson-Guptill, 1981. Look beyond particulars of style for important ideas found nowhere else assembled in concise form.

Millard, Howard, with Andrew Davidhazy and Henry Horenstein. "The Polarizer," in *Modern Photography,* 49:7 (July 1985): 43–58.

Mueller, Conrad G., and Mae Rudolph. *Light and Vision,* Life Science Library. New York: Time-Life Books, 1966.

Piene, Nan R., "Light Art" in *Art in America,* 55:3 (May–June 1967): 25–29.

Rainwater, Clarence. *Light and Color.* New York: Golden Press, 1971.

Scientific American, entire issue on light and vision, 219:3 (September 1968).

Perception and psychology

Allman, William F. "Mindworks," in *Science 86,* 7:4 (May 1986): 23–31.

Baby Talk, PBS Television, NOVA #1207, (C) 1985 WGBH Educational Foundation. A program on how children acquire language. WGBH Transcripts, Boston, Mass.

Bornstein, Marc H., and Lawrence E. Marks. "Color Revisionism," in *Psychology Today,* 16:1 (January 1982): 64–73.

"The Colors of Behavior," in *Psychology Today,* 16:9 (September 1985): 66.

Dember, William N., and Joel S. Warm. *Psychology of Perception,* 2d edition. New York: Holt, Rinehart and Winston, 1979.

Dodwell, Peter C., and Terry Caelli, editors. *Figural Synthesis.* Hillsdale, N.J.: Erlbaum, 1984.

Finke, Ronald A. "Mental Imagery and the Visual System," in *Scientific American,* 254:3 (March 1986): 88–95.

Fischman, Joshua. "Color My World," in *Psychology Today* 20:4 (April 1986): 6.

Gazzaniga, Michael S. *The Social Brain: Discovering the Networks of the Mind.* New York: Basic Books, 1985.

Gregory, Richard L. *Eye and Brain.* New York: McGraw-Hill, 1966.

———. *The Intelligent Eye.* San Francisco: McGraw-Hill, 1970.

Hagen, Margaret, editor. *The Perception of Pictures,* Volume I. New York: Academic Press, 1980.

———. *The Perception of Pictures,* Volume II. New York: Academic Press, 1980.

Held, Richard, editor. *Image, Object and Illusion,* readings from the *Scientific American.* San Francisco: W. H. Freeman, 1974.

Kaufman, Lloyd. *Perception: The World Transformed.* New York: Oxford University Press, 1979.

Luckiesh, M. *Visual Illusions: Their Causes, Characteristics, and Applications.* New York: Dover Publications, 1965.

Ramachandran, Vilayanur S., and Stuart M. Anstis. "The Perception of Apparent Motion," in *Scientific American,* 254:6 (June 1986): 102–109.

Rivlin, Robert, and Karen Gravelle. *Deciphering the Senses: The Expanding World of Human Perception.* New York: Simon & Schuster, 1984.

Rock, Irvin. *Perception.* New York: Scientific American Books, 1984.

Tysoe, Marion. "What's Wrong with Blue Potatoes?" in *Psychology Today,* 19:12 (December 1985): 6–7.

Space

Gardner, Martin. "Illusions of the Third Dimension" in *Psychology Today,* 17 (August 1983): 62–67.

Mulvey, Frank. *Graphic Perception of Space.* New York: Van Nostrand Reinhold, 1969.

Vries, Jan Vredeman de. *Perspective.* Replica of original edition published in 1604. New York: Dover Publications, 1968.

See **Perception:** Hagen, Margaret.

Vision and visual illusions

Curtiss, Deborah, *Introduction to Visual Literacy: A Guide to the Visual Arts and Communication.* Englewood Cliffs, N.J.: Prentice-Hall, 1988.

The Invisible World: Sights Beyond the Limits of the Naked Eye. Boston: Houghton Mifflin Company, 1981.

Kavner, Richard S., and Lorraine Dusky. *Total Vision.* New York: A & W Publishers, 1978.

Lanners, Edi. *Illusions,* trans. and adapted by Heinz Norden. New York: Holt, Rinehart and Winston, 1973.

Livingstone, Margaret S., "Art, Illusion and the Visual System," in *Scientific American,* 258:1 (January 1988): 78–85. Also see "What Explains Subjective Contour Illusions, Those Bright Spots That Are Not Really There?" by Jearl Walker, pp. 96–99, same issue.

Nelson, George. *How to See.* Boston: Little, Brown, 1977.

Pirenne, Maurice Henry. *Optics, Painting and Photography.* Cambridge, England: Cambridge University Press, 1970.

Sinclair, Saundra. *How Animals See: Other Visions of Our World.* New York; Oxford, England: Facts on File, 1985.

Wade, Nicholas. *The Art and Science of Visual Illusions.* Boston: Routledge and Kegan Paul, 1982.

Zurer, Pamela S. "The Chemistry of Vision," in *Chemical and Engineering News* (November 28, 1983): 24+.

General information

Burke, James. *The Day the Universe Changed*. Boston: Little, Brown, 1985. Note Chapter 3, "Point of View," pages 55–90, which deals with the discovery of Renaissance perspective, and also see the discussion of perception in Chapter 10.

"The Chemistry of Art," series of articles on the topics of color, light, ceramics, safety, pigments, and metal artifacts. The *Journal of Chemical Education*, 57 (April 1980): 255 + . Art Reprint, *Journal of Chemical Education*, 238 Kent Road, Springfield, Pa. 19064.

Hours, Madeleine. *Conservation and Scientific Analysis of Painting*. New York: Van Nostrand Reinhold, 1976.

Judson, Horace Freeland. *The Search for Solutions*. New York: Holt, Rinehart and Winston, 1980.

O'Brien, James F. *Design by Accident*. New York: Dover Publications, 1968.

Proctor, Richard M., and Jennifer F. Lew. *Surface Design for Fabrics*. Seattle and London: University of Washington Press, 1984.

Index

Boldface italicized page numbers refer ONLY to illustrations or to their captions.

Artists